Orchestrating the Nation

Orchestrating the Nation

The Nineteenth-Century American Symphonic Enterprise

Douglas W. Shadle

OXFORD
UNIVERSITY PRESS

OXFORD
UNIVERSITY PRESS

Oxford University Press is a department of the University of
Oxford. It furthers the University's objective of excellence in research,
scholarship, and education by publishing worldwide.

Oxford   New York
Auckland   Cape Town   Dar es Salaam   Hong Kong   Karachi
Kuala Lumpur   Madrid   Melbourne   Mexico City   Nairobi
New Delhi   Shanghai   Taipei   Toronto

With offices in
Argentina   Austria   Brazil   Chile   Czech Republic   France   Greece
Guatemala   Hungary   Italy   Japan   Poland   Portugal   Singapore
South Korea   Switzerland   Thailand   Turkey   Ukraine   Vietnam

Oxford is a registered trademark of Oxford University Press
in the UK and certain other countries.

Published in the United States of America by
Oxford University Press
198 Madison Avenue, New York, NY 10016

This volume is published with generous support of the AMS 75 PAYS Endowment
of the American Musicological Society, funded in part by the National
Endowment for the Humanities and the Andrew W. Mellon Foundation.

Library of Congress Cataloging-in-Publication Data
Shadle, Douglas W., author.
Orchestrating the nation : the nineteenth-century American
symphonic enterprise / Douglas W. Shadle.
pages cm
Includes bibliographical references and index.
ISBN 978–0–19–935864–9 (hardcover) — ISBN 978–0–19–935865–6 (ebook)
1. Symphony—United States—19th century.   2. Music—United States—19th century—
History and criticism.   I. Title.
ML1255.S53 2015
784.20973'09034—dc23
2015013939

9 7 5 3 1 2 4 6 8
Printed in the United States of America
on acid-free paper

CONTENTS

ACKNOWLEDGMENTS

This book is indebted to many individuals and institutions. Several provided direct material aid: Vanderbilt University's Vice Provost for Research Dennis Hall and Assistant Provost Elizabeth Rapisarda, who provided a generous subvention to defray the costs of permissions and an index; the Graduate School of the University of North Carolina (UNC) at Chapel Hill; Dr. Thomas S. Royster Jr. and Caroline Royster, who funded my graduate fellowship at UNC; the music department at UNC; and the Library Company of Philadelphia and the Historical Society of Pennsylvania, which jointly supported a month-long residency. Oren Vinogradov provided research assistance at key moments. Elena Avalos-Bock helped me with sound clips for the website.

Several libraries and librarians made my work much easier: Mark Dickson (interlibrary loan requisition expert), James Procell, Matt Ertz, and Donald Dean at the University of Louisville Anderson Music Library; Holling Smith-Borne, Sara Manus, Jacob Schaub, Robert Rich, and Michael Jones at the Vanderbilt University Potter Music Library; Phil Nagy of Vanderbilt University's Special Collections Division; Connie King and James Green of the Library Company of Philadelphia; Sara Borden of the Historical Society of Pennsylvania; Gabe Smith at the New York Philharmonic Archives; Sharon Thayer and Jeff Marshall at the University of Vermont; Jackie Penny at the American Antiquarian Society; the Library of Congress Music Division and Newspaper Division; the New York Public Library for the Performing Arts Music Division; the Houghton Library at Harvard University; and the New England Conservatory Archives and Special Collections. Phil Vandermeer, Diane Steinhaus, and Carrie Monette at the University of North Carolina Music Library deserve the lion's share of thanks for getting me started.

A number of receptive and collegial groups invited me to share thoughts related to the book with them: the School of Music and Center for Collaborative and International Arts at Georgia State University; graduate musicology colloquia at Michigan State University and the University of Kentucky; the University of Louisville Faculty Humanities Forum; the Society for American Music; the South-Central and Midwest chapters of the

American Musicological Society; and the organizers of nineteenth-century music conferences on two continents—a fitting transatlantic experience.

My doctoral dissertation committee helped get this work off the ground, as did several members of the Society for American music, all of whom gave valuable and constructive criticism at various points along the way. In particular I thank Denise Von Glahn, Michael Broyles, John Graziano, and Nancy Newman for their insights. The anonymous readers for Oxford University Press, who graciously revealed their identities to me later, made great suggestions for improving every aspect of the book. James Davis and Patrick Warfield generously agreed to read a draft of the full manuscript before final submission and offered invaluable advice. Friends whom I bugged to read various smaller sections include William Gibbons, Glenda Goodman, Kevin Bartig, and Marie Sumner Lott. I owe them. (And now I've paid back Ryan Raul Bañagale.)

My colleagues at Vanderbilt's Blair School of Music—Melanie Lowe, Joy Calico, Jim Lovensheimer, Gregory Barz, Robbie Fry, and Ryan Middagh—provided me with much needed moral support and professional guidance (as well as a few read-throughs—thanks again, Joy!) as the book neared completion. Blair School Dean Mark Wait likewise offered his unbridled support. Suzanne Ryan at Oxford University Press got behind this project during its earliest stages, and I will be eternally grateful for her sustained confidence and assistance. Her assistants, Jessen O'Brien and Dan Gibney, made the process easy for me. Production editor Mary Jo Rhodes and copy editor Bonnie Kelsey cleaned up the messes in my manuscript and transformed them into this beautiful volume.

A handful of others deserve individual recognition. Jack Ashworth became one of my closest friends as I wrote the book. Travis Stimeling and Laurie McManus acted as sounding boards almost daily. They define friendship. Evan Bonds's generosity as a mentor has been matchless. It was also his seminar on the nineteenth-century American symphony that inspired me to pursue this research. Joe Vick and Jim Hatch of Little Rock, Arkansas were my first string teachers. They fed my passion for orchestral music from a very young age. Violists Timothy Nelson, Larry Wheeler, and Evan Wilson, my private instructors over a period of nearly fifteen years, only made that passion stronger. Finally, my wife Karen and I discussed every idea in this book during many miles of walking together. The final product certainly bears her imprint, though I was never able to convince her that Fry's music is better than Bristow's.

ABOUT THE COMPANION WEBSITE

http://global.oup.com/us/orchestratingthenation/
Oxford University Press has created a website to accompany *Orchestrating the Nation* that includes supplemental items designed to enhance the reading experience. First, the website features recorded clips of the works highlighted in the text, where available. Since many of the printed examples are reductions of large orchestral scores, these clips will allow the reader to experience the music's full orchestral palette. The recordings also eliminate the necessity for readers to have an advanced level of note-reading ability. Second, I have included supplementary web links and source notes that will be useful for researchers and musicians interested in pursuing new leads related to the subject matter. In both cases, new items will be added as they become available. Readers are encouraged to check for updates often.

Orchestrating the Nation

Introduction

Why do American orchestras play so many German symphonies? Does German music wield special powers? A few years ago, I gave a pre-concert lecture on music and national identity for a major professional orchestra. Works by Sibelius and Rachmaninov were on the program. It was my type of lecture: no notes necessary. I regaled the audience with stories about the diversity of national musical traditions and wowed them with arguments about the historical contingency of national identity. Or so I thought. During the discussion period, one gentleman asked, "But what about Beethoven? *His* music is universal. It will bring world peace." I was stunned. His statement directly opposed every point I had made. Anxious that I had not communicated my thoughts well, I could think of only one reply: "Beethoven was German." Perhaps I should have noted that the matter of world peace is still unresolved.

The subjects of Germany and Beethoven are good points of departure for a book about the history of orchestral music in the United States. The most enduring and popular symphonies in this country, many of which Beethoven himself wrote, are of German cultural origin. How this situation arose has come under increasing musicological, historical, and sociological scrutiny over the past three decades. It is a complex story of canon formation.[1] While interrogating canons, however, we have failed to see something right under our noses: the American symphonic enterprise of the nineteenth century. Between 1800 and 1900, more than fifty composers born or living in the United States wrote roughly one hundred symphonies in all (see table I.1). The numbers are truly astonishing given how little we tend to know about the music.

The prevailing assumption about this repertoire, if one exists, is that a fair portion is "bad" by conventional standards. (And it certainly does not

Table I.1. BRIEF CATALOG OF NINETEENTH-CENTURY AMERICAN SYMPHONISTS. NAMES IN BOLD INDICATE FIGURES HIGHLIGHTED IN THE BOOK

Name	Life Dates	Symphonies from Period
Filippo Trajetta	1777–1854	1803 (lost)
Anthony Philip Heinrich	1781–1861	1830s–1850s (x13)
Leopold Meignen	1793–1873	1845
Paul Emile Johns	1798–1860	1824 (lost)
Charles Hommann	1800–1872	ca. 1821–1823
Eduard Sobolewski	1804–1872	1845 (before U.S. immigration)
William Cumming Peters	1805–1866	1831
Simon Knaebel	1812–ca. 1880	1851 (lost)
William Henry Fry	1813–1864	1852 (x2); 1853; 1854 (x3); n.d.
Robert Stoepel	1821–1887	1859
Charles Callahan Perkins	1823–1886	1850 (lost)
Frédéric Louis Ritter	1824–1891	pre-1868; 1868; after 1868 (x2)
George Frederick Bristow	1825–1898	1848; 1853; 1858; 1872; 1893
Ellsworth C. Phelps	1827–1913	1874/78; 1880 (lost)
Edward Mollenhauer	1827–1914	1870 (lost)
Carl Hohnstock	1828–1889	1853–1854
Louis Moreau Gottschalk	1829–1869	ca. 1851 (lost); 1859; 1869
Leopold Damrosch	1832–1885	1878
Charles Crozat Converse	1832–1918	n.d. (lost)
Charles Jerome Hopkins	1836–1898	1856
Constance F. Runcie	1836–1911	n.d. (lost)
Benjamin Johnson (B. J.) Lang	1837–1909	n.d. (lost)
Philip Gottlieb Anton	1839–1896	ca. 1888; n.d.
John Knowles Paine	1839–1906	1875; 1880
Robert Goldbeck	1839–1908	1863
Henry E. Browne	Unknown	1865
Calixa Lavallée	1842–1891	ca. 1885 (lost)
George Elbridge Whiting	1842–1923	ca. 1888 (lost)
Caryl Florio (W. J. Robjohn)	1843–1920	1887 (x2)
Asger Hamerik	1843–1923	1881; 1883; 1885; 1889; 1891; 1897
Otis Bardwell Boise	1844–1912	1875
John Nelson Pattison	1845–1905	n.d.
William Wallace Gilchrist	1846–1916	1891
Silas Gamaliel Pratt	1846–1916	1871; 1875; n.d.
Horace Wadham Nicholl	1848–1922	n.d.; 1882
Albert Augustus Stanley	1851–1932	n.d. (lost?)
Louis Maas	1852–1889	1883
George Whitefield Chadwick	1854–1931	1881; 1883–1885; 1893–1894
Arthur Bird	1856–1923	1885
Johann Heinrich Beck	1856–1924	1875–1877

Name	Life Dates	Symphonies from Period
George Templeton Strong	1856–1948	1886; 1888
Henry Schoenefeld	1857–1936	1893 (lost)
Frederick Zech Jr.	1858–1926	1883 (x2); 1885; 1893; 1895
Harry Rowe Shelley	1858–1947	1897
Carl Busch	1862–1943	1898
Ernest R. Kroeger	1862–1934	number/dates unknown
Horatio Parker	1863–1919	1885
William E. Haesche	1867–1929	ca. 1890s
Amy Beach	1867–1944	1896
Gustav Strube	1867–1953	1896
Howard Brockway	1870–1951	1894
Henry Kimball Hadley	1871–1937	1897
Frederick Shepherd Converse	1871–1940	1898
Charles Ives	1874–1954	ca. 1898–1902

have any special powers.) A handful of potential readers may be so put off by this reputation that they will skip this book altogether merely after reading the title. Unfortunately, they will never know that the book is actually about them since it examines the very processes through which listeners confer value upon composers, pieces of music, and the act of composition itself. But, to clarify, the inherent musical value of individual symphonies does not concern me here. Instead, I am focused on the accrual of what sociologist Pierre Bourdieu has called cultural and symbolic capital—noneconomic assets that grant prestige within a given social context.[2] In the context at hand, participants in the American symphonic enterprise generated little of either.

What speaks to me about this repertoire, then, is that the public forgot it virtually as soon as it was created. It failed to launch. Many of the scores still lie dormant in archival boxes and for all practical purposes might as well not exist. Why? It was not because their initial audiences didn't like them. By and large, the public enjoyed the music immensely. As we shall see, however, even popularity could not elevate the status of this music. Brandishing their symbolic capital as recognized musical experts, critics could always toss audience pleasers into the "populist dustbin," leading later generations to think that the music naturally belonged there.[3]

How these pieces became our cultural detritus is revelatory for understanding the general condition of orchestral music and the status of its composers in the United States today. The immediate, decisive, and at times violently willful acts of forgetting that sequestered this repertoire and its creators relied on certain intellectual dispositions of the nineteenth century that persisted well into the twentieth and locked away the past. The gaping hole in our collective memory, not the music itself, is precisely what makes this repertoire relevant. My presumption is that the vast majority of orchestral music enthusiasts don't even *know* they don't know anything about it. *Orchestrating the Nation* reveals why.

Although the symphony as a genre is much older, the story in *Orchestrating the Nation* is fundamentally of the nineteenth century, an era marked by the distinct rise of musical nationalism. Throughout the period, German-speaking musicians persistently claimed universal ownership of the symphony, and even of music itself. In doing so, they created an orbital model of musical culture in which non-Germans stood at the periphery around a Germanic center.[4] At key historical junctures, thinkers and musicians in the United States with highly visible public platforms, such as the critic John Sullivan Dwight and the conductor Theodore Thomas (to say nothing of ordinary listeners, like the gentleman at my lecture), insisted on the truth of this model. Some were Germans themselves and required little convincing. Consequently, there were moments when critics unfairly lampooned American-born composers who challenged this stance or when performers quietly passed them over in favor of German music. These composers then fell quickly out of the public eye as the one-sided views of their detractors maintained a significant presence in public discourse. The struggle for power and public representation among the various pro-German and pro-American factions appearing across the century stands at the heart of my narrative. The distinction between the two factions, I might add, was not always clear.

The academic discipline of musicology—itself a German invention—did little to loosen German music's preeminence in the public imagination during the first half of the twentieth century.[5] An accompanying devaluation of nineteenth-century American musical culture has changed little since then. The discipline's persistent valorization of the idealist aesthetic of autonomy, another outlook associated with nineteenth-century German thought, has not helped the matter.[6] To be sure, contemporary scholarly overviews of the symphony display much greater breadth than today's concert programs, but even the most inclusive favor a select group of so-called masters and masterworks, usually German, while giving far less attention to works by others.[7] As non-Europeans who appear to have been vanquished by a judicious marketplace of public opinion, nineteenth-century American composers have remained practically silent in scholarly discourse.

Given such a state of affairs, one may not realize that U.S. composers participated actively in the broader symphonic enterprise of the nineteenth century—the work of Schumann, Mendelssohn, Brahms, Bruckner, and Mahler. Most listeners today will likely never hear an American symphony composed before 1930 unless it is by Charles Ives. The popular American symphonic works that once coalesced into some sort of canonical status—pieces by Aaron Copland, Samuel Barber, Roy Harris, and others—date primarily from the period between 1930 and the end of World War II. This period formed an ostensible golden age for the genre in the United States. Listeners today appreciate these works in large part for their so-called American sound. As I demonstrate, however, this era was one of the last bursts of symphonic composition between 1835 and 1950, and writers did not begin to privilege the idea of a distinctly American sound until the turn of the twentieth century.[8]

The historiography of American music more generally has accentuated the neglect and misunderstanding of this repertoire. Taking for granted that German music was a universal standard and therefore the most valuable, the first generation of American music scholars assumed that any orchestral music composer should share this belief. German musical preeminence went unquestioned.[9] The next scholarly generation began to dismantle the German intellectual bulwark by emphasizing the distinctly local aspects of the country's musical culture, especially its vernacular styles and practices. This attitude left nineteenth-century symphonic composition in an awkward position because the genre did not originate in the United States. Gilbert Chase, for example, believed that European cultural dominance throughout the nineteenth century rendered most compositional activity from the period irrelevant. "Take it out," he wrote, "and nothing vital is lost [. . .]."[10] Chase did not seem to acknowledge that although the concept of orchestral music itself was tied inextricably to German culture, a wide array of composers and listeners in the United States considered it a tool for asserting national cultural autonomy and believed it would be the cornerstone of an authentically national musical culture.[11] (And as we shall see, this belief was resisted by musicians who considered orchestral music a tool for asserting *German* cultural autonomy and musical authority on American shores.) Tempering the universalist and patriotic extremism of the past, recent overviews of nineteenth-century American music have shifted focus away from composers and onto the social dimensions of music-making, especially performance.[12] But with composers and the act of composition merely lurking in the background of these studies, fundamental questions about the production, function, and meaning of nineteenth-century American symphonic music remain unaddressed.

Orchestrating the Nation is the first book to approach the nineteenth-century American symphonic enterprise from a holistic vantage. I have unearthed a kaleidoscopic array of characters, documents, and events that no one has scrutinized together through a broad interpretive lens. This book offers a fresh paradigm for understanding the repertoire by examining several interlocking parts in tandem: composition, performance, listening, and writing. My first goal is to historicize the functions and possible meanings of this music within its original contexts.[13] From there, I demonstrate how shifting perceptions of the repertoire eliminated it from public consciousness.

Looking through this same lens, it is also apparent that the story of American orchestral music is both national and international. The realities of cultural and material exchange within the United States and across the Atlantic deeply affected the individuals appearing in the book. With the rapid circulation of people, objects, and ideas across the ocean, and with a large body of performance repertoire that was shared with European orchestras, the American symphonic enterprise of the nineteenth century was one of the most vibrant intercultural exchanges in all of Western music history. By approaching the subject from multiple angles and highlighting moments of transatlantic dialogue, this book challenges many common assumptions about Western Europe's orchestral music culture as well.[14] Canonical European composers depended on nineteenth-century American performers and audiences for their longevity, and I illustrate how American composers fit into this transatlantic process of canon formation.

The repertoire's size makes it unwieldy. Its multifaceted character resists totalizing interpretations. To render it more manageable, I had to make difficult choices about whose music to include. In general, I have highlighted the composers whose careers had the widest intersection with musical institutions that later defined the mainstream, such as the New York Philharmonic and the Boston Symphony Orchestra. I have also distilled three interrelated themes that carry through the book's chronological narrative: the question of national musical identity, the rhetorical roles played by the German symphonic tradition, and the changing landscape of musical institutions. In each case, I have chosen to examine these topics in national and transatlantic contexts in order to challenge the longstanding tendency to favor purely national accounts of the nineteenth century.[15]

THE NATIONAL IDENTITY CRISIS

Eighteenth-century Romantic theorists of nationhood, such as Johann Gottfried Herder (1744–1803), had a profound impact on Western musical thought during the nineteenth century. For Herder and others, particular cultural groups called "nations" possessed identities forged by a shared linguistic and cultural heritage.[16] Within this framework, particular types of music (what would later be called "folk songs") appeared to be the natural possessions of such national groups. During the nineteenth century, writers often extended this line of thought to include genres of so-called "cultivated" music, as long as it was imbued with a national or folk "character."[17] Recent thinkers have argued that the early theorization of these culturally defined nations converged with a rapidly evolving global economy and shift-ing conceptions of the political state during the nineteenth century, thereby constructing full ideologies of nationalism. This politicized nation-building process filtered into every corner of Western culture. Public figures across the political spectrum, including musicians, considered political might an extension of ethnic and cultural superiority.[18]

Throughout the nineteenth century, however, the nation was always a fluid category. Consequently, the ways in which musicians participated in nation-building discourses varied dramatically from one location to the next, and even across generations within a given community.[19] In the United States, where geographical boundaries shifted constantly, early debates about national identity, at least among the English-speaking majority, tended to revolve helically around broader demands for the coun-try to enter the international cultural marketplace on the one hand and a strong desire to create a domestic national community on the other. From the first moments following political independence, the country consti-tuted the geographic periphery of the West. It also lacked key elements that philosophers like Herder believed could evince a distinct national identity: a homogeneous ethnic makeup, a shared linguistic heritage, and static geographical boundaries. Romantic conceptions of nationhood did not readily apply.[20]

Augmenting this amorphous sense of national identity and mitigating claims of independence, robust cultural and economic ties to Great Britain persisted well into the nineteenth century. The awkward postcolonial con-dition in which Americans found themselves at the turn of the nineteenth century led many of them to believe they were experiencing an identity cri-sis, musical and otherwise.[21] Unsurprisingly, certain Americans believed that this problem needed to be fixed. Over the course of the century, the rhetoric of Jacksonian democracy, a belief in the inevitability of aggressive westward expansion, and strategic global imperialism proved to be power-ful forces for asserting national political autonomy on a global scale.[22] But the country retained wide channels of cultural exchange with Western Europe, particularly in music, and thus maintained a distinctly cosmopoli-tan cultural ethos.

When considering the construction of national musical identity in the United States, it is tempting to frame the narrative as an inexorable quest for a "true" American musical style. Guided by a work-centered con-ception of nationalism, those adopting this historiographical approach have tended to take for granted that a specific composer or style—Aaron Copland or Charles Ives, for example—created an ideal American sound. With a specific endpoint in mind, these writers have narrated the develop-mental steps leading up to the concrete moment when this ideal was sup-posedly achieved.[23]

This approach does capture a certain animating principle driving the changing tastes and aspirations of American musicians and listeners throughout the nineteenth century and beyond. Each successive generation publicly asked questions about what an American style might sound like or what role European styles should play in the development of a national musical culture. But the predominantly twentieth-century premise that any one style might be more American than another is questionable. It reifies a fixed national musical identity that in truth was and is only a chimera. And it discounts national identity formation processes that were not focused directly on style. As German musicologist Bernd Sponheuer has argued, national identity is not "an empirically demonstrable musical trait derived from style criticism."[24] Rather, it is constructed.

Composer and critic Virgil Thomson addressed such concerns in the middle of the twentieth century when he stated, in his inimitable way, that to write American music, one must simply be American and "then write any kind of music you wish."[25] The solution seems elegant. The concrete person writing music matters more than the sound of the music itself. But this perspective was acutely problematic in the nineteenth century. Immigrant musicians, especially from German-speaking lands, arrived on American shores in massive waves and were confronted with pointed questions about national identity. Should they assimilate into the culture of the English-speaking ruling class? To what extent should they retain Old World cultural practices, including those related to music? Were they American at all? (English speakers often asked these questions of Germans more anxiously than Germans asked them of themselves.) Other American residents—indigenous peoples and those of African heritage, for example—also played little role in these discussions until the end of the century, and only then primarily as objects under discussion, not participating subjects within it. Defining musical nationhood often entailed exclusion, because who was "truly" American remained a perennially open question.

Musicologist Charles Hiroshi Garrett has argued in favor of considering American national musical identity a contested moving target, rather than a monolithic entity, since individuals and groups with different agendas will tend to conceive of it differently from one another.[26] This paradigm also applies to the nineteenth century, when conceptions of national identity were certainly more diverse than the two described above. Critic John Sullivan Dwight (1813–1893), for example, declared flatly in 1845 that a symphony by Beethoven was the music "of this [American] age." His implication was that even music written in Vienna by a German could somehow be American through a process of cultural appropriation. In a certain sense, the claim seems hard to dispute because Beethoven has been an integral part of the American musical landscape for two centuries.[27] Following a different line of thought altogether, cultural historian Daniel Cavicchi has recently illustrated how changes in listening habits at mid-century contributed to emerging conceptions of national musical identity that were more closely related to internal processes of self-fashioning than to external modes of expression. In other words, listeners constructed the nation from the inside out.[28]

Orchestral concerts and the genre of the symphony became vital parts of public musical life throughout Europe and the United States during the early decades of the nineteenth century. For that reason, every component of the symphonic enterprise—composition, performance, listening, and writing—potentially served as a locus for national identity formation. Each chapter illustrates how these elements shaped competing visions of American identity.[29]

THE BEETHOVEN PROBLEM

The second guiding concept in this book is what I call, after musicologist Walter Frisch, the Beethoven problem.[30] As soon as Beethoven's works first crossed the Atlantic in the early nineteenth century, musicians hailed them as superior models of what orchestral music, especially symphonies, ought to be. If an ideal already existed, attempting to match or surpass it must have felt like a daunting task for aspiring composers. On both sides of the Atlantic, moreover, critics frequently greeted new symphonies with direct comparisons to Beethoven or others whose compositional authority went undisputed in public forums. Accusations of imitation or outright plagiarism could stifle a composer's future. The resulting imperative to generate an individual compositional identity created a palpable sense of anxiety among symphonists. Sharing this anxiety, hand-wringing critics often called the symphony's future viability into question as well.[31]

The circular transatlantic flow of music, musicians, and ideas during the early decades of the nineteenth century led to the simultaneous elevation of the genre's status on both sides of the ocean. Municipalities in Europe and the United States alike hosted orchestral concerts at an increasing pace during this period. In the United States, critics expressed awe and reverence toward the symphony as early as the 1830s, not long after such attitudes had become commonplace in Europe. German-speaking musicians, the primary engines driving this change in status, also brought over the nascent idea that the symphony could express a national identity, project distinct political connotations, and serve as an agent of cultural uplift and ennoblement. With this aesthetic framework in mind, American musicians and music lovers frequently perceived the symphony as a vessel that should contain specific types of creative energy.

In nineteenth-century American musical discourse, problems of aesthetics, compositional technique, and national identity were not unique to the symphony. Opera and vernacular song, for example, had long helped to construct national identities in European regions, and they would continue to do so in the United States.[32] The symphony, however, had no such established position or cultural role in the United States—and to a certain extent even in Europe—at the turn of the century. Its relatively benign status nevertheless changed rapidly as the authority purportedly granted to it by respected "masters" such as Beethoven began to raise its international appeal.[33]

How to approach such a potent and expressive vehicle remained a challenge for aspiring composers since performing organizations continued to present works by the roster of perceived masters in fresh listening contexts; critics in turn reinterpreted the meaning and value of these same works, thereby entrenching them in the public imagination. Whether in Europe or in the United States, new symphonists could never avoid Beethoven even if they tried. But aside from any problems brought on by the looming specters of tradition and convention, which might have led composers to abandon the genre altogether, the symphony remained a vital medium of expression in the United States across the nineteenth century, much as it did throughout Europe.

One might assume that the lack of general knowledge about the composers discussed in this book may be attributed to their failure to address the Beethoven problem effectively. Perhaps they merely copied greater masters or were simply crushed under the weight of tradition. This has been a commonly held perception of their music—and rightly so, because certain symphonists did indeed follow traditional paths; they had no compelling reason not to. Even so, other symphonists chose to break radically from convention, often to assert an American identity with programmatic tools such as evocative titles, narrative forms, or national themes. They attempted to capitalize on the symphony's full expressive potential.

Potentially liberating as it was, the turn toward concrete modes of expression introduced a challenging new transatlantic element into the American symphonic enterprise: the Wagner problem. Wagner's increasing visibility in American musical culture following the Civil War (a phenomenon described in chapter 8) complicated what had previously been a simple dichotomy between classicism and innovation as composers engaged with a broadening range of stylistic and conceptual possibilities for the symphony. Skeptical critics leveled accusations of Wagnerism (or similar epithets) in addition to their accusations of plagiarism, all of which at times became proxies for anti-American sentiment. Ultimately, then, the Beethoven problem and the Wagner problem coalesced into a "German music problem" that would have permanent ramifications for American composers. Navigating the marketplace was not as simple as convincing audiences to buy tickets. Style mattered.

THE INSTITUTIONAL HURDLE

But tickets certainly mattered as well. The symphony became a central component of nineteenth-century Western musical culture because a transatlantic surge in the development of musical infrastructure allowed it to flourish. Philadelphia musicians organized one of the country's first successful standing orchestral societies in 1820, only seven years after London's Royal Philharmonic and shortly before the Paris Conservatoire offered a regular series of public orchestral performances. The Philharmonic Society of New-York (as it was then called) was founded in 1842, the same year as its counterpart in Vienna. American orchestras tended to be concentrated in large northeastern urban centers, but cities as far west as Milwaukee, St. Louis, and even San Francisco had hosted several symphonic performances by 1870. Entrepreneurial conductor Theodore Thomas's touring orchestra led a breathtaking number of concerts across the country from 1870 through the 1890s. The founding of permanent orchestras in Boston, Chicago, Cincinnati, and Pittsburgh—and Berlin for that matter—marked the last stage of development during the final quarter of the century. Yet none of these orchestras served as an incubator for American symphonic composition.

That one can speak of an identity crisis or a Beethoven problem, then, is a result of the extraordinary fact that American composers chose to write symphonies at all. The number of symphonies written during the period is truly arresting when one considers that the country's musical landscape was so inhospitable toward them. Even with orchestras dotting the landscape, there was virtually no money to be made writing symphonies. In fact, composers often incurred devastating losses because hiring an orchestra for just one performance—to say nothing of renting a hall or copying parts—proved to be a prohibitive cost that was difficult to recoup with ticket sales. Beyond the cost, mustering enough interested players was also a distinct challenge. The publication of such works, another potential avenue for profit, was largely out of the question. Writing symphonies was simply not a practical endeavor.

Each symphonist listed in table I.1 faced unique challenges depending on his or her relationship to institutions. In addition to composers born in the United States, there were immigrant symphonists from France, Germany, Bohemia, Poland, England, and Canada. Most symphonists operated in and around Boston or New York, but several lived in Philadelphia, Chicago, Cleveland, Saint Louis, San Francisco, or smaller cities such as Ann Arbor, Michigan; still others left the United States and settled abroad. Most were men, but two women joined them despite the widespread belief at the time that women were incapable of composing in larger forms. The majority of these symphonists did not earn enough income from composition to be self-sufficient. Some had full-time careers outside of music, but most were also talented instrumentalists and conductors. Roughly one-fourth of them taught music at the college level, and at least two worked in grade schools; another still was a pioneer educator of young children. And the careers of some, such as George Bristow, outlasted those of canonical European figures such as Johannes Brahms.

Both the Beethoven problem and the national identity crisis were intimately bound to practical dimensions of the orchestral enterprise in the nineteenth century. A composer's status relative to institutional powerbrokers had a significant impact on his or her success. How an orchestra's programming decisions were made, for example, or how it was organized had a significant impact on the repertoires it chose to perform. Which individuals made the decisions also mattered a great deal. German immigrant musicians formed a significant core within the ranks of several major orchestras. Sympathy for German repertoires, and in some cases clear antipathy toward Americans, understandably ran high among this group. In turn, a persistent conflict between German- and English-speaking musicians that spanned virtually the entire century called into question the very possibility of creating a single national musical culture, especially in the orchestral music marketplace. Complicating the matter further, the high esteem in which most resident Americans seemed to hold German music ran counter to the low esteem in which many Anglo-Americans seemed to hold German-speaking people.

Fanning the flames of this conflict in any direction it chose, the musical press also played a significant institutional role in shaping attitudes about the symphony. Writers contributed most directly by reviewing performances of new works, but their import within the broader tapestry of musical culture extended far beyond this function. Readers invested critics with a type of cultural capital that they could then divest onto musicians with their critical remarks. As in the golden age of American criticism during the first half of the twentieth century, nineteenth-century critics could make or break a musician's career.[34]

Despite such importance in local and national contexts, the American musical press occupied only a small corner of the Atlantic world's web-like print culture whose networks extended across the globe. Print was the dominant method of information exchange throughout much of the nineteenth century, and it was vital for processes of knowledge construction and identity formation among readers within a given community. German historian Jürgen Osterhammel has explained that print materials facilitated contact with ideas and artifacts that were previously inaccessible and therefore expanded a reader's cultural horizons, or "reference density."[35]

The phenomenon of increased reference density had a direct bearing on the American musical landscape. A theoretical understanding of music and knowledge about current musical events in Europe became tools that writers and readers could use for building or destroying ideas and aspirations. As we shall see, print materials published in several languages had a significant impact on the careers of the musicians featured in this study. And responding to pervasive biases concerning the power of particular critics, especially John Sullivan Dwight, I have collected a kaleidoscopic array of critical voices in order to illustrate their diversity.

OVERVIEW OF CONTENTS

Spanning the entire nineteenth century, *Orchestrating the Nation* has a long narrative arc that is punctuated at key points. Focusing on the first third of the century, chapter 1 traces the intellectual and cultural strands that would continue to color symphonic composition in later decades: a general receptivity toward European culture and ideas, concomitant changes in perceptions of the symphony's aesthetic value and expressive capacity, and a developing sense that a national mode of musical expression was achievable.

Chapters 2 through 6 trace the intertwined careers of three prolific antebellum composers: Anthony Philip Heinrich, George Frederick Bristow, and William Henry Fry. Each one approached questions of national identity and musical style in their symphonies while negotiating demands made by resistant institutions and mercurial critics. Although their musical styles diverged greatly, none of them found much critical success in this inhospitable environment; audiences, on the other hand, tended to like them. This section reaches its culmination with the introduction of a final antebellum symphonist, Robert Stoepel, a German immigrant whose reputation and pedigree were not enough to thwart negative criticism. Following a brief interlude addressing the Civil War, chapter 7 introduces Louis Moreau Gottschalk, whose career bracketed the war and whose symphonies captured his idiosyncratic philosophical beliefs. These works earned him high acclaim—but only in Spanish America, not the United States.

Two forces altered the course of symphonic composition in the decades following the war: the rise of Wagnerism and the desire for a folk-derived national style, elements that simultaneously affected musical life throughout Europe. In addition to their effects on new compositions in the United States, these changing interests provided writers with excuses to minimize the accomplishments of earlier composers. Chapters 8 through 10 follow the careers of three symphonists—Bristow (who lived well into the 1890s), John Knowles Paine, and Ellsworth Phelps—as they grappled with conflicting public attitudes toward the morality of Wagnerism. Only Paine managed to leave the conflict unharmed.

As soon as Paine's position as a compositional leader seemed secure, however, the critical terrain shifted rapidly under his feet as a new widespread focus on the construction of a folk-based style—an idea Antonín Dvořák articulated publicly and forcefully in 1893—once again lulled critics into a state of amnesia, even in regard to the recent past. Chapters 11 and 12 illustrate how George Whitefield Chadwick, Amy Beach, George Templeton Strong, and (again) Bristow failed to achieve much critical acclaim despite widespread approbation from audiences.

The story of nineteenth-century American symphonic enterprise was like a winter that never turned into spring. Crocuses and tulips peeked out of the soil only to discover that temperatures remained below freezing. In this case, the icy chill was the selective amnesia brought on by diverse ideological agendas—from the rejection of works that did not appear to be symphonies to the denial of any national identity at all. Composers, critics, performers, and audiences forged uneasy alliances and frequently worked at cross purposes, often to the detriment of most of the figures that appear in this book. Ultimately, these composers and their music froze before they could bloom.

CHAPTER 1

✢

The Launch of the Enterprise

Symphonies have occupied preeminent places on American concert programs for over a century and a half.[1] It makes sense that a symphony
orchestra would choose to highlight the genre that inspired its name. But
there are of course more compelling reasons. Symphonies are typically long.
Today they occupy the entire second half of a concert. Some, such as Mahler's
Resurrection, are so long that they can reasonably comprise the first half as
well. The sheer temporal scope of these works gives them an air of grandeur
on par with cathedrals, novels, and magnificent frescoes. Symphonies are
also complex. The limitless combination of orchestral timbres allows for a
degree of expressive variety not found in other instrumental genres. And the
symphony's conventional multi-movement arrangement, with or without a
text, can house engaging musical narratives that allow listeners to ascribe a
wide range of connotative meanings to the work.[2]

These intrinsic elements help explain the symphony's persistence on concert programs, but we should not assume that listeners would necessarily
value them. The fact that the symphony ever held pride of place is not a consequence of its inherent musical properties alone. Historically contingent
cultural processes that occurred rapidly on both sides of the Atlantic during the early part of the nineteenth century dramatically transformed the
musical public's perceptions of the symphony. How this change unfolded in
Europe is well known. The American story is less so.[3]

After hearing Beethoven's Fifth, one listener remarked, "Saturday evening I heard one of Beethoven's great symphonies. [. . .] What majesty,
what depth, what tearful sweetness of the human heart, what triumphs of
the Angel Mind!" Reading these words, we may be struck by how thunder-
ously they echo E. T. A. Hoffmann's ecstatic 1810 review of the same work.[4]
In the years following the review, Hoffmann's ideas and quasi-religious

language gained remarkable traction among European musical writers while Beethoven achieved a near godlike status as a composer capable of probing the inner depths of reality.[5] This listener's ecstatic response to the Fifth is especially compelling because it was penned in 1841 by a young American woman, Margaret Fuller (1810–1850), who had never been to Europe and who had probably never read Hoffmann.[6]

Fuller's Hoffmanesque effusions did not arise out of a vacuum. She was no stranger to European, and especially German, aesthetic thought. When she heard the concert in question, she had been copiously researching the life of Johann Wolfgang von Goethe (1749–1842) and was in the midst of translating an oration on the relationship of nature to the plastic arts by F. W. J. Schelling (1775–1854).[7] Regardless of its specific source of philosophical inspiration, her response reveals that the status of Beethoven and his symphonies in the United States, at least in certain corners, had begun to synchronize with Europe by the 1840s. And how Fuller came to formulate the response in the first place is a microcosmic portrait of how the symphony as a genre came to play an important role in American musical life during the early part of the century. In both cases, it was a transatlantic process.

Beyond the fact that the symphony awakened new emotional feelings, the genre's rising transatlantic stature had real consequences for the country's creative pulse. For many listeners, the German symphony represented the pinnacle of instrumental music, and the symphonies of Beethoven were the most awe-inspiring specimens of all. As one scholar recently put it, the symphony became "the most influential genre on the transatlantic music highway."[8] The country's apparent preference for imported music was not favorable for American composers who contemplated the prospect of writing a symphony. The iron-fisted rules of supply and demand created an atmosphere in which orchestras offered only the music that subscribers and financiers felt comfortable backing or that the musicians themselves wanted to play. For their part, critics tended to support the reproduction of older music over experiments with new works. But these barriers did not deter American composers from writing symphonies anyway. This chapter accounts for the factors that led them to make this choice and describes the environments in which they lived and worked.

COSMOPOLITANISM ASCENDANT

The United States was born with an identity crisis. Following the Constitution's ratification in 1787, the federal government had a blueprint for its own organization along with rules to follow, structures to build, personnel to assemble, and many other actions to take. This document was the world's first republican constitution. It allowed aspects of the new country's political identity to be fixed from the beginning. But the freshness and relative stability of this political framework did not immediately spur sweeping cultural changes. Important facets of American culture that were independent of national politics did not change at all. Americans, at least those of the privileged classes, still spoke English and drank tea, and, under the explicit protection of the Bill of Rights, could enjoy reading newspapers and singing psalms more than ever. Daily life after ratification was practically no different than it was before.

The rift between sweeping political change and cultural inertia created a lingering condition shaping artistic creation throughout the first half of the nineteenth century that some scholars have diagnosed as "postcolonial anxiety."[9] Like their counterparts in decolonized nations of the twentieth century, post-Independence writers, visual artists, and musicians began to assert their cultural autonomy by directly confronting this anxiety. Their responses generally appeared in one of three guises: idealistically attempting to reject outside influences altogether, embracing the reality of the nation's economic and cultural dependence on Europe (especially Britain), or, as was most common, some combination of the two.

The distance across this spectrum elicited tension. In the world of letters, for example, novelists James Fenimore Cooper and Washington Irving engaged in several spiteful exchanges that epitomized the impulse certain authors felt to create a national literature. Cooper repeatedly and unfairly accused Irving of Anglophilia, a harsh and politically devastating accusation at the time. But such accusations did not help answer the question of how an author was supposed to eliminate English literature—everything from Shakespeare to Keats—from the American creative lexicon. These practicalities at times escaped certain thinkers, such as Ralph Waldo Emerson, who later fueled the fire by condemning American authors for their apish dependence on European ideas and warned them that they were "suspected to be timid, imitative, tame." Emerson's criticism notwithstanding, it was a difficult enterprise for authors to assert a specifically American identity without echoing well-established and familiar models.[10]

Such anxiety was a pervasive malaise among musicians as well, and the symptoms were similar. Beginning around 1800, Americans widely believed that the country needed to develop its musical identity. Daniel Dana (1771–1859), who would later become president of Dartmouth College, told the Essex (MA) Musical Association in 1803 that the nation's musical character was "scarcely formed" and "still in its infancy." Five years later, Caleb Emerson (1779–1853), a prominent newspaper editor, sent a similar message to the Amherst (NH) Handellian Musical Society. "Though favorable to the general diffusion of knowledge," he noted, "the United States [. . .] affords little encouragement to the vigorous cultivation of any particular science," including music.[11]

Despite this agreement about the problem, their solutions were opposite. Like their literary colleagues, they suggested that Americans follow one of two paths. Dana proposed that Americans quickly fashion their musical development on current British taste, especially the "immortal" composi-tions of Handel, Arne, Milgrove, and any others "who have imbibed their spirit." Emerson, however, felt that Americans should bow to no outside authority in matters of taste or skill. He claimed that musicians needed to combine "natural genius" with arduous study; only then would "distin-guished *American* composers" appear on the horizon. Though subtle, the dif-ference between the two solutions was critical. One focused outward, the other inward.[12]

Over the next several decades, Dana's cosmopolitan solution—one defined by openness to cultures outside U.S. borders—came to dominate musical life throughout the country. Powerful institutions and influential musi-cians, many of whom came from London or elsewhere in Europe, supported this solution. In concert halls from Boston to Charleston and as far west as Lexington, Kentucky, the country's first ensembles fed audiences a steady diet of imported music. For example, Boston's Handel and Haydn Society, whose name is a testament to just such a cosmopolitan outlook, maintained and marketed cultural ties to the Old World. The society's leaders wanted it to be a national organization that brought great works to mass audiences and served as a model for all American cities. Echoing Dana, they enshrined their desire to solve the country's musical ailments with a prescription of Handel and Haydn directly into the society's constitution:

> While in our country, [. . .] the admirers of musick find their beloved science far
> from exciting the feelings, or exercising the powers, to which it is accustomed
> in the old world. [. . .] The undersigned do hereby agree to form themselves
> into a society, by the name of the HANDEL AND HAYDN SOCIETY, for the
> purpose of improving the style of performing sacred musick, and introducing
> into more general use, the works of HANDEL, HAYDN, and other eminent
> composers.[13]

The document left no provision for cultivating music written by local composers.

Writers fawned over the group's approach. Commenting on a concert from 1819, one listener observed that "the celebrated chef d'oeuvre of art, 'Haydn's creation,' has been performed at Boston by the *Handel and Haydn Society*. Such performances will remove the vulgar error that we have no taste for music."[14] John Rowe Parker (1777–1844), a Boston-based music business-man and editor of a musical magazine, agreed wholeheartedly. Reviewing a series of published collections of the society's choicest repertoire, he gushed at the contents while criticizing American composers. "Many fine specimens of compositions from the works of *Handel, Haydn, Mozart, Pleyel, Beethoven* and other Foreign and English composers," he claimed, would remove the "defects" of American psalmody—one of the only areas of composition in which locals had been active.[15] Idealistic as the group's founders might have been, they were also eminently practical. They took what had worked in Europe to cultivate taste—or at least so they believed—and hoped it would work equally well in the United States.[16] Developing local creativity would be nothing more than a side effect.

Such institutionalized cosmopolitanism was not unique in the early part of the century, nor was it limited to the Boston area. The leaders of Philadelphia's Musical Fund Society, founded in 1820 (not long, incidentally, after Vienna's Gesellschaft der Musikfreunde), also showcased popular European composers rather than cultivate local works. Replicating the British and continental trend of mixed-genre performances, the society's first concert included excerpts from symphonies, concertos, and overtures by Andreas Romberg, Bernhard Romberg, Gioachino Rossini, Étienne Méhul, Pierre Rode, and even Beethoven—the very composers whose music was popular throughout Europe. As in London, lighter vocal pieces such as English glees, airs, and choruses were interspersed among these heavier works.[17] Over the next several years, the society's library saw manifold increases because of its financial ability to import scores. The group quickly tackled staple oratorios performed by Boston's Handel and Haydn Society, from whom the Philadelphians frequently borrowed music. In order to educate audiences during performances, the society also provided thick booklets containing a work's texts along with critical commentary taken from leading English historians such as Charles Burney, John Hawkins, and Thomas Busby.[18] Matching London, rather than distinguishing Philadelphia, was the group's implicit aim.

Such transplantation and continuation of Old World musical culture nurtured a paradigm of compositional emulation among the resident composers who attempted to enter the local marketplace. In this cosmopolitan environment, the most practical choice for composers was to write firmly within European conventions. They may not have considered other possibilities at all since no expected them to do otherwise. Filippo Trajetta (1777–1854), for example, one of the most prolific composers working in the United States after the turn of the century, wrote three biblically themed oratorios, several cantatas, at least two sinfonias, and a violin concerto, all in traditional idioms. His republican political outlook, which brought him to the United States, did not inspire him to seek other musical shores, particularly not by constructing a uniquely American musical style.[19]

Another successful composer, Charles Hommann (1803–ca. 1870) of Philadelphia, wrote the country's earliest symphony in the increasingly popular four-movement Viennese mold. It was idiomatically identical to noteworthy late eighteenth-century European works and should have attracted attention from performing groups. Though Hommann was a respected professional member of the Musical Fund Society, he instead dedicated the work to the nearby Philharmonic Society of Bethlehem, an ensemble of Moravian settlers. The reasons behind this decision are unclear because the core repertoire of the Moravians was also European. But even after the benevolent Philharmonic premiered the symphony, the Musical Fund Society inexplicably never performed it despite its resemblance to works by Haydn. Favoring the music of now forgotten figures like Andreas Romberg, the group evidently found no special reason to program pieces written by locals.[20]

The Musical Fund Society eventually became more cordial toward local composers when it began to offer prizes for works by resident Americans. But the directors were not interested in compositional innovation. "Certainly if the sphere of emulation, and improvement shall become once aroused," they explained, "we may be allowed to indulge a hope, that in music as well as in the other branches of the Fine Arts, our Country shall one day attain an elevated rank."[21] Instead of generating an outbreak of interest in composition, the competition had the opposite effect. The society's directors bemoaned declining interest in its activities and attributed this deterioration to a rival society of amateurs that had offered its own liberal prizes for composition, one of which Hommann himself won.[22] The Musical Fund Society's prize, awarded over a year after the turmoil, went to Antonio Bagioli (1795–1871), an Italian-born composer and singing master living in New York whose works were also idiomatic for the time.

Despite their neglect of local composition, these institutions did not consider their activities unpatriotic; quite the opposite. Many musicians believed that the performance of European masterworks would serve to uplift American culture and would in turn become a means of asserting national musical autonomy. Following a celebration of George Washington's birthday in 1815, during which a large Boston chorus programmed works by Handel alongside hymns of peace, one witness emphatically remarked that "nothing but a 'Te Deum Laudamus' could satisfy the emotions of that hour [. . .] and a performance of the Dettingen Te Deum and the Hallelujah Chorus of Handel were executed by two hundred and fifty vocal and instrumental performers."[23] Handel, an ostensible symbol of the English monarchy, had been reinterpreted as an expression of American patriotism in this new context.

Such practices manifested what has recently been called "rooted cosmopolitanism"—being "attached to a home of one's own, with its own cultural particularities, but taking pleasure from the presence of other, different places that are home to other, different people."[24] Boston critic John Sullivan Dwight found this pleasure in German music. Commenting on Beethoven's symphonies early in his career, he wrote:

The truth is, Beethoven's is the music of this age; it gives voice to the impris-
oned soul and aspiration of this age. Spiritually and essentially, it can be better
comprehended by unmusical Americans in Boston now, than it could in Vienna
when it was born. It was prophetic of the great world movement [democracy]
that now stirs so many hearts. [. . .] The child will study what it loves; and we
apprehend it is our destiny in this age and in this land to love Beethoven.[25]

In this formulation, Beethoven's was the music of democratic America despite
the fact that it was deeply enmeshed in aristocratic Habsburg Vienna. And
his message to composers was clear. Since European works could develop a
new national patina, the country had enough music. If Dwight had his way,
composers had no need to write symphonies at all.

MAKE WAY FOR THE SYMPHONY

Musical cosmopolitanism was a fact of life throughout the nineteenth century, but it entailed more than the performance and enjoyment of European
music on American soil. The belief systems underlying European musical
thought, particularly the high valuation of instrumental music, also found a
welcome home in the United States. By 1827, the year of Beethoven's death,
the symphony had garnered widespread acceptance in Western Europe as the
most learned and difficult instrumental genre. It attained a similar status in
the United States around 1830, when critics and audiences asserted a status
for instrumental music rivaling that of the oratorio, which for decades had
occupied a position on both sides of the Atlantic as the most revered genre
of music.[26]

The American Revolution coincided with an age during which the symphony enjoyed a high status as entertaining music within the courtly environment of Europe, particularly in Vienna—an environment antithetical
to revolutionary principles. Without nobility serving as patrons, the early
United States did not have a well-developed infrastructure for supporting
symphonic composition. As in Britain, American concert life acquired a
more public character than it had in Vienna and elsewhere. But even in
the Austrian capital, the turn of the century marked a dip in symphonic
productivity as older networks of patronage began to unravel, causing
Beethoven himself to experience the public marketplace's relative hostil-
ity toward the genre.[27] Before the 1820s, there was no good reason why
the American public would demand symphonies, or why composers would
write any.[28]

Within a short time, though, American attitudes would change, partly
because of the rapid canonization of Viennese composers in Europe. In 1831,
an anonymous writer for a New England magazine exhorted readers to

contemplate the high degree of skill that composing orchestral masterworks required:

> Read an overture by Haydn or Mozart, or listen to it, simply as a study of human intellect, and you will confess that the mind which could invent those airs and harmonies, could, in each note, as it was written, calculate the precise effect of an orchestra of a hundred instruments, give to each its proper office, combine, interweave, and separate and reunite them, so as to produce that matchless result by which you are entranced, is of the rarest order of human genius.[29]

The appearance of more performing ensembles devoted to orchestral music fed this desire for intellectually challenging concerts. Not long after Boston's Handel and Haydn Society had become established as one of the country's leading choral ensembles, prominent Boston musicians and civic leaders attempted to cultivate an appreciation for European orchestral music as well. Initially founded in 1833 as an educational institution, the Boston Academy of Music soon emerged as the city's chief advocate of orchestral music under the guidance of Boston's mayor, Samuel Atkins Eliot (1798–1862).

Although the Academy was originally intended to promulgate sacred choral music—much like the Handel and Haydn Society—Eliot eventually enlisted the help of a semi-permanent orchestra to assist the choir in its performances of large-scale works.[30] This innovation was the first in a series of maneuvers to transform the Academy into an exclusively orchestral organization and to distance itself from the older ensemble's mission. A mere three years later, critics began to opine that despite Eliot's efforts, there was still *not enough* orchestral music in Boston. Theodor Hach, a magazine editor and critic who had recently arrived from German lands, complained that "orchestral music is neither understood and appreciated by the public, nor is it ever brought out in that style of uniform and effective performance, that commands attention and interest."[31] Hach also urged the Academy to cultivate instrumental music even more than vocal "because the former is at present in a lower condition among us."[32]

Eliot and the Academy took this advice and resolved to make orchestral music their primary focus. "In fact," Eliot wrote in the Academy's ninth annual report, "the organization of the orchestra, as regards both skill and disposition, was such as we desire to see perpetuated; and the only change we could wish would be to increase the proportion of well-played string instruments." Just a year later, he believed the Academy had succeeded in swaying public taste in favor of orchestral music. In language reminiscent of the anonymous critic quoted above, he congratulated Boston audiences for discerning that "solo performances [. . .] are discovered to be matters of less interest and effect, in general, than the combination of many instruments, a whole orchestra, in the performance of great compositions of musical genius." The Academy disbanded in 1847 but had left an indelible mark on the city.[33]

New York musicians orchestrated a similar transformation. Unlike in Boston, it was more than a purely intellectual and experimental venture. The German-speaking community, led by waves of recent immigrant musicians, directly fostered interest in symphonies and gave the city's orchestral music culture a more distinctively German character. The Philharmonic Society of New-York, founded as a cooperative venture in 1842, quickly became the city's most visible organization promoting instrumental music. Roughly half of the fifty-two original performing members of the Philharmonic were Germans, leading one historian to remark that they were the "prop" of the organization and that "without them an orchestra would have been an impossibility."[34] Beethoven and Mendelssohn were the most frequently performed composers, followed by Spohr, Weber, and Schumann, and then by lesser-known figures such as Heinrich Marschner, Johann Kalliwoda, and Peter Josef von Lindpaintner—all Germans. The Philharmonic's German contingent brought more than music from their homeland; they also brought a love of the symphony. In the first three seasons alone, the orchestra performed Beethoven's Third, Fifth, and Seventh twice, his Second and Eighth once, and other symphonies by Mozart, Spohr, and Haydn—in nearly all cases as the opening work, as was customary.[35]

The strategies taken by Eliot in Boston and the Philharmonic in New York had a palpable effect on listeners, many of whom, like Margaret Fuller, began to develop reverent attitudes toward the genre. Louis Madeira (1819–1896), longtime secretary of Philadelphia's Musical Fund Society, believed that the city's growing taste for fine music hinged on the group's ability to perform symphonies. Americans should follow the lead of the Germans, he insisted, because they (unlike Americans) had never let Italian opera overshadow the symphony's inherent beauty.[36] The society's board of directors believed that the orchestra and its patrons had finally reached maturity after "the largest audience ever gathered in the walls of the Musical Fund Hall" showed enthusiastic appreciation for the group's stellar rendition of the "complicated yet expressive harmonies" of Beethoven's First.[37]

John Sullivan Dwight shared this sentiment when he dreamily claimed that symphonies make us "forget that there is any other world. [. . .] And a true symphony, a deep work of art in that form, will be more or less to the minds who hear it, in precise proportion to their own depth, just as nature is."[38] New Yorkers followed suit. Reviewing an 1849 performance of Spohr's dramatic Seventh Symphony given by the Philharmonic, critic Henry Cood Watson praised the work as "truly metaphysical" and, echoing Hoffmann, added that "its depths must be sounded to find the full scope of its power and meaning."[39] A performance of Beethoven's Fifth left the typically prolix diarist

George Templeton Strong awestruck and speechless: "It's hardly worthwhile to write any grandiloquencies on the subject. [. . .] So, to save trouble, I simply write a '!' and anybody who'll have the goodness to dilute the same over six closely written pages will possess my views and sentiments about *Beethoven's Symphony in C minor.*"[40] Symphonies quickly enraptured American audiences and drew them to continue favoring a cosmopolitan musical climate.

A BREWING CONFLICT OVER EXPRESSION

European debates over the symphony's future also spilled onto American shores and colored local discussions about the genre's future. In the years following Beethoven's death, the symphony continued to be a ripe topic for criticism and analysis in European newspapers and music periodicals. "We find imitations" of Beethoven's symphonies, Robert Schumann lamented in 1839, "and, oddly enough, principally of his earlier symphonies, as if each one needed a certain time to be understood and copied."[41] Schumann's vexation with "imitators" epitomized the Beethoven problem facing aspiring symphonists, for how to remain expressive in well-tried forms was not an easy question to answer. Discussions about the symphony's expressive potential nevertheless consolidated around two related issues: the musical representation of extramusical content and the stylistic boundaries of the genre itself. Both issues heavily shaped the genre's growth and reception over the next several decades and created distinct musical camps among the musical intelligentsia throughout Europe.[42]

European musicians from the period tended to believe that instrumental music had the ability to express or suggest content outside of music itself. For some, such content included descriptive or representational elements in which musical sounds could suggest a vivid visual image or sequence of events. Writers captured this idea in the ubiquitous German terms *Tonmalerei* and *das Tongemälde* (both of which mean "tone painting," the first as an act and the second as an object).[43] For others, music could express interior emotions, feelings, or sentiments—in a word, an ethos—but little else. Beethoven's description of his Sixth Symphony's first movement, "Erwachen heiterer Empfindungen bei der Ankunft auf dem Lande [Awakening of Cheerful Feelings upon Arrival in the Country]," became one of the most famous examples of this concept. And, for others still, even abstract music bearing no descriptive title could evoke an ethos.[44]

Disagreements about the suitability of musical representation created two roughly defined camps that, for convenience, might be called the "ethos" camp and the "tone painters." The ethos camp included composers who wrote symphonies untouched by pre-compositional literary narratives or poetic images. Robert Schumann, Felix Mendelssohn, and Niels

Gade tended to fall into this group, as did the forgotten (but once important) George Onslow, Franz Berwald, and Johann Kalliwoda.[45] Tone painters, including Hector Berlioz, Félicien David, and at times Louis Spohr, wrote symphonies heavily laced with narrative connotations that were spelled out in printed concert programs.[46] The two camps were not always friendly, or even neutral, toward one another. Critics associated with the ethos camp repeatedly panned the excessive literary dimension of the tone painters, the most notorious example of which was Robert Schumann's review of Berlioz's *Symphonie fantastique*. He claimed with national chauvinism that "all Germany greeted [the program] thus: such signboards always have a touch of unworthiness and charlatanry."[47] A suggestion of the music's meaning—a mere hint at its ethos—would have been enough for any German.

Differences concerning the genre's form further sharpened the divisions over narrative and pictorial content in symphonies. Two camps that fell along similar lines also began to take shape around this issue. Composers from the ethos camp utilized and expanded Beethoven's advanced formal techniques—cyclic integration, the choral finale, and lengthy sonata forms—but their experiments were mild. Of all the members of this camp, only Mendelssohn truly tested the genre's conventional boundaries in his *Lobgesang*. The tone painters, on the other hand, aggressively pushed the envelope. David's *Le Désert*, spoken passages and all, is barely classifiable as a symphony (he called it an "ode-symphonie"). And few composers attempted the physical theatricality of the dueling orchestras in Spohr's grandiose Seventh, subtitled *Irdisches und Göttliches im Menschenleben (The Earthly and Divine in the Life of Man)*. In his review of Berlioz's *Symphonie fantastique*, Schumann had suggested that the form and structure of Beethoven's Ninth provided the outer limits of the genre and that further experimentation was not only unnecessary but detrimental to its progress. These composers did not take heed.

Critics from the period stimulated the benign factionalization found in these compositional trends by introducing contentious political language into their writings. In an 1834 review of two overtures by Kalliwoda, for example, Schumann made direct comparisons between musical factions and political parties. "Just as in politics," he asserted, "one may divide the musical into Liberals, Moderates, and Royalists, or into Romantics, Modernists, and Classicists."[48] Two years later, another *Neue Zeitschrift für Musik* critic, writing from St. Petersburg, praised the inexorability of the unification of politics and music.[49] Swept up by such rhetoric, critics often used political language in their interpretations of specific works, especially symphonies. In German-speaking lands in particular, listeners increasingly began to hear the genre as a model of a democratic society and an expression of the political ideal of German unification. *Neue Zeitschrift für Musik* critics, such as Wolfgang Robert Griepenkerl, Ernst Gottschald, and Franz Brendel, used these interpretive strategies throughout the 1830s and 1840s.[50]

As early as the 1820s, moreover, the symphony in German-speaking lands had become an accepted means of distinguishing German national identity from French and Italian because listeners often considered it a distinctly German genre. Reviewing Mendelssohn's *Scottish* Symphony, for example, critic August Kahlert (1807–1864) claimed, with distinct national pride,

> The domain of the symphony has, for a long time, indisputably belonged to the Germans, a nation that generally dominates the realm of instrumental music, wherein the symphony is the most distinguished province. Despite all the effort they give, France and Italy do not understand this dream world of tones that the German has created, where there is no need for words to guide the listener's imagination to definite concepts, but where free forms of the tonal design elevate themselves to a governing authority.[51]

As Kahlert's chauvinist pronouncements demonstrate, critical discussions about the symphony could move fluidly from content and formal structure to questions concerning national identity.[52]

Political interpretations of the symphony traveled across the Atlantic, and few nineteenth-century American writers championed them more ably than John Sullivan Dwight. Influenced heavily by the aesthetic writings of Friedrich Schiller, Dwight believed firmly in music's ability to model both right living and the ideal political state.[53] He thought the symphony was an especially valuable model because it could blend and orchestrate disparate ideas into a unified and ordered whole. "Each note in the great world-symphony," he told a Boston audience in 1844, "is a whole, a unit in itself, and must assert its individuality, insisting on its own peculiar sound, at the same time that it reverently dedicates itself and helps fulfil beyond itself the harmony of the whole."[54] For Dwight, Beethoven's symphonies were the most valuable model of all. Beethoven, he claimed, was "the seventh note in the scale" toward an abolishment of human hierarchies.[55] The United States already embodied many of Dwight's democratic social ideals. It was only natural, then, that he would hear an image of his home country in the sounds of a Beethoven symphony (in this case the Sixth): "'we are all *one*, though many,' [the notes] seem to say."[56] The reference to the national motto adopted in 1782, *E pluribus unum*, would have been unmistakable to his readers.

For its part, tone-painterly music confounded critics like Dwight, who did not know how to integrate it into a political and aesthetic theory that relied on musical abstraction. Dwight's friend George William Curtis once lamented that Beethoven's representational battle symphony, *Wellingtons Sieg*, was "a sad disappointment." He wrote in a letter to Dwight in 1843 that it "was merely a musical picture of the battle—a battle of Prague for the orchestra! [. . .] Imagine me, a fervid worshipper of Beethoven, rushing in to hear a symphony where, with all orchestral force, the old song, L-a-w, Law, was banged into my ears."[57] Outside of its original compositional context, the piece's representational elements had lost all meaning for Curtis. And Margaret Fuller, who was enraptured after hearing Beethoven's Fifth, claimed that the more descriptive Sixth, the *Pastoral*, "does not require a depth in the life of the hearer, but only simplicity to feel its beauties." The symphony was, as she put it, "only one hour of [Beethoven's] true life."[58]

Comments such as these laid the early groundwork for resistance to descriptive orchestral music in the United States (which was later called "program music" after Liszt invented the term in 1855). The Beethoven problem facing aspiring symphonic composers in Europe, along with its potential for descriptive and nationalized expression, had arrived in full force in the United States by the 1840s. With Dwight, Fuller, and many others placing Beethoven and his symphonies at the summit of a musical Olympus, local composers faced a significant quandary: Since Beethoven could reportedly speak for the American people, even *being* American could not necessarily help them gain a foothold. Compounding this issue, the works that were ostensibly solving the Beethoven problem in Europe—symphonies by Mendelssohn, Schumann, and Spohr—were the very symphonies that introduced the American public to the genre in the first place. For nearly a quarter century, they were practically the only symphonies Americans knew.

A NATION RESOUNDING

Drawing from a nascent national pride of their own, certain American composers turned toward patriotic modes of expression during the earlier part of the century. Caleb Emerson had argued that the exploitation of Americans' "natural genius" would bring about a new era of the nation's musical life. But thinkers like Emerson rarely articulated practical steps for composers to follow. Benjamin Carr (1768–1831) and James Hewitt (1770–1820), two English-born composers who immigrated permanently to the United States, nevertheless offered one solution that would have remarkable endurance throughout the century: the use of descriptive, patriotic musical elements—precisely the tools that confounded Curtis and Dwight.

Hewitt's *The Battle of Trenton* (1797), a solo piano work, depicts George Washington's famous 1776 crossing of the Delaware River and subsequent trouncing of enemy Hessian forces. It bears a remarkable resemblance to the highly popular *Battle of Prague* (ca. 1788) by František Koczwara (ca. 1750–1791), a potboiler that commemorated a Bohemian military victory against Prussian forces in 1756.[59] Drawing from the work's unabashedly patriotic sentiment, Hewitt borrowed several of its musical elements, including rumbling bass notes depicting cannon fire and rapid chromatic sixteenth-note figurations that suggest intense action. He also added enough musical Americana to alter its character substantially. The appearance of "Yankee Doodle" in the place of "God Save the King" near the work's rousing conclusion gives it an unmistakably American character. With the tableau narrative style used to commemorate an important national event and his clever use of national tunes, Hewitt had created a musical monument to America's achievements in war and international politics (see table 1.1).

Hewitt employed similar patriotic strategies in *Fourth of July* (1801), a piano work evoking the annual celebration of the country's most important and distinctly national holiday. In the period following the American Revolution, a shared sense of national identity emerged in the exuberant repetition of local patriotic celebrations around the country, especially on Independence Day.[60] Hewitt's sonata musically depicts a parade of troops walking through town for a Fourth of July celebration. After the parade passes, sustained major chords signify the "shouts of the populace," which are immediately followed by a rousing rendition of "Hail Columbia," one of the country's unofficial national anthems at the time. There was nothing particularly innovative about the work, but it captured the spirit of patriotic celebration and created a vivid musical portrait of a national occurrence that transcended any specific locale.

Although these and similar works mirrored European styles, they participated in broader attempts at national identity formation that swept the country after the Revolutionary War. Commemoration of the war and the signing of the Declaration of Independence quickly spread into every corner of national life and served as a means for constructing a uniquely American identity. Even before the war's end, printers released engraved pictorial accounts of the early battles along with biographies of the leading officers. Novelist Hugh Henry Brackenridge (1748–1816) penned a five-act commemoration of the Battle of Bunker Hill in 1776, just a year after the battle itself.[61] Shortly after victory was declared, artist Charles Willson Peale (1741–1827)

Table 1.1. STRUCTURALLY SIMILAR FINALES

F. Koczwara, *The Battle of Prague* (1788)	J. Hewitt, *The Battle of Trenton* (1797)
"Cries of the Wounded"	"Grief of the Americans . . ."
"Trumpet of Victory"	"Yankee Doodle"
"God Save the King"	"Quick Step for the Band"
"Turkish Music, Quick Step"	"Trumpets of Victory"
Finale—Allegro	Allegro—"General Rejoicing"

attempted to construct a triumphal arch in downtown Philadelphia and painted portraits of famous military personalities. Former officers in the war established the Society of the Cincinnati in 1783 with the express purpose of preserving the war's memory, and citizens from the city of Boston incorporated an organization to build an enormous physical monument to the Battle of Bunker Hill, which stands above the city still today.[62]

The prevailing attitude surrounding these activities was one of reverence for sacrifice and united effort. The Americans who publicly consumed commemorative artworks were to model their own growth as citizens on the virtues of American soldiers. Patriotic musical works certainly suited this purpose. Hewitt depicted the "ardor of the Americans at landing" with a breathless triplet figuration found nowhere else in *The Battle of Trenton*, for example, while the Hessians flee from the Americans not once but twice after being defeated. But resident American composers such as Hewitt did not attain widespread approbation, or longevity, among the musical elite. Throughout their careers, their works were overshadowed by the great oratorios of Handel and Haydn.

While such patriotism was primarily a compositional phenomenon, it partnered well with the activities of certain musicians who traveled to the United States from elsewhere and wanted to connect with local culture—the reverse of Dwight's "rooted cosmopolitanism." Around March of 1848, a group of musicians in Berlin, the Germania Musical Society, resolved to form an egalitarian orchestra and departed for the United States "in order to enflame and stimulate in the hearts of these politically free people, through numerous performances of our greatest instrumental composers, [. . .] love for the fine art of music." Their motto: "One for all and all for one." Inspired by the democratic ideals fueling the revolutionary insurrections taking place in Berlin, they believed that the United States would be the perfect home for their orchestra—indeed the only home—precisely because the new country more heartily embraced their worldview than any other.[63]

Like many American listeners in the 1840s, the Germanians esteemed instrumental music above all other forms and associated musical performance with political life. Enacting Dwight's ideal of the individual uniting with the whole, they avoided showy displays of virtuosity and became known for their especially pristine performances. The society's historian, Henry Albrecht, compared this approach favorably to European common practice, in which "everybody in the orchestra seeks (with few exceptions) to exhibit himself through the assertion of exceptional mannerisms in performance; because of this, of course, a performance rarely appears totally flawless."[64] Finding a home and a welcome community of democratic music lovers, the Germanians toured the United States for six years and, according to one estimate, gave over nine hundred concerts with more than one million listeners in attendance; critics widely praised their idiosyncratic approach to performance.[65] The group's erstwhile leader Carl Bergmann (1821–1876) would become a powerful advocate for American-born composers later in his career, but the Germanians did not actively support symphonic composition in their new home.

ORCHESTRATING THE NATION

Composers considering the possibility of national expression with symphonic music had no blueprint showing them how to do it. Hewitt's blatant patriotic approach was not the obvious choice. At the time, thinkers tended to consider musical technique an ineffable manifestation of a national character, or "genius" as it was often called, that had little to do with historical themes such as the Revolution. A recent Yale graduate named Ichabod Skinner contended in 1796 that "the Italians have for many years excelled, and perhaps still excel all other nations in music.—The Germans also have carried it to a great degree of perfection.—The former are most highly favored by nature and climate, but the latter have nearly equalled the former, by industry and application."[66] Differences in style were the natural consequences of differing characters and climate conditions, he thought, not individual agency.

Common formulations like Skinner's did not typically specify what sort of music might manifest a national character: folk songs, sacred music, instrumental music, a combination of these, or something else entirely. Even so, questions concerning national musical types came under increasing scrutiny in both American and British musical circles after the turn of the nineteenth century. Two general concepts drove the philosophical approaches to these questions. "National music" typically referred to songs with vague origins that had inhered in the popular consciousness through long-term historical processes. Writers frequently referred to Scottish folk melodies or the Swiss *Ranz des Vaches* as ideal examples of this type. The second concept, "scientific music," referred to music with an identifiable authorial source and a sound that somehow demonstrated the composer's inventiveness; writers frequently called this category "cultivated music" when emphasizing its dependence on literate pedagogy.[67]

The relative value of each musical type was a source of debate. National music enthusiasts believed that its rootedness in a community ensured its "purity," whereas advocates of scientific music argued that it could transcend its national origin and was therefore superior. One such advocate, a writer for *Blackwell's Edinburgh Magazine*, a Scottish monthly with articles that were reprinted frequently in the United States, argued in 1819 that national music "may operate with peculiar effect on the feelings of the natives; but this is no reason why any man should refuse to extend his taste, and enlighten his views, so as to be able to relish scientific music."[68] A community's ultimate goal, therefore, should be to elevate itself with exposure to more scientific music. Samuel Atkins Eliot of Boston, among others, would adopt this very position over the next two decades.

The distinction between the two musical types was not always sharp. Many thinkers believed that scientific music could possess nationalized traits, an idea mitigating the notion that learning and cultivation were universal experiences. Only a few months after the *Blackwell's* piece, for example, an article in John Rowe Parker's *Euterpiad* asserted that German national music must not have been "reasonably striking" because "the pure German school of composition, however profound, is more adapted to the learned few, than for the feeling many, and is somewhat deficient in grace and melody." Only those German composers such as Mozart, who had "ingrafted the Italian style upon their own," had produced any masterpieces worthy of the name.[69] According to this frame of mind, national music had been supplanted (but not erased) by cultivated music, and so-called masterworks could acquire a national (and even transnational) character through technical means. But specifically *how* a composer might go about creating nationalized music remained unaddressed.

René La Roche (1795–1872) of Philadelphia, a distinguished physician, founding member and violinist of the city's Musical Fund Society, and owner of one of the country's largest libraries of musical literature, continued to address these issues in a series of articles written for the *American Quarterly Review* between 1827 and 1837. Early in the series, La Roche adopted the commonly held position that the music of each nation possesses "some peculiarity depending on the taste and disposition of the people, and by which it is distinguished from that of every other country."[70] The next several articles treated these two topics—disposition and taste—in some detail. In a review of published lectures given by the English composer William Crotch (1775–1847), La Roche noted that "[n]ations, like individuals, when of a serious turn of mind, or engaged in serious pursuits, will naturally prefer music of a corresponding character [to its disposition]; while others, of a different disposition or differently occupied, or the former, if a change takes place in their pursuits, will give the preference to music of an opposite stamp." Such sustained effort, La Roche argued elsewhere, can bring about "notorious changes" in a nation's taste over a long period of time.[71]

La Roche considered the history of French music an apt illustration of this phenomenon. Commenting on the culturally "mixed" system of French composition, he attributed its peculiarities to its wealth, central geographic location, and mild climate, as well as the serendipitous circumstance that "reform and innovation" were "intrusted to several great masters of the two schools of Italy and Germany." Emphasizing the element of sustained effort, he added that the "almost daily performances of the best productions of the two countries" had contributed to the development of French musical sophistication. Extended serious exposure to great music could cultivate taste within a community, he claimed, and France was his proof.[72]

When commenting on the question of an American national music (of any kind), writers turned dour. One New Englander bemoaned, "As a people, it may be regretted that we have displayed no musical genius, and not much musical taste. We not only have no national music,—we have scarcely a single composer."[73] La Roche agreed, claiming, "It would be highly unreasonable to look for any music in our own country, which deserves to be called national." He explained that the country's ethnic heterogeneity limited its ability to forge a common musical heritage. And to make matters worse, whatever folk music America's "yeomanry" had seemed to adopt tended to be "debased" renditions of operatic tunes or favorite instrumental pieces.[74]

But all hope was not lost, at least for La Roche. He observed that hymnody had become a fledgling national music in the United States because of its communal character. Large festivities centered on national feelings, he claimed, might also inspire authentic national poetry and music—creations that "could speak to the inmost heart of the common man, and [. . .] instead of casting every thought into the transatlantic mould, should embody the national feeling in words that burn."[75] Of course, wishing this process to unfold and willing it were two separate issues. Although La Roche did not make the connection explicit, the process by which French music had attained its unique character could very well help the United States:

> [I]n our opinion, the French may be considered as possessing a school of music in many respects peculiar to them. If this be conceded to us, it will follow that the number of schools now extant in Europe, amounts to three; the German, the Italian, and the French; that the two first differ materially from each other; [. . .] and finally, that the French school, though approximating on some points to each of the preceding—uniting the nervousness of the first [German] to the gracefulness of the second [Italian], possesses characteristic features calculated to establish its independence of them both.[76]

For Americans, establishing such independence was only a matter of time and exposure since even a conglomeration of cultures, such as that found in France, could develop musical autonomy.

The dramatic irony of all this theorization was that Germans themselves were experiencing a similar anxiety about how to define a national musical identity. Americans tended to take for granted that German musical identity had long since been fixed. Between the middle of the eighteenth century and the middle of the nineteenth, however, prominent German writers as diverse as Johann Joachim Quantz, Johann Karl Friedrich Triest, Ernst Ludwig Gerber, and Franz Brendel all asserted that French and Italian music occupied distinct cultural spaces that could be melded into a cosmopolitan

German conglomerate. After the turn of the nineteenth century, the supposed profundity and "spiritual depth" of German music—traits described in particular by E. T. A. Hoffmann—would allow it to transcend its constituent parts. Into the 1820s, Berlin critic A. B. Marx would lament (much like his American counterparts) that the state of German music had fallen into disarray at the hands of an uncultivated public. Despite these points of intellectual contact, American thinkers seemed oblivious and operated under the assumption that German music had attained an essential distinctiveness.[77]

Hoping to help his compatriots attain this level of distinction, New England author Henry Russell Cleveland (1808–1843) took La Roche's line of thinking further while offering an even more robust prescription for the development of American national musical expression. In an 1840 essay published in the *North American Review*, Cleveland attempted to reconcile the country's supposed lack of a national "folk music" with its desire to create a distinctly national "school" of composition.[78] Like La Roche, Cleveland believed that a truly national music, or "traditionary music" as he called it, arises spontaneously only at the moment of a nation's cultural and political coalescence; it then becomes more refined as generations pass. Nations with a colonial history, including England and the United States, faced significant barriers to this process since colonizing forces had wiped out any original style that might have taken root. The desire for an American folk tradition on par with Scottish or Swiss songs was thus ultimately misplaced, he thought.

But this was not to say that the United States would be doomed to have no distinct musical culture forever. Echoing La Roche, Cleveland contended that a "national taste" would serve as an intermediate step and could be developed through widespread encounters with many different types of cultivated music. Through increased educational efforts, even foreign musical styles could become domesticated and nationalized, much as the English had adopted Handel's music as their own. "The democratic spirit of the country," Cleveland argued further, was particularly conducive to the creation of a national music, as long as the music in question was "addressed to the people" (i.e., in an appropriate style) and "received by the people at large" (i.e., suited their collective character).[79] He targeted the Boston Academy of Music in particular as an especially valuable institution since it both trained students and staged performances. Cleveland envisioned a musical environment much like that of the German-speaking lands, which supported both *Bildung* (or formation) and the creation of a cultivated music partaking of a *Volk* essence.[80] For Cleveland, that essence was democracy.

In such a formulation, exposure to the works of great masters would serve to elevate the populace. The next stage in the nation's musical development, as the argument went, had to entail the production of a cultivated music that would manifest American values. Given the symphony's newly raised status, its increasing presence on concert programs, and now the fertile desire for a national music that would speak directly to the people while forming their collective taste, it was presumably one of the most suitable vehicles for moving the country toward the widely shared ideal of international musical prominence. One key ingredient was missing: symphonists ready to lead the charge.

CHAPTER 2

࿓

Anthony Philip Heinrich,
Hapless Wanderer

The first American symphonist to lead the charge toward international musical prominence was Anthony Philip Heinrich (1781–1861), an eccentric Bohemian immigrant. But he failed miserably. Despite being one of the country's most prolific symphonists, Heinrich died broken and penniless on the cusp of the Civil War and would be forgotten until Oscar Sonneck of the Library of Congress discovered his voluminous collection of manuscripts and memorabilia over fifty years after his death.

This conclusion would have seemed preposterous to Heinrich when he began his professional life as an import-export merchant in the Austrian empire. The devastation wrought by the Napoleonic Wars destroyed the firm and prompted him to reconsider his professional ambitions. This was only the first in a long series of tribulations Heinrich would face throughout his career. Ultimately deciding to forge a new professional identity, he sailed for the New World in 1816 and settled for a brief period as the music director of a Pittsburgh theater. Heinrich later left this position and traveled on foot to Kentucky, where he lived until 1823. It was there, while living in a log cabin near Bardstown, that he began composing seriously. In his own words, he was "thrown, as it were, by *discordant events*, far from the emporiums of musical science, into the isolated wilds of nature, where he invoked his Muse, tutored only by ALMA MATER."[1]

While living in Kentucky, Heinrich published dozens of compositions in two large volumes, the size of which surpassed any previous collection of secular pieces by an American resident composer. As he developed this collection, he recognized that styling himself as an adopted American despite his cultural heritage as a Bohemian might be a successful marketing strategy.

In a letter thanking *Euterpiad* editor John Rowe Parker for a notice of the first volume, he explained,

> From a sincere attachment to America, my newly adopted Country, especially Kentucky, thought I proper to exert myself in Order to prove an honest warm hearted spirited national Minstrel—Small indeed is the Number of Composers in our young musical Commonwealth—Not one yet, I presume has here stept forward to produce a Volume of Compositions, presented in a Toute ensemble of Varieties of any Magnitude, and calculated to travel or exhibit Itself abroad—I have at all events attempted it, and under Privations, Difficulties, and Hardships which might almost raise me to a musical Martyr of Patience & Sufferance if to nothing else.[2]

Parker later praised the volume and created a moniker that would follow the composer for decades: "He may, therefore, justly be styled *the Beethoven* of America, and, as such he is actually considered by the few who have taken the trouble to ascertain his merits."[3] Heinrich was not the first American resident to be compared to a great European composer. Supply Belcher (1751–1836), a distinguished psalmodist, was also known as "The Handel of Maine."[4] With a title of national stature in mind, though, Americans expected not only great music from Heinrich's pen, but that it—and he—would represent the nation to the rest of the world.

Heinrich capitalized opportunistically on these expectations throughout his career, often by cultivating a specifically American persona.[5] Shortly after he left Kentucky for Boston in 1823, one newspaper report noted, "Mr. A. P. Heinrich [. . .] is indeed the first regular or general *American* composer—the first who [. . .] has almost exclusively devoted himself to the sublime study of harmony."[6] Beyond acquiring a dubious cachet as "the first" American composer, Heinrich also persistently attempted to validate his authenticity as a *genuinely* American composer by writing works, including symphonies, with uniquely and overtly American themes, the strategy adopted by James Hewitt half a generation earlier. Even so, Heinrich (figure 2.1) wrote several symphonies that did not manifest unadulterated patriotic sentiment at all. Indeed, the United States was not his sole allegiance. He was a wandering Bohemian longing for *Heimat* but acted as a shameless self-promoter when it suited his purposes. His music reflected this self-imposed rootlessness.

THE WANDERER ABROAD

Heinrich remained itinerant for much of his early musical career. He traveled primarily to bolster his professional reputation but also to seek the companionship of his estranged daughter, whom he had abandoned when

A.P. HEINRICH.

The western Minstrel.

Figure 2.1: Anthony Philip Heinrich. Library of Congress Prints and Photographs Division, Washington, D.C.

he immigrated to the New World. Except for a brief return to Boston, the composer moved throughout Europe between 1826 and 1837 in order "to satisfy my friends in America, that no exertion on my part has been spared to prove, that their country cultivates this science as well as others, which have distinguished her in the eyes of the Englishmen." Believing that "no professor was in higher reputation," he thought of himself as an American musical ambassador.[7]

Heinrich's experiences abroad would become emblematic of his long and disaster-laden career. On his first journey back to Europe, for example, his violin was crushed in an unfortunate accident that also left him with a broken finger. Upon his arrival in England, he attempted to publicize his compositions and managed to eke out a living as a violinist—crooked finger and all—in the orchestra of Drury Lane Theatre. The London musical establishment noticed his presence, and he was able to publish several new songs that garnered favorable reviews.

While in London, Heinrich also corresponded with celebrated figures such as the famous Irish poet Thomas Moore (1779–1852). Writing such letters was a lifelong preoccupation for Heinrich. If his correspondents did not reply as he wished, he would become cranky and take his grievances to the press. In a letter to a theater manager that was reprinted in the United States at Heinrich's behest, he wrote, "Even among the rude you would be a paragon of rudeness. Your insolent neglect and taciturnity prove you unworthy of the elevated station you held, but the gods know how obtained."[8] His effusiveness, in prose and in music, knew no bounds, and he did not mince words.

During a brief return to Boston, Heinrich established another pattern that would recur throughout his career: balking at performances of larger compositions. Over a period of several weeks, the Boston press touted a benefit concert to honor the return of the city's "adopted native," but it was mounted only after a series of delays. The slated keynote work, a symphony honoring the centennial of Washington's birth, was nowhere to be found. Heinrich had nevertheless managed to finagle performances of several other pieces in the meantime, which gave him ample public exposure and raised his local profile.[9]

Upon returning to London a second time, Heinrich resumed his crotchety antics. After learning that the Drury Lane management intended to renege on contractual obligations to the orchestra, he threatened to resign. "If you [. . .] have any better message to furnish than sending me to the Realms of the Devil," he wrote in a huff, "then will I cheerfully come again to the harmonious regions of the Orchestra, if not, it remains for me, to bid you all an affectionate farewell for the <u>Finalissimus</u>."[10] Finding himself out of work, Heinrich managed to complete an impressive array of compositions in 1834, including one of his first symphonies, a work memorializing the poet Friedrich Schiller (1759–1805).

Schiller began life, appropriately, with the subtitle *overture poëtique*. Heinrich later appended new sections to the work in order to fill out its final shape as a five-movement *grande sinfonia dramatica*. After a slow but brief introductory movement, the second movement functions as a traditional symphonic allegro. It is not in sonata form and instead exhibits Heinrich's idiosyncratic sense of melodic design, which features subtle changes of detail as the treatment becomes increasingly elaborate (example 2.1). The slower fourth movement showcases Heinrich's unconventional approach to solo writing (example 2.2), while the others make use of techniques that he had explored in *The Dawning of Music in Kentucky*, his first published volume, including adventurous harmonic peregrinations (movement three) and a musical palindrome (movement five).

Example 2.1: Idiosyncratic Melodic Design. Heinrich, *Schiller*, II: Allegro patetico concer-tante, mm. 1–18 (flute and violin unison).

Beyond the work's title, Heinrich left no indication concerning why he chose to celebrate Schiller in particular. An updated edition of Thomas Carlyle's *Life of Friedrich Schiller* appeared in 1833, and the renewed public interest in Schiller's writings that came in its wake might have inspired Heinrich. Reviews of the book, which often included panegyrics on Schiller's great-ness, appeared widely throughout the United States and would have trav-eled to England, where Heinrich was residing. To honor Schiller's birthplace, Heinrich dedicated the work to Wilhelm Friedrich Karl, King of Württemberg (1781–1864), a choice that reflected his misguided diplomatic pretensions. There is no evidence that the king, one of Heinrich's many royal dedicatees, knew the piece existed or that it was ever performed.

Nearly a year after completing *Schiller*, Heinrich submitted another sym-phony (likely his *Gran sinfonia eroica*) to a competition held by the famous Concert Spirituel of Vienna. A win would serve as external validation of his efforts. The competition was stiff, however, and the committee gave the final award to Franz Lachner (1803–1890), a Munich *Kappellmeister*.[11] Though gripped by illness, Heinrich soon traveled to the continent, where his self-promotion paid dividends. With information evidently gathered from Heinrich himself, the Leipzig *Allgemeine musikalische Zeitung* wrote a lengthy report of his activities in Europe, including his entry into the Vienna

Example 2.2: Unusual Contrapuntal Texture. Heinrich, *Schiller*, I: Adagio misterioso, mm. 7–11 (principal string solos plus solo winds).

competition. The journal described his music as "entirely idiosyncratic, especially in rhythm" ("ganz eigenthümlich, namentlich im Rhythmischen") and noted that the principal reason for his continental journey was to reunite with his daughter, not the symphony competition.[12] When he reached Bohemia, however, he found that she had traveled to the United States in order to find *him*; more bad luck.[13]

This final leg of Heinrich's trip included stops in Prague, Vienna, and Graz. In this last destination, he arranged to have several of his larger works performed by the Styrian Musik-Verein under the direction of Anselm Hüttenbrenner (1794–1868), who had been a close personal friend of Franz Schubert and an acquaintance of Beethoven. The program included a selection from a new symphony called *Der Kampf des Condor, amerikanisch charakteristisches Tongemählde* (*The Conflict of the Condor, American Characteristic Tone-picture*), which Heinrich would later rename *The Ornithological Combat of Kings*. The program mentioned only the first movement, suggesting that the symphony was not completed at the time of its performance. What was heard remains a mystery, but it is clear that Heinrich utilized music from the *Gran sinfonia eroica* as the basis for the first two movements of *The Ornithological Combat*. He probably used this material at the concert.

In any case, Heinrich described the completed symphony as "four movements united into one" since each successive movement borrows and reworks passages found in earlier movements (in the manner of leitmotifs) and it contains a single narrative arc from beginning to end. If the work was indeed intended to depict an epic conflict, however, the music belies this purpose since the musical drama rarely rises to the level found in battle pieces such as Beethoven's *Wellingtons Sieg*. Certain effects nevertheless grant Heinrich's symphony a picturesque quality, particularly the brooding opening and a delicate violin duet in the second movement that refashions a theme introduced in the first. After a rousing finale, the piece concludes with a cadenza for solo flute. Heinrich would frequently employ this framing device to great effect in several of his later works (example 2.3).

The sole known review of the concert focused on the work's representational dimension, which was a persistent concern for European critics in the 1830s. "The most striking achievement," wrote August Mandel, secretary of the Musik-Verein, "was the Symphony, The Combat of the Condor, in which the cooperation of all known orchestral instruments is required to represent the strength of the gigantic bird as it wings its way over the topmost peaks of the Andes." After noting that the work acquainted listeners with "American folk melodies" (though none exist in the final version of *The Ornithological Combat*) and that it might not "please every ear," he rhapsodized that Heinrich had

> sought out Nature in her workshop where she produces her mighty works, where great bridges of rock are thrown across streams; where rivers, broad as seas, flow out of undiscovered sources over hundreds of miles to the ocean itself; where great lakes plunge with deafening roar to the depths below, and the tornado, with its crashing strength lays bare the impenetrable secrets of the primeval forests.[14]

Lest readers believe this trait was an American idiosyncrasy, Mandel added that esteemed European composers had also written works of such tremendous scope. Heinrich, he concluded, had not sought "reinforcement by bells and cannon" and had thereby achieved a truly artistic level of musical representation rather than "mere effect."

Mandel's cautiously optimistic, if overwrought, review situated Heinrich close to the leading edge of orchestral composition. Although he acknowledged Heinrich's American inspiration, his commentary did not mark the music as somehow completely removed from the European tradition and therefore in need of a separate set of standards for evaluation. *Der Kampf des*

Example 2.3: Heinrich, *Ornithological Combat of Kings*.
(a) Stormy Opening. I: The Conflict of the Condor in the Air (Allegro moderato), mm. 1–8.
(b) Lush Violin Duet. II: Repose of the Condor (Andante sostenuto quasi Adagio), mm. 54–62 (solo violins 1 and 2).
(c) IV: Victory of the Condor (Adagio), final measures (flutes 1 and 2 accompanied by strings).

Example 2.3: (Continued)

Condor had convinced Mandel, and perhaps some of his fellow listeners, that musical art had taken root in the United States. If so, Heinrich had accomplished his ultimate musical goal for the journey.

THE WANDERER RETURNS HOME

The professional success Heinrich obtained in Graz was not enough to counter the bad luck that continued to plague him throughout his travels. As he wended his way back to the Atlantic coast, he coped with extended bouts of sickness and was robbed several times, including at a hotel in Bordeaux, where he completed yet another orchestral work as he convalesced,

Example 2.4: Heinrich, *The Columbiad*, Colorful Variations on "Yankee Doodle."
(a) String tremolo, mm. 149–152.
(b) Alternating arco and pizzicato, mm. 206–213.

The Columbiad, Grand American National Chivalrous Symphony. This piece was his first explicit symphonic homage to the United States. Following the patriotic title, it includes quotations from "Hail Columbia" and colorful variations on "Yankee Doodle," all interspersed with contrapuntal sections that heighten its grandeur (example 2.4).[15] He left no dedication but noted at the end of the score that he hoped it would "be found worthy of public patronage, especially in the United States." Reflecting on his mortality, he added that he wished the piece could benefit his daughter or some other charitable purpose if he died before it could be produced.[16] Unlike many of his other works, the symphony does not demand virtuosic performance capabilities, but there is no evidence that Heinrich attempted to produce it himself or that anyone performed it after his death.

Heinrich's brief glimpses of mortality in Bordeaux apparently had no predictive value. He returned to the United States soon thereafter and would remain a New York resident for the next two decades. During this period of his career, he acquired a reputation as a wizened naïf and earned the moniker "Father Heinrich."[17] Whether public attitudes toward his personality and music were genuine or cloying is hard to assess. He was easily the country's most prolific composer of large-scale works, after all, and continued to expose his peevish temperament in the press. Not long after returning, for example, he engaged in a feud with critic Henry Cood Watson (1816–1875), whom he called a "quack reviewer."[18] Yet when a group of interested musicians, including Watson, decided to establish a cooperative orchestra dedicated to cultivating musical taste in the city, they elected Heinrich to preside over the organizational meeting held in 1842. This group would become the Philharmonic Society of New-York. Neither of these incidents suggests that Heinrich was ingenuous.

That same year, Heinrich mounted a musical festival at New York's Broadway Tabernacle. It featured an uncharacteristically large ensemble, as well as musical luminaries from the newly formed Philharmonic. Selections from his oratorio *The Pilgrim Fathers* were highlights. Reviews were generally quite favorable and noted the audience's unbridled enthusiasm, but Heinrich remarked to the press that the concert did not recoup his financial outlay.[19] Seeking recompense, he attempted to secure financial subscriptions in order to publish the oratorio in a sumptuous bound score of over five hundred pages. The advertisement noted, with his characteristic patriotism and rhetorical flourish, "The entire work [. . .] will be presented as a LEGACY to the Country he has adopted,—THE LAND OF WASHINGTON!!"[20] Heinrich's efforts were not successful.

Undeterred by the failure, Heinrich completed several more symphonies during the 1840s, including three that reflected his abiding interest in Native American culture and history. These subjects had already inspired him to compose non-symphonic works with titles such as *Pushmataha* (1831), *The Treaty of William Penn* (1835), and *Pocahontas* (1837). Providing additional inspiration, valuable printed sources about Native American life appeared during the very period when Heinrich wrote these symphonies: *Travels in the Interior of North America* (1843) by German naturalist Prince Maximilian von Wied-Neuwied (1782–1867) and *The Origin of the North American Indians* (1843) by ethnographer John McIntosh. The particular subjects of the symphonies bear the imprint of these writings, and Heinrich even appended a quotation from Prince Maximilian's volume to one of the scores.

The title for the first of these works, *Manitou Mysteries, or the Voice of the Great Spirit* (with the subtitle *Gran sinfonia misteriosa-indiana*), seems drawn from a chapter on Native American religion in McIntosh's study that describes an omnipotent deity, "the Great Spirit," as well as lesser spirits whom Algonquin peoples called "manitous."[21] Despite the elaborate title and mystical subject, the symphony is Heinrich's most traditional. It follows a standard four-movement plan and contains no subheadings suggesting descriptive content, but the general character of the symphony is rustic. The third movement, a lush adagio, begins with the framing technique used to close *The Ornithological Combat* (which Heinrich completed around the same time). Here, however, the gesture sets off a broad melody doubled by a solo horn and the first violins (example 2.5). It is as if a thick fog gives way to the voice of the Great Spirit. The rest of the symphony is eminently playable, but no evidence suggests he attempted to secure a performance of it.[22]

The idea for Heinrich's second Native American symphony, *The Indian Carnival, or "The Indian Festival of Dreams"* (*sinfonia eratico-fantachia*), also

Example 2.5: Broad Melody Depicting the Great Spirit. Heinrich, *Manitou Mysteries*, III: The Adagio, mm. 9–14 (French horn and violin 1 accompanied by strings).

derived from McIntosh. During a fifteen-day "festival of dreams" (described by McIntosh), which might have reminded Heinrich of the Carnevale season of his Bohemian homeland, participants "act at this time all kinds of fooleries, and every one runs from cabin to cabin, disguised in a thousand ridiculous ways; they break and overset everything, and nobody dares to contradict them. [. . .] To be freed from this persecution, one must guess dreams, which often no one can form any conception of."[23] Heinrich attempted to capture the vividness and drama of McIntosh's description with the same musical framing device he employed in *Manitou Mysteries*. Slow and flexible cadenza-like figures lead into a raucous allegro that gradually intensifies into a full-blown instrumental maelstrom marking the culmination of the festival. Upon its conclusion, a misty andante restores the semblance of order (example 2.6). Like readers of McIntosh's narrative, listeners are to become viewers as Heinrich weaves the story with music.

Heinrich called his third and largest Native American symphony *The Mastodon*. The title bears little relation to the subject matter of the individual movements and may serve instead as a metaphor for the work's size.[24] He

Example 2.6: Narrative Frame. Heinrich, *The Indian Carnival*, Coda quasi Presto, mm. 102–114 (full orch.).

named the outer two movements after figures from Native American history: *Mackkatananamakee* ("Black Thunder") and *Oskanondonha* (sometimes called "Shenandoah"). These two leaders had become famous for giving speeches to U.S. government officials once publishers distributed their orations widely in various print sources between 1815 and 1843.[25] The inner movement of the sympmhony refers to a religious ceremony described by Prince Maximilian in which a large pyramid is constructed out of elk antlers.[26]

In each movement of *The Mastodon*, Heinrich made specific compositional choices that appear to build layers of meaning that extend beyond their titles. The first movement, for example, contains a lengthy quotation of a piano

Example 2.7: Interlocking Lines Depicting the Elkhorn Pyramid. Heinrich, *The Mastodon*, II: The Elkhorn Pyramid (Adagio), mm. 233–251 (strings).

piece composed at roughly the same time, "Tyler's Grand Veto." The title does not refer to a political act, but to President John Tyler's rebuff of Heinrich's request for presidential patronage.[27] In Heinrich's mind, this negative experience placed him in solidarity with *Mackkatananamakee*, whom President James Madison had once mistreated. In the second movement, a strange passage marked "fugato" may be, as one writer has suggested, Heinrich's attempt to depict the elk horn pyramid's "tightly interlocking structure" (example 2.7).[28] Finally, in the movement referencing *Oskanondonha*, whose well-known speech was an introspective reflection on his old age, Heinrich adopted the storyteller pose taken in his other two Native American symphonies with the inclusion of cadenza-like framing gestures at both ends (example 2.8). Rapidly shifting moods and tempos grant the movement a cinematic quality.

While completing these works, Heinrich had earned the friendly confidence and professional support of Lydia Maria Child (1802–1880), a prominent abolitionist and women's rights activist who had also penned sympathetic fictional and nonfiction accounts of Native American life.[29] In a letter

Example 2.8: Cadenza Frame. Heinrich, *The Mastodon*, III: Shenandoah (Larghetto), mm. 727–734 (string soloists).

written to the press late in 1845, Child wrote a touching portrait of Heinrich and compared him sympathetically to a lead character in novelist Edward Bulwer-Lytton's *Zanoni* (1842). The character, an eccentric old violinist and composer named Pisani, lived through interminable struggles but, like Heinrich, maintained a genial outlook:

He had composed other pieces, of larger ambition and wider accomplishment, and, chief of these, his precious—his unpurchased—his unpublished—his unpublishable and imperishable opera of the "Siren." This great work had been the dream of his boyhood—the mistress of his manhood; in advancing age it stood beside him like his youth. Vainly had he struggled to place it before the work.[30]

Had anyone recalled this passage from the novel after glancing through Child's letter, the parallels to Heinrich would have been perfectly clear. He even had a "Siren" of his own: the oratorio *The Pilgrim Fathers*.

When the press announced that Heinrich would mount a second festival the following spring, variations of Child's letter resurfaced. She urged her fellow New Yorkers to patronize his efforts so that "his sunset might be a warm and golden one."[31] Notices of the concert appeared widely, and Child remarked that the evening's centerpiece would be a new symphony, *To the Spirit of Beethoven*. Heinrich had written the work in response to the highly publicized unveiling of the Beethoven monument in Bonn just a few months earlier. Unlike the majority of his other symphonies, *To the Spirit of Beethoven* depicts the ceremony itself in minute detail, from the "assembling of the musical profession and the people" to "the uncovering of the monument" and "the enthusiastic admiration and praise of the convocation." A single gong strike separates each scene from the next. As a whole, the musical language is not much different from his earlier works, but he chose musical *topoi* befitting the subject matter of each movement (example 2.9).

Why Heinrich chose this particular event for detailed musical depiction is unclear, but it fit with his general program of asserting a cosmopolitan persona with connections to contemporary world events. In this case, his goal seemed to be for German musicians to encounter the work as a sign of goodwill from the United States. He called the first section "Hail to the citizens of Bonn," for example, which suggests an authorial voice from abroad. Pleading on Heinrich's behalf before the concert, Child added that the work had been composed "in a comfortless garret, tormented with insects of all sorts." Most surprising of all, Henry Cood Watson, Heinrich's erstwhile foe, provided program notes for the audience that included a detailed description of the symphony. There was only one problem: "there were not instruments enough for its execution," which led Heinrich to scrap the work from the performance. And he never sent a copy of the score to Bonn.[32]

Omissions aside, the evening pleased the audience, which regaled Heinrich with tokens of appreciation. As one report described the scene, a bouquet of flowers was "immediately followed by a wreath of laurel, thrown by a lady-poetess [Child], distinguished by her ultra-transcendental enthusiasm in musical matters, and the incomprehensibility of her 'superlatively splendid' notices."[33] A review in the *Tribune* described the music as "grand,

Example 2.9: Topical Scenes. Heinrich, *To the Spirit of Beethoven*.
(a) No. 4: The Commotion of the Multitude Discovering the Royal Cortege (Allegro moderato), mm. 1–6 (full orch.).
(b) Transition into No. 8: Hail to Beethoven! (Andante grandioso), mm. 1–4 (full orch.).

glorious—sublime" and added that "the Creator has evidently developed in close conjunction with sublimity the manifestations of a full, joyous and unrestrainable mirthfulness, which breaks out in most grotesque and unexpected fashion—thus helping to keep Nature's face decked with smiles." Though reluctant to comment on musical details beyond Watson's remarks, the reviewer concluded that "Heinrich is undoubtedly ahead of his age; and we believe that his music will be far more popular long after he is dead than now."[34] As in 1842, the concert did not make a profit, and the critic's prophecy did not come to pass.

THE WANDERER'S CRITICS

When Henry Russell Cleveland was developing his theories of national music in 1840, only a smattering of audiences had heard a symphony composed by an American. Heinrich had produced portions of one overseas, but his abortive efforts in Boston and New York prevented locals from forming an opinion of his symphonic works. Even so, audiences likely would have been on their own since music critics of the day tended to emphasize the quality of a performance rather than a piece's musical content. This focus served a vital function by helping listeners decide how to allocate their money and time within an increasingly diversified musical marketplace. Gossip about star performers also proved to be an insatiable public thirst.

For the musical organizations that directed their efforts specifically toward the cultivation of taste, such as the Boston Academy of Music, "taste" eventually came to include not only a discriminating ear for correct performance, but also for musical works invested with the power to disclose deeper meanings. As we have seen, instrumental pieces engendered sentiments of awe and reverence among a wide cross-section of listeners in the 1830s and 1840s. Certain critics in turn attempted to create a discursive space in which they served not only as judges of a performer's correctness, but also as interpreters of musical secrets. Adopting this new role allowed them to reify a perpetually uncultivated public by chastising average listeners for lack of appreciation.

European critics had not performed this function for long by the time American writers took this work-oriented turn.[35] Music editors who believed in this critical function, such as Theodor Hach of Boston, were able to translate and reprint European essays concerning individual works while retaining their conventional roles as commentators on performance quality and the general state of local musical culture. But when it came to assessing works that had never been heard before—in other words, when they were responding to premieres of American pieces—critics developed new techniques for asserting an authoritative stance, not only over audiences, but also over composers themselves. A power struggle over public opinion and representation was poised to erupt.

Following the ill-fated New York concert of 1846, a disappointed Heinrich set his sights on Boston. Sympathizers in the press pitched a potential benefit concert as a contest: Surely Boston could do better than New York in terms of gathering receipts for the aging composer. And it did. By all accounts, the proceeds of the concert were significant. Another of Heinrich's confidantes, Cornelia Walter (1813–1898), editor of the *Boston Evening Transcript*, remarked that "the pecuniary rewards, however large, will be but an inadequate reward for the toils and deprivations of the most unselfish creatures ever born into a world of care—of an old man of many misfortunes, but with a great soul and the heart of dreaming youth!"[36] The concert had been a success but had not included any symphonies; selections from *The Pilgrim Fathers* were natural headliners. But as a keynote event in Boston, it inevitably drew a response from critic John Sullivan Dwight, which was his first extended engagement with music by a local composer. Its negativity would set the tone for the rest of his long career.

During the months leading up to the performance, Dwight had been preaching about the American qualities of Beethoven's symphonies. In his review of Heinrich's music, he let readers know where the Bohemian stood in comparison. While admitting that the lack of rehearsal and the poor performance were forgivable, Dwight focused his comments on Heinrich's proclivity for writing descriptive music. "In efforts to describe things," he began, "to paint pictures in the hearer's imagination, music leaves its natural channels, and forfeits true unity which would come from the simple development of itself from within *as music*. Beethoven had no *programme* to his symphonies, intended no description, with the single exception of the *Pastorale*; yet, how full of meaning are they!" Then, tempering Heinrich's (and the audience's) patriotic enthusiasm, he unleashed his full fury against the concept:

> We are sorry to see such circumstances dragged into music as the "Indian War Council," the "Advance of the Americans," the "Skirmish," and "Fall of Tecumseh." Music, aiming at no subject,—music composed with no consciousness of anything in the world *but* music, is sure to tell of greater things than these. It is true that every thing about America and American history was ideal to the warm-hearted and liberty-living enthusiast when he came here. [. . .] This was so far well, and can be conceived to have cooperated finely with his musical labors, had he only composed from the sentiment with which they filled him, instead of trying to compose tone-narratives and tableaux of them.[37]

Historical events might make a good story, he granted, but "it does not follow that just that series of subjects, translated into so many musical themes or passages, will still have unity as music." For Dwight, Heinrich was certainly not the Beethoven of America. And by taking this position on the question of musical representation, Dwight made far fewer concessions to Heinrich's aesthetic than had August Mandel, the critic in Graz who actually seemed to enjoy it.

Heinrich fumed. If readers believed it, Dwight's screed would have invalidated a significant portion of the composer's entire output. In a letter to a friend, he responded with characteristic acidity and lambasted Dwight's position while scoffing at the critic's isolation on the Fourierist Brook Farm commune:

> Mr. Dwight is a happy wight, for he lives in serene solitude at Brookfarm among the chirpings of some innocent insects, and the Concertos of Bullfrogs, the latter like the symphonies of Beethoven needing no programmes, speaking for themselves to the mind of that contemplative gentleman. [. . .] Mr. Dwight is really very distantly local from full good orchestras, and has probably heard very little of orchestral effects, combinations and professional tactics.[38]

After complaining that Dwight had glossed over the meat of the production by excoriating the performers and unleashing a diatribe about musical description, Heinrich disparaged him further:

> Should it ever be my melancholy lot to compose a doleful ditty for some departed disciple of the *Fourier System* I promise faithfully to introduce nothing but *Sordini* and dampers of all sorts to make reparation to the gentle, susceptible Mr. Dwight of the rural philanthropic social spot of Brookfarm, of which Eldorado full of the Beethoven works I should indeed like to be *Maestro di Capello*.

These remarks revealed the darker side of Heinrich's supposedly childlike demeanor, and the suggestion that Dwight's opinions had developed in relative isolation was not far from the truth. He might have read books and articles about music and musical aesthetics, but he could not have experienced nearly as many live orchestral performances as the globetrotting Heinrich.

Heinrich also maintained that Dwight's emphasis on musical description had missed the point, for he had "never taken any pattern from Beethoven or anyone else." As far as he was concerned, originality was the prevailing musical currency, not abstraction. With a snide dismissal of his own, the seething composer concluded that

> Mr. Dwight judges a great deal by faith and musical superstition. He discovers so much meaning in Beethoven. I congratulate him upon so important a discovery at my expense. [. . .] He rails gently at my programmes whilst all the while he makes in his speeches all sorts of metaphysical metaphors and creates wonderful imagery, far beyond my summersets.[39]

Heinrich was not naïve. He understood that a critical paradigm treating Beethoven as an ideal would necessarily devalue any new composition, particularly if it strayed from well-worn stylistic paths. And he knew that Dwight's complaints over musical description obscured his otherwise clear preference for older compositions. Heinrich had written a prodigious amount of orchestral music in just over a decade, only a small fraction of which audiences would eventually hear. But the responses to what little was performed—cautious optimism in Graz and outright dismissal in Boston—would establish patterns for the reception of American symphonies across the rest of the century. Composers often needed to go elsewhere for their music to be appreciated.

CHAPTER 3

☙

William Henry Fry, Operatic Translator

Whereas Anthony Philip Heinrich responded to John Sullivan Dwight's attacks on his music privately, William Henry Fry (1813–1864), another of the century's most prolific composers and writers, rarely spared an opportunity to take his artistic grievances with critics into a public forum. Like Heinrich, he also had a particular way with words. Even the sharp-tongued pianist and composer Jerome Hopkins, whom we'll meet again in chapter 6, thought Fry was a windbag. "Called on Mr. Fry," Hopkins once wrote in his journal, "who bored me for an almost interminable length of time with the most conceited and egotistical effusions. I was <u>disgusted</u>. But I endured them all for he promised to uphold my proposed new musical society in his paper, the Tribune."[1] It should be no surprise, then, that Fry also had a notable career as a firebrand antislavery activist, for this political issue was the most divisive of the day.

Fry died of tuberculosis in Santa Cruz only a few months before the end of the Civil War. He contracted the disease while giving stump speeches during the 1860 election season. For the campaign, he also wrote a lengthy pamphlet that detailed slavery's long history and served as an election guide explaining why the Republican Party—and presidential candidate Senator Abraham Lincoln—favored the institution's dissolution. In the pamphlet, which Fry sent to Lincoln himself, he targeted the Southern Democrats who justified slavery with the claim that all great civilizations had tolerated its existence and therefore the United States should as well. He wondered how the position could hold muster in the face of widespread recognition that treating human beings as property was intrinsically evil.[2]

So he dismantled this position with surgical precision and great rhetorical flourish. Shamefully, he concluded, the United States was the only country in the West that continued to tolerate slavery, much less be a home to those who would defend it:

> Other nations beckon us on: England [. . .] struck the chains off all her slaves, and each rising and setting sun does homage to the majesty of the achievement, over the hills and vales of her happy islands. Russia, with twenty million serfs, is, at the fiat of her best Emperor, about to touch them with the Ithuriel spear of emancipation, so that their moral nature may reach the skies. Shall we, then, with such glorious examples of the good, the generous, and the right, retroäct, absolve ourselves from the gallant past, cut off our brilliant future, and be stifled in essential barbarism?[3]

Writing these words must have pained Fry deeply because he had spent his professional career arguing that the rest of the world should look to the United States as a model of cultural superiority and that Americans should harness the power of liberty for creative ends.

The question he posed in his antislavery treatise resonated strongly with his general outlook on musical culture and his overarching goals as a composer. In order to assert American cultural superiority, Fry's chief strategy was to be a musical translator—someone who could take received knowledge ("glorious examples of the good") and transform it into innovative creativity ("our brilliant future'). In a review of a symphony written by his composition teacher and musical mentor, Fry described how this process might take shape within a specifically musical context:

> We consider the whole basis of prosperous and triumphant Art in this country to rest upon Originality of Production. We may, and must, import true models from Europe; but taking as our standard the recognized excellence or perfection of the masters in Art of that country, we must then originate, re-create, and accord our derived taste and skill to the genius of our own hemisphere. It is alone by this double process that we can make our country the actual mother, as well as the double foster mother of Art.[4]

Echoing Henry Russell Cleveland's nationalization idea, Fry argued that, beyond merely cultivating audience taste, composers should work with their materials until they create a distinctly American style. Though easily misunderstood as emulation, the "double process" Fry described was the art of translation—using a filter to transform something distinctly *not* American into something that is.

Fry's teacher, Leopold Meignen (1793–1873), had a profound influence on Philadelphia's musical culture for three decades and affected the young Philadelphian's approach to compositional style. Born in France, he began his career as a bandleader in Napoleon's army and later attended the Paris Conservatoire before immigrating to the United States. Upon arriving in Philadelphia in 1828, he cobbled together a career as a composer, conductor, private tutor, and publisher. The Musical Fund Society appointed him chief conductor in 1844. In this role he steadily shifted the society's repertoire away from the mixed-genre concerts of the 1830s and toward programs that featured the orchestra, thus aligning the group's programming more closely with that of other fledgling American ensembles.[5]

Meignen's position also afforded him the opportunity to premiere his symphony without interference, a luxury that Charles Hommann and Anthony Philip Heinrich had lacked. And although Meignen promoted music by Beethoven, his own symphony was stylistically different. It comprises only two movements and depicts a detailed narrative derived from his experiences as a serviceman in Napoleon's army. As Fry described the story, a soldier on guard at midnight thinks longingly about his home but falls asleep. Then he "dreams of a battle, which is gloriously represented by the confusion of a *double figure* [fugue], as it is called by musicians; the battle ceases; the retreat bugle sounds; and the dreaming sentinel awakes to the sound of a drum."[6] While there is nothing that seems particularly American or even national about the work, Meignen's choice to let its narrative plot determine its unique architectural shape would become a central component of Fry's translation project.

The idea that Americans should translate a European artistic language into something distinctly American percolated far beyond musical culture at the time. Writer John L. O'Sullivan (1813–1895), for example, remarked that American authors might happily use the literature "of our mother language," but "without abusing it by utterly submitting our minds to it." The relationship between Europe and the United States that Fry and O'Sullivan were proposing had strong parallels to the relationship between the ancient Greeks and Romans. As Romans translated Greek literary and scientific works into Latin, authors found it necessary to create new words and even new modes of expression. Their creativity enriched both the language itself and the collective knowledge of the subject at hand. "It may not be amiss," Cicero once argued, "after you have read the [original] author, to become, as it were, his rival and attempt something of your own upon the same subject, then to make careful comparison in order to determine whether you or he is the better."[7] This competitive spirit animated Fry (figure 3.1) throughout his compositional career. He was a Roman, and the so-called European musical masters were his Greeks.

Figure 3.1: William Henry Fry. Courtesy of the New York Philharmonic Leon Levy Digital Archives.

TRANSLATING OPERA

While the middle-aged Heinrich was in London during the 1830s, Fry came of age hobnobbing in Philadelphia's elite social circles. Inspired by the city's litterateurs, he pursued a lifelong career as a journalist. His father, William Fry (1777–1855), was one of the country's finest printers, and his father's newspaper, the *National Gazette and Literary Register*, was a model across the country.[8] William Henry learned the trade from his father's business partner, Robert Walsh (1785–1859), a belletrist and statesman who edited the newspaper and the *American Quarterly Review*, the magazine that published René La Roche's articles on national music (see chapter 1). Walsh also pioneered the inclusion of meaty artistic and musical coverage in the daily press.[9] Shortly after Walsh retired from his position in 1836, William Henry assumed the task of reviewing Philadelphia's musical events for the newspaper.

Fry's efforts to translate foreign musical styles into an American language began with opera. By the time his compositional career started in earnest during the 1830s, opera had begun to develop a distinct cachet in the United States as an appealing form of theatrical entertainment.[10] As a critic, Fry gained behind-the-scenes access to Philadelphia's stunningly diverse musical culture. French and Italian operas, sometimes performed in their original languages, but more often in English, filled the air.[11] By 1840, Fry had already composed two full-length operas of his own, *The Bridal of Dunure* and *Aurelia the Vestal*, both with English libretti by his older brother Joseph Reese Fry (1811–1865); neither was produced.[12] At this point in his career, Fry had expressed no particular interest in symphonies, but his experience with opera over the next several years would prove to be crucial in the development of his symphonic philosophy.

After failing to produce *Aurelia*, the Fry brothers pursued a more direct cultural translation strategy with the country's first English adaptation of Vincenzo Bellini and Felice Romani's *Norma*. Joseph provided the translation while William Henry adapted the music, and together they staged the work according to their own dramatic vision. *Norma* would quickly become one of American audiences' most beloved operas.[13] By all accounts, however, ticket sales did not recoup their generous outlay for lavish costumes and scenery, a large chorus and orchestra, and a leading cast headed by Ann and Joseph Wood, one of the most famous operatic duos active in the United States. To make matters worse, a rival impresario staged a competing version of *Norma* translated by the husband of his company's star that siphoned off potential profits for the Fry brothers.

Despite these financial losses, the rival staging proved to be a boon for the brothers as Joseph's excellent translation immediately became the production's distinguishing feature.[14] After hearing the premiere, Philadelphia businessman Joseph Sill wrote extensively about it is in his diary and praised it effusively:

> Mr Fry obligingly sent me a Copy of the Libretto, done into English by him, which, having read attentively, has given me much pleasure. He has succeeded in presenting us with a pleasing metrical version of the Italian which I have little doubt is as correct as it is pleasing.[15]

Sill attended the rival production the following evening and remarked that it "won't compare ... with the other house."[16] The competition sparked by the rivalry nevertheless caused both houses to go bankrupt, which prompted the Woods to leave the country altogether.[17]

With each side picking up the pieces, the rivalry spilled over into New York City, where the Fry brothers again emerged as victors.[18] A writer for the *Knickerbocker* remarked that "the verse is smooth and flowing; and the reader is not annoyed by indifferent and unmeaning passages, such as largely disfigure the *libretto* of nearly every opera we ever heard. The translation is in all respects creditable to the care and skill of Mr. Fry."[19] Following a new production of their translation in New York, critic Henry Cood Watson (who had developed a love-hate relationship with Anthony Philip Heinrich) could hardly have been more generous: "Norma, as translated by Messrs. Fry, [. . .] is superior in versification, truthfulness, and just accentuation; and the present performance, with one exception, is so infinitely superior to that of the past season, that it will not admit comparison."[20] Phase one of Fry's translation project was complete.

THE TRANSLATOR'S CRITICS

The new production of *Norma* fit into Fry's general program of cultural translation because he was combating what he perceived as a widespread belief that English was an unsuitable language for opera, especially in the grand Italian style with accompanied recitative. The Scottish music critic George Hogarth had recently written that composer Thomas Arne (1710–1778) had unsuccessfully adapted the Italianate style of accompanied recitative to English in his opera *Artaxerxes* (1762) and had therefore put the issue to rest. "Italian speech," Hogarth argued, "can be made to take a musical form [. . .]; and thus the dialogue of the Italian opera may be sung, or rather spoken, in recitative: but in no other language is this practicable."[21] The idea had died with Arne, he thought.

James Rush, a Philadelphia doctor, took Hogarth's argument further by disputing the legitimacy of recitative altogether, English or otherwise. His lengthy 1827 philosophical treatise on the human voice included a thoughtful analysis of recitative that left no comment about its efficacy or value. But second and third printings—from 1833 and 1845, respectively—took a much firmer stand. Using language suggestive of racial miscegenation, Rush argued that recitative was an abomination. "As embracing within itself the characteristic expression of both speech and song," he claimed, recitative "does, by this vain design to effect a combination of incompatible functions, really destroy the peculiar and delightful nature of each."[22] The critical success of Joseph Fry's mellifluous English translation of *Norma* had openly called such a position into question.

Building on the momentum of *Norma*, the Fry brothers quickly began working on the next phase of their program: staging their own original opera. At its 1845 premiere, they touted *Leonora* as the first grand opera by any

U.S. composer and librettist. With its seamless orchestral accompaniment, it offered a concrete challenge to the anti-recitative positions of Hogarth and Ruth. Despite the Fry brothers' dogged interest in settling this dispute, the issue was not taken up in press reviews, which focused instead on Fry's penchant for "borrowing" turns of melody from Bellini or on the historical implications of creating a truly American opera. These were not unimportant concerns, but they were also not the duo's primary focus.

Such lack of interest irritated William. In the preface to the piano-vocal score of *Leonora*, published in 1846, he contended that the construction of an American national musical identity was tied inextricably to the employment of accompanied recitative, and therefore to grand opera more generally. Grand opera, he claimed, "is essentially the high, complete, and classic form" since "it imparts proper uniformity of style to the entire declamation; does not confound the strictly musical with the acting drama; and with an artistic performance confirms the interest of the representation."[23] Because English composers had failed to create such an opera, successfully doing so would become a national accomplishment. It would allow Americans to best their English rivals.

Although Fry expressed this patriotic stance quite forcefully in a rousing peroration, a defense of English-language recitative occupied the bulk of his remarks—an unusual gesture given the esoteric nature of the subject and the press's general disregard. But the argument Fry made in his preface to *Leonora* was personal. In a scathing series of reviews, Henry Cood Watson, who had praised the *Norma* translation, excoriated the new opera by calling the concept of English recitative a "monstrosity." He suggested caustically that *Leonora* would die long before Arne's *Artaxerxes*, which of course was dead anyway.[24] Fry rebutted such remarks in the preface by claiming that audiences would delight in recitative and that he had "too much admiration for the resources of the English language, to admit of the supposition that it is excluded, by its nature, from the highest form of opera."[25]

Fry also responded to Rush's pointed attack. Rush had blamed the persistence of recitative in opera on "the fatal influence of that vampire of classic authority, which, whilst fanning us into a learned and vain-glorious stupefaction, has for ages been drawing out the life blood of our intellectual independence."[26] These comments must have seemed like a direct attack to Fry, who knew Rush's treatise and was the only prominent local figure defending English recitative.[27] After a lengthy description of how English is indeed an operatic language, Fry closed the preface with a bit of his own characteristically puffy rhetoric:

> The mists of antiquity and the divination of the future; the abodes of the gods, of fairies, and of demons, as well as of men; earth, air, sea, and sky are searched for the facts and imaginings of the dramatist. To fight against such a material and immaterial array, is like a war upon the seven prismatic colors, upon the seven essential sounds, upon the very spirit of ideality which clothes all visible things

with romance and beauty. To destroy dramatic music is to endanger all music; to bring back monkish formality and abused mathematics in the science.[28]

Fry considered himself a countervailing force, a savior of drama.

Curiously, though, Fry added that "the chief interest of all instrumental music," a topic unrelated to the matter at hand, "lies in the dramatic expression derived originally from the universal lyrical delineations of the stage." As if portending the future, he had articulated the first seeds of his symphonic philosophy: that a symphony should somehow draw from opera's inherent drama. To complete his patriotic mission, he needed to devise a way to make the symphony into an American genre, to translate it, just as he had translated the Italian grand operatic style into an American work like *Leonora*.

THE TRANSLATOR ABROAD

To translate is to filter. When Fry wrote an Italianate opera using English recitative, he filtered the bel canto style through his own American mind but gave no indication concerning the specific musical function this filter actually performed. After moving to Europe in 1846 (around the time that Heinrich had mounted his ruinous New York festival), Fry articulated what he believed the American mind possessed that others did not: the "baptism" of democracy. His philosophy of democracy had a significant impact on his later compositional strategies and helped clarify the purpose of his earlier artistic efforts.

Fry's journalistic career (now for Philadelphia's *Public Ledger*) gave him the opportunity to travel to Paris, where his former mentor Robert Walsh had taken up residence as the U.S. Consul-General. Late in 1849, the prominent New York editor and social reformer Horace Greeley (1811–1872) also enlisted Fry as a Parisian correspondent for the *Daily Tribune* of New York, one of the city's leading papers. Fry immediately began an epistolary feuilleton called "Europe by an American." As the series continued, the scope and quality of Fry's coverage expanded noticeably.

Numbering in the hundreds, his highly detailed letters to both newspapers chronicled major political events, including the widespread revolutions that began in 1848 and cultural affairs such as performances (and intrigue) at the Paris Opéra. Fry compared life in Europe with life across the Atlantic, and one country always managed to stand a head above the rest—sometimes quite literally. Commenting on a group of dancers at an opera performance, he boasted, "The tallest girl of the dancers was American—typical, doubtless, of the greatest extent of territory."[29] Though laced with national chauvinism, his comparisons of American and European political structures were remarkably accurate.

Fry rarely relinquished an opportunity to tout U.S. democracy at the expense of his French hosts. Eerily foretelling Louis-Napoléon's establishment of the Second French Empire, he noted with characteristic condescension that "sudden and fierce revolutions seem in Europe to change tyrants and leave reforms for the most part untouched. [. . .] But an American, who has the baptism of Democracy, can read the French character."[30] Unlike the ruggedly individualistic and vibrant democracy found in the United States, Paris was "manured into feculent splendor by a system of centralization exceeding the rapacity of ancient Rome, swarms with a bureaucracy, an army of office-seekers, and a whole pandemonium of do-nothings and eat-alls." After his prophecy concerning the empire had come to pass just over two years later, he was certain that the change had been inevitable: "A great people, the French, and as fit for liberty as ****."[31]

Fry was no friendlier to Britain's ruling aristocracy than to France's power-hungry centralized government. If anything, it was worse:

> [G]ood feeling among nations can never exist between privilege and democracy any more than between evil and good. And it is precisely because there is no good feeling between the hereditary lords of the English people and soil, and the American democracy, that in England and in America there are constantly made such flowery official pretensions of mutual respect. Full hearts, few words.[32]

He equated American economic and political ties to Britain with treason and the "compromise of our national genius and destiny." In other letters, he went so far as to blame British taxation and trade policies—and the American government's complicity with them—for the persistence of American slavery and the sectional struggles that would culminate in the Civil War.[33] Throughout his letters, he equated American democracy with goodness and righteousness, and autocracy and aristocracy with evil and confusion.

Building on this pro-democracy stance, Fry also probed questions about what roles European culture should play in the expression of a uniquely American identity. The misappropriation or mistranslation of European models would be a disastrous mistake. The "persevering ugliness" of American cities especially grieved him. American cities, he argued, could begin to thrive only after their leaders accepted roles as "double foster" parents looking simultaneously outward and inward. Lambasting Philadelphia as a "Quaker abortion," he complained that planners of American cities slavishly followed European designs without accounting for the natural beauty and grace of the American landscape. New York was no better, as its "solemn, stupid squares, its stereotyped forms, [and] its wretched plagiarisms of city plans" were designed for climates and natural conditions completely different from those found in the United States. What worked in one locale was not necessarily the best solution in another. Everything required careful translation.[34]

Beginning in August of 1850, Fry also contributed occasional missives to the *Message Bird*, a prominent New York music journal.[35] Conscious of the journal's specialized audience, Fry limited his discussions primarily to musical matters but used it as a vehicle to push his political agenda. Maintaining his aim at the evils of Europe, he continued to promote American democracy in this new context by equating composers working under the despotic regimes then ruling Europe's musical capitals with "upper domestics" and "petted servants." This condition harmed composers' psyches to such a degree, he claimed, that Beethoven's storied "misanthropy" was a result of the cognitive dissonance induced by the combination of beauty and authoritarianism, which Fry called the "science of havoc." His solution was predictable: "If Art, musical Art, be rendered a profession for a heroic nature, to be accepted as a harvest of social dignities, as well as a means of wealth or fame, it must be under a Democracy like our own."[36]

In Fry's formulation, democracy was a necessary condition for music to flourish, but it was not sufficient. Attitudes toward art and life, even within a democracy, also had to become more congenial to aesthetic pleasure. He insisted that aesthetic enjoyment must fully replace the oppressive vices of authoritarianism and greed:

> When we shall have shaken off the heavy load of English tradition which bears down upon art, [. . .] then all will strive to be artists. [. . .] I see no hope for Art, but in the extinction of the principle of Force and Privilege, and the substitution of its attractions in their stead. The settlement of political questions, the diminution of the powers of the government, and of the importance of the politician [. . .] these things are all necessary to work out the artistic mission.[37]

Fry urged Americans to sever their European musical ties. If they did not, the consequences would be truly dangerous for composers and society at large. This message was especially radical for a country whose musical culture was hurriedly becoming the purview of the moneyed elite, as well as a cultural enclave for German immigrants—a situation that Fry had yet to experience firsthand.

Radical as his ideas might have been for American musical culture, though, Fry's was not a lone voice in the desert. In literary corners, others believed that America's "genius" was fully manifested in its form of government and that success in artistic endeavors relied on democracy. Led by John L. O'Sullivan, the group of novelists, poets, and journalists calling themselves "Young America" loudly promoted the development of a uniquely American literature defined by its democratic spirit. Their numbers included canonical literary figures like Nathaniel Hawthorne and Herman Melville.[38]

Paralleling Fry's ideas, O'Sullivan called for a radical separation from English literature, which "enslaved" writers. He assured his readers that "the vital principle of an American national literature must be democracy." And like Fry, he admitted that shirking English models entirely was an impossible task. These models must instead be manipulated to suit a peculiarly American sensibility:

> No one will misunderstand us as disparaging the literature of our mother language—far from it. We appreciate it with a profound veneration and gratitude, and would use it, without abusing it by utterly submitting our own minds to it; but we look upon it, as we do the political system of the country, as something magnificent, venerable, splendid, and powerful, and containing a considerable infusion of true principle; yet the one no more suitable to be adopted as our own, or as a model for slavish imitation, than the other.[39]

In the same way that the shared musical languages of tonality and orchestral instrumentation prevented American composers from creating a symphonic style out of thin air, the structures of the English language forced a relationship between American and English literature. With the spirit of democracy always at their disposal, however, writers and composers could create a distinctly American art by translating the old into something fresh. They had to become "double foster" parents who raised their children on a diet of freedom. American audiences were waiting.

THE TRANSLATOR RETURNS HOME

Fry had not found much luck as a composer in Europe, where he had tried to find a new venue for *Leonora*. And despite the bitterness he had expressed toward other cultures in his Parisian letters, he was rife with optimism for the future. If democracy continued to be the principle animating American life, he maintained, the nation's potential for greatness—in politics, science, and the arts—was limitless. Americans lacked only originality and independence of thought, and these defects could be corrected by moving away from European trends and focusing on what was truly American and good.

Eager to show his readers that his vision could become a concrete reality, Fry advertised a series of lectures on the history and theory of music that he intended to lead upon his return to the United States. "The aim of these lectures," one ad claimed, "will be to present, in a condensed but clear form, an illustrated history of the rise, progress and present state of all departments of instrumental and vocal music."[40] The historical trajectory presented in the lectures served to create a sharp distinction between his own originality—the ideal future of American music—and music of the past. By hearing Fry's music alongside more familiar pieces by favorites like Haydn and Rossini, audiences would have ample opportunity to learn the differences between his new American style and the supposedly undemocratic music of bygone ages.[41] He had set up a platform for the public to evaluate his Ciceronian ideas.

The first nine lectures went according to plan, but Fry had to scramble for the tenth after his musicians canceled for another engagement.[42] In a bonus eleventh lecture, however, he returned to his initial plan and, in a stirring peroration, called for a declaration of independence in American art. Savvy listeners would have known that this statement crowned his epistolary efforts of the previous six years. Aghast at American audiences' worship of European composers, a circumstance brought on by the cosmopolitan musical institutions that had blossomed around the country during his absence, he complained that "the American public are too fond of quoting Handel, Mozart, Beethoven, and European artists generally, and decrying whatever is not modeled after their rules." But a composer should not "allow the name of Beethoven, or Handel, or Mozart to prove an eternal bugbear to him." Instead, he urged composers to "strike out manfully and independently into untrodden realms, just as his nature and inspirations may incite him, else he can never achieve lasting renown."[43]

Critic Richard Storrs Willis (1819–1900), who had studied in Europe for six years, took offense at the suggestion and retorted that "a nation's homage—the esteem and admiration and love of the whole artistic world is worth a *life* of toil. The Muses will not descend from Olympus to crown every aspirant for that honor—not, at least, at his first awkward, and perhaps impertinent summons."[44] And just as Dwight had implied in his review of Heinrich's music, Willis argued that moving too far away from musical norms placed a composer's reputation at risk. From his perch in Boston, Dwight himself entered the fray and took an even more reactionary position. He asserted that supporting local composers might actually detract from the appreciation of masterworks. And if that were the case, he added, "we think the worthy public shows its common-sense in cleaving to the former [Beethoven] and letting the latter [native aspirants] abide their time, as genius of all kinds has had to do in all times and places."[45] In Dwight's understanding of the musical world, works of genius were destined to become recognized with time regardless of the concrete circumstances in which they appeared in the first place. He and Willis saw no reason to believe that American composers might face obstacles to success that stood beyond their control.

Although he attracted large audiences and assembled an all-star cast of musicians that included the best singers, conductors, and orchestral players in New York, Fry's lectures ultimately failed. No fellow composer rushed to his defense, and critics remained unconvinced. Dwight had agreed that American musical culture was experiencing increasing Europeanization but claimed that this change was in fact good—certainly not a problem that needed fixing.[46] Fry, on the other hand, believed that critics like Dwight perpetuated American dependence on foreign music by consistently fawning over the works of Mendelssohn, Beethoven, and Handel. He equated their adoration of European works to a composer's servile dependence on European models and resoundingly denounced their efforts, much as Heinrich had done in his private letter. Truly original criticism, Fry asserted, was not the easy and glib repetition of "the words or ideas of Europeans on European compositions," but interpretations of a piece of music stemming from the critic's ability "to take an original score and read it and understand it"—and then to translate it for listeners.[47] If composers had to be held to standards of originality, so should critics. But in Dwight's case, as Boston critic William F. Apthorp later contended, no one was sure if he was capable of analyzing a score.[48]

Convincing key critics of his seriousness and legitimacy proved to be a constant challenge for Fry. The lecture series had not helped despite the audience's general appreciation. Maybe he had not articulated questions of style very clearly or had allowed his national chauvinism to overwhelm the substance of his ideas. Whatever the source of his disappointment, he needed an even better platform to make the case that a truly American music could become a reality. When the famed French conductor (and London resident) Louis Antoine Jullien (1812–1860) arrived in New York in 1853, that platform materialized. He commissioned Fry to write a new symphony for his virtuosic orchestra. After a well-attended Christmas Eve performance of Fry's *Santa Claus: Christmas Symphony*, Willis and Dwight, the same critics who rankled him after his lectures, incited the composer to defend his views once again. This time, however, he was able to demonstrate how musical style fit into his plan for American artistic independence—how he could translate European sounds into an American musical language.

CHAPTER 4

୦⅄୦

George Frederick Bristow,
American Stalwart

A s William Henry Fry was gathering information for his lecture series, critic John Sullivan Dwight was busy making preparations to launch an educational periodical devoted to the day's most important musical topics. Founded in 1852, six years after Dwight had needled Anthony Philip Heinrich over his descriptive fantasies, the journal was called, appropriately, *Dwight's Journal of Music*. It would become his longstanding critical platform.

Shortly into the enterprise, Dwight took his mission overseas by attempting to alter European perceptions of musical life in the United States. He was a well-established Boston critic with a Harvard pedigree. If anyone could do it, presumably he could. So he sent a package to the editorial office of the *Neue Zeitschrift für Musik* in Leipzig that included several issues of his journal along with a listing of music performed in Boston during the 1852–1853 concert season (which, incidentally, included several performances by the Germania Musical Society, now in its fifth year in the United States). His goal, simply put, was to illustrate the broadness and sophistication of Boston's musical taste, and in so doing, impress the leading intellectuals of the German-speaking musical world. Unlike Fry, who had just moved on from his lecture series, Dwight was not seeking American artistic independence.

The Germans welcomed the package harmoniously. By that time, the journal's editorship had transferred from Robert Schumann to Franz Brendel (1811–1868), an ally of Richard Wagner and Franz Liszt, composers whose music was practically unknown in the United States. Brendel commissioned Richard Pohl (1826–1896), another Wagnerian, to respond to Dwight in an open letter that appeared in the *Neue Zeitschrift* and that Dwight reprinted in English after receiving a copy in Boston.[1] Dwight was a translator too, but the more literal kind.

Writing under the pseudonym Hoplit, Pohl lauded Dwight for his efforts to promote good musical taste. The city of Boston, he claimed, had avoided the cosmopolitanism and "humbug" (a code word for infatuation with Italian opera) of New York City and had subsequently emerged as an international center of high culture. He remarked in particular on the number of symphonies heard in Boston, a result of the Germanians' diligent efforts. Evidently Dwight had succeeded: Pohl was convinced.

The letter quickly took a dramatic political turn, however, as Pohl expressed "a certain feeling of fatherland's pride, at having found in the 'far West' an important center for our native and to us sacred tones, for German ways of feeling and for German art." Much to Pohl's surprise, the United States had quickly surpassed Great Britain in its ability to appreciate the "modern" music of Beethoven, Mendelssohn, and Schumann, as opposed to the crusty Handel and Haydn revered by the British. Pohl was also impressed that Bostonians had advocated vigorously for Schumann and Wagner (whose music had recently been introduced by the Germania Society) by offering fair-minded criticism of their latest works. This attitude, he claimed proudly, had opened the United States to a new era of musical understanding:

> Where one sees such fruits, there must one shout out a glad and truly-meant "Glucksauf!" to the fresh and vital New World, and with joy greet in spirit a man who, while geographically our antipodes, is yet in tendency and in endeavor our confederate. The sympathies of the Art-related stand higher than those of the birth-related, for they are of a more spiritual sort. And the genuine cosmopolitanism reigns in the kingdom of the Ideal![2]

Dwight, ever the Germanophile, likely fed on this paragraph gleefully, for it seemed to affirm his mission.

Attempting to win over Dwight and his readers with this friendly expression of cultural kinship, Pohl then revealed his true aim much more forcefully: the spread of Wagnerism. He noted with special interest that Bostonians had given sustained attention to Schumann and Berlioz, two of the most advanced composers of the age. Coupled with a strong appreciation for the choral finale of Beethoven's Ninth, a linchpin in Wagner's vision of the future (or as Pohl called it, "that effective mediator between yesterday and today, between the *this side* and the *that side* of one-sided Art"), Boston's strong interest in modern music was proof that "all the very elements calculated to prepare one for the Wagner art" had already coalesced in the United States. "And therefore," he added in an appeal to American patriotism,

"I already see in spirit the bridge thrown across the ocean, which, though it be tens of years hence, will lead the Wagner art-works over into the land of freedom!"[3]

After dubbing Wagner "the man of free Art" who would "one day rise up anew and find an abiding foothold in the land of freedom," Pohl closed his letter with another appeal to Americans' inchoate sense of Manifest Destiny. Throughout history, he contended, the westerly movement of progress—from Asia to Europe, and now from Europe to the New World—had been inexorable and unstoppable. The United States was the only logical place for Wagner's music to land next: "America needs scarcely ten years for a transformation," he asserted with great flourish, "which in our effete Europe would occupy an entire generation of men. Perhaps we shall, within a shorter time than we ourselves imagine, meet again 'over there,' to witness the first performance of Wagner's *Tannhäuser* in Boston, and to cry out with new confirmed conviction to the land of the Future: WESTWARD MOVES THE HISTORY OF ART!"[4]

Dwight must have been speechless when he first read the letter. His printed response was a mixture of excitement and bewilderment. He thanked Pohl for his high opinion of the country's "catholicity" and appreciation of a variety of musical styles. But he felt that his German confrère was overestimating Americans' readiness to receive new music, even if they were especially progressive thinkers. "Our very love of the classics," he insisted, "is with us the ground of the most unfailing Progress. [. . .] O for long life on this earth, or in conscious communication with it, that we may hear and hail the MUSIC OF THE FUTURE!"[5] Dwight sincerely wanted to remain open to Wagner and other moderns, but he was reluctant to associate himself with their ideas before coming to know them more fully—and especially before comparing them to his ideal models of high art, Beethoven, Mendelssohn, and the other "classics."

George Frederick Bristow (1825–1898), a New York composer and conductor who had helped direct the ensemble performing in William Henry Fry's lecture series, was probably speechless as well. His name did not appear once in the transatlantic correspondence despite being the country's most promising young composer. A statement of the country's musical accomplishments surely should have included information about its composers. For all its detail, however, the exchange reflected Dwight and Pohl's shared focus on music that was already in circulation, rather than the creation of new works. They believed the United States should be a passive receptacle for European art and that it would mature with time. Indeed, they thought it might even surpass the Old World in its refinement. On a deeper level, the multilingual and transatlantic character of the exchange also articulated the rapidly widening rift between cosmopolitan thinkers such as Dwight and figures who directed their attention more squarely on local matters. How a composer was supposed to navigate this environment proved to be a vexing question for Bristow.

A writer of five symphonies, Bristow (figure 4.1) nevertheless became the country's most distinguished composer throughout the second half of the century. And as far as he was concerned, European music did not need any translation—a position that placed him in direct opposition to the more progressive Fry. Throughout his career, Bristow's compositional style aligned closely with contemporary European trends, but critics still asserted their authority over him while using an impressive array of rhetorical strategies for diminishing his efforts. Ignoring such fickle behavior, Bristow the stalwart became increasingly interested in musical depictions of American subjects and pursued other interests that kept him out of the spotlight that Fry seemed to relish. He died while on the job at one of New York's public schools after serving as a music instructor to grade-school children for several decades.[6]

Figure 4.1: George Frederick Bristow. Courtesy of the Historical Society of Pennsylvania.

THE STALWART IN CONFLICT

Bristow's career began just as Anthony Philip Heinrich was making headway in New York. After performing alongside his father in a theater orchestra for several years, he joined the first violin section of the Philharmonic Society in 1843, only one season after Heinrich had helped establish it. But things did not get off to a good start. As he recounted later in life, the teenaged Bristow was prone to pranking his fellow musicians. On one noteworthy occasion, he inadvertently poisoned his father with lamp oil that he had poured into the community snuff box, stuffed a herring in the bell of a French horn (causing the player to wretch in disgust), incited a scuffle between the horn player and a flautist who unfairly took the blame, and greased the bow of a drunk cellist—all in one night.[7]

As an aspiring composer, however, Bristow treated the Philharmonic's bylaws, especially Article VII, much more seriously. "If any grand orchestral compositions," the article began, "such as overtures, or symphonies, shall be presented to the Society, they being composed in this country, the Society shall perform one every season."[8] The directors drafted the article in order to promote resident composers by affording them the rare and valuable opportunity for a capable orchestra to perform their works. These leaders understood that having such an opportunity was the best way for a composer to grow.

With longstanding familial ties to the New York music scene, Bristow was a natural choice for compositional grooming. In January of 1847, only a few months after Heinrich's ill-fated festival and Fry's departure for Paris, the Philharmonic allowed Bristow to conduct his first orchestral work, a concert overture. Although the work received attention from the press, the performance quickly became a distant memory as onlookers soon accused the Philharmonic of willfully neglecting its pro-American mission. Hermann Saroni (1824–1900), an influential critic and aspiring composer himself, noted that he had "heard of the rejection of some valuable 'active members,' simply because they happened not to belong to the clique in power." These members were so upset that he believed they intended "to secede from the mother institution and to found a new society by themselves."[9] Bristow was likely among these malcontents, for another writer snarled that "our *patriotism* is becoming a little pricked in anticipation" of a performance of "a certain symphony which cost a talented member of [the Society] ... some four years of hard study."[10] The ink was still drying on the manuscript of his First Symphony.

The situation soon worsened. Saroni later reported that certain members of the Philharmonic believed it was failing its mission of cultivating taste and had turned into a vehicle for profiteering.[11] Bowing to internal and external pressures to reinstate the neglected article, the Philharmonic eventually performed Bristow's new symphony and an overture by Theodore Eisfeld (1816–1882), a German immigrant and subscribing member, at an extra public rehearsal given in May of 1850. Critics received Bristow's symphony more favorably than his overture, which was certainly a credit to advocates of local composers and a stain on the Philharmonic's reputation. The board of directors contemplated restructuring the contentious article of the bylaws so that it would be even more favorable to Americans, but while some changes were made on paper, nothing changed in practice. The speculation and insinuation in the press soured Bristow toward the Philharmonic for years.[12]

By the time discussions concerning the orchestra's treatment of local composers were winding down in May of 1851, xenophobia over the matter had bubbled to the surface and added a more sinister dimension. One critic made the open accusation that "clannish cliques are formed in our midst by alien artists, musicians, and actors. [. . .] Why, then, do foreigners set themselves apart, practically saying to us 'We are more holy than ye?' Why are they illiberal? Why do they not appreciate our talent?" And, with a final accusation of cultural separatism, "Why, if they are truly men of genius, do they band themselves together, and establish lines of nationality in our midst?"[13] Although it died quickly in this instance, the belief that the German contingent of the Philharmonic not only looked down upon Americans but also sought to separate from them would resurface several times over the next three decades.

THE STALWART'S CRITICS

Fortunately for Bristow, such divisive politics did not color the critical reception of his early works. In fact, writers pegged Bristow as a compositional imitator from the outset but waffled about how he should remedy the problem. Reviewing the 1847 premiere of Bristow's concert overture, Henry Cood Watson perfunctorily claimed that he "possesses much talent and promises much in future compositions," but the work was "wanting in individuality" and exhibited little "evidence of original thought." To his credit, Bristow had demonstrated familiarity with the "power and resources of the orchestra" and had filled his music with "reminiscences of the Italian, German, and French schools"—a testament to his ability to assimilate a wide variety of styles. Yet Watson urged the young Bristow to "model himself upon Mozart's instrumental work, which will be found the safest of all models."[14] While appearing to offer guidance, such a suggestion mainly served to reinforce Watson's public persona as a knowledgeable mediator and tastemaker.

Other writers dispatched similarly mixed messages, about both whom to copy and by how much. Richard Grant White (1822–1885) believed that Bristow had followed Auber, Weber, and Mendelssohn down a promising path despite being unable to find much individuality.[15] George Templeton Strong remarked in his diary (and thus not directly to the composer) that the overture was "made up of reminiscences of Weber and Spohr, though perhaps it was rather a mixture of their respective styles than any appropriating of what they had written."[16] Bristow had clearly studied a variety of scores, but such study only seemed to work against him.

Like any aspiring novice, Bristow absorbed the advice he was given and tried to implement it in his First Symphony, which premiered at the Philharmonic's pacifying rehearsal of local compositions in 1850. With a nod toward Watson's recommendation to follow Mozart, Bristow opened the piece in a manner similar to Mozart's Symphony No. 39 in E♭, K. 543. Since the Philharmonic had performed it in an earlier season, modeling it would have been a straightforward choice. The slow introduction contains sudden dynamic contrasts amid the strong rhythmic drive of dotted eighth-sixteenth figures (example 4.1). Also like its model, the opening builds to an intense climax that turns into a soaring martial tune followed by a quiet and myste-rious chromatic expansion of the dominant (example 4.2). The strong resem-blance to Mozart ends there, however, as the first movement allegro begins in cut time, not the triple meter of the earlier work. It was a close imitation but not overly faithful.

Such attentive modeling still bothered certain critics. Saroni, who had advocated for Bristow in his journal, heard such a mish-mash of styles that he compared it to a "musical chessboard, with a field for each composer from

Example 4.1: Stately Opening. Bristow, Symphony No. 1, I (slow introduction), mm. 1–8 (full orch.).

Example 4.2: Chromatic Conclusion. Bristow, Symphony No. 1, I (slow introduction), mm. 55–62 (strings).

the time of Haydn to Mendelssohn-Bartholdy."[17] A composer himself, he gave Bristow only one suggestion for improvement: give up altogether. He urged the aspirant to "be content with compositions of less extent. If former masters have began [sic] their career by writing symphonies, they did so at a time when that form was not developed by the master hand of a Mozart, Beethoven, etc., etc." In essence, the symphonic canon had already closed.

Displeased with the vague reminiscences of earlier composers dotting the symphony, Saroni also demolished the music's syntax. He complained about "the utter want of connection between the different ideas. Almost every sixteen bars, the composer seems to have come to a dead halt. He begins a new melody, and goes again over the same ground, suddenly drops the theme and begins a new one, which has not the remotest connection to the former."[18] Structure and syntax were likely fresh on Saroni's mind. He was in the midst of creating an English translation of German theorist Adolf Bernhard Marx's popular treatise on composition, which would be available for American audiences for the first time.[19]

And Saroni was not off the mark. Following the introduction, the allegro's opening melody is a delightful tune reminiscent of Haydn or Mozart but harmonized with a chromaticism that was more characteristic of Spohr's style. It ends peculiarly on a diminished seventh sonority (example 4.3). As Saroni suggested, the following sections bear no relation to the opening until the primary theme is stated once more by the full orchestra in a seemingly needless repetition. A secondary theme in the dominant key appears after a typical transition, but the melody is insipid and repetitious (example 4.4). Summing up his impressions, Saroni remarked that the symphony as a whole is "too long by half" and has a monotonous character, "which is anything

Example 4.3: Opening Theme. Symphony No. 1, I: Allegro vivace, mm. 63–78 (strings).

but pleasant." Throughout the work, Bristow did indeed have the remarkable tendency to double the length of a phrase by repeating it with a new orchestration. And since three of the four movements are all in the same key, the symphony is literally monotonous.

Other critics enjoyed the symphony, however, and commented freely on Bristow's originality. Frederick Nicholls Crouch (1808–1896) believed it was "an achievement withal so respectable, and of so much higher grade [. . .] than anything heretofore attempted in this country" and therefore deserved extended commentary.[20] He justified the effort by extolling Bristow's credentials as both an experienced orchestral performer and a composer of excellent shorter works. In a more thorough review printed the following week, Crouch then insinuated that Saroni, who had never written a symphony of his own (and never would), was simply jealous. The second movement, he claimed, "happily illustrates [Bristow's] unreserved and innate conceptions and peculiar temperament better then [sic] any other portion of the symphony. There is a dreamy romance and placid beauty in this strain, which attracts and soothes the listener, almost in spite of his will."[21] Scored in a rich A♭ major, the luscious opening melody (example 4.5) is judiciously ornamented and spans well over an octave, giving it the dreamy quality Crouch detected.

Example 4.4: Insipid Second Theme. Bristow, Symphony No. 1, I: Allegro vivace, mm. 149–164 (full orch.).

Writing after a later revival of the symphony's minuet movement, Henry Cood Watson noticed a marked improvement over the overture and described the minuet as "rich in melody, brilliant, and effective."[22] But never shying from comparing it to the European masters, he also echoed Saroni's complaints that the work's ideas are "reminiscences of old familiar themes" by pointing out that "the *tema* very greatly resembles Mozart's accompaniment to *Deh vieni alla finestra*, from 'Don Giovanni.'" The movement's opening melody does indeed contain the same arched melodic gestures found in Mozart's aria (example 4.6). Lest his readers assume this was high praise, Watson added faintly that a listener "might find some fault with the scoring and arrangements; but in consideration of Mr. Bristow's antecedents and peculiarities, we cannot but admire it as a meritorious and genial work."

Bristow had followed the advice he was given by copying some of the most highly esteemed symphonic masters, including Mozart, but this effort was not enough. According to critics, he needed to improve significantly before they would concede that his music rivaled the quality of his

Example 4.5: Italianate Opening Theme. Bristow, Symphony No. 1, II: Adagio, mm. 1–8 (strings).

Example 4.6: Mozartean Reminiscence. Bristow, Symphony No. 1, III: Minuetto, mm. 1–8.

European counterparts. Crouch urged him to "study sufficiently; write simply, without aiming to accomplish too much at the outset; don't be impatient of *many* experiments, nor shrink from the severest tests, before producing publicly."[23] Nodding in agreement, Watson's next round of advice was more forthright: "If Mr. Bristow would go for a year or two to Spohr, Hector Berlioz, and others, or attend the great Philharmonic and other Grand Concerts and Festivals at the *Gewandhaus* and similar places on the European Continent, he would become a Composer [. . .] of whom the country might be proud."[24] They never thought to compare his music favorably to works of "lesser" Europeans such as Johann Kalliwoda, whose music the Philharmonic had performed unapologetically.

Determined to succeed without help, Bristow did not follow this advice. He stayed put. His self-confidence as a composer grew between 1851 and 1853 as other orchestras, including the ensemble that accompanied the famous soprano Jenny Lind (1820–1887) on her cross-country tour, programmed his overture and selections from his symphony.[25] By refusing to seek the approval overseas, he had declared independence from Europe, but in a manner far different from Fry, who focused on style. As in Fry's case, however, Louis Antoine Jullien's 1853 arrival in New York would prove to have a profound impact on the young composer's career. In the months following Dwight's exchange with Richard Pohl, the landscape of the American symphonic enterprise would change dramatically.

CHAPTER 5

✑

The Rivalry of Nations

While Anthony Philip Heinrich was composing furiously, William Henry Fry was soaking up Paris, and George Frederick Bristow was struggling to find venues for his music, other resident composers were transforming the dramatic patriotism of James Hewitt's instrumental works into theatrical sensations. Late in 1850, for example, the year the New York Philharmonic gave Bristow's symphony at a public rehearsal, Robert-Nicholas-Charles-Bochsa (1789–1856), an ostentatious harpist, composer, and conductor, staged a series of "Promenade Concerts" elsewhere in the city. He intended his programs to combine enlightenment with entertainment. At one of these events, he adapted Beethoven's descriptive *Wellingtons Sieg* into an American battle memorial with "Yankee Doodle" in place of "God Save the Queen," a strategy taken directly from Hewitt's playbook. If the original work by Beethoven confounded highbrow listeners like George William Curtis, one wonders how they would have responded to this showy patriotic concoction.[1]

Bochsa's arrangement paled in comparison to a new symphony by Simon Knaebel (1812–ca. 1880), a German immigrant who joined the Philharmonic in 1842 as a charter member and violinist. Knaebel wrote the giant piece, called *The Battle of Bunker Hill*, for the battle's seventy-fifth anniversary in 1851. It required two full orchestras, each of which represented an army, the Continentals and the British, and it comprised twenty instrumental movements that followed a choral setting of a well-known poem by Lydia Sigourney (1791–1865). As in James Hewitt's battle pieces—and Beethoven's, for that matter—each movement depicted the battle in realistic detail (see table 5.1). Although it received scant notice and mild praise from critics in music periodicals, one daily newspaper declared it a resounding triumph. "It is enough to say," wrote the *Brooklyn Daily Eagle*, "that its effect upon the vast auditory

---

Table 5.1. PROGRAM FOR *THE BATTLE OF BUNKER HILL SYMPHONY* (1851)
BY SIMON KNAEBEL.

---

1. General Putnam's March
2. Digging Fortifications after midnight (in the mean time, the British cry, "All's Well") to be represented by the Horns as a duet
3. Astonishment of the British, discovering the fortifications
4. First Cannon by the British
5. Signal to Fire
6. Second Cannon
7. Tremendous Fire from the Floating Batteries
8. Colonel Prescott's Quick Step
9. Horses galloping at a distance; Artillery approaching, etc.
10. Drum beats to arms
11. Order for attack
12. Cannon by the Americans
13. Signal to advance
14. Heavy fire by the Americans
15. General fire on both sides
16. The fall of General Warren. Marcia funerale preceded by a choral of four Trombones
17. Thundering cannonade by the British
18. Charlestown on fire
19. Cries of the wounded
20. Finale—March and Combat between both Orchestras on the National Airs

---

[of around 3,000 listeners] was such as to call forth, at the close of each succeeding phrase, the most unqualified applause; and the whole received the 'broad seal' of perfect success."[2] John Sullivan Dwight and George William Curtis, the Beethoven worshipers, undoubtedly would have hated it.

Rather than rallying the city into a frenzy of national unity, these extravagant patriotic displays masked the bubbling turmoil concerning the status of immigrant musicians. German speakers entered the United States at a greater pace than ever before in the wake of the failed revolutions of 1848–1849. Like any large immigrant group, they established close-knit communities within cities and entire regions. These tight local bonds allowed them to maintain Old World cultural practices, including participating in the Turner gymnastics movement and singing in Liederkranz societies, with relative ease.

In the Klein Deutschland neighborhood of New York City, German immigrants also constructed hundreds of entertainment venues such as theaters, dance halls, and beer gardens, all of which required the services of instrumental musicians.[3] German players who fled the revolutions found that earning a living as a musician in the United States was not difficult. Those who also wanted to hone their skills while playing more challenging repertoire could seek membership in the Philharmonic Society. Since the orchestra drew its roster from the best theater musicians, the rapid infrastructural development of the German musical entertainment industry flooded the market and swelled the society's ranks of German musicians. Ethnic and linguistic isolationism—problems portended by Dwight's communication with the *Neue Zeitschrift für Musik*—ultimately became a source of bitter conflict for Bristow and Fry.

THE STALWART SNUBBED

Bristow's rocky relationship with the Philharmonic did not end with the conciliatory performance of his symphony in 1850. Two years later, Englishman George Loder (1816–1868) announced his retirement as the orchestra's principal conductor. The board of directors became hopelessly deadlocked in its decision concerning a replacement. Now the orchestra's concertmaster, Bristow decided to enter his name for consideration. If he controlled the reins, he could ensure that the bylaws would be taken more seriously and that his compositional aspirations would be fulfilled. Unfortunately, because he did not receive a clear majority of the vote, the directors dropped him from consideration in favor of Theodore Eisfeld, a revolutionary-era immigrant from Brauschweig whose overture had also been featured on a Philharmonic program. Eisfeld subsequently conducted the orchestra solely or in a shared capacity for the next thirteen years.[4] This new position gave him considerable clout.

The snubbed Bristow directed much of his attention elsewhere. He assumed the directorship of the newly reorganized Harmonic Society, a chorus akin to Boston's Handel and Haydn Society. The group received wide public exposure after Bristow offered its services to William Henry Fry for his series of lectures and to the noted German soprano Henriette Sontag (1806–1854), who mounted a series of festival concerts around the same time.[5] Bristow's choice to assist at the lecture series was risky because he did not know Fry very well; Fry had only just arrived from Paris. But it benefited his compositional career since Fry programmed the finale of his languishing symphony as well as a selection from *Eleutheria*, a patriotic cantata by American composer George Henry Curtis (1821–1895) that Bristow had orchestrated. With this kind of publicity, Bristow's stock as a versatile musician was rising rapidly.

Bristow's visibility within the greater musical community paid big dividends when Louis Antoine Jullien and his virtuosic orchestra came to New York in the autumn of 1853, just two months after Dwight's printed exchange with the Wagnerian Richard Pohl. Shortly after his arrival, Jullien invited Bristow to join the violin section of his orchestra, and Bristow in turn shared his symphony with Jullien, who immediately began programming the minuet movement. Falsely (but cleverly) billing Bristow's work as a "New Symphony," Jullien performed it in New York at least three times before taking it on the road during a tour along the eastern seaboard. He eventually programmed it again upon his return to New York City in December.[6] Returning the favor, Bristow offered the services of his Harmonic Society (recently renamed the Sacred Harmonic Society) to Jullien, who with Bristow's assistance directed a monumental performance of Handel's *Messiah* on the night after Christmas.

A few days later, Jullien staged a performance that he billed as a "Grand American Night." Bristow's popular minuet appeared on the program along with two of Fry's symphonies, which he had used as illustrations during his lecture series and had re-orchestrated for Jullien. The orchestra also premiered the first movement of a new symphony by Bristow, which advertisements claimed had been composed "expressly for this occasion." Within a matter of months, then, Jullien had commissioned Bristow to write a symphony and performed excerpts from his works at least a dozen times, an impressive number that far exceeded the Philharmonic's meager support.

Although Bristow's relationship with the Philharmonic had turned cold since his rejection as its new conductor, the fact that Jullien found his music worthy enough to perform, not just once but several times, rekindled public ire. Following Jullien's initial performance of Bristow's music, in October, Fry began stoking the anti-Philharmonic flames by filling his editorial column in the *Tribune* with anti-German vitriol directed at the orchestra. Claiming that Bristow's music was "quite as well written as the last German symphonies played by the Philharmonic," which had included Schubert's Ninth, Beethoven's Fifth, and Schumann's First, he declared that the orchestra ought to leap at the opportunity to perform the complete work; mastering it would be a credit to any ensemble's reputation. Comparing the country's musical establishment to "low provincials" for esteeming European works simply because they were European, Fry urged listeners to show more pride in native musicians. "Is not New York as large as Vienna and larger," he asked, "Then why defer to any German town?"[7] Apparently little had changed in the months after his final lecture.

Using Jullien's open acceptance of local music as proof of its high quality, Fry fired a second salvo at the orchestra a few weeks later. "[D]eference to European dictation" was degrading to any American composer, he argued, and it was shameful that "the chances for an American to put before the public any work of musical High Art, depend, in this country, upon the accidental presence of such a liberal-minded man and consummate musician as M. Jullien."[8] Without the support of well-established institutions, composers left their livelihood to the whims of visitors. Fry's position was self-interested but it was not without merit.

Before a local response to Fry's attacks appeared, John Sullivan Dwight, the Bostonian, stepped into the conversation. Spouting off about the universality of beauty, he deflected Fry by suggesting that a composer's lack of success is more properly attributed to the public's lack of interest in the music. He also managed to wrangle Bristow into the discussion in order to make the point: "Mr. Fry and Mr. Bristow are sure to be accepted, [. . .] just so soon as their audiences shall feel that there is genius, inspiration, beauty, poetry of music in their symphonies, at all proportioned to the audacity and oddness of their designs." Reiterating a claim he had made in his response to Fry's patriotic lecture the previous winter, he emphasized that genius would "convert us to itself by its own proper magnetism." Time, Dwight insisted, would be the ultimate arbiter of greatness.[9]

But Dwight's suggestion that audiences would, in time, simply prefer "great" works over others flew directly past Fry, who was arguing that powerful cliques, not disinterested audiences, were the root cause of the Philharmonic's neglect of American composers. And if American composers were never given a chance to be heard, Fry wondered, how could audiences make an informed decision? Meeting Dwight on his own terms, Fry retorted that if critics and the Philharmonic wished to reject new music on purely stylistic grounds, then they had no reason to treat Bristow poorly since his symphonies were "strictly classic" in form and design.[10] (Fry's, as we shall see, were not.)

With his name now in the open air, Bristow felt compelled to join the discussion. In a letter addressed to Richard Storrs Willis's *Musical World and Times*, Bristow confirmed Fry's accusations that the Philharmonic had never tried to fulfill its mandate to support local music. Noting that his overture was the only American piece it had ever performed, "either by mistake or accident," he roundly criticized the group for its systematic avoidance of American works. "As one exception makes a rule stronger," he deduced, "so this single stray fact shows that the Philharmonic Society has been as anti-American as if it been located in London during the revolutionary war, and composed of native born English Tories." Not forgetting his fleeting moment in the spotlight after the so-called premiere of his symphony in 1850, Bristow piquantly alluded to the story of Tristram Shandy by reminding readers that the work had merely been *rehearsed* in public, not performed: "So Uncle says—'Our army swore terribly at Flanders'—but that army did not fight."[11]

Bristow contended that the Philharmonic's neglect of its mission was rooted in a toxic mixture of anti-Americanism and German chauvinism. He called the society's very purpose into question:

Now, in the name of the Nine Muses, what is the Philharmonic Society [. . .] in this country? Is it to play exclusively works of German masters, especially if they be dead, in order that our critics may translate their ready-made praises from German? [. . .] Is there a Philharmonic Society in Germany for the encouragement solely of American music? Then why should there be a society here for the encouragement solely of German music; unless, as Mr. Fry says, the object be to render us a Hessian Colony, which we most incontestably are?[12]

Readers would have winced at the caustic reference to Hessians, who had served as mercenaries for the British army during the American Revolution. The source of Bristow's frustration, which had been building for at least four years, could not have been more evident: Germans.

The tirade did not stop there. Not merely dissatisfied with the Philharmonic's programming philosophy, Bristow urged the wholesale replacement of its directors with parties sympathetic to his cause, and, with a decidedly political and prejudicial tone, shooed the current administration back to Europe:

> If all their artistic affections are unalterably German, let them pack back to Germany and enjoy the police and bayonets and aristocratic kicks and cuffs of that land, where an artist is a serf to a nobleman, as the history of all their great composers show [sic]. [. . .] While America has been thus far able to do the chief things for the dignity of man, forsooth she must be denied the brains for original Art, and must stand like a beggar, deferentially cap in hand, when she comes to compete with the ability of any dirty German village.[13]

Concluding that the Philharmonic's attempt to snuff out American music was "just short of a conspiracy," Bristow insisted that the orchestra was as *un*-American in its governance as it was *anti*-American in its orientation. Enraged, he resigned his place as a violinist in the orchestra, as well as his position on the board.

Fry, meanwhile, had focused his energy on Dwight's contention that genius would make itself known through the clear preferences of paying audiences. In a letter to *Dwight's Journal*, he explained at length that so-called "genius" composers like Handel, Haydn, Mozart, and Beethoven had been rejected by critics in one city while being overwhelmed with praise elsewhere. More to the point, however, he added that American composers had not been afforded the same opportunities to be heard as their European counterparts. A symphony, he claimed, "when composed, until repeatedly played, has for mankind about as much absolute existence as a statue or painting would have, if the moment it came from the artist's hand and unseen by other eyes than his, it were buried in the ground and left there to rot." Using Dwight's own contention that frequent performances were an "essential condition for correcting errors of opinion" concerning large and complex works, Fry argued vehemently that those very conditions had not been "awarded" to him.[14]

While Fry was occupied with this exchange, the conversation following Bristow's opening gambit continued to unfold in the pages of Willis's journal over several weeks. The Philharmonic's treasurer William Scharfenberg and an anonymous board member published cursory replies, but the board itself decided to offer a public and supposedly collective rebuttal arguing that Bristow's accusations were patently false.[15] The orchestra, they claimed, had performed not one but eleven works by Americans, and the idea that there was a "conspiracy" against American composers was absurd. Yet Ureli Corelli Hill (1802–1875), a founding member who was then serving as the board's vice president and who had supported Bristow throughout his career, declared shenanigans when he wrote to Willis claiming that his name had been signed to the rebuttal letter without his permission.[16] No conspiracy indeed.

Using Hill's exposé as irrefutable proof of his accusations, Bristow responded formally to the board's rebuttal by reiterating his claim that only one American work written for full orchestra—his overture—had ever appeared in a true Philharmonic performance. And even it, he added, was performed "due to the influence of Mr. Hill," rather than through a collective agreement. In the peroration of this second letter, Bristow publicly tendered his resignation and stated his intention to form "The American Philharmonic Society, which I trust will be free from all *cliques*, and whose aim will be, to promote, and cultivate the Divine Art, regardless of any *national* prejudices."[17] Unsympathetic readers might have noted the irony that Bristow's proposal to form an orchestra devoid of "national prejudices" stemmed from his apparently anti-German feelings.

Despite Bristow's fiery close, the argument continued for several more weeks as still more commentators attempted to impugn Bristow's judgment. Bristow had asserted that the Philharmonic began as a strictly American organization and only later transformed into a tightly knit German-controlled body. Germans, he claimed, "had obtained complete sway over the direction [of the Philharmonic], and had the power [. . .] to show their contempt for everything American."[18] Protesting this point, an anonymous correspondent to *Dwight's*, calling himself (or perhaps herself) "Pegan," claimed that the Philharmonic "originated in the desire of the German resident musicians to keep up their knowledge of and taste for the music of their native land and in the wish of Americans to know the music of which they had heard and read so much."[19] And as such, "its performances are to be of music by composers of high and acknowledged standing," not novices and aspirants.

Pegan's presumptuous history lesson irritated Bristow, who responded the following week by redoubling his original assertion that the Philharmonic was intended be an American organization, "*there not being a single German concerned in [its] formation.*"[20] (He left no comment on the Bohemian Anthony Philip Heinrich's involvement.) Then, after quoting a lengthy passage about the orchestra's origin taken from one of the Philharmonic's recent annual reports, he concluded decisively that,

> According to the above, it will be seen that, the Philharmonic was originated by Mr. Hill with the assistance of Messrs. A. and H. B. Dodworth, and that the

constitution was framed by Messrs. Hill, Penson, Walker, Dodworth, whom I take to be Americans, and Englishmen, and *not Germans*. [. . .] Does this look like being originated "in the desire of the German resident musicians," for the purpose of performing none but German music? No! The Philharmonic Society commenced upon a good American foundation: but from time to time, the old members, those who had actually built up the Society, have been literally thrust out. [. . .] Thus it will be seen, that twelve years ago, the Philharmonic Society was American; at the present time, it is German, and wholly devoted to German interests.[21]

Since the Philharmonic's original purpose was "the proper performance of great orchestral music" regardless of its national origin, Bristow's argument seemed bulletproof.[22] With such an emphatic closing, the dispute quickly faded into the background. The Philharmonic continued its work unmoved—without Bristow's violin.

Except for Dwight's occasional sideline commentary, the bitter exchange had little to do with music. Instead, Bristow filled his missives with anti-immigrant invective characterizing Germans as conniving, cliquish, and, worst of all, abusers of American political independence. Such rhetoric reflected the broader nativist sentiment called "Know-Nothingism" that was sweeping the country as local political parties converged around anti-immigrant feelings. Know-Nothings were suspicious of the overwhelmingly large numbers of Irish and Germans entering the United States and believed they would re-erect Old World institutions on American soil.[23] One widely circulated manifesto claimed that Free German Associations were openly promoting constitutions "under the direction of Romish despots, to destroy our liberties."[24] Although there is no evidence demonstrating that Bristow belonged to one of these parties, the rhetorical connection is clear. He perceived the Philharmonic's dogmatic promulgation of German works as the musical equivalent of colonization. And his ideology was so apparent to nineteenth-century onlookers that Henry Krehbiel, a knowledgeable critic and Philharmonic historian, conferred the Know-Nothing label on Bristow in an obituary written over forty years after the controversy.[25]

Even so, Bristow was not the only participant in the discussion whose national chauvinism was on full display. "Pegan" had also belittled American composers with an array of ethnic slurs. "America is on the point of throwing off allegiance to Germany," Pegan's letter claimed, and "in vocal music the victory is already achieved. Three negro minstrel bands draw nightly crowds of devotees to their temples, while a German four-part *Lied*, or an old English Glee, is unknown." Bristow scoffed at the comparison of symphonists to negro minstrels,[26] but this was only the first of Pegan's taunts:

Imagine the conflict; the Teutonic army drawn up in martial array, furnished with ammunition by Captain Mozart, and on the other side one or two violins, perhaps reinforced by some of our *American* instruments. *Nun geht's los!* ["Here we go!"] With an awful shock the quadruple fugue in Mozart's C Major Symphony meets in mid air a strain from—from—but we will not specify.[27]

Unsatisfied with the creation of an orchestra devoted solely to American works, Pegan suggested that French, Italian, and even Chinese musicians— "now, alas, selling tobacco and cigars, or distributing advertisements in the streets"—might as well start *their* own orchestras, too. ("I shall go strong for the latter—blessed be their long queues!") Piling on the invective, Pegan closed by comparing Fry to a fictional Chinese musician named "Chan Yong, who has the cigar stand at Park Gate," and claiming that Fry would never be able to write a traditional symphony in a matter of days, as he had recently asserted.

Pegan's personal barbs notwithstanding, Bristow had just cause for his grievances when considered in the light of the Philharmonic's bylaws. The acrimonious tone in his missives nevertheless revealed a deep animosity toward many of the individuals in his immediate musical circle, and the responses suggested that the feelings were mutual. In his list of the orchestra's founders, he had conveniently characterized English immigrants as pro-American and presented them as patriots equal to native-born Americans. But Germans had constituted the largest ethnic proportion of the orchestra's roster (if not its board) from the beginning. Bristow certainly knew this statistic but failed to mention it. From his perspective, these musicians were not likely to hold American values, and from Pegan's perspective, Americans had no business writing symphonies.

THE TRANSLATOR AT WORK

William Henry Fry, who had started the trouble in the first place, became embroiled in still another controversy during Jullien's residency. In this case, it was in fact about musical style. Anxious to test his translation theories concerning the relationship between operatic drama and instrumental music, he wrote seven symphonies within a short timeframe. This flurry of activity was a clear consequence of Jullien's extended presence in the country.

Fry gave each of his symphonies a title evoking a picturesque scene or dramatic narrative: *A Day in the Country* (1852), *The Breaking Heart* (1852, also known as *Adagio Sostenuto*), *Santa Claus: Christmas Symphony* (1853), *Grand Symphonie: Childe Harold* (1854), *Niagara: A Symphony* (1854), *Sacred Symphony No. III—Hagar in the Wilderness* (1854), and *Dramatic Symphony—The Dying Soldier* (n.d.).[28] These titles and subjects (*Niagara* notwithstanding) may seem incongruous with the nationalist program that Fry had been developing since the 1840s. And as a mélange of European cultivated traditions, the music itself may not initially sound "American" to contemporary ears either.[29] But Fry was a translator, not an originator. His final public statement before leaving for Europe—the preface to *Leonora*—was that instrumental music's chief goal should be to aspire to the dramatic expression of the lyric stage. He had already tried translating Italian opera into an American form but soon considered ways to translate it into other genres as well.

The idea continued to occupy Fry after his departure to Europe. Writing from Paris to the *Message Bird* in 1851, he ruminated at length on the impracticality and difficulty of producing an opera compared to writing a symphony: "To write a good opera is the most difficult of musical undertakings; because the ideas are controlled by the words, and the compass and possibilities of the voice."[30] In an opera, he suggested, the libretto and stage action wield absolute authority over the work's musical expression, leaving the music unable to point beyond the staged action. The symphony, however, allows for much greater freedom of the imagination, a fact illustrated by Beethoven's "dislike to be tied down with words and preference for the untrammeled *Sinfonia*." Echoing E. T. A. Hoffmann's seminal review of the Fifth, Fry was suggesting that Beethoven, who wrote only one opera but nine symphonies, must have been searching for the ineffable in his instrumental music.

This distinction between the two genres suggested that symphonies could become laden with a mixture of musical and extramusical symbolism, which, Fry believed, opera could not. Fry's dramatic sensibility and a vivid imagination reinforced his conception of the symphony as a musical pathway to these symbolic worlds. Without a text exerting influence over his compositional choices, he approached each new work as if he were painting a vignette or writing a story, not composing music for its own sake or for pure entertainment.

The construction of his symphonies reflects these two approaches, which might be called "painterly" and "narrative." The painterly symphonies include *Hagar, The Dying Soldier, The Breaking Heart*, and *Niagara*. Each comprises a single movement divided into distinct episodes. A general lack of melodic contrast among the sections projects a feeling of relative stasis. The image moves, but the story seems frozen in time. In contrast with these works, the narrative symphonies, *A Day in the Country* and *Santa Claus*, contain several movements that depict specific scenes outlined in a printed program; Fry then stitched these movements together with colorful musical transitions. Time passes in the story world through changes of scenery and depictions of morning, evening, and nightfall. The difference between these two structures loosely matches the fixed quality of diorama displays and the narrative quality of panoramic paintings, both of which were popular entertainments at the time.

The descriptive themes of Fry's symphonies would have had great cultural resonance among his audiences and in most cases would not have required much explanation. *Niagara* evoked one of the most widely recognized images of the country's natural splendor, and Americans increasingly perceived Niagara Falls as a symbol of democracy.[31] As an oblique metaphor for American slavery, the biblical story of Hagar played a central role in exegetical justifications for proslavery and antislavery positions throughout the first half of the century. Her story also entered the public consciousness through poems depicting her plight, the most notable of which was *Hagar in the Wilderness* by Nathaniel Parker Willis (1806–1867), brother of the composer and critic Richard Storrs Willis, whose magazine hosted the Philharmonic fiasco. *Childe Harold* had well-known literary origins in the epic verse of Lord Byron.[32]

Fry's other symphonies contained stories that he developed himself. Based on a an unpublished song with words by his brother Joseph, *The Dying Soldier* portrays a man wounded in battle whose last wish is that slaves be freed. *A Day in the Country* depicts rustic festivities in the summer heat, and as evening descends, "a recruiting party arrives, the soldiers join the dance, and more rude and boisterous becomes the mirth as the symphony concludes with a Finale stretto." The seemingly maudlin title of *The Breaking Heart* belies the utter seriousness of his metaphorical intent. Drawing from the deep well of American public piety, it presents a young woman dying of heartbreak as she approaches the altar in a cathedral, "that materialized home of eternity—where the senses of the neophyte in religion or architecture, are appalled." According to the program, "Angel Whispers" and "Spirit Wanderings" swirl around her before she falls "as the organ peals forth with the last pulsations of the breaking heart."[33]

The religious metaphors in *Santa Claus* are richer still. The symphony reaches one dramatic climax with the death of a vagrant at the stroke of midnight on Christmas morning as Santa Claus, a symbol for Christ, emerges from the snowstorm in his sleigh with toys. The music supposedly illustrates death and life, sin and redemption—points made clear in the detailed and instructive 1,300-word printed synopsis he distributed at performances, perhaps at Jullien's request. The degree of descriptive and musical detail found in the synopsis far surpassed the programs of earlier works such as Berlioz's *Symphonie fantastique*, which, in any case, was virtually unknown in the United States.[34] After the vagrant's death in the midnight snowstorm, for example,

> The Violins, at the final stroke of twelve, instantly mount up into their highest regions, which are among the novelties of the instrumentation of this day, being an addition to the upper portion of the orchestral Violin unused by composers a few years since. While they so discourse the recollections of a new birth in the thin treble of infancy, suddenly is heard in a lower region of the

scale, a fresh intonation. This is the Bassoon of Mr. HARDY, which instrument besides its other qualities is at the pitch where it is here taken, the most quaint of all in the orchestra, and hence is chosen to describe SANTA CLAUS. It gives an air in double time like the trot of a horse, accompanied by sleigh bells, and the cracking of a whip.[35]

Such detailed descriptions required little musical understanding in order for a listener to make connections between the story and the sounds of the symphony.

Just as Robert Schumann had wagged his finger at Berlioz's program, however, critics frowned on Fry's adoption of the practice. One even groaned with a sentiment reminiscent of Rousseau's complaint about descriptive music: "[W]e hold it derogatory to the cause of art. It seems like an inscription below a painting, informing the beholder 'this is a horse.'"[36] (No one was immune from this sort of criticism: George William Curtis had responded similarly to a Philharmonic performance of Spohr's *Die Weihe der Töne* the previous year. "If I were a composer of a symphony," he sneered, "I should certainly not apprise you in a schedule of general heads what I meant to express in it.")[37]

All sneering aside, the editor of the *Albion*, a leading literary magazine, recognized that the principal value of Fry's printed synopsis was to educate the listening public. At the height of the symphony's popularity, he justified reprinting it in full for his readers: "It seems to us that [Fry] has therein exhibited a remarkable skill in expounding the peculiar vagaries of his Fancy, and in making technical terms of Art intelligible to common understandings."[38] By making instrumental music's capacity for dramatic narrative expression more intelligible with the synopsis, the editor suggested, Fry had targeted ordinary and inexperienced listeners, not the critics who had claimed that such aids were superfluous.

Beyond its vivid descriptions of dramatic action, Fry's synopses also pointed to his music's intensely soloistic dimensions. He devised several related strategies of solo instrumental writing, all of which figure prominently in his symphonies. The first is the most conventional. One section of the orchestra, typically the highest in an instrumental grouping, soars above a boilerplate accompaniment pattern. This strategy pervades *The Breaking Heart*, in which a single expressive melody recurs in several different orchestrations (example 5.1a). Suspensions, chromatic inflections, and lush string writing contribute to the ethos of heartbreak. And even Fry's most skeptical critics remarked on the work's sustained emotional impact. "There is warm feeling in it," Richard Storrs Willis noted, "and the theme expresses emotions which music is perhaps better able to express than poetry. Mr Fry has produced in it a veritable elegy." [39] In *A Day in the Country*, a horn quartet sings a similarly expressive hymn to nature that welcomes daybreak (example 5.1b).

Fry's also used timbre to paint pictures with solo instruments that embody individual characters with specific or idiosyncratic personality traits—a double bass as the dying vagrant or a bassoon as Santa Claus (example 5.2). At times, Fry endowed such coloristic experiments with even greater lyricism when these instrumental characters appear to sing miniature arias complete with subtle Italianate decorations (example 5.3).[40]

On the surface, none of these strategies was new. Rather, Fry had translated them from opera into a purely orchestral medium. At times he coupled Italianate ornaments with a fermata or "colla parte" instruction. Other moments resemble standalone orchestral interludes or expressive introductions to cavatinas. Still others have a distinctly vocal character despite their unusual instrumentation. Fry's listeners detected the music's vocal qualities in abundance. Reviewers tended to single out cantabile passages such as

Example 5.1: Operatic Instrumental Passages.
(a) Expressive Melody. Fry, *The Breaking Heart* (Adagio sostenuto), mm. 9–16 (strings).
(b) Hymn to Nature. Fry, *A Day in the Country* (Adagio), mm. 15–24 (horns).

Example 5.1: (Continued)

(b)

Example 5.2: Lyrical Solo Passages.
(a) Dying Vagrant. Fry, *Santa Claus*, Largo grave, mm. 60–69 (double bass solo).
(b) Santa Claus. Fry, *Santa Claus*, Allegro non tanto, mm. 3–10 (bassoon solo).

Example 5.3: Italianate Melodies.
(a) Angelic Herald. Fry, *Santa Claus*, Andante maestoso, mm. 30–46 (cornet).
(b) Dying Soldier. Fry, *The Dying Soldier* (Largo), mm. 9–16 (saxophone).

the "magnificent execution of a horn quartet, representing the Hymen [sic] of nature" and "the description of a snowstorm, with a traveler perishing," which was "excellently realized."[41] A detailed review of *Childe Harold* likewise focused on these elements:

> Very soon out of the arid desert of feeling, ascends a minor melody, played on the Saxophone by WUILLE, as the impersonation of the *Childe* or *Knight* Harold of the middle ages: the Saxophone being the *Corno musa* of the middle ages—the instrument of BLONDEL, perchance—and renders songs of chivalric lorn love better than any other wind instrument.[42]

No critic, however, captured the essence of Fry's music better than Charles Burkhardt in comments on *Santa Claus*: "Its style and formation are not of the high school of art; they are of a modern Italian or French pattern, devoid of the severe but effective simplicity of Mozart or Beethoven. The Solo, Duo, and Trio parts for instruments, appear like Donizetti-ish vocal parts."[43] Whether he liked it or not, Burkhardt had perceived the music as translated opera.

Certain critics argued that these operatic traits diminished Fry's claims that his works were symphonies at all. Burkhardt had dubbed *Santa Claus*, Fry's favorite, a mere "*pièce d'occasion*," while Willis considered it "a good Christmas piece: but hardly a composition to be gravely criticized like an earnest work of Art."[44] These comments raised Fry's ire, particularly after his recent fulminations about the Philharmonic's neglect of American composers. Now, he thought, critics were creating excuses for the orchestra under the façade of style critiques. In a lengthy letter to Willis occupying nearly four tabloid pages, he retorted, "I believe that *Santa Claus* is the longest instrumental composition on a single subject, with unbroken continuity," and was therefore worthy of legitimate, detailed critique.[45]

Fry considered *Santa Claus* a generic hybrid—both symphonic and lyrical, instrumental and dramatic. In the letter, he disparaged Beethoven for writing symphonies lacking dramatic unity since each of his movements was typically unrelated to the others. Fry's own manifestation of the genre, by contrast, had created a seamless dramatic garment from beginning to end. The conservative minded Willis did not take kindly to such effrontery—challenging Beethoven's authority. He responded to Fry's letter by claiming that "there may be *literary* unity in the *story* which you connect in your own mind with the music. [. . .] But there is no *musical* unity."[46] Fry's works would more properly be called fantasias, he claimed, not symphonies. Just as the Bristow controversy would spin out of control, so did the argument over the nature of the symphony, which covered both formal design and Fry's proclivity for musical description. If he read the printed exchange, the fight would have reminded Anthony Philip Heinrich of his spat with Dwight almost a decade earlier.[47]

Throughout the debate, Willis did not understand that Fry, the translator, was engaging with the German symphonic tradition in strategic ways. As Fry was formulating his opening gambit to Willis, the Philharmonic had premiered Robert Schumann's Second Symphony. The performance afforded Fry a separate opportunity to share his thoughts on the nature of symphonic music. "We hold it to be an inflexible rule in the philosophy of Art," he began in his review for the *Tribune*, "that it must assume new forms, or if old ones are adhered to, they should be improved upon in the spirit of the works bearing such an antique construction." Schumann, he claimed, had not done so, leading Fry to call the work "a sheer waste of powder."[48]

Fry also offered a critique of the work's lack of overtly dramatic elements, a central component of his own compositional philosophy:

> There is a great deal of mosaic detail in Schumann. If the piece had been descriptive (which we think all music should be, dramatically), we might be able to say more about it, than we can now, as it was simply symphonic—without any definite idea—beyond symmetry, rhetoric, light and shade, and classic forms.[49]

Here Fry had laid out a concrete blueprint for translating past symphonies into his new dramatic vision: escaping old formal constraints while imbuing the music with drama. This formula is precisely what he attempted to manifest in his own works.

An example of this specifically symphonic translation occurs in a scene midway through *Santa Claus*, where a depiction of a family reciting the Lord's Prayer at bedtime appears as a measured, almost chant-like, instrumental recitative (example 5.4). This technique had become a marker of symphonic innovation following its famous appearance in the fourth movement of Beethoven's Ninth Symphony, where the cellos and contrabasses foreshadow the vocal recitative that introduces Schiller's text. Sensing its expressive potential and admiring its use in the Ninth, several composers later employed it. In Berlioz's *Roméo et Juliette*, for example, it integrates the voices and the orchestra while providing dramatic intensity to the story.[50] Liszt often used it as an abstract gesture evoking strong, agitated emotions.[51] But Fry used the technique in yet a different way. The music conjures the familiar words of the prayer and likely evoked a host of meaningful associations in his audiences—individual and collective piety, prayer with family and fellow believers, and humility before God.

A second example of symphonic translation occurs at the end of the work, where Santa's incessant sleigh bells slyly morph into a stratospherically high

Example 5.4: The Lord's Prayer Recitative. Fry, *Santa Claus*, Andante sostenuto, mm. 13–26 (strings).

Example 5.5: "Adeste fideles." Fry, *Santa Claus*, Allegro, mm. 1–16 (violins).

tremolo rendition of the famous Christmas hymn "Adeste fideles" (example 5.5). Functioning structurally like the cello section's quiet initial presentation of Beethoven's "Ode to Joy" theme, this passage sets the stage for a rousing choral finale, though it is wordless.[52] Instead of entering a series of variations, the music quickly cuts to a scene depicting Christmas morning. After a broad tutti major chord representing the dawn, a lone clarinet enters with a jolly tune vaguely reminiscent of a Christmas Eve dance heard earlier in the piece. Noisemaking toys and toy instruments soon join the dance as children play happily with their Christmas presents. Finally, sounding at full volume, the entire orchestra returns to "Adeste fideles," which serves as one last reminder to the audience that Christmas celebrates the birth of Christ. Blinded by what he perceived as frivolity, Willis did not recognize these connections to Beethoven's music.

THE STALWART MISUNDERSTOOD

Meanwhile, Bristow had faced his own struggles with perplexed critics even before his protracted argument with the Philharmonic began. Throughout this period, Jullien had been performing his music alongside Fry's. Disagreements over how Bristow's more conventional approach should fit into the larger symphonic tradition intensified in the critical response to his latest symphony, which he dubbed *Jullien* in honor of the conductor.

Richard Storrs Willis praised it highly following the work's partial premiere at Jullien's American event late in 1853: "It is a good specimen of the musical abilities of this gentleman. He writes easily, his thought is clear, translating

Example 5.6: Primary Theme. Bristow, Symphony No. 2, *Jullien*, I: Allegro appassionato, mm. 8–14 (bassoon solo and cellos).

itself in round forms and phrases, and moving always at an expeditious pace. The main idea, entrusted first to the violoncelli, is well conceived and skillfully developed, and the connecting episodes come in naturally and are well adapted to the subject" (example 5.6).[53] As in Bristow's previous effort, this movement adheres to the standard sonata-allegro framework. But, departing from the earlier work, he extensively developed motives and melodic ideas from the opening without rote repetition or plodding intervening passages—a marked improvement by virtually any traditional standard. Willis had noticed.

Beyond its well-crafted design, Willis also claimed he detected the emergence of an individual compositional voice. Earlier critiques had not granted Bristow this sort of accomplishment. Noting that the work had been composed expressly for Jullien's all-American concert and was thus intended to exhibit a touch of American identity, he added that "had no mention been made of this it were easy to perceive it: for it exhibits a noted modification in the style of the author."[54] Although Willis did not mention a specific passage in the movement, he was probably referring to the secondary melody (example 5.7). It exhibits the Italian bel canto style with juicy suspensions, subtle chromaticism and ornamentation, and an arched shape—hardly a traditional symphonic sound, but one with which Fry was experimenting as well.

Willis did not state why he believed the movement's character was distinctly American, but Fry, ever the patriot, agreed with his overall assessment. Following a revival of the complete work given by the Philharmonic in 1856, Fry theorized at length about what musical features lent it this specifically national character. Although it "is safely in the beaten track," he pointed out, "with the tonic and dominant relations, the four separate movements, and so forth," the second movement (allegretto) had a truly innovative spirit:

> In place of having a minuetto—which was in Haydn's and Mozart's time the dance, and as such suggested to every auditor what a polka does now—Mr. Bristow has, according to a hint we expressed long ago, for the laws of progressive aesthetics in music, adopted the spirit and the accent of the polka instead of the now vitally unsuggestive minuet. [. . .] It indicates emancipation of the musical intellect so far as it goes.[55]

By replacing the standard minuet (or scherzo) with a polka, Bristow had updated the conventional structure to please his American audiences, who at the time adored the dance. Jullien himself had written dozens of polkas and

Example 5.7: Secondary Theme. Bristow, Symphony No. 2, *Jullien*, I: Allegro appassionato, mm. 83–99 (strings).

had been one of the primary catalysts for the genre's popularity in the United States. Making the connection, Willis commented that the movement's main theme had "truly a slight reminiscence of Jullien."[56] Bristow did not need to write with patriotic bombast in order for Fry and Willis to detect a national flavor.

Despite the subtle traces of a national identity that Willis and Fry perceived, other critics still decried the music as too derivative of European models. One reviewer called the work "a serious mistake." Echoing Fry's admiration of the second movement but finding little else to compliment, this writer added that "persons afflicted with an over action of the memory must have found themselves unpleasantly familiar with too many of our 'tone-poet's' imaginations"—a thought tantamount to an accusation of plagiarism.[57] Along similar lines, one of Dwight's New York correspondents echoed Hermann Saroni's remark concerning the earlier symphony that Bristow's style was like a chessboard of musical history:

Its chief fault is a pretty serious one: a decided want of originality. It is full of reminiscences of other composers; Weber, Mendelssohn, Spohr, Haydn,

Mozart, and I know not what others, seem to be playing ball with snatches of their melodies, and tossing them to and fro in merry confusion. In listening to it, I found myself constantly thinking: "What is that? Where have I heard this? I surely know this melody," etc.[58]

Like the others, this critic most enjoyed the polka but felt it "savored of Mozart and Haydn" despite its "freshness and originality."

Theodore Hagen (1823–1871), a German-born critic who had previously contributed to Schumann's *Neue Zeitschrift für Musik* before immigrating to the United States, penned the harshest review of all. He complained sardonically that "the motivos [main themes] are quite common, lacking entirely in nobility of expression, [and] there even seems to be no striving for fine traits in instrumentation and in the polyphonic treatment of the work, if the noble art of polyphony can be applied to the harmonic development of Mr. Bristow's motivos."[59] The melodies were so poor in Hagen's estimation that they could not bear any development. And instead of hearing traces of the German masters in the symphony, Hagen, who was appalled at the substitution of a polka for the minuet, thought the music "reminded us of the so-called symphonies of Küffner, and similar composers, whose compositions were formerly played by some bands of amateurs, or in some garden-concerts."[60] A polka had no place in a work of high art. He recommended that American composers would be better served by having their music performed between the acts of a play than at concerts devoted to "the purest taste and greatest finish."

The repetitive and ambivalent comparisons of Bristow's music to other composers reflected the molasses-like pace at which American critics developed a framework for assessing and evaluating new compositions, especially those that tested the boundaries of symphonic conventions. Much like aspiring symphonic composers, they too were burdened by the Beethoven problem: What was a new symphony supposed to sound like? What exactly made a symphony good? That Bristow was an American only added to the difficulty, for premieres of "new" works by composers like Mendelssohn and Schumann were usually anticipated by European reviews that were reprinted (or parroted) in the local press. With these reviews to guide them, critics could "steal" impressions from European listeners (as Fry frequently accused them of doing). Of course critics could also take any opportunity to display their supposed knowledge of European repertoire, even if they had read it in a German magazine a few hours before a local premiere.

Given that the well-respected German symphonists of the 1840s were also heavily and noticeably indebted to Beethoven, it hardly seemed fair for American critics to complain about hearing bits and snatches of familiar melodies or orchestration patterns in works by their compatriots. Bristow's emulation had come at their behest, after all. Fairness aside, critics rarely pinpointed specific passages that could have served as Bristow's models, thereby avoiding accusations of outright plagiarism (which they leveled at Fry from time to time—undoubtedly a quid pro quo). With sporadic live concerts rather than careful study of scores as their primary sources of musical knowledge, most critics had no way of affirming how original or unoriginal Bristow's music truly was. Knowledge of the repertoire was only beginning to take shape in the 1850s, and critics were not able to assess Bristow's music with the advantage of a broad perspective. They also failed to answer the question of just how a symphonist was not supposed to sound similar to other symphonists. Like their European counterparts, they set an impossible standard.

Bristow's contemporaries did not recognize or acknowledge the degree of his early creativity, especially when compared to the closed system of works in the Philharmonic's rotation. In the *Jullien* Symphony, Bristow experimented with the advanced technique of cyclic integration. The primary melodies in each of the first three movements share an opening syncopated tie followed by a gently sloping downward motion, while the finale places similar syncopations in the middle of the phrase (example 5.8). Beyond this obvious attempt to unite all four movements, the occasional recurrence of an unusual sonority—a solo trombone, including a strikingly lyrical theme in the third movement—integrates the work more subtly (example 5.9). Older composers, particularly Haydn, had exploited cyclic integration, but post-Beethovenian writers expressed a heightened appreciation of the supposedly organic unity that the technique engendered.[61] The fact that Bristow employed it at all suggests that he engaged critically with a wide array of scores and understood its currency.

Example 5.8: Cyclic Integration in Bristow, Symphony No. 2, *Jullien* (see also example 5.6)
(a) II: Allegretto, mm. 1–6 (violin 1).
(b) III: Adagio, mm. 17–20 (violin 1).
(c) IV: Allegro agitato, mm. 3–7 (violin 1).

In addition to this advanced organizational strategy, the *Jullien* Symphony also contains localized moments of technical complexity and sophistication. Like the slow movement of Mendelssohn's Third, Bristow's adagio movement has a distinctive rhythmic richness, most notably in a re-orchestrated statement of the primary theme (example 5.10). Noting its resemblance to

Example 5.9: Trombone Melody. Bristow, Symphony No. 2, *Jullien* III: Adagio, mm. 9–16.

Example 5.10: Rhythmically Dense Section. Bristow, Symphony No. 2, *Jullien* III: Adagio, mm. 101–108 (strings).

Example 5.10: (Continued)

Mendelssohn's work, a British reviewer claimed its "melodial phrases are graceful and expressive, and his instrumentation clear and musician-like."[62] The resemblance was an asset, not a liability.

Although none of these strategies was truly original, their presence should have demonstrated to listeners that Bristow was attempting to distinguish himself while remaining firmly within the conservative, Mendelssohnian strain of symphonic writing. The fact that Jullien chose to perform Bristow's music repeatedly upon his return to Great Britain, where it was greeted enthusiastically, also should have made the Philharmonic board think twice about its treatment of locals. Jullien's concertmaster wrote to Bristow after the orchestra's departure and notified him that, in Britain, "you are known as the American composer."[63] A year later, the New York correspondent to *Le Ménestrel* of Paris noted in an otherwise quotidian report that "at the last Philharmonic concert, [the orchestra] performed a symphony by Bristow, American composer."[64] Bristow had an easier time acquiring a sound reputation abroad than he did within his own musical community.

THE WANDERER FALLS AGAIN

Anthony Philip Heinrich could sympathize, for that was precisely his experience with critics. Between his successful Boston concert and Jullien's arrival, he had occupied himself with other projects, including a literal musical monument to Mendelssohn, which he called *Tomb of Genius, to the Memory of Mendelssohn-Bartholdy, Sinfonia Sacra for Grande Orchestra*. It is a relatively short work that he wrote after the German composer's untimely death in 1847. The symphony exudes somberness, particularly with the addition of an organ obbligato and sustained rolling timpani throughout much of the piece. It comes to an emotional climax in a brief section labeled "cadenza dolorosa," which is then followed by an intense allegro finale (example 5.11). Heinrich also appended the following verse to the score on the page preceding the cadenza:

More brightly became my inner life,
More beautiful, since I met you,
Since a similar exalted striving
"So closely united heart with heart."

(Heller ward mein innres Leben
Schöner seit ich dich erkannt
Seit ein gleiches hohes Streben
"Herz mit Herz so eng verbannt." [sic, *verband*])

Written by an obscure poet named Agnes von Calatin (1813–1845), the stanza originally appeared in a love poem, but in this context, it suggests that Heinrich identified with Mendelssohn in their mutual "striving" toward musical beauty. Lying far outside Heinrich's national program, *Tomb of Genius*, like his earlier Beethoven monument, functioned as a tool for asserting a cosmopolitan bond to events in the Old World. Likewise, no ensemble ever performed it.

Outside of his compositional activities, Heinrich had also engaged in his own spats with the Philharmonic, the very orchestra he had helped to establish. As in Bristow's case, his relationship with the ensemble did not get off to a good start. In September of 1842, just a few months after its formation, he canceled his membership after discovering he had been fined for an absence from a rehearsal. His animosity would only grow with time. He approached the Philharmonic in 1845 to inquire if the orchestra would be interested in performing *The Pilgrim Fathers*, his chef d'oeuvre. A mere two days later, he withdrew his request, apparently having changed his mind.

In a similar episode, he tried to convince the Philharmonic to perform a new symphony, *The Empress Queen Maria Theresia and the Magyars* (1848), a strange work depicting Maria Theresia's appeal for aid to the Hungarian Diet during the early stages of the War of Austrian Succession. Heinrich dedicated

Example 5.11: Cadenza Dolorosa. Heinrich, *The Tomb of Genius*, Adagio, mm. 1–12 (full orch. and organ obbligato).

the work to the nation of Hungary, perhaps in response to the revolution led by Lajos Kossuth. After repeated inquiries to the Philharmonic that went unanswered, Heinrich sent his correspondence to the press. Invoking the contentious Article VII of the Philharmonic bylaws, he proposed that the orchestra could "perform it at [its] fourth concert of the season as an American production" in order to prepare it for a more polished performance at a "farewell concert." He was even willing to put up half the money in advance. Whether Heinrich's persistence annoyed the board, or the board found the music lacking, the Philharmonic never relented.[65]

But neither did Heinrich. At some point during the exchange, he distributed copies of a piece called "Valentine to the New York Philharmonic Society," dated February 14, to each musician in the orchestra. The society's secretary thanked Heinrich (sarcastically), but Heinrich was unimpressed. Anticipating Hermann Saroni's complaints about the orchestra, he responded,

> I am glad that you cling to the works of celebrated masters, but pardon my taking the liberty of advising you as true musical Republicans to allow young aspirants plentiful aid and hearing. For myself you turned once a deaf ear to my earnest and enthusiastic offer. This is enough. I never retrograde like Crawfish, and am a philosopher after my own fashion, whether I obtain followers or not. I find myself perfectly contented in my twilight situation "Entre Chien et Loup."[66]

The appeal to republican broadmindedness was especially pointed given the rapidly devolving political situation in the German lands. At this point in his career, Heinrich probably felt that supporting the work of others would be more fruitful than continuing to struggle solely on his own behalf.

As Fry was giving his lecture series, Heinrich decided to mount a third large benefit concert in New York in order to finance a trip to Europe, his last wish. Another well-known figure, the composer Augusta Browne (1820–1882), once again lent aid with a message imploring the public to subscribe. "In short," she wrote, "though it grievously shocks my sensitiveness to utter the word—money,—I do hope that a goodly weight of that vulgar terrestrial convenience, which artists are wont to scorn as dross, may spirit itself into his treasury." As a musician herself, Browne also spoke with authority about the projected program, particularly a "new" symphony entitled *National Memories; or, Gran Sinfonia Britanica*, the score of which she had scrutinized "with deep admiration," leading her to believe that it would "command the approbation of the most erudite *cognoscenti* of Europe."[67]

National Memories began life in 1844 as a "royal symphony" called *Victoria's and Albion's Young Hope, the Prince of Wales*, but had been shelved until 1851. At that time Heinrich sent it to Queen Victoria under the title *The American Eagle's Musical Flight to the World's Fair*. He intended it to be an American musical gift to London's Great Exhibition. Unlike most of his other works with prominent dedicatees, the queen's royal entourage accepted it. By the time it reached Browne's hands, it had changed names once again but had retained most of the same musical features, particularly a set of variations on "Rule Britannia" and "God Save the Queen" (example 5.12). She claimed that Heinrich had "treated [the tunes] with a novel freshness and artistic skill that might cause a zealous Briton to shout aloud, and throw himself at the composer's feet in patriotic ecstasy."

Example 5.12: Variation on "God Save the Queen." Heinrich, *National Memories*, I: Andante, mm. 17–26 (strings).

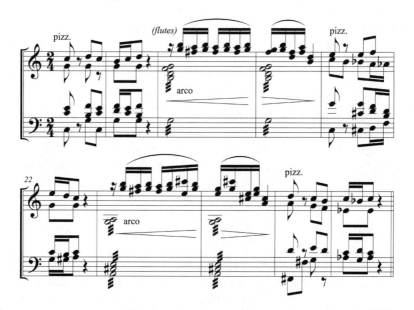

Browne also remarked at length on the second movement, Andantino Romantico, calling it "one of the most exquisite imaginings to which I have ever listened." Believing it depicted the British countryside, she described it as a "rural landscape, breathing of dewy meads, murmuring rivulets, and sylvan tranquility, while through the scene float the tender cadences of a shepherd's pipe." The movement features a monumental clarinet cadenza. As with several of Heinrich's other large pieces, *National Memories* had to be cut because of poor preparation. But one wonders how well audiences would have responded to a patriotic work celebrating Great Britain. Composers and critics were in the midst of arguing about national musical autonomy, after all. And this issue would continue to color the careers of Fry, Bristow, and Heinrich even as this chapter of their lives drew to a close with Jullien's departure.

CHAPTER 6

✺

The End of an Era

A s fate would have it, the American Philharmonic that George Frederick
Bristow vowed to form in 1854 never materialized. He returned to the
ranks of the Philharmonic Society violin section just over a year after the
dust settled.[1] Shortly after Jullien's departure, however, Bristow engaged
in another enterprise that reflected deepening divisions along ethnic
lines within New York's musical community. In 1855, the year after the
Philharmonic controversy, Charles Jerome Hopkins (figure 6.1) proposed
to create a chamber music society devoted to compositions by native-born
Americans. Hopkins (1836–1898), a pianist and composer, was a precocious
nineteen-year-old who had become a musical celebrity in his hometown of
Burlington, Vermont, and wanted to make a name for himself in New York.
He hoped to capitalize on the acclaim that followed Jullien's masterful per-
formances of William Henry Fry's and Bristow's symphonies.

Briefly referencing the Philharmonic kerfuffle, Hopkins pitched the idea
in an open letter to Richard Storrs Willis's magazine:

> It is the opinion of many, and it has often been asserted, more especially by
> foreigners, that America can boast of no classical music. [. . .] But heretofore
> there has been no chance for a native composer to place his music before the
> public in such a manner as to have it fairly tried and impartially judged. [. . .]
> We have already in our possession [. . .] instrumental pieces from the pen of
> Mr. George F. Bristow. [. . .] But to all those who object to it on the ground that
> American music is not good music, it is un-classical, plagiaristic, or unfit to be
> compared with German productions, we would say, "Give it a fair trial."[2]

Hopkins echoed Fry's contentions that Americans could compose at least
as well as Europeans but simply needed opportunities for their music to be

Figure 6.1: Charles Jerome Hopkins. Courtesy of the University of Vermont Libraries, Special Collections.

performed and heard without prejudice. The letter's specifically anti-German angle also likely appealed to Bristow, who might have heard a similar pitch from Hopkins in person before agreeing to lend him one of his scores.

Commentators immediately applauded Hopkins's efforts. Giving notice of the first concert sponsored by the organization, now called the New-York American-Music Association, critic Charles Bailey Seymour remarked in the *New York Times* that "an investment of fifty cents may be profitably made in what we believe to be a deserving undertaking. [. . .] There are in our midst men who are capable, we believe, of giving to art a new and national impetus.

They have waited their opportunity in vain. Tonight they try to seize it. Give them a helping hand."[3] With much-needed critical support, the enterprise quickly earned a key stamp of approval.

It also apparently needed active members and a more organized structure. Midway through the first season, Willis publicly urged Hopkins to solidify the organization with bylaws, a constitution, and officers.[4] As it stood, the association was merely an ad hoc group of composers and sympathetic performers. For his part, Bristow operated behind the scenes after Hopkins turned to him for support. The pair conferred about how to structure the organization, and Bristow eventually signed a document promising his participation during the second season. After acquiring the signatures of Louis Moreau Gottschalk and William Mason, two of the city's foremost pianists and composers, Hopkins used this document to woo performers to appear at the group's concerts.[5] In the weeks leading up to the second season, affiliated individuals finally held a meeting to elect officers and establish a consulting committee. *Dwight's* reported that "Charles J. Hopkins [. . .] was elected President" and that the consulting committee "includes the well-known names of Richard Storrs Willis, of the *Musical World*, Geo. F. Bristow, and George H. Curtis."[6] But for some reason, they did not draw up an official constitution.

Despite agreeing to be one of several public faces for the organization, Bristow gave Hopkins a considerable headache. When Hopkins asked Bristow if he would pay a fee to have his works performed, he reportedly replied, "Now Hopkins you know that I have nothing to do with it, but call upon me next week and I will give you a —— dollar!!!"[7] Bristow also allegedly dodged meetings scheduled to produce a constitution and bylaws. Hopkins finally confronted him about the lack of interest, but Bristow flatly refused to be involved "since we have determined not to confine ourselves to the performance of Native music but also to bring forward that composed by foreigners residing in the country, provided their principles are republican."[8] Not wanting to sever all ties, he nevertheless "promised to take part in the quartet playing" as a violinist—a feeble token gesture of support.

The situation deteriorated completely, however, when Bristow later rescinded his offer to perform as a violinist. Hopkins was irate: "Where is the end of these constant drawbacks, and discouraging instances of bad faith! Bristow you are a <u>Blackguard!</u>"[9] Since he had begrudgingly paid Hopkins's fee, Bristow allowed his arias to appear on the organization's first and second concerts of the season, but never again before the group's demise in the spring of 1858. Bristow soured toward the enterprise so quickly because he opposed the inclusion of immigrant or foreign compositions on the programs. Over ten years Hopkins's elder, he knew this new policy had not been the group's original intent and perceived it as a bait-and-switch.

Hopkins, musicians affiliated with the organization, and the press (including familiar characters such as Richard Storrs Willis and Theodore Hagen) sparred over the issue of whether or not the group should include foreign works on its program. Its mission seemed to change drastically when pianist William Mason performed a piano reduction of Liszt's *Les Preludes* at a concert in March of 1857. At that point, Bristow stood to gain little, if anything, from involvement with the organization. Having one of his works performed on the same program as one of Liszt's most recent pieces was no honor for him—and more like a personal affront. He had already competed against European masterworks for a decade and a half. The young Hopkins was green when it came to such matters and probably saw nothing wrong with it.

Bristow's absence nevertheless puzzled some onlookers. Not privy to the fact that Bristow had turned a cold shoulder to Hopkins (a point revealed only in his private journal), Willis was upset by the poor quality of American compositions on the organization's later programs and wondered why Bristow was missing:

> While we wish to see the native music of America advanced in this community, we think that the director might find better compositions to bring before the public . . . while we have such *good* native composers among us as G. F. Bristow and Wm. H. Fry, among others.[10]

Bristow might have felt he had no compelling reason to supply the fledgling organization with his compositions when he could use the Philharmonic as a tool for achieving much greater publicity and acclaim—a choice he most certainly made in 1859, when the orchestra performed his latest symphony. He was winning a battle against German music on his own terms, even if he had to muddle through an onslaught of negative criticism in the process.

THE MEANING OF TRANSLATION

Following the purported demise of Hopkins's organization in 1858, *Times* critic Charles Bailey Seymour wrote despondently that "the American musician unfortunately is wholly indifferent to nationality in art. As a general thing he is nothing but a superfluous appendage to the skirts of Germany; he sings German songs, plays German music, and drinks German lager beer." Choosing to emulate German music would oppress a composer's psyche, because "he distrusts himself. [. . .] It is very foolish for a man to think that he can do everything better than another, but it is deplorable to find a man who thinks that others can do everything better than he."[11] William Henry Fry did not suffer from this anxiety. Although he did not write much instrumental music after Jullien's departure, memories of its effects lingered in the public imagination for years. At the height of summer in 1857, the editor of *Harper's Weekly* pined for "a cool symphony, like Beethoven's *Pastorale*" and asked, "Why does not Mr. Fry compose a Polar Sonata, with reminiscences of icebergs, hummocks, frozen fingers, and white bears? With the thermometer at a hundred in the shade, it would obtain a *succès fou*. Who is there that would not go to be harmonically cooled off?"[12]

Despite lacking the patriotic bombast found in works like Jullien's hugely popular *American Quadrille*, Fry's music spoke to his audiences in a direct way.[13] His high aesthetic valuation of opera reflected its status as shared cultural property among American listeners. And his insistence that democracy uniquely defined the nation's social fabric resonated with their increasing desire for experiences that would allow them to enact selfhood. Fry's symphonies provided audiences with opportunities to come into contact with the very values that helped shape them into a national community in the first place. It was through the filter of these values that he attempted to translate older European styles into an American musical language his listeners could understand.

Prevailing antebellum attitudes about national musical identity focused on "nationalization," not distinct stylistic Americanisms, and if any style of European music had become nationalized by the time of Jullien's arrival, it was Italian opera. Henry Russell Cleveland, a spokesman for nationalization, had complained in 1840 that Italian opera was a "mere hot-house plant," a luxury "open for the wealthiest classes alone, which has no influence beyond its own walls, or the saloons of the aristocracy."[14] Writing at the time when the Fry brothers were preparing their translation of *Norma*, he could not have anticipated that Italian opera would make front-page headlines a decade later as the soprano Jenny Lind took the country by storm for many months and sang her way into listeners' hearts.[15]

The American thirst for opera continued unabated after the Lind tour as other leading stars, such as Henriette Sontag, Marietta Alboni, Catherine Hayes, Giulia Grisi, and Giovanni Matteo Mario, launched successful American tours between 1852 and 1854. The sounds of Italian opera had also become an integral part of the country's musical soundscape in more subtle ways, especially in urban areas, through the proliferation of operatic numbers arranged for wind band or solo voice and piano, in the Italianate trappings of parlor songs (including those by Stephen Foster), in street organ grinding, and in the burlesques of minstrel troupes. Even *Leonora*, Fry's American grand opera, had found its way onto the minstrel stage.[16]

Despite such ubiquity, Italian opera's status as an Americanized national art form remained an open question into the 1850s. Was it democratic enough? Richard Storrs Willis rejoiced when Alboni and Sontag were both available for low single-ticket prices: "We have it, at last. Italian Opera is established in New York on a *democratic*, and, consequently, on a paying basis. [. . .] Nothing can be established in this country except upon a democratic and popular basis, with chances and advantages equally open to all classes."[17] Willis's exuberance was well founded, but Fry pointed out in a lecture five days later that "our whole concern in music appears to be to hear an individual singer. Whether such singing is a permanency in the country; whether it places us beyond vulgar provincialism is not an open question at all. Whether such singing stimulates the production of American musical works is never considered."[18] (He also noted that the six hundred thousand dollars spent on Jenny Lind alone could have been used to establish a national conservatory guaranteeing the nation's future musical prosperity and international status.) Just as Cleveland had once suggested, merely listening to good music, even if it were financially accessible to a wide populace, would not be enough to spur the development of a national music. It needed to be imbued with a democratic spirit.

Fry believed that he himself could accomplish this goal by addressing the problem through the lens of comprehensibility. Could a listener understand the music immediately or not? Fry's careful attention to this question was plainly evident in his preference for English-language opera and his choice to provide detailed descriptive synopses of his instrumental works. Musical intelligibility also appeared as a recurring motif in his musical criticism, in which he decried "Young Germany" for having "no command of melody" and scoffed at Handel's use of fugues in his oratorios.[19] Fry preferred the clear melodic structures and light accompaniment prevalent in bel canto—a distinct alternative to what critic Charles Burkhardt had called the "severity" of Beethoven and Mozart. For Fry, this alternative was also distinctly American.

Fry's concern for musical Americanization ran more deeply than purely stylistic translation. He was also eminently concerned with the relationship between listeners and performers—a fact evident in compositional strategies that accentuated the act of performance itself. Fry had first encountered such strategies at concerts led by the American bandmaster Francis Johnson (1792–1844). After witnessing promenade-style concerts in Europe early in 1838, Johnson began to lead his own soirées in Philadelphia and advertised them as "*à la [Philippe] Musard.*" Like Musard and his erstwhile Parisian competitor Louis Antoine Jullien (the same Jullien who premiered Fry's symphonies), Johnson featured operatic arrangements and dance numbers that he occasionally decorated with nonmusical elements such as sleigh bells and other theatrical effects. This style dazzled low-paying and "unsophisticated" audiences (unsophisticated in the estimation of critics such as Dwight, that is).[20]

Even though a certain segment of American music lovers disliked their theatrics, Johnson, Musard, and Jullien refined a performance technique that highlighted well-drilled ensemble playing interwoven with solos that demonstrated superior technical ability. This technique appealed to "sophisticated" listeners as well. Responding to Jullien's first set of performances in New York, for example, Richard Storrs Willis singled out this technique as one of the ensemble's "strong points":

> The marked characteristics of Jullien's orchestra, those which distinguish it from every other in the world, continue to produce a proportionate impression upon the public. These characteristics are the *solo* performers of this splendid instrumental combination, and the *vocal* element, of which Jullien avails himself in instrumental music. It is well known, that Jullien has in his orchestra a group of the best solo players, upon different instruments, in the world. Consequently, in arranging his music he can give, in one piece, if he choose, each soloist an opportunity for display, subordinating the whole orchestra to him, for the time being.[21]

Hearing Jullien's performances for the first time must have given Fry a sense of nostalgia for Johnson's soirées in Philadelphia. It also must have given him a fair amount of inspiration: All of the symphonies he wrote or retooled specifically for Jullien's orchestra capitalize precisely on this performance characteristic.[22] It was also this very characteristic that helped audiences construct a national identity through the process of listening. The concept of a "national taste," articulated by Cleveland and others, was dependent on listeners sharing responses to a given style, and it is clear that listeners of the era were especially concerned with music's *effects* on them. By this point in the century, Americans had begun to understand listening as a participatory musical act distinct from performance, rather than an idle pursuit.[23] Summing up his description of Jullien's strong points, Willis added, "The *relieving* effect of this, in a long instrumental piece, is of course very great. It also arrests the attention, and strikes the audience powerfully."[24] It was through such aural participation that Fry's music provided avenues for the construction of an enacted, shared national identity.

Attending concerts often functioned as a tool of self-transformation for middle-class American listeners, especially in larger urban areas such as those where Jullien stopped along his tour. A drive to fashion the self was a fundamental element of nineteenth-century American life; a republican polity, a primarily Protestant religious milieu, a market economy, and a culture of literacy all reflected a value system privileging individuality and autonomy.[25] Within urban musical culture, this drive toward self-construction involved making unique choices in a rapidly widening marketplace. Responding to the public's search for selfhood, musicians and their agents began marketing their physical images and offstage personalities (not necessarily their purely musical talents) in order to woo increasingly discriminating consumers. The dialogue between potential listeners and performing stars occurring in advertisements moved into the concert hall and colored the musical experience itself. Individual audience members began to develop a sense of communion with the performers through the vehicle of music.

This potential connection or bond explains why reviewers, including Fry himself, repeatedly named Jullien's soloists in print despite the strong likelihood that audiences would not recognize the names. Like actors, these soloists embodied other personas on stage: Hardy the bassoonist became Santa Claus and Bottesini the bassist became the dying man. Listeners wanted to be led into the fictional world of the music by the musicians themselves. They were thus presented with believable and captivating models of selfhood that reinforced their own inward processes of personal identity formation.[26]

The construction of a national identity followed from this experience. Unlike performances featuring a single star, Jullien's orchestra provided audiences with models of cooperation and the republican value of subordinating the self to the common good. German listeners as diverse as Heinrich Christoph Koch, Robert Schumann, and Gottfried Wilhelm Fink perceived the orchestra (particularly when performing symphonies) as a metaphor for republican participation.[27] As we have seen, these politicized interpretations of instrumental music had gained traction in the 1840s among New England Transcendentalists like Dwight, and they persisted through the 1850s:

> Music is the only art which, requiring the concerted action of numbers, in different spheres, can exemplify and enforce that principle of order and subordination of one thing to another, and of one man to another, without which harmony, whether in music or in politics, cannot exist. [. . .] So in politics he must contribute, according to his place and ability, to the success of the government under which he lives; he must be aware that his share in the whole is but a small one, but he is bound to contribute that little to the benefit of the whole.[28]

Jullien had perfected this political system: After hearing a performance of Beethoven's Fifth, Dwight himself remarked with a shred of gleeful incredulity: "Was it not something to hear that scrambling bass passage in the Scherzo of the C minor symphony, brought out into the bold, broad outline by the nine double-basses, with BOTTESINI among them!"[29] Even the most virtuosic performer had to play for a team.

Fry's symphonies displayed his deep engagement with this system of values, which directly countered the critics who preferred abstract music. Audiences demanded encores of his symphonies, sometimes more than once on the same evening. They appreciated the music's dual symbolic capacity—the solos that catered to their desire for communion with an individual and the colorful orchestral effects that maximized the ensemble's collective unity. To Fry's dismay, however, not one critic remarked openly about these democratic qualities (at least in his music specifically), preferring instead to comment on each piece as if it were a crystalline work to be contemplated, not an animated being capable of affecting a listener concretely. Their values were different.

In his lengthy letters to the musical press during the *Santa Claus* controversy, Fry shied away from asserting a distinctly national identity for the music itself. He was more concerned with the importance of listening. Instead of discussing national identity as an inherent property of the score, he focused on audiences: "If, then, my compositions are correct grammatically and rhetorically, all that the critic can award to or take from me, is the possession of the original power which moves the public, makes its mark upon the work, and causes it to live"[30] Fry in fact said little throughout his career about music's direct capacity for expressing a national identity. One of the only instances occurred in a review of his teacher Leopold Meignen's symphony: "Every work like that of the symphony in question, being produced here by an American citizen, is a national work. [. . .] If we wish our community to be anything beyond a beggarly, cent-per-cent, money-grubbing concern, we must spiritualize it by a worship of the sublime and the beautiful."[31] With his focus on music's concrete effects on listeners and their ability to appreciate translation, Fry provided just such an opportunity.

THE WANDERER ABROAD

As the 1854 controversy over *Santa Claus* was waning, a critic for *Putnam's* (likely the Beethoven fanatic George William Curtis) suggested that any discussion about a composer's own national identity, much less the music itself or how an audience responded to it, was moot: "Has Mr. Fry, and those who complain of over-much German in the selections of this Society, yet to learn that art is not, in any limited sense, 'national?'"[32] The idea that art somehow transcended nationality, which Americans would hold more widely over time, was anathema for Fry. By this point, he had been arguing in favor of a national music culture for a decade. From his alternate perspective, national identity was in fact a problem of global proportions: "I make common cause with Americans, born or naturalized, who are engaged in the world's art-struggle, and against degrading deference to European dictation, such as if I am rightly informed, is a part of the musical faith of the performers and some of the subscribers of that Society [the Philharmonic]."[33] Only Americans held the keys to music's future progress.

Although Fry was probably not thinking of Heinrich, the Bohemian had been engaging in his own artistic struggle with national identity—emphasis on the struggle—both at home and abroad during this same period. Heinrich finally returned to Europe during the second season of Charles Jerome Hopkins's venture. It was a dream come true for the septuagenarian, who had been trying to raise funds for the trip for over a decade. To his credit, the trip was successful. His music was featured on three separate concerts given in Prague for his fellow Bohemians. This time, his oratorio *The Pilgrim Fathers* faded into the background as three of his symphonies finally came to light in performance: *The Empress Queen and the Magyars* (which had been rejected earlier by the New York Philharmonic), *National Memories* (which had been aborted at his Grand Valedictory Concert in 1853) and *The Columbiad, or Migration of American Wild Passenger Pigeons*, which, as we shall see, had already made its European debut.

The Empress Queen is aligned most closely with *To the Spirit of Beethoven* in its general concept; each section depicts a specific narrative event. Although three of the four movements illustrate a rousing battle scene, the most captivating moment occurs in the opening section, when Maria Theresia makes her appeal for aid in front of the Hungarian Diet. Several virtuosic passages for solo violin marked *recitativo imposante*, each of which is punctuated by sustained chords for the entire orchestra, signal the queen's entrance. Representing her impassioned appeal, the violin continues over light accompaniment (example 6.1). In Heinrich's program notes appended to the score, he wrote that Maria Theresia's plea, delivered while holding her infant son (later Emperor Joseph II) in front of the noblemen of the Diet, made such an impact that it "called forth the strength and valour of the Hungarian Armies, gathered from all parts of the Empire, which by their peculiar manner of fighting and their ferocity spread terror and dismay through the whole French and German armies."[34] The concert was given scant notice, but Heinrich was fortunate to hear a work that had been gathering dust for nearly decade. It was the crowning achievement of his long career.

The other major symphony performed in Prague, *The Columbiad*, was not new either. For this piece, Heinrich borrowed and reworked significant portions from two earlier works: *The Ornithological Combat of Kings*, his other avian-themed symphony, and the patriotic *Columbiad*, the work written in Bordeaux that included quotations from "Hail Columbia" and "Yankee Doodle" (see chapter 2). According to Heinrich's notes, he intended the symphony to depict the migration of passenger pigeons, birds whose bodies were so densely packed in flight that they wrought devastation, including their own collective demise, as they traveled across the country. Ornithologists John James Audubon and Alexander Wilson famously described this distinctly American phenomenon in exacting detail.[35] The symphony was a compositional summit for Heinrich since it combined a national subject, nature

Example 6.1a: Violin Cadenza. Heinrich, *Empress Queen and the Magyars*, No. 2: The Empress Queen Enters, Bearing Her Infant, Enters the Hall of the Diet, Followed by Her Cortege (Recitativo imposante), unmeasured.

Example 6.1b: Heinrich, *Empress Queen and the Magyars*, No. 3: Maria Theresia's Appeal (Adagio sostenuto), mm. 1–6 (solo violin accompanied by strings).

imagery, narrative elements, and patriotic tunes. These traits had appeared only in smaller combinations in earlier works.

Heinrich's listeners did not realize they were hearing some of the same music that audiences in Graz had enjoyed two decades earlier. Much of the material that Heinrich had borrowed from *The Ornithological Combat* came from the portions likely performed there (see example 2.3), thus providing him with a rare opportunity to experience two critical perspectives on the same music separated by twenty years.

The response to the concert revealed changes in aesthetic thought that had occurred in the interim between the performances. Writing in the 1830s, August Mandel had heard the raw power of nature in Heinrich's score. A Prague commentator agreed but used newer terminology to describe the music:

> In a certain way we see here the primitive beginnings of that form of musical description which at present seems to have attained a high degree of justification in the art world under the name of program music; and indeed in this case it depends for its effect upon immediate and objective impressions—as of course it must do, since that can be the only possible means of expression of a personality like this, so absolutely untouched by any fundamental art culture such as is obtained through the study of theory and musical literature, but forced to rely solely upon its own exceedingly sensitive and innately expressive spirit.[36]

Franz Liszt had coined the term *Program-musik* only two years earlier to describe works that unite music with a poetic idea.[37] This writer believed that Heinrich had approximated the concept. Heinrich's excursions through the wilds of North America had allowed him to delve into deeper, more truthful poetic meanings despite the lack of a polished technique. "It cannot be denied," the reviewer added, "that on occasion we find not only true spiritual essence, but also its eminently worthy expression." Writing nearly twenty years apart, European critics had remained remarkably open to the idea of Heinrich's vivid style of musical portraiture. John Sullivan Dwight, by contrast, had refused to hear Heinrich's music on its own terms when given the chance.

THE SOUNDS OF *HIAWATHA*

Robert Stöpel (1821–1887), a German-born composer, would give Dwight another chance to reflect on the value of descriptive music composed by a local musician. After developing a sound reputation as a composer and theater orchestra director in London, Stoepel (as he became known among English speakers) took a position at Wallack's Theatre, one of the most prestigious houses in New York, in 1850.[38] During the early part of the decade, he would have been able to attend Fry's lectures, hear Jullien's concerts, read the ensuing debates, and assess the Philharmonic situation, all without becoming involved in the controversy. Some of the Philharmonic players might have worked for him during the week. He had the perfect professional vantage.

Much like his fellow American composers, however, Stoepel found himself at the center of a firestorm when he tried his hand at writing a symphony. Heinrich had self-destructed. Bristow had weathered ethnic struggle and insinuations of plagiarism. Fry had endured scathing criticism of his radical ideas. Stoepel, though the most obscure of the four today, wrote a symphony that received the most attention of all. Native American culture fascinated Stoepel, as it had Heinrich. For his symphony, he chose to write a massive choral-orchestral setting of Henry Wadsworth Longfellow's popular *Song of Hiawatha* (1855). Called variously a "Romantic Symphony," an "Indian Symphony," and an "Indian Legend," Stoepel's music took Boston, New York, and London by storm on the eve of the American Civil War.

Stoepel began thinking about the project around 1857, by which time Longfellow's poem had achieved large sales figures and had penetrated into the public consciousness through countless recitations (and parodies). The poem also traveled across the Atlantic to London, where readers greeted it with responses ranging from fascination to disdain. Musical imagery abounds in the poem itself. One of the main characters, Hiawatha's friend Chibiabos, is a musician. Furthermore, the sing-song trochaic meter of the text lends itself well to a musical setting. An experienced theater musician, Stoepel likely saw the poem's potential as a medium of dramatic musical expression, while its decidedly national story would draw large crowds. It was both inspiring and practical.

Stoepel's setting, which survives today only in a published piano reduction with ample annotations concerning orchestration, is by no means a symphony according to the traditional definition touted by critics such as Richard Storrs Willis. Resembling a cantata more than a conventional symphony, *Hiawatha* has fourteen tableaux, each of which depicts a particular canto of the poem and contains words taken directly from Longfellow's text. Stoepel scored each section variously for orchestra alone, accompanied solo vocals, or orchestra and choir.

The scope of the work was exceptionally large for the time. At its initial performances, Matilda Heron (1830–1877), a famous tragedienne who was also Stoepel's wife, recited the remainder of the poem between movements. With her dramatic readings, performances could take three hours. The only piece of similar structure and size known to American audiences was Félicien David's first "ode-symphonie," *Le désert* (1844), though a typical performance did not last nearly as long. (David's *Christophe Colomb* [1847], whose subject, incidentally, was appropriately national for Americans, was virtually unknown in the United States.)

Stoepel's evocative music suited the subject matter well. The orchestral prelude, for example, depicted the "Solitude of the Wilderness" with a foggy string progression followed by the faintly "exotic" warbling of a flute and clarinet (example 6.2). After a swift section for winds and strings representing the smoke of the peace pipe, Stoepel's rendition of the opening canto concludes with a stunning aria for baritone (here embodying the Great Spirit) accompanied by the low brass (example 6.3). The rest of the symphony illustrates Stoepel's versatility, particularly the soothing lullaby sung by Hiawatha's grandmother (example 6.4) and the two scenes from Hiawatha's wedding. In Pau-Puk-Keewis's beggar dance, pulsating open fifths and a snappy but sinewy oboe melody capture the mischievous dancer's catlike movements (example 6.5). In Chibiabos's song of love and longing, the warbling flute gesture from the opening returns as an accompaniment to the singer's haunting melody (example 6.6).

Hiawatha premiered in Boston in January of 1859 and moved to New York a few weeks later. The Boston performance posed a special set of challenges for critics that works by Fry and Bristow had not. First, Stoepel was German and, though not a recognized master, had a strong reputation both overseas and in the United States. Fry's and Bristow's lack of European training and their heritage as native-born Americans were strikes against them in the eyes of many critics, but Stoepel's cultural heritage and musical training were iron-clad. Second, the work was essentially sui generis despite its title. Typical complaints about the wrong way to compose a symphony would not hold water since Stoepel made no pretense that *Hiawatha* was traditional. Finally, there were no public rehearsals, which prevented advance critical reports. Without potentially negative murmurs prejudicing critics, they had to pay careful attention to the performance. The stage was set for the fair criticism that Heinrich, Fry, and Bristow had long desired.

Critics left the premiere unsettled, but not because of any weird or unintelligible music. By all accounts, Stoepel had crafted the work elegantly and had followed all grammatical rules. But they still found a glaring fault: It was not a masterwork. One correspondent for *Dwight's* claimed several times that there was nothing at all wrong with the piece, "but it is hardly anything more." Another was more enthusiastic but cautioned against rushing to judgment after only one hearing.[39] Yet they all agreed that it would not stand the test of time despite providing no real criteria for making this determination.

A similarly unsettled Dwight decided to focus his critique on a spate of positive reviews found in local newspapers, rather than on the composition itself.[40] "Let us, at least, avoid all such extravagance," he whined, "Better for the artist that his work fail to meet due recognition all at once, or for a long time, than that it go forth coupled from the first with such pretentions.

Example 6.2: Stoepel, *Hiawatha*, No. 1: Solitude in the Wilderness (Andante), mm. 1–9.

Example 6.3: Stoepel, *Hiawatha*, No. 1B: The Great Spirit's Allocution to the Tribes (Andante maestoso), mm. 1–13 (baritone soloist and trombones).

Never was any Beethoven or Mendelssohn, in countries where they *do* appreciate such efforts, greeted on a first production in such terms."[41] Even so, he seemed to enjoy the work, having "listened to the whole with great, with unexpected pleasure." It was "deeply interesting to the end," he added, and had a "peculiar, wild charm." But he also claimed it had a monotony that "consisted rather in the absence throughout of what we should call imaginative vitality." In sum, Dwight would prefer that a work fail rather than succeed

Example **6.4**: Stoepel, *Hiawatha*, No. 3: Cradle Song (Andante con moto) mm. 5–13 (vocal soloist and full orch.).

after an initial performance because only time could determine greatness. Whether or not he himself enjoyed the piece was inconsequential, if he could decide in the first place.

Other reviews printed in *Dwight's* waffled about the work's overall quality. It was "good," they claimed, but lacked a certain *je ne sais quoi* making it "great." Following the New York premiere, by contrast, reviewers praised *Hiawatha* to the skies. A critic for the *Evening Express* was eulogistic, calling it "sweet, touching, romantic" and "a work whose entire impression is very definite and very favorable; one which indicates in its author the possession of that genuine feeling which is at the bottom of all real art." And, gushing further, "the symphony possesses the marked merit of originality; [. . .] There is very little to suggest other music; very little to recall familiar strains; indeed, we know no recent musical work so nearly original."[42] Stoepel had

Example **6.5**: Stoepel, *Hiawatha*, No. 7: Pau-Puk-Keewis' Beggar Dance (Allegro moderato), mm. 1–6 (oboe solo, timpani, and strings).

successfully avoided the criticisms that had plagued Bristow after the premieres of his first two symphonies: lack of individuality, lack of originality, and even lack of inspiration.

Other New Yorkers saw the work's craftsmanship and originality as signs that the country had finally established a legitimate musical culture. Theodore Hagen, who had skewered Bristow's previous symphony, claimed that "Mr. Stoepel was therefore right, to produce the only symphony which, in our opinion, ought to be written nowadays, that is, the one which is based on a distinct subject, well apt to put the descriptive powers of the composer in motion."[43] An enthusiastic Richard Storrs Willis claimed that "one fails to detect [. . .] any special nationality," but only because "it is a singular blending of all styles." Countering Dwight's position, he added that "aside from the attractiveness of the music of 'Hiawatha,' there is that in the theme—its newness, its purely American character—which will give it something more than an ephemeral popularity."[44] A writer for *Leslie's Illustrated Magazine* took Willis's position one step farther by commenting on the possibility that Stoepel had created a distinct American style. The writer suggested that a composer's natural inclination to borrow musical ideas directly from Native American sources would lead nowhere. Stoepel, however, had "drawn from rude sources material for the beautiful, and [had] colored it into exquisite shapes in the mint of his brain."[45] He had translated them.

As one might expect, William Henry Fry, translator extraordinaire, was ecstatic with joy after perusing the score. Not only was it a work by an American worth hearing (he claimed that he indeed considered Stoepel an American), but it also illustrated "modern art, which of course, in many

Example 6.6: Stoepel, *Hiawatha*, No. 8: Love Song (Chibiabos) (Andante con moto), mm. 9–16 (tenor soloist and full orch.).

details is in advance of the classics." Like Richard Wagner (and Fry himself), Stoepel was moving composition into the future, Fry thought. Taking a swipe at critics of Dwight's conservative ilk, he added, "We mention this incidentally in reference to the ordinary braying about the classics." Dwight later responded to Fry's needling (over a slightly different issue) and the two were once again at loggerheads—seemingly a perpetual state of affairs.[46]

This fight was no mere clash of personalities. The chasm between the responses of the cautious Bostonians and the enthusiastic New Yorkers epitomized the plight of antebellum American composers by crystallizing two radically opposed visions for the future of music in the United States. One side believed that praise should be reserved only for recognized masters who had survived the sanctions of time. How they survived in practical terms was never in question. What mattered was that their works, presumably through the sheer force of divine inspiration, had been able to transcend time and place. The other side believed that legitimate praise should be given when due. If a work pleases the listener, let the listener enjoy it—many times, if necessary—because only listeners hold the key to the sanction of ages. This battle was ideological, and the stakes were not inconsequential for composers.

The public knew as much. One avid reader wrote to Dwight and complained about his reluctance to praise Stoepel and *Hiawatha*, particularly after admitting that he found pleasure in the work. In a remarkably measured tone, "H." (as the letter was signed) deconstructed Dwight's ideology piece by piece while Dwight responded to each assertion in footnotes. The letter contained three main points about Dwight's initial critique that the author believed were unjust or undeserving: that the work did not signal a new era in the country's musical advancement, as certain newspapers had reported; that the work did not exhibit the highest levels of technical accomplishment; and that Stoepel had not demonstrated "creative genius." This remarkable document encapsulated one of the central conflicts enveloping American composers, critics, and listeners at the time.[47]

H. contended first that "of all musical works originally produced in this country, Mr. Stoepel's is so incomparably the best that no other can be named with it. Hence it is right to assert that when such a composition, claiming comparison with those of acknowledged European masters, is written and first performed in America, an event which has never before occurred, an era in our musical history is marked." Dwight replied snidely that practically any event *may* mark a new era, but "the consequence of an event must be somewhat unfolded before we common mortals can proclaim an era." He cautioned H. to "wait and see what influence it will have, and whether it will shape or color much the musical future of our country: then it will be time enough to say it marks an 'era.'" Dwight's idealism clouded the fact, apparent to any practicing composer, that a work could exert influence only through performance, distribution, and fair assessment, not through the strength of its own transcendent will.

H. argued further that Stoepel's technical resources were indeed on par with European masters. Dwight's criticism that *Hiawatha* did not include any fugues was a non-starter, for example, because Stoepel used counterpoint to an appropriate degree: "Their absence," H. noted, "is rather to be set down to his credit, since such effects would be wholly out of place in a piece of this character." Dwight again resorted to the authority of transcendence to support his claims:

Who is the man among us, unless we had a Mendelssohn or Beethoven, that is *competent*, on a few hearings, or a reading of a score, to pronounce a composer's contrapuntal resources "without limit?" One must have exhausted all the possibilities of Art to be able to say that S. can do all that Bach or Handel did! *We* should not dare say that at once of any man, even if he were another Bach.

And he reiterated the point when discussing H.'s praise of Stoepel's orchestration:

> Were Mendelssohn to say [that no orchestral writing is better], we should place some trust in the opinion. But who of *us*—nay, how many, think you, even of our best musicians, are really competent, from simply reading score with score, to say of a new work, that it is equal to the best orchestral writing of the greatest masters?

Taking this position put Dwight in a bind because his status as a cultural broker depended on readers granting him authority over musical matters. If it took a Mendelssohn to make any pronouncement on music, then what did Dwight think *he* was doing? Rather than offer fair commentary, all a mere mortal could do was to say that time would determine winners and losers, which is precisely all that Dwight did.

Finally, H. broached the subjects of inspiration and creative genius, certainly important qualities for any composer seeking a corner in the musical marketplace. A historical realist, H. claimed that Mozart, despite having one of the greatest musical minds of all time, was "so deficient in imagination that his music very often fails to express the meaning of the words to which it is applied, and sometimes exhibits an entirely opposite spirit." Beethoven, likewise, had exhibited a high degree of "imaginative genius," but neither he nor Mozart had attempted to depict "a subject of such new and extreme difficulty as the one which Mr. Stoepel has chosen, and I very much doubt whether either would have succeeded better." Dwight once again refused to engage with the actual argument:

> To question Mozart's "imaginative genius" because his music means more than the trash of words to which he often wrote, or to attribute the highest order of such genius to Mr. S[toepel] because he has been happy in the musical illustration of a more difficult poetic subject, than Beethoven ever undertook, shows, in either case, a very superficial notion of "imagination," "genius," "creative faculty," &c. We have no room to discuss it. Mozart wanting in imagination! Much as we are pleased with Mr. Stoepel's music, we find more imagination in one of Zerlina's little songs than in the whole of "Hiawatha;" we appeal to mankind. But our critic seems to waver in the re-assertion of his own strong statement.

If a monumental work like *Hiawatha* exhibited no more inspiration than a tiny aria by Mozart, why would anyone compose at all? Just as Hermann

Saroni had suggested to Bristow after the premiere of his First Symphony in 1850, Dwight was in essence saying that composers should simply give up. The masters had no more seats at their table.

THE STALWART STANDS FIRM

New Yorker George Frederick Bristow, meanwhile, had not given up. Nor did he succumb to the inferiority complex that New York's Charles Bailey Seymour felt was the destiny of American composers. Time having healed old wounds, evidently, Philharmonic members joined forces with Bristow's Harmonic Society two months after the *Hiawatha* performances in order to offer the composer a "Grand Testimonial Concert" that featured a movement from the *Jullien* Symphony and his overture to *The Winter's Tale* (1856).[48] Soon thereafter, the Philharmonic also premiered his latest symphony at a concert on its regular subscription series. Carl Bergmann (1821–1876), the former Germanian who shared the role of lead conductor with Theodore Eisfeld, directed the orchestra.

Bristow continued to refine his conventional style in this new symphony but also included short poetic passages in the printed program that reflected the character of the music (table 6.1). He borrowed this strategy from Spohr's Fourth Symphony (*Die Weihe der Töne*), which the Philharmonic had performed most recently in November of 1857.[49] The expansive first movement reflects the poem's inner tension between darkness and the joy of music. A brooding unison melody in the lower strings (the primary theme) contrasts with a series of bright, rolling scalar passages in the first violins and clarinet accompanied by a harp (example 6.7). Following a lengthy development of material taken from the exposition's transitional passages, including a fugal

Table 6.1. POEMS ACCOMPANYING GEORGE FREDERICK BRISTOW'S SYMPHONY NO. 3, OP. 26

Movement 1:	Movement 2:
My soul is dark—oh! quickly string	Gay being, born to flutter through the day;
The harp I yet can brook to hear. [. . .]	Sport in the sunshine of the present hour:
And now 'tis doomed to know the worst	On the sweet rose thy painted wings display
And break at once—or yield to song.	And cull the fragrance of the opening flower.
Movement 3:	Movement 4:
Pure was the temperate air, and even calm	Next Anger rushed, his eyes on fire,
Perpetual reign'd, save what the zephyrs bland	In lightnings owned his secret stings,
Breathed o'er the blue expanse	In one rude clash he struck the lyre
	And swept with hurried hand the Strings.

Example 6.7: Contrasting Poetic Moods in Bristow, Symphony No. 3, I: Allegro.
(a) Primary Theme, mm. 1–8 (cellos and basses).
(b) Secondary Theme, mm. 42–50 (clarinet 1, violin 1, and harp).

treatment reminiscent of Mendelssohn's Third Symphony, the movement's middle section concludes with a restatement of the secondary theme accompanied by harp arpeggios, lending the passage a cadenza-like quality. The movement closes with the opening theme in its dark unison presentation, granting it an arched shape. Bristow would employ this technique again in his next symphony.

The remaining movements illustrate Bristow's command of orchestral color. The second, a scherzo depicting a butterfly, exhibits the fairylike style made famous by Mendelssohn and Berlioz (example 6.8).[50] One reviewer noted that it did not "fail of a well-pronounced encore" at the premiere, which had been a common reaction to Mendelssohn's similarly effervescent music for Shakespeare's *A Midsummer Night's Dream*. The third movement is a calm nocturne in which the main melody appears in a series of subtle variations of color and mood. The symphony concludes with a stormy finale in F♯ minor that, according to the poem, depicts a personification of Anger violently striking the strings of a lyre. Straying from the character of the poem, however, Bristow closed the movement with a triumphant coda.

In a sharp reversal from the past, critics did not tend to remark on the work's similarity to others, suggesting that they had come to consider Bristow a unique contributor to a larger tradition. Although there was ample

Example 6.8: Fairylike Character. Symphony No. 3, II: Scherzo, mm. 1–7 (strings).

opportunity, the long notice in *Dwight's* did not mention other composers at all. The reviewer claimed instead that it was "a vast improvement upon his former work of like character [. . . and] his work has the happy quality of being popular enough to please the multitude, and yet possessing sufficient depth and intrinsic worth to preserve it from being trivial."[51] *Times* critic Charles Bailey Seymour did not particularly enjoy the piece and accused Bristow of debasing the symphony by "surrendering himself" to the "pleasant inspiration" of dance themes, but he at least seemed to recognize an individual compositional voice: "With more opportunities to have his works performed, there can hardly be a doubt that Mr. Bristow would do much better than he has done in this work."[52]

Other critics praised the work highly. Theodore Hagen, who had disparaged Bristow's earlier *Jullien* Symphony as reminiscent of Küffner (but had praised Stoepel's *Hiawatha*), was much more encouraged by this production. "Mr. Bristow's Symphony was well received," he noted, "and deservedly so, for it points, on the part of the author, to hard studies, which we feel confident will be crowned with ultimate and legitimate success."[53] Willis approached each movement on its own terms. In sharp contrast to his criticisms of Fry's music five years earlier, he used Bristow's ability to manifest the character of the poems as a measure of the work's success. Commenting on the fairylike scherzo, he remarked that "delicate contrasts of shading, skilful alternations of string, brass, and wood instruments, sharp crispy phrasing, all subdued, producing a soft, fluttering, airy gaiety, were the prominent beauties at once discernible." Ever the mercurial patriot, he also broached the subject of American identity:

> The fact that it included a creditable composition, in classic proportions, was, of itself, a good and commendable feature; not simply because the composition was good, nor because it was of American origin, but because it was American and good. [. . .] The work as a whole is very commendable, and perfectly convinces one that the author is a thorough musician, and possesses a mastery over orchestral mysteries.[54]

It was not until Bristow seemed to find a sufficiently original voice that his attempts to work within the symphonic tradition garnered recognition not as music by an American but as American music. It was American *and* good. There is no evidence that Dwight ever had a chance to hear it.

INTERLUDE

THE COUNTRY DIVIDED

As the music of Fry, Bristow, Heinrich, and Stoepel stirred controversy in the country's musical centers throughout the 1850s, it soon faded to the background as the war over slavery ripped the country in two. These composers all favored the Union during the war. Bristow wrote patriotic works, including a large overture titled *Columbus*. To honor Fry's efforts during the 1860 election, President Lincoln appointed him to the post of secretary of legation at Turin in order to serve U.S. interests in the newly unified kingdom of Italy, but he had to withdraw due to ill health. He instead returned to composition and premiered a new opera, *Notre Dame de Paris*, at a Sanitary Commission Fair in Philadelphia just a few months before his death. Stoepel had taken *Hiawatha* to London early in 1861, where critics received it with high praise. They also dubbed it a representative American national work and had finally come to believe that musical culture in the United States had matured. Two years later, *Hiawatha* returned to New York, where it was performed both in regular halls and as part of benefit performances for wounded soldiers. Heinrich, who had been Franz Schubert's elder by sixteen years, died within days of the first shots at Fort Sumter. Another prominent admirer, John James Audubon's widow Lucy (1787–1874), claimed Heinrich's body and interred it in the family vault. And following Lincoln's death in 1865, the German-dominated Philharmonic paid tribute by omitting the "Ode to Joy" finale at a performance of Beethoven's Ninth after opening the concert with the funeral march from the "Eroica."[1]

Of the composers previously mentioned, only Bristow maintained an active career as a symphonist into the 1870s, and virtually no new composer began a fresh symphonic career during the war. In terms of pure statistics, the 1860s punctuated the end of an era for the American symphonic enterprise, much as the war had for the country's political and social life. The war incited an intellectual shift that reconfigured discussions of national identity. The label "American" could no longer be defined over and against foreign and faraway cultures alone. On the one hand, the war forced residents of the Union and the Confederacy to rethink what it meant to be part of a regional section, in both cultural and patriotic terms. On the other hand, the political issues leading to the split, chiefly the abolition of slavery, elicited new conceptions of American identity that cut across the geopolitical divide.[2] Once the war was over, Americans were once again compelled to rethink what it meant to belong and just *who* might belong to the nation.

The war's devastation rendered older belief systems obsolete and left a wounded open space for new modes of thought to replace them.[3] The prevailing wisdom concerning the culture of classical music in the postbellum era is that practices of so-called sacralization and art worship filled the hole left by the Civil War. These practices had roots in the cosmopolitan ideologies of critics like John Sullivan Dwight and Richard Storrs Willis, as well as the founders of the Handel and Haydn Society and the New York Philharmonic. Supported by a faith in music's ability to serve as an agent of uplift, the postbellum cult of art worship crossed class barriers and ideological lines throughout the period as it fed on charismatic and "priestly" performers such as Anton Seidl (1850–1898) and Theodore Thomas (1835–1905). These men were genuine believers, as were their ardent fans.[4]

The cosmopolitan ethos pervading the country's classical music culture changed shape after the war. Certain factions maintained a distinct desire for new, foreign, and especially German, cultural products. Certain thinkers also openly asserted a German-American cultural unity that would have been anathema to Fry or Bristow (or even the German immigrant Hermann Saroni) in the 1850s.[5] Whether or not these individuals favored sacralization was not always correlated to their perspectives on these issues.

Complicating matters further, Germany was not a monolithic cultural entity in the latter part of the century despite political unification in 1871. Like the United States, its national musical identity was hotly contested. The conflict between Wagnerians and anti-Wagnerians concerning the future of German music spilled over onto American shores in full force during the 1870s, and the place of Wagnerism would become one of the most pressing musical issues of the day on both sides of the Atlantic. How local American composers fit, or were supposed to fit, into this rapidly changing musical climate was not always clear.

Composers faced two central problems—one concerning the past and one concerning the future. On the one hand, the desire to assert national musical autonomy, a feeling that animated the works and ideals of all the composers highlighted in previous chapters (albeit in different ways), ran counter to the cosmopolitan worship of transcendent art that took hold in certain quarters. For many onlookers, the antebellum era thus represented a moment of infancy rather than anything one should take seriously. From this perspective, composers like Fry were merely finding their way. Consequently, it became easy for powerful public figures such as critics and conductors to neglect or forget older American music. Without works in the performing canon, older (and deceased) American composers had no voice in the musical marketplace. They remained in and of the past as they were literally silenced.

On the other hand, composers also had to grapple with the question of how to meet the competing demands made by these same figures, who were divided into four primary (and occasionally overlapping) ideological factions: those who denied the possibility of a national musical identity altogether and wanted Americans to write within the classical tradition or give up; those who wanted Americans to remain at the forefront of European compositional trends, particularly Wagnerism; those who believed Wagnerism (or classicism) would grow organically into a national American style; and those who believed that Americans should create a national style based on folk songs. While scholars have lavished the most attention on the last of these factions, headed by critic Henry Krehbiel (1854–1923), the first two dominated musical discourse throughout the 1870s and 1880s.

Composers aligned their efforts with the demands of all four factions, but critics could always find reasons to be dissatisfied. If works were too "American," they were not serious enough; if they were too "European," they were not original enough. Criticisms also frequently had nothing to do with the work itself, but rather with personal animosity. There can be no doubt that the sacralization of art, fueled by the desire for German music (of whatever brand), left a lasting imprint on the culture of classical music that is still with us today. What is not apparent to us now, however, is the turmoil that composers faced as they tested hostile waters that were virtually impossible to navigate. Older composers vanished. New composers took their places but soon vanished as well.

CHAPTER 7

ᴄᴧᴏ

Louis Moreau Gottschalk,
Pan-American Republican

Throughout the antebellum era, composers followed several divergent paths toward the construction of a national musical identity. Anthony Philip Heinrich found inspiration in a multitude of experiences from across the world but focused intently on Native Americans (and birds). Critics such as William Henry Fry and Richard Storrs Willis perceived American traits in George Frederick Bristow's music despite its traditionalism. Bristow's own ethnicity seemed to matter most to him. Fry developed a patchwork style that translated an array of older European elements into new configurations, and the music's democratic ethos appealed greatly to his audiences. Robert Stoepel gave a musical voice to a distinctly American literary subject; even across the Atlantic, listeners perceived a certain national patina.

Antebellum approaches to the Beethoven problem were similarly kaleidoscopic. Bristow conceived of the symphony in the most conventional terms by employing the traditional four-movement arrangement, standard tonal planning, light orchestration, and a balance between melodic beauty and motivic development. Stoepel appended the term "symphony" to *Hiawatha*, a choice reflecting his idiosyncratic conception of the genre's outer limits. Fry and Heinrich tended to write works with narrative plots that determined their external forms. And Fry even articulated a well-reasoned defense of why his newer vision should supersede the old: to do so would be progressive, and therefore American. From his perspective, he was writing a national "music of the future."

Beyond questions of national expression and musical style, the broader culture of classical music in the United States also stood at a major crossroad at the dawn of the Civil War. Would it or would it not support American composers? Fry, Bristow, and Stoepel had proven to critics and audiences alike that it was a project worth pursuing (and even Heinrich had acquired a motley circle of admirers). Detractors such as John Sullivan Dwight and members of prominent performing ensembles saw no pressing need. They were content with the status quo. Dwight believed that a work of art could transcend the time and place in which it was written. If it were great, it would be destined to be perceived as such. But even though Dwight, along with everyone else, recognized the need to hear works several times before the whole could be grasped adequately (to say nothing of its finer details), he did not seem to recognize that a great work could never emerge from obscurity without performances. Composers continually had to finance productions of their own works in order for them to be heard at all.

Dwight's argument that orchestras simply preferred great works was tautological: They had refused to perform anything else.[1] Most regular audience members, by contrast, listened for the sensual pleasures of music or admired the physicality of musical performance, not necessarily the experience of coming into contact with a transcendent work of art graced by a universal master. (Some, like George Templeton Strong and Margaret Fuller, certainly did.) American composers were able to cater to both desires in the sophisticated genre of the symphony, but they were unable to generate a positive consensus. A Louisiana-born virtuoso pianist and composer, Louis Moreau Gottschalk (1829–1869), packed his belongings and found more receptive audiences for his symphonies at the gigantic musical festivals he mounted throughout Spanish America (figure 7.1). There he became a hero.

THE REPUBLICAN AS NATIONALIST

Whereas Fry, Bristow, and Heinrich attained only limited acceptance among critics, widespread acclaim seemed effortless for Gottschalk. After a successful early performing career in Paris and just before his return to the United States in 1853, one commentator placed Gottschalk alongside historian George Bancroft, poet Edgar Allan Poe, novelist James Fenimore Cooper, essayist Edwin Percy Whipple, and sculptor Hiram Powers as an icon of the country's superior cultural achievements.[2] Such accolades would follow him over the next twelve years as he toured throughout North and South America. In 1865, he fled the United States in public disgrace over alleged indiscretions with a female student in San Francisco (allegations he denied), but success followed him during his exile in South America, where he died unexpectedly four years later.[3] He received a hero's welcome when his body was interred in Brooklyn following a spectacular funeral at St. Stephen's parish in New York.[4]

Figure 7.1: Pictorial Rendition of Louis Moreau Gottschalk's Music Festival Held in Rio de Janeiro on Nov. 24, 1869. Reproduced from "650 Musicos!" *A Vida Fluminense* 2, No. 101 (Dec. 4, 1869): 1075. Prints and Photographs Division, Library of Congress, Washington, D.C.

Following his U.S. debut recital, which took place as Fry was in the midst of his lecture series, one writer hailed him as a genuine American original: "His 'Bamboula,' 'Bananier,' &c., are truly original specimens of a new and delightful, a purely American, or, if you please southern Creole school, the Gottschalk school, as it may yet be called. The warmth, the feeling, the poetry of the compositions [. . .] are Mr. Gottschalk's own, are legitimate, national, and classical and will hereafter be identified with his name."[5] Although this writer understood Gottschalk's early works as American, the conclusion was especially remarkable because commentators often took great pains to note that he was a Louisianan-American of mixed European descent—a Creole. His style reflected an interethnic cultural milieu that was a far cry from the Anglo-Saxon, northeastern learned culture of Bancroft, Cooper, Whipple, and Powers—what many antebellum thinkers believed America truly was.[6]

Critical emphasis on the vernacular characteristics of Gottschalk's output obscured the fact that he also produced two large-scale, bombastically patriotic American works. In both *Grand National Symphony for Ten Pianos, Battle of Bunker Hill* (1853–1854) and *L'Union* (pub. 1863), he constructed an identity using conventional stylistic means that dated to the era of James Hewitt.[7] Gottschalk quoted recognizable patriotic songs in both works in order to represent national characters. Several of his American predecessors, including Hewitt, Simon Knaebel, and Anthony Philip Heinrich, employed this stock technique. Beethoven did as well. The score for *Bunker Hill* is lost, but contemporary accounts revealed that it depicted the opposing English and American forces in battle by combining their respective national tunes, "God Save the Queen" and "Yankee Doodle," amid the thunderous roar of pianistic cannon fire. It concluded with a rousing contrapuntal rendition of "Hail, Columbia" and "Yankee Doodle" as a sign of American victory.[8]

Reviewers of *Bunker Hill* did not write about the work with the overtly politicized or partisan interpretations of symphonies that were becoming common in Europe, but one critic did hear the sounds of an American national identity: "We commend Mr. Gottschalk, not the less for his supreme artistic power, than for that good judgment which tells of his country's power—*E pluribus unum*."[9] Gottschalk wrote the work in order to capitalize on the fervor surrounding the battle's seventy-fifth anniversary, and it participated in the longstanding tradition of nationalist commemoration that followed in the wake of the Revolutionary War, just as Hewitt's music had in its own day. *L'Union* contained similar patriotic musical elements. Since Gottschalk unveiled it in performance during the Civil War, it served as a rallying piece, but in this case, it stood for the war-torn republic (or as a point of antagonism for supporters of the Confederacy).[10] Dwight, the arch-classicist, would have scoffed if he had ever heard the piece.[11]

Gottschalk's "American" works, whether vernacular or patriotic, by no means comprised the entirety of his nation-oriented output. In addition to several smaller pieces inspired by his voyages to Latin America, Gottschalk also composed two symphonies for full orchestra, both of which contained Latin American themes and imagery: *Symphonie romantique: la nuit des tropiques* (1859) and *À Montevideo: 2me symphonie-romantique pour grand orchestre* (1868).[12] Like many of the symphonies by his contemporaries both in the United States and abroad, these pieces participated in nation-building processes, and the identities constructed in both works reflected the complex political situation underpinning Gottschalk's career. He was a pan-American republican who sought to "ennoble" the country's neighbors to the south. And although his symphonies were not the first to garner international attention, he was one of the first American-born musicians to harness the country's status as an emerging international political power.

THE REPUBLICAN AS INTERNATIONALIST

Unlike many of his compositional compatriots (Fry being a notable exception), Gottschalk articulated strong opinions on a wide variety of political topics, primarily in his memoirs and letters. His interest in politics also ran much more deeply than allegiances to any single organized group. He believed in the goodness of the republican form of government, for example, and his dedication to these principles compelled him to free his slaves in the early 1850s, just as the issue of slavery was becoming white-hot on the national political stage. These political inclinations were inextricably intertwined with his musical career at home and abroad.

Despite his generally progressive political leanings and apparent support of the political and social uplift of the poor, Gottschalk was not a quintessential Jacksonian who embraced the inherent nobility of ordinary people.[13] He expressed mild antipathy toward African Americans, calling them "morally inferior" to whites. He also complained in his memoirs about the negative effects that unchecked democracy can have on educated society. In one colorful episode, he ranted about having to sit next to rowdy hooligans on train cars. "One can be a republican," he noted, "and not like the society of those who drink every five minutes, pick their teeth with their penknife, use their fingers for handkerchiefs, and eat sausage and keep you in remembrance of it through its odor a long time after the sausage has disappeared."[14] All of the socially unacceptable behavior, such as spitting in public, was "absurd and unworthy of us," he continued, and "in fifty years will have disappeared."

His understanding of the young country's growing pains filtered into his opinions of the even younger Spanish American republics. Most of the Spanish American regions that Gottschalk visited during his career were embroiled in efforts to be released from colonial governance (Cuba) or were fledgling countries that had recently won their independence from Spanish or Portuguese rule (Uruguay and Brazil). Reflecting on his visits, Gottschalk frequently recognized the historical similarity between the colonial and postcolonial conditions of Latin America and the United States and felt a certain political kinship with members of these other cultures. The pianist's support of progressive reforms at home mirrored his efforts to support marginalized persons abroad. In a letter to *Watson's Art Journal*, for example, Gottschalk indicated that he had received medals and other honors from a variety of philanthropic institutions in Spanish America, especially orphan asylums and public education reformers.[15] His support for these institutions stemmed from republicanism. "Of all the forms of government," he wrote in a letter to the Society of Friends of Popular Education in Montevideo, "the republic is that which exacts from the people the greatest degree of enlightenment: under it each citizen ought to actively participate in its destinies; as he constitutes, so to speak, a fraction of the government itself." Later in the letter, he explained that every citizen has an inalienable right to education and that even "the most obscure farmers of the 'Far West' ought to be able to share ideas for the benefit of all."[16]

Gottschalk did not have a generally high opinion of the citizens or the leadership of the young Spanish American republics, however, and displayed no reservation when expressing his aversion. After a trip through Peru in 1865, he wrote that he found "the most unbridled corruption in every branch of government, the most shameless venality among all classes, everything is sold, everything is bought." As if recalling the seven deadly sins, he added, "Sloth, ignorance, and hatred of the foreigner, these are the only beliefs profoundly rooted in the heart of this race, debauched physically and morally. Sad spectacle!" Criticizing each in turn, he then dwelt on the weaknesses of other republics: Nicaragua, Guatemala, and Ecuador all "belonged to the clergy"; Honduras and El Salvador were "supernumerary subalterns"; Peru and Bolivia were ruled by merciless killers; and, ironically, "the Republic of Paraguay is governed by a hereditary president for life (?)—a republic!" If those countries were not bad enough for him, the so-called Argentine Republic was the worst of all. Its people were "the source whence flow all turpitudes, all corruptions, and every bad human passion. In this nation all are abandoned by Providence."[17]

The reason for Gottschalk's annoyance and disdain, as he noted in the case of Paraguay, was the abuse of the word "republic." For such an ardent American patriot and believer in the fundamental goodness of U.S.-style republicanism, the use of the word to describe a state ruled by military leaders or clergy seemed especially brazen to him:

> [T]he word "republic" (an outrage on the elevated principles this word represents) serves them as a cloak under which they give themselves up to every kind of despotism and vileness . . . this is the Argentine republic. Alas! I might also say, behold the Spanish-American republic; for, except Chile, all the governments of these agglomerations of bandits which sully the banner of American liberty, and which call themselves republics, from Mexico to Cape Horn, are nothing but brigandage, theft, barbarism and cruelty—organized and unpunished.[18]

Yet Gottschalk held out hope that true republicanism would take hold in Spanish America, and he considered himself a partner in the struggle. In a letter that was widely disseminated in the Buenos Aires press, he expressed empathy for his fellow republicans:

> As a son of the great republic to the north, I grew accustomed from earliest youth to considering the entire Western Hemisphere, irrespective of language or latitude, as the common fatherland of all who desire progress and liberty. As a citizen of the United States, I find myself profoundly grateful for your divination of the basic Americanist urge [republicanism] that drives me forward.[19]

His documented philanthropic support of public education throughout the region most clearly manifested this belief in a common future.

But public education was only part of Gottschalk's equation for cultural uplift. "Civilizing" forces to counteract "boorish tendencies" also played a central role. For Gottschalk, one of these forces should be good music, especially grand works such as symphonies. Commenting on the lack of refinement among American listeners, he once asked, "Do you pause [when listening to a Beethoven symphony] to observe if the performers are in full dress, if the piccolo has his hair carefully combed, and if the violinists in the front rows have their boots blackened?" To which he replied, "Certainly not, and it is fortunate, for your pleasure would often be diminished."[20] A symphony was worthy of respect.

PAN-AMERICAN CULTURAL TIES

Gottschalk's unofficial cultural diplomacy in Spanish America reflected broader economic and political realities. In Cuba, for example, the United States asserted an enormous amount of control over the island at mid-century, both commercially and culturally. Novelist and world traveler Anthony Trollope (1815–1882) noted after a trip to the West Indies that "the trade of [Cuba] is falling into the hands of foreigners—into those principally of Americans from the States. Havana will soon become as much American as New Orleans. It requires but little of the spirit of prophecy to foretell that the Spanish rule will not be long obeyed by such people."[21] Gottschalk agreed, pointing out that Cuba's "business is almost exclusively with the United States." But the relationship between the United States and Cuba entailed far more than mutual commercial interests. He added that the United States "is at the head of every enterprise and all the progress that for some years past have transformed ancient Cuba, and made of her today one of the richest, most civilized, and most beautiful countries in the world."[22]

The United States and Cuba indeed experienced a rich period of musical and cultural exchange during the 1850s. The famed Swedish soprano Jenny Lind left New York in 1850 for a southern tour that included Baltimore, Washington, Charleston, and eventually Havana.[23] Opera impresario Max Maretzek (1821–1897) likewise engaged singers on American tours that included Havana as a regular stop. More important, he also used his time in Havana to recruit singers for the Astor Place Opera House.[24] This strategy created a reciprocal cultural exchange that Americans began to notice. So many Cubans came to New York and enjoyed the city's musical culture that one observer claimed that roles had been reversed: "Instead of annexing Cuba to themselves, we should say that the United States were on the point of being annexed to Cuba. [. . .] Every steamer that comes from the sunny South discharges new hordes of savage Carribbeans [sic] on our undefended coast."[25] With these close cultural ties, Cuba was part of the national community of the United States (at least as far as many U.S. residents were concerned), whether it was annexed politically or not.

Gottschalk's extensive travels and concertizing throughout Central and South America nevertheless had a distinct political tenor. The despotic military regimes leading parts of South America would have construed his support of reform organizations as subversive, if not outright revolutionary. But in countries that were more receptive to U.S. values, Gottschalk was hailed as a diplomat and an icon of American-style republicanism. Just before leaving after an extended stay in Buenos Aires, he gave a speech to the political luminaries at his farewell banquet, and one witness remarked that "after Gottschalk's speech, those who were merely admirers became friends and those who were already his friends felt still prouder of being designated as such. In the great artist they had found a noble soul."[26] He could be an enemy, but he could also be ally.

THE REPUBLICAN AS MUSICAL EMISSARY

Gottschalk considered himself not only a political diplomat, but also a musical emissary, a leader from abroad who could elevate the status of music in developing countries. "The artist [is] the privileged instrument of a moral and civilizing influence," he once stated.[27] In several of the Latin American regions where he concertized, he effected what he believed was just such a moral and civilizing influence by organizing lavish musical festivals reminiscent of Hector Berlioz's and Louis Antoine Jullien's monster concerts. Gottschalk's extravagant festivals tended to include large newly composed works that he based on local musical traditions and scored for a dazzling array of native musical instruments in addition to those of the traditional Western orchestra. One such festival in Ponce, Puerto Rico, included a piece scored for a brass band from the local militia, four pianists, a handful of violinists, eight maraca players, and eight guiro players.[28]

Although much of the music he composed for the festivals is now lost, two of his most important works, his surviving symphonies, were products of these musical spectacles. Both works celebrate the respective locales in which they were written by evoking a picturesque sonic panorama of the surrounding landscape that eventually dissolves into the sounds of local styles. Unlike his Creole piano works or his smaller Latin American dance pieces, the two symphonies also constructed identities extending far beyond local color. In each work, Gottschalk instantiated his pan-American idealism by interweaving regional elements with compositional techniques from the Western European tradition.

Despite the views of those critics who heard an authentic national identity in his character pieces, constructing a distinct American national sound was not one of Gottschalk's lifelong musical aims. Instead, a more abstract mode of thought underlay his general approach to composition. He expounded upon this line of thinking in a remarkably profound essay that he wrote for the *Atlantic Monthly* near the end of his career. This essay outlined a philosophy of music resting on the notion that it "answers to that innate, undefinable feeling which every one possesses, *the Ideal*."[29] Drawing sporadically on language reminiscent of German idealist and Romantic philosophers, Gottschalk explained that music has a threefold effect upon listeners: physical, moral, and psychological (or "complex," as he called it). Each of these, in turn, contributes to music's simultaneously objective (or tone-painterly and superficial) and subjective (or emotional and deep) qualities.

Gottschalk argued that the effect of music's physical sounds on our passively listening bodies alerts us to its objective, sensory dimension and causes us to respond physically. Music "influences our whole physical economy," he claimed, because it "quickens the pulse, slightly excites perspiration, and produces a species of voluptuous and transient irritation in our nervous system."[30] At the same time, music also allows listeners to "discover in [the music's] general character an agreement with our psychical state and assimilate it."[31] In this respect, it is equally subjective and objective. Unlike words, which limit our imagination, music mirrors our innermost selves:

> Play a melancholy passage to an exile thinking about his distant country, to an abandoned lover, to a mother mourning her child, to a conquered warrior, and be assured that each one of these various griefs will appropriate these plaintive harmonies to itself and will recognize in them the voice of its own suffering.[32]

This reflexive moral effect is felt all the more strongly when listeners hear their own national music. "Play to a Creole of the Antilles one of his dances," he asserted, "with its quaint rhythm, its plaintive and dreamy melody, and immediately you will see him filled with enthusiasm." Music's final property, its psychological agency, causes listeners to be captured—in a sense, taken out of themselves—or even have their suffering alleviated. To that end, "[music] is one of the most powerful means of ameliorating and ennobling the human mind, of elevating the morals, and, above all, of refining the manners of people."[33] In sum, it is a civilizing influence.

Such cultural uplift was the precise function that Gottschalk intended his two symphonies to fulfill in Cuba and especially in Uruguay, a country that he believed was in desperate need of moral support and refinement. Each work takes unique advantage of the three properties described in his essay in order to achieve the desired effect. Beyond pandering to his audiences' desire for spectacle, as Gottschalk was undoubtedly wont to do, both pieces transform the use of local color into noble monuments of nationhood. By creating tonal pictures of the local landscape, he likely hoped the music's physical agency would awaken a sense of reflexivity and national pride within his listeners. Transported by these emotions, they would leave a performance less crude (as he might have put it) than when they arrived. They would become ennobled.

THE REPUBLICAN IN CUBA

Gottschalk composed the first of these two pieces, called *Symphonie romantique: la nuit des tropiques*, in 1859 while living in Matouba, a remote area on the island of Guadaloupe, a colony in the French Antilles. He orchestrated the work over a period of several months and then continued on his travels to Cuba.[34] On Christmas Day, 1859, the Havana press got wind that Gottschalk intended to produce a grand festival to honor the inauguration of Cuba's new captain-general, or colonial ruler. With the assistance of musical illuminati from the around the city, Gottschalk assembled roughly 650 musicians, including a band of Afro-Cuban drummers from the distant city of Santiago, to perform three of his works, including the symphony. According to reports, roughly four thousand people filled the famous Teatro Tacón while countless listeners also gathered outside the hall.[35] The total number of musicians far surpassed that of the festival Gottschalk mounted in Puerto Rico; the audiences at Jullien's New York concerts, who heard symphonies by Fry and Bristow just a few years earlier, paled in comparison.

Though Gottschalk used it as a subtitle for the entire work, the phrase *La nuit des tropiques* ("Night in the Tropics") actually describes only the music of the first movement, a leisurely andante in $\frac{6}{8}$ that depicts a thunderstorm rudely interrupting a peaceful island evening before leaving as quickly as it arrived.[36] The movement is divided into four large sections: the calm of night, the storm, the aftermath, and the restoration of calm. It combines conventional tone painting techniques that reflected Gottschalk's belief in music's physical agency with more advanced compositional strategies that, according to his philosophical scheme, were designed to pull listeners into an active engagement with the material. The music itself follows a broad trajectory that moves through the gamut of physical, emotional, and psychological states described in Gottschalk's essay.

The movement's opening captures the tropical countryside that Gottschalk had come to love while living in the Antilles. After returning to New York, he pined wistfully: "I slept for weeks the sleep of the spirit, so delicious, so poetical, in the midst of the voluptuous, enervating atmosphere of those happy lands of the *dolce far niente*, whose lazy breezes murmuring softly bear on their wings the languid, distant harmonies of the countryside."[37] A counterpoint between the first flute and the first violins supported by dreamy pulsations in the cellos, basses, and French horns gives way to an aimless melody in the violins suggesting a lazy breeze (example 7.1).

Example 7.1: Languid Duet. *Symphonie romantique*, I: Andante, mm. 8–16 (flute 1 and strings).

Example 7.2: "Civilizing" Cornet Solo. *Symphonie romantique*, I: Andante, mm. 48–56.

A solo played by the *cornet à piston* rises above the rolling accompaniment and momentarily disrupts the scene. The languid ambiance persists, but with the addition of this unnatural (and characteristically French) timbre to the texture, a touch of "civilization" seems to encroach upon the peaceful tropical atmosphere. Unlike the opening, this new melody has a clear shape and is supported by sophisticated harmonies. Much like the *cornet à piston* solo in Fry's *Santa Claus* (example 5.3a), tasteful appoggiaturas and carefully constructed hemiola figures give it the character of an Italian bel canto melody (example 7.2).

The second section, depicting the storm, unfolds much like the first. A rumbling C-minor melody in the orchestra's lower register emerges underneath blustery syncopated figurations in the violins (example 7.3). The music returns to its painterly mode and arouses the sensory imagination by depicting a storm with thunder, rain, and wind. After a reprise of the storm melody and a short variation, the music takes a dramatic turn into the key of E♭ major, and the entire orchestra sounds a triumphal variation of the storm melody underneath the continued breathless sixteenth-note figurations in the strings and upper woodwinds.[38] The fright aroused by a wicked tropical storm transforms into a deeper, sublime awe of nature's power and beauty (example 7.4).

Example 7.3: Storm Theme. *Symphonie romantique*, I: Andante, mm. 73–80 (strings).

The moment might have been inspired by the analogous portion of Beethoven's *Pastoral* Symphony. Gottschalk once remarked, "Beethoven, taken as a symphonist, is the most inspired among composers, and the one who composes best for the orchestra. The instrumental effects he combines on paper are always realized in the orchestra as he has conceived them."[39] Though less scary than Beethoven's, Gottschalk's storm is far more glorious.

Example 7.4: Storm Apotheosis. *Symphonie romantique,* I: Andante, mm. 93–101 (full orch.).

The final two sections of the movement work together to manifest music's role as the complex agent of moral uplift. As the storm dies away, the triumphal E♭ major melody from the previous section and the languorous pictorial lines from the opening unite and undergo a series of thematic transformations reminiscent of a sonata-form development. The complexity of this section surpasses all that came before it and almost demands rapt attention. Following a brief transition that recalls Mendelssohn's fairylike music, all sounds melt into tremolos in the highest registers of the upper strings. The opening *cornet à piston* melody returns with the support of languid pulsations. With this ethereal accompaniment, the tune's character becomes transcendent. At its conclusion, the *cornet à piston*, joined by a solo cello's contrapuntal line, continues with an apotheosized version of the storm melody. The violins persist with their stratospheric tremolos, and the music dissolves into nothingness, as if the island has been transformed from an earthly into a heavenly paradise.

Example 7.5: *Cinquillo* Rhythm.

Gottschalk revived the symphony several years later in Santiago, Chile. As was his custom, he edited it to suit local audiences. In this case, he removed the Cuban-inflected second movement and retained only the first. One of the sole extant reviews of the work printed in English appeared after this performance. The writer commented precisely on the ennobling effect generated by the first movement's conclusion:

> It was beautiful in every sense, and would exhaust the vocabulary of technicalities in describing its distinctive merits. It was written in the modern romantic style, not quite Richard Wagnerish, as the ideas of Gottschalk are fresher and more clear than those of the eccentric "musician of the future," but equal to the works of that great "Novator" as far as the instrumentation and novel effects are concerned. The latter part of the symphony was especially deserving of mention. Its object is to depict the dawn of day, when the violins accompany with a soft mysterious *tremolo* the principal melody heard through the chord formed by the horns and bass clarionets, producing a most poetical and impressive effect.[40]

Through careful coloristic effect and clear delineations of character, the music had transported the audience.

The symphony's second movement is a raucous dance called *Une fête sous les tropiques* ("A festival in the tropics"). As before, the overarching structure creates an experience of musical ennoblement, but unlike the preceding movement, it does not include suggestive pictorial representation. The opening third of the movement is built on a single ostinato, the *cinquillo*, an African-derived rhythm that followed the patterns of diasporic movement throughout the Caribbean during the eighteenth and nineteenth centuries and subsequently became a fundamental rhythm in national musical styles throughout the region (example 7.5).[41] As the *cinquillo* traveled to Havana in the 1850s, it came to be associated with lasciviousness and with the lower-class Afro-Cuban sectors of the city.[42] Since Gottschalk specifically sought out La Tumba Francesca, an Afro-Cuban drumming ensemble from far-away Santiago, this stigmatized dimension of Cuban culture, as opposed to the more "civilized" Spanish dimension, is almost certainly what he wished to evoke.

The opening section of the movement climaxes with a tutti statement of a triumphant *cinquillo*-based melody celebrating the dance. The tune's

Example 7.6: Rhythmically Vital Dance Theme. *Symphonie romantique*, II: Allegro moderato, mm. 140–147 (full orch.).

juxtaposition with a habanera accompaniment makes the moment even more festive (example 7.6). After a lengthy transitional area, this section concludes with a rapid cadenza-like passage in the first violins. Reflecting what Gottschalk wrote about Creoles hearing music of the Antilles, the purpose of this dancelike section was presumably to arouse the pure enthusiasm of his "native" listeners.

The movement's second section differs drastically in character. Its predominant theme blends the Cuban sound of a fragmented *cinquillo* rhythm with an American flavor reminiscent of Stephen Foster, especially the "doo dah" motive of his song "Camptown Races," and a generic parlor song accompaniment in the lower strings (example 7.7).[43] After several statements of modified versions of the melody, Gottschalk transformed its basic shape and rhythms into a fugue subject (example 7.8). At the height of its contrapuntal complexity, the fugue involves four voices but does not reach a true climax until the full orchestra participates in a three-voice fugato using the same subject. This out-of-place fugal passage seems to ennoble the local *cinquillo* rhythm by introducing traces of both a learned Western practice and Foster's Americanism. In Gottschalk's philosophical formulation, the fugue should have taken the audience's experience of the music beyond reflexive identification with the dance style to a realm of the imagination that would strengthen their character.

Unlike the first movement, the second does not conclude with a transcendent apotheosis. It returns instead to a triumphal statement of the *cinquillo* melody that opened the work and ends with a bombastic tutti bang. Leaving the peak of "moral uplift" to a more subtle moment in the middle of the work, Gottschalk might have thought that this ending would elicit the most

Example 7.7: "Doo Dah" Figure. *Symphonie romantique*, II: Allegro moderato, mm. 207–214 (strings).

Example 7.8: Fugue Subject. *Symphonie romantique*, II: Allegro moderato, mm. 258–263 (violins).

approval from his audience. Commenting on the work several years after Gottschalk's death, the composer's eulogistic biographer and friend Luis Ricardo Fors remarked,

> The grandiose symphony "Night of the Tropics" [is] a work of gigantic conception, of sparkling genius, of the vastest plan, in which Gottschalk, despite showing the most elevated degree of aesthetic and select beauty, molds it, in its rhythms and nature, to all the characteristic expressions of the nation, to the point of satisfying the most demanding musical taste.[44]

In its appeal to a wide public, Gottschalk would have been hard-pressed to find a more effective way to celebrate a nation and its people.

Yet who, or what, exactly Gottschalk was celebrating is not clear. Once described as a blend of "Parisian elegance and American democracy,"[45] the mixture of cultivated European and vernacular American musical styles in the symphony, underpinned by the local sounds of Cuba, strongly exudes the Americanization of Cuba that had already taken place by the time of the work's composition. The subtle quotation of a transfigured "Camptown Races" created a reflection of the cultural reality in Cuba that Anthony Trollope and even Gottschalk himself plainly recognized. As Gottschalk suggested in his treatise, audiences would hear themselves in the music, but the presence of U.S. tourists and traders throughout Cuba radically affected who they, the listeners, really were: part of a nascent American cultural empire. From the perspectives of the composer and his listeners, the work was steeped in the hemispheric thinking that drove U.S. relations with Cuba for decades.

THE REPUBLICAN IN URUGUAY

Gottschalk's second symphony, *À Montevideo*, presented an even sharper portrait of pan-Americanism than his Cuban work. Like his earlier effort, it was also not without subtle imperialist overtones. He wrote *À Montevideo* in 1868 for a grand musical festival held at the Teatro Solís in Montevideo, Uruguay. Like the event in Havana, this festival required the services of hundreds of musicians, including several military bands, two theater orchestras, and dozens of unaffiliated instrumentalists.[46] Although it comprises only one movement, the work contains three primary sections: an introductory andante in $\frac{6}{8}$, a dashing presto in $\frac{2}{4}$, and a section in $\frac{4}{4}$ marked "Maestoso."

The character of *À Montevideo*'s picturesque opening is similar to that of *Symphonie romantique*. After a brief introduction featuring the clarinets and horns, the first clarinet and violas play a languid and sinewy counterpoint recalling the violin melody in the earlier work (example 7.9). At the conclusion of this theme, the oboes and clarinets take over with a new melody vaguely reminiscent of the Italianate *cornet à piston* tune (example 7.10). In a progressive ennoblement of the mood, the violins eventually take over the melody accompanied by the full orchestra. With this tone-painterly opening gesture, the music engages the objective, sensuous side of Gottschalk's ideal listening experience only to suggest a deeper moral realm as the melody emerges in full.

Following a fast-paced section written in a lighter theatrical style reminiscent of French comic opera (which Uruguayans craved), the symphony takes a triumphal turn in the Maestoso finale.[47] The new section begins with a broad statement of the Uruguayan national anthem, "¡*Orientales, la patria o la tumba!*," appearing first in the trumpets and trombones before traveling through a colorful orchestral palette (example 7.11). Functioning much

Example 7.9: Languid Duet. *À Montevideo*, Part I: Andante, mm. 9–15 (clarinet 1 and viola).

Example 7.10: "Ennobled" Duet. *À Montevideo*, Part I: Andante, mm. 17–24 (full orch.).

Example 7.11: Uruguayan National Anthem. *À Montevideo*, Part III: Maestoso, mm. 2–5 (brass).

like the *cinquillo* in the Cuban work, the initial presentation of the anthem was almost certainly intended to fill Gottschalk's listeners with raw enthusiasm. After this statement, the first violins take up the melody but quickly enter into a fugato with the second violins and violas. As in the fugue from *Symphonie romantique*, the moral and sentimental dimensions of the music morph into the complex psychological dimension by providing a learned context that compels listeners to engage with greater alertness.

The finale continues with presentations of the anthem interspersed with dark passages suggesting turmoil. The anthem returns in a final triumphant moment supported by the full orchestra playing fortissimo. But just as the piece seems to reach a rousing conclusion, the music suddenly shifts to a tutti fortissimo rendition of "Hail, Columbia," a distinctly American national tune, which is then followed immediately by a statement of "Yankee Doodle," another song having a long tradition as a symbol of the United States that Gottschalk himself had used to great effect in *L'Union* and *Bunker Hill*.[48] To close the circle, *À Montevideo* ends with a final bombastic statement of the Uruguayan anthem.

À Montevideo musically transforms the country's natural landscape into an object of moral reflection, but in this case, Gottschalk also chose to include the ultimate moral agent, a national anthem—a musical genre symbolizing independence that was not yet available to the colonial Cubans. He had commented in his essay that hearing national airs could bring even the most hardened of generals to tears, quite an appropriate image for the war-torn Montevideo of 1868.[49] But if Gottschalk's only goal were to move the hearts of his listeners, the inclusion of "Hail, Columbia" and "Yankee Doodle," both of which have equal weight in the piece, would seem counterproductive. The shared placement of each tune suggests that Gottschalk was redefining the concept of national music: It was not purely local.

The coalescence of the three songs in the symphony's finale declares the republican fellowship of Spanish Americans and U.S. citizens for which Gottschalk had tirelessly campaigned. As the crowning moment of a symphony that moves from objectivity to subjectivity according to the course Gottschalk had outlined, it presents the picture of his pan-American, republican ideal: Uruguay and the United States side by side. One reviewer remarked,

> Suffice it to mention that they [the works, including the symphony] were received by endless applauses. The best proof which their merit produced in the public. Gottschalk may well be proud of the triumph which he obtained last night. [. . .] Well does he deserve the praise of being the man who has given the greatest and most successful concert ever heard in this part of South America. May he, in his brilliant career, remember now and then his grateful and sincere admirers in Montevideo.[50]

With a vision that united North and South, Gottschalk became one of the first American composers to assert the country's cultural authority concretely in international arenas—and to achieve success while doing so.

Just before his death, Gottschalk noted that his efforts to civilize and Americanize the Spanish republics were beginning to bear fruit and would inevitably succeed. In a letter to the *New York Times*, he asserted boldly that "these South American republics understand that, sooner or later, the United States will be the arbiter of taste, and Brazil, though ruled by monarchical institutions, is, in point of fact, the most liberal of all these countries, and the most disposed to avail itself of the impulse we have given to civilization."[51] Music had played a central role in these cultural changes, which Gottschalk himself attempted to spur with his symphonies. Gigantic music festivals had proven to be the perfect venue for pursuing his lofty ideals.

CHAPTER 8

⌁

John Knowles Paine,
Universal Classicist

Everyone loves gigantic music festivals. At least that is what bandmaster Patrick S. Gilmore (1829–1892) convinced himself during the 1868 election season, when he planned a grandiose festival called the National Peace Jubilee. Though the Civil War had ended three years earlier, General Ulysses S. Grant campaigned for the presidency with the motto "Let us have peace." In February of that year, President Andrew Johnson had been impeached in retaliation for changing course on reconstruction policies. He was one "guilty" vote away from being removed from office. The larger problem, however, concerned the treatment of former Confederate soldiers and slaveholders and, most important, freed slaves. The South and the government were in turmoil, but peace was Grant's promise and Gilmore's obsession.

The bandmaster's initial plans for the event called for one thousand instrumentalists, ten thousand mixed voices, twenty thousand children vocalists, and a hall that would hold fifty thousand people. In all, it was supposed to cost two hundred thousand dollars and serve an audience of over a million visitors, a very grandiose plan indeed. After several fits and starts, and against vehement opposition from certain quarters, Gilmore finally marshaled enough support to stage the event in Boston in June of 1869. About half the planned number of musicians participated. Describing his feelings to a group of visitors the day before it started, Gilmore presented himself as a mere vessel destined to channel great music: "Yes gentlemen, I derive a sweeter pleasure from music than all the money in the world could give; it is the food of my soul, and under its heavenly influence I have forgotten many cares and trials. Though the humblest of its representatives, I have been one of its most ardent worshippers from childhood."[1] He hoped the festival would ignite a spark of musical worship throughout the land.

One would think that John Sullivan Dwight, now ten years removed from the *Hiawatha* affair (see chapter 6), would welcome such spiritualization. Though he adored the sounds of the "silvery voices of seven thousand children," which he described as "purity itself, like the white ray of 'holy light' divided by the prism," Dwight believed that the mingling of patriotic bonanzas with symphonies (programmed only to "conciliate the musical") had destroyed the very idea of music. "We have seen how the two got on together; how the anvils killed the Symphony, and how hard was abstinence from anvils when a classical programme was for once allowed its course." But the National Peace Jubilee had provided the tens of thousands of visitors with "a new belief in Music; a new conviction of its social worth; above all, of its importance as a pervading, educational and fusing element in our whole democratic life." It had done this "incalculable good," Dwight thought, despite itself.[2]

Henry Cood Watson, one of Dwight's New York counterparts, felt differently. He was taken by the event's magnitude. From his perspective, the scope of the Jubilee was a sign of immeasurable forward progress, not only for the country's musical culture in general but for new orchestral music specifically:

> Compare the scores of the early writers with those of Haydn, of Haydn with Beethoven, and Beethoven with some of our modern scores. Observe the progress of expansion, as one after another new means were developed and perfected. And it is absurd to suppose that even we have reached the ultimate in orchestral resources and effects.[3]

As Gilmore had hoped, Watson had fallen under the spell of the festival's magnificence. "We can only bow down our head in admiration," the critic observed reverently, "and thank God that we had knowledge enough, and heart enough, to appreciate the beauty, the grandeur, the sublimity, the Religion, of the greatest offering at the shrine of Music that the Christian world has ever witnessed."[4] In all of the moment's patriotic fervor, however, no one seemed to mind that only one piece by an American, an *Overture Triumphale* by Charles Crozat Converse (1832–1918), appeared during Gilmore's five-day festival. Little had changed for local composers in over half a century.

THE CLASSICIST ABROAD

Because of his success as a symphonist and his influence as a Harvard professor, a writer for the *Nation* once called John Knowles Paine (1839–1906), a native of Portland, Maine, "the Nestor of American composers."[5] The musical sage of Cambridge died of pneumonia after lying bedridden for several weeks. Like William Henry Fry, Paine had struggled with chronic illness for years—in this case with diabetes mellitus, which, like Fry's tuberculosis, could be treated only minimally with the medicine of the day. Paine's works in progress, including a tone poem called *Lincoln* (Fry's political champion), sat on his desk unfinished. His completed chef d'oeuvre, an exotic opera with the title *Azara*, remained unperformed. At least Fry had been able to see his last opera fully staged before his death.[6]

Throughout his career, which began in earnest only after the Civil War, Paine became acutely aware of the precarious place homegrown composers occupied within the German-dominated musical quarters of the United States. Gilmore's Jubilee epitomized the predicament. Unlike older New Yorkers such as Fry and Bristow, however, Paine did not have firsthand professional experience with the tumultuous early 1850s, when native-born musicians had perceived Germans as a real threat to the development of an authentic national musical culture. Instead, Paine considered Germans potential allies. His first teacher and mentor, Hermann Kotzschmar, was a German immigrant who was younger than both Fry and Bristow. Far-away New York, with its ethnic mudslinging, might as well have been another country.

Under Kotzschmar's tutelage, Paine organized a series of organ concerts designed to defray the expenses of studying in Europe, an opportunity that Fry and Bristow never had.[7] These concerts, held in 1857 and 1858 (and thus overlapping with the final season of Charles Jerome Hopkins's concert series in New York), piqued Dwight's interest. Shortly after leaving Portland for Boston, Paine met and befriended Alexander Wheelock Thayer (1817–1897), a member of the city's elite musical circles and a scholar who had spent considerable time in Europe researching Beethoven's life. Thayer was also a Harvard alumnus and had been one of Fry's adversaries in the contentious debates of the early 1850s. On a trip to New York in late June of 1858, the two New Englanders likely crossed paths with Fry. At that time, the city was hosting a large festival featuring a massive performance of Beethoven's Ninth Symphony. Over 40,000 people attended, and Fry was a featured guest speaker. His remarks focused on the universal brotherhood of humankind, undoubtedly a touchy subject given the explosive political climate preceding the outbreak of war.[8]

In any case, Paine and Thayer then traveled to Europe and established residence in Berlin, where the aspiring composer studied organ at the Neue Akademie der Tonkunst (New Academy for Music), an institution modeled on Mendelssohn's Leipzig Conservatory. Not immune to the factionalized musical politics at mid-century, such institutions were typically strongholds of conservatism. Paine's student compositions reveal a thorough immersion in the older music of J. S. Bach, not the chromaticism and experimentation of progressives like Wagner or Liszt, who consistently railed against the conservatories.[9] Paine's involvement in the German conservatory milieu served him well, however, upon his return to Portland in 1861. While there, he performed privately for the editor of the *Boston Musical Times*, who commented favorably on their time together and noted Paine's penchant for Bach, which he had acquired in Berlin:

> [Paine] revels in the wealth of the life-long labor of the illustrious master. He would have the world love Bach as he loves him, and he sincerely believes that the world has only to know him as he knows him to love him equally well. He is a missionary of Bach, and Bach has no more enthusiastic a worshiper, nor so admirable an interpreter in the United or Disunited States of America.[10]

The editor also hinted that Paine would receive a warm welcome if he were to move to Boston. The organist obliged, and his debut recital a few months later, which featured four works by Bach and three by Paine himself, was a success.[11]

Upon winning the approval of the city's leading musical intelligentsia, Paine quickly secured a salaried position at a local church, where he worked until he became college organist at Harvard in 1864. In the intervening years, he continued his missionary activities by performing Bach's music in recital alongside pieces by composers with more established reputations in the United States, such as Mozart, Mendelssohn, and Handel. Paine also slowly introduced his own music, including small organ pieces and a substantial mass. Dwight responded positively to the mass and praised its religiosity, claiming it bore the imprints of Bach, Mendelssohn, and Beethoven.[12] Such kind remarks about the work's serious and churchlike ethos inspired Paine to return to Europe in order to secure a full performance, which would potentially bolster his career at home. Dwight had found a musical and intellectual protégé.

Though initially rebuffed by the Berlin musical establishment, Paine set about organizing a chorus himself and hired an independent orchestra that gave a full performance of the mass just six months into his stay. It was an unqualified success. Critics commented approvingly on the work's strong connections to the classical tradition. Upon examining the score, influential critic Flodoard Geyer noted that "a genuine German spirit breathes through the work, which, built up in the school of Bach and Handel, yet reveals throughout the writer's own creative power."[13] One of Paine's Berlin companions, George Osgood, relished in the moment: "We were proud to know that at least we had our representative in this most beautiful of arts; and to see the phlegmatic German at length heartily acknowledging that in America we not only have time and ability to make money, but that we can send forth artists, and those too who bid fair to stand in the very front rank."[14] For Osgood, the high quality of Paine's music was proof of American greatness, but from Godard's perspective, it was good only to the extent that it was German in character.

ROMANCING GERMAN CULTURE

The responses to Paine's mass revealed just how facile the conflation of "German" with "universal" could be by the late 1860s, even among Americans. Such sentiments would have been unthinkable to William Henry Fry, who had died a little more than two years earlier. But over the course of his career, Fry could not have avoided recognizing that the sentiment grew in tandem with Americans' persistent love affair with Beethoven. As early as 1819, a group of amateur musicians in Portland had organized a Beethoven Society, so named because Beethoven "stands second to none of the masters of melody who have arisen and shone upon the present age." In contrast to Handel and Haydn, they claimed, Beethoven was a composer "whose genius seems to anticipate a future age, and labors for the benefit of posterity."[15] Foreshadowing Dwight, this prophetic language hinted that the society's founders also heard the sounds of democracy, the ultimate marker of an inexorable future, in Beethoven's music.

By 1856, not long after the Philharmonic controversy with George Frederick Bristow, passion for Beethoven's music had become blisteringly hot, particularly in New England. That year marked the inauguration of a large bronze statue of Beethoven by the noted American sculptor Thomas Crawford (1814–1857) at the Boston Music Hall, the city's best concert venue and the eventual home of the Boston Symphony Orchestra. William Wetmore Story (1819–1895), himself a sculptor and poet, recited a lauda-tory verse at the ceremony that transformed Beethoven from a prophet into a Christ-like messiah, with the statue standing, literally, as a bronze idol: "Clay no longer—he has risen from the buried mould of earth,/To a golden form transfigured by a new and glorious birth." Story's poem echoed Dwight's insistence that Beethoven's music would serve to uplift Americans from what he thought was a state of utilitarian incivility:

Never is a nation finished while it wants the grace of Art—
Use must borrow robes of Beauty, life must rise above the mart.
Faith and love are all ideal, speaking with a music tone—
And without their touch of magic, labor is the Devil's own.
Therefore are we glad to greet thee, master artist, to thy place,
For we need in all our living Beauty and ideal grace,
Mostly here, to lift our nation, move its heart and calm its nerves,
And to round life's angled duties to imaginative curves.[16]

Conflating the beauty of Beethoven's music with the presence of Crawford's awe-inspiring statue, the poem gave its hearers hope that the nation would rise to a glorious future filled with the master's tones.

Just a year after Patrick Gilmore's National Peace Jubilee, the country's eyes turned once again toward Beethoven in order to celebrate the centennial of his birth. Out of metropolitan pride, New Yorkers concocted a scheme to outdo the National Peace Jubilee but failed miserably. Beethoven's Fifth Symphony opened and closed the event, but, as in the earlier festival, most of the program consisted of vocal and choral selections. Curiously, these were not by Beethoven. Turning the spotlight away from Beethoven, Gilmore himself even programmed Jullien's *Grand Quadrille of All Nations* at an affiliated performance. Infighting among the musicians and financiers, coupled with lack of interest from patrons, nearly led to the entire event's collapse. Complementing the official efforts, however, Bristow led a separate Juvenile Beethoven Centennial Celebration that featured hundreds of his public school students from the heavily German tenth ward, aged seven to fourteen, in rousing performances that the press praised heartily. Unlike the official event, it was a complete success.[17]

In other cities, Beethoven centennials took an openly political turn. Earlier expressions of reverence had focused primarily on Beethoven's universality and suggested that his presence in America was a divine intervention designed to uplift the nation. Centennial festivals, by contrast, often acknowledged the political outlook that led to his ascendance in the United States: cosmopolitan republicanism. In an appropriately dated issue of his journal, December 17, Dwight modeled an essay introducing the upcoming Boston festivities on Christian martyrologies: "One hundred years ago today, in the Electoral city of Bonn upon the Rhine, of humble parentage, was born the Great Musician, [etc.]." In this saintly story, Beethoven led a select host of compositional masters who prefigured not only the musical ascendancy of Germany, but the political might of the German Empire:

> United Germany, peaceful and strong, intelligent and just, foremost in high ideals and good works, shall be but the fulfillment of the song of all her great tone-prophets. How could a people whose civilization has been all impregnated with such deep, earnest music, fail at last to triumph over more shallow, baneful civilization whose chief ideal was "*la gloire*" and evermore aggressive?[18]

Over the course of the century, Germany's powerful cultural influence, manifested most clearly in Beethoven's music, had crossed national borders and taken over the world. But, he noted, "The music of the modern master was particularly sympathetic to the ideals, the whole spirit of the young, free republic." This was by now a familiar refrain for Dwight: Beethoven's music was American.

In Chicago, Unitarian minister Robert Laird Collier (1837–1890) delivered a centennial oration that resonated strongly with Dwight's, but he envisioned an even stronger cultural union between the United States and

Germany. As the "symbol of unity and brotherhood," he argued, music (especially Beethoven's) would become the glue binding the two nations together:

> The Rhine shall not divide nor the channel separate, neither shall the great
> ocean be broad enough to keep continent from continent. We shall be one people, with one language in all the earth. Beethoven was a republican, and liberty
> shimmered through all his nature, and floats afar out upon the weird measures
> and marvels of his music. The calendar of a century closes today over his name,
> and the genius of freedom for which it stands is the magic wand uniting the
> New America to the old Germany.[19]

The correspondent for *Dwight's* who sent the report noted that the oration was "received with great enthusiasm." Beethoven had apparently conquered Chicago as well.

THE CLASSICIST'S HISTORY

Dwight, an elder statesman of the musical intelligentsia, had far outlived the likes of Heinrich, Fry, and Gottschalk (though not Bristow), and his efforts to imbue Beethoven's music with a distinctly American identity were able to fall afresh upon a new generation, Paine's generation. Expressions of American and German cultural unity were in fact quite common in the years following the Civil War, both inside and outside musical contexts.[20] Unlike Fry and Bristow, for example, Gottschalk had sympathized openly with the German cultural heritage of his music. To honor the assistance of German musicians at one of his South American festivals, he noted:

> The sincere, austere, and deep worship the German nation has for music, is
> one of its most glorious titles in the history of civilization; therefore, in devoting today my talent to a German audience, 9000 miles away from home, I am
> pleased to render an homage to the nation of the greatest geniuses, as well as
> the people who always knew so well how to encourage, understand, and reward
> all the great celebrities of the art.[21]

Fry would have scoffed at such syrupy froth.

Paine, however, would make similarly elevated statements after his return from Berlin. His sermonizing began at a large national convention for many of the country's most important musicians (a direct outgrowth of Gilmore's National Peace Jubilee), where he pled forcefully for the public support of composers. His speech was a concatenation of ideas that figures of the previous generation had espoused forcefully. "Surely the devoted artist with lofty ideals and untiring zeal will be rewarded with new revelations," he argued with the fervor of Charles Jerome Hopkins, "and we Americans have a right if not a duty to compete in this trial."[22] Then, as if channeling Fry, he insisted that the diligent cultivation of craft and technique would raise the esteem in which the public held composers—and that support from the wealthy would be a necessary component. Under this new system, he naïvely added, "All narrow and ignorant prejudices against [composers] will vanish." Americans had heard all of these arguments before, yet they still held composers in low esteem.

But one final component of Paine's message was truly unique, at least coming from a composer. He asserted that American culture was an extension of European civilization, not exceptional or even distinct:

> America has had the reputation of being a country without art. The excuse commonly given is, that "this is a new country." But as we have wealth enough to foster art, though we are a young nation, it seems to be more the fault of the will and habit of the people than its so-called youth. If we are young in years we are old in experience. What is this, apparently, but a continuation of European civilization?[23]

Here for the first time, a prominent composer, rather than a critic or other public intellectual, argued that the identity crisis facing American musicians was really no crisis at all. The United States was simply Europe on the western side of the Atlantic. Fry would have scoffed at this notion as well.

In another striking parallel to Fry's career, Paine led an elaborate series of lectures on the history of music for Boston audiences. Paine's eighteen lectures, compared to Fry's eleven, were much more learned (rather than showy), but they were no less politically motivated. The series, delivered from December of 1870 through the following April, displayed Paine's impressive command of broad historical narratives and detailed minutiae (despite being filled with what we would now consider bias and error).

Paine's historical narrative rested on the theory that a familiar cast of master composers performed one of two functions. Either they stood as the summit of an era's musical development or they served as the springboard to a new era. Bach's music was "the culmination of Protestant church music," for example, while Handel had "reconciled" sacred and secular music in the oratorio.[24] Handel's ability to synthesize these opposites confirmed his status as a "universal master," a designation that Paine also conferred upon Mozart:

> This unparalleled universality is not only displayed in his complete mastery of every kind of musical composition, vocal and instrumental, from a popular song to a grand symphony, from a simple dance to a solemn requiem, but in the rare adaptation of different national peculiarities of style to his own individuality. It was his mission to unite and beautify the national elements of music, which hitherto had remained apart.[25]

Through sheer strength of will and raw musical talent, the most widely recognized masters had been able to develop a musical language that spoke to all people. They were universal.

Paine's urge to connect "universality" to assimilation and amalgamation was not unusual. Writing in 1863, German music historian Joseph Schlüter had also claimed that Handel was "the most universal musician before Mozart" and, like Mozart, had to acquire success by negotiating public taste and artistic freedom—and reconciling the two.[26] Schlüter likewise considered Mozart the "sole heir" (*Universalerbe*) to all that came before him, a sign of his ability to assimilate several styles into an individual musical voice.[27] Frédéric Louis Ritter (1834–1891), a composer and professor of music at Vassar College, had likewise contended that "when these two characteristic qualities, which distinguish the German mind, are found combined, though very rarely, [. . .] then art reaches that point of universal excellence which makes its works the aesthetical expression of no single nationality, but the spirit of the whole age." Ritter's representatives of this unification were Palestrina, Lassus, Handel, and Mozart.[28]

The concept of transcendence, an idea with deep roots in the German intellectual tradition, accompanied Paine's concept of universality and provided his historical narrative with an additional structural pillar. Bach, he argued, was the first composer whose music stood outside the confines of time and place, despite his inarguable identity as a German. Unlike the cosmopolitan Handel, Bach did not travel throughout Europe but flourished in isolation. Fleshing out this image of a reclusive genius, Paine noted that Bach was misunderstood in his own time, "even by his sons and disciples." Comprehending his music required the passage of time since he was "the most intellectual musician who ever lived." And such inaccessibility is precisely what separated Bach's music from Handel's, which had "become antiquated, because he incorporated into it some conventionalities of the prevailing schools" (the precise feature that made his music "universal"). Bach's music, by contrast, "cannot grow antiquated" because it is timeless and transcendent.[29]

Paine used the image of Bach as a misunderstood genius to draw a comparison to Beethoven: Together, they were "the most subjective" composers. Following this thread in a lecture focused on Beethoven, he argued that music history had tended to move steadily from the objective to the subjective, and that Beethoven could not have emerged at any other moment in time. Like Bach, he had withdrawn from the world as a performer "to give himself up to an ideal world" as a composer. Removal from the social life of humankind had allowed his music to appear transcendent.[30] Whereas Mozart had manifested universality by subsuming national styles into a single, unique whole and had thus punctuated a significant moment in the history of music, Beethoven had laid the foundation for music's future by crystallizing and perfecting transcendent musical forms.[31] Bach had taken harmony and counterpoint to new heights, but Beethoven had shaped the very vessels, such as the sonata and the symphony, that could harness music's full expressive power.

In this familiar narrative, told only a few months after the Beethoven centennial celebrations, the great composer stood as a giant whose shadow shrouded the musical world in darkness for much of the century. The image that Paine drew in his final two lectures was bleak. "Through the controlling power of Beethoven's genius," he claimed, "the various forms of concert and chamber music have remained the central point of all subsequent development as represented by the younger masters, Schubert, Mendelssohn, Schumann, Chopin, and others." Beethoven had elevated the forms of Haydn and Mozart to match his larger-than-life personality, but "no successor has yet appeared to carry the dimensions of the art beyond the limits he set."[32]

Keeping Beethoven's flame alive must have been difficult. Paine found specific reasons to eliminate highly regarded composers from the line of succession. The popular Mendelssohn had exercised "genius" in "almost every form of musical composition" but had failed because he did not move beyond the national into universality and transcendence. Schumann suffered from a similar weakness. "It is doubtful," Paine surmised, "whether [his] music will ever be liked in Italy and France, where Mozart and Mendelssohn find a place, and even the English who are allied by race with the Germans have not fully accepted Schumann's or Sebastian Bach's music."[33] Ritter, incidentally, would agree: "Though composers like Schubert, Mendelssohn, and especially Schumann, succeeded in creating genial works in this direction, they cannot be considered in the sense of progress beyond Beethoven's achievement."[34] If all of them had failed, who was left to carry the banner of universalism? Brahms, whose name did not appear in the lectures, was still working on his First Symphony in 1871 and had been active in Vienna since the mid-1860s, not the Berlin familiar to Paine.

MUSIC OF THE AMERICAN FUTURE

Paine's final lecture addressed questions of music's future and who would shape it. His answers were provocative. He blamed the untimely deaths of Mendelssohn and Schumann for the withered condition of contemporary European musical life. "Had these leaders of the musical world lived to the present hour in the active practice of their art," he speculated, the relative prominence of later musicians like Wagner and Liszt would

> doubtless have been modified by their living influence and example. No one can doubt that Mendelssohn would have exerted all his power and influence in

a different direction. Before his death, the various public attempts by Berlioz and Wagner failed to strike any root.[35]

Berlioz's penchant for programmaticism was misguided, Paine added, because his overreliance on the printed word intellectualized music, the proper domain of which was emotion. And Wagner's revolutionary ideas were so inimical to the measured progress of history that he would be remembered as a wild dreamer whose ramblings simply could not pass muster against a rational critique.

Paine's vision of history was not unusual, but his explanation of contemporary European musical life was ideologically driven. Since he had firsthand experiences overseas, he was in a small class of powerful brokers who controlled the dissemination of information about Europe to the American public. The typical American music lover had no way of learning about musical developments across the ocean without the aid of these brokers, thus creating a situation in which information streams often diverged significantly from life on the ground.[36] *Dwight's Journal*, for example, frequently cast Brahms in a negative light by reprinting lukewarm or damning reviews from European periodicals. The heightened sense of anticipation that had marked the twenty-year span between Schumann's famous "Neue Bahnen" article in the *Neue Zeitschrift für Musik* and the premiere of Brahms's First Symphony was absent from the American national consciousness. As a result, American perceptions of the European musical landscape were guided increasingly by premieres of pieces emanating from the Wagnerian, "New German," or "modern" camp (as it was variously called), or at least from the composers whom they considered a part of that camp, rightly or wrongly.[37] During the 1860s, Americans were not yet aware of what ramifications the European controversies surrounding "music of the future" would have on musical life at home, but Paine's 1871 lecture was a loud warning.

Many listeners had not responded kindly to this new music when it was performed in the United States for the first time. Commenting on a New York Philharmonic performance of Franz Liszt's *Festklänge* in 1860, critic Edmund Remack described it as "undoubtedly very odd, and it seems as if the composer, in his endeavor to be original, carefully avoided every flash of melody or natural harmony; the phrases are disconnected, the work abounds in musical contra-positions, and reminds one, so to speak, of a musical contortionist."[38] Henry Cood Watson reacted even more fitfully to the first movement of Liszt's *Zwei Episoden aus Lenaus Faust*:

Liszt's "Nachtliger Zug" is a weary, dreary, senseless stringing together of patches of irreconcilable discords, which mean nothing, being but a pedantic display of his knowledge of harmony and instrumental combinations and effects, without one idea or salient thought. Considered as music, it is disgusting. [. . .] It is a waste of time to produce these grim, fantastic absurdities, for they occupy the places which would otherwise be filled by sound, intelligible music.[39]

With limited space and limited time, he wondered, why would New York Philharmonic conductor Carl Bergmann choose such pieces over others? Rhetoric like Watson's and Remack's left readers with lingering concerns about the value and morality of Wagnerism.

New music also challenged critics to develop new modes of thought for processing it. The typically conservative Dwight programmed Niels Gade's First Symphony and Carl Goldmark's *Sakuntala* overture (which was hot off the presses) at Harvard Musical Association concerts during the season when Paine delivered his lectures. He smiled at the symphony's "perfect unity" and even heard an American ethos: "The romantic Northern seashore spirit that pervades it [was] in the strong *Finale* like a summoning of all the clans, with a heroic, grand Bardic song ringing through it, which one of our brave regiments might well have marched to, singing, in the war of the rebellion."[40] This fusion of the work's national identities—German, Danish, and American—recalled his contention during the Beethoven centennial that music could unite humankind. The overture, on the other hand, "has not lifted us, as all great music does, into that free ideal element of thought and feeling, where we seem to be at one with all and nearer to the universal heart." Instead, he grumbled,

> The music wanders, too woe-begone and self-oblivious *for music* [. . .]; A nightmare spell weighs heavily on each tremendous strain of the whole orchestra to get out what it has to say, but nothing comes. Again and again with loud solemnity of emphasis, with startling attitude and gesture, the orator begins his all-important statement, while you listen breathless; "but," "*but*," "BUT," he says:—but nothing comes.[41]

Dwight's complaints reflected the negative animus he felt toward representational music of any kind, but they also revealed his distaste for sudden changes of character, prolixity, lack of motivic development, and unconventional form—all features typically associated with the music of Wagner, Liszt, and Berlioz.

Despite Dwight's complaints, Bergmann and Theodore Thomas (1835–1905), the country's two leading conductors, kept trying. Between 1870 and 1873, they introduced American audiences to a host of recent symphonies and other orchestral works by Liszt, Berlioz, Goldmark, Anton Rubinstein and, most important, Joachim Raff. These pieces became staples of their repertoires over the next several years.[42] Critics, including Dwight, often framed their responses to this music in terms of classicism and modernism, and they had sincere doubts about the musical future. Referring to works by Beethoven, for example, the *Brooklyn Daily Eagle* remarked that "it must be confessed that there is not a popular fondness for the musical classics. The genuine liking for works which convention compels an artistic respect is limited to a comparative few." The critic then attempted to educate readers about other paths:

> But there is a new school of artists who insist that the classical composers have by no means exhausted the subject. They say that the forms of musical expression are more varied and manifold than those of any other art, and that, as the emotions stimulated by music are subtle and undefinable, so there are innumerable methods of reaching those emotions. [. . .] Yet the new school survives ridicule and denunciation and is steadily progressing. There is truth hidden somewhere in its obscure incoherencies.[43]

The writer went on to argue the Goldmark's "original and striking" *Sakuntala* could take a place alongside Wagner's overture to *Tannhäuser* as a lasting example of modernism. The final work on the program, however, Berlioz's *Les franc-juges* overture, "is the music of the noisy school, [. . .] and which disguises poverty and barrenness with the scramble of stringed instruments, the blare of trumpets, the hoarse cries of trombones, the thunder of drums."

Listeners needed a middle path, and Joachim Raff (1822–1882), a neglected composer today, provided it.[44] New York critics responded with skepticism to his Second Symphony, which premiered in 1870, by harping at length on its resemblance to Mendelssohn, as well as its failure to live up to Mendelssohnian standards. George Frederick Bristow might have sympathized. In any case, Watson remained optimistic: "It certainly is not a work of striking genius, for it indicates [. . .] no erratic rush into the Wagnerian regions, that antipode to pure, serene, and lofty heights of the truly aesthetic in the musical art. [. . .] He is rather the poet of the art, than the erratically inspired seer."[45] The symphony marked cautious progress in the right direction.

Raff's openly programmatic Third Symphony, *Im Walde*, on the other hand, secured his U.S. reputation. It premiered in New York in January of 1872 and had become "decidedly popular" by March of 1873, according to John Hassard (1836–1888), critic for the *New York Tribune*. After a performance directed by Carl Wolfsohn (1834–1907) in Philadelphia earlier in the year, a critic for the *Inquirer* claimed, "We can say of it more emphatically than we did before, that in many respects no other symphonies we have heard, except Beethoven's, are equal to it." Reporting on the same concert, a correspondent for *Dwight's* assented by pronouncing that "the genius and active talent of Raff have wrought into form this valuable contribution to the 'noble army' of Symphonies, and well up in the line must its place be."[46]

With Raff's programmatic Fifth (*Lenore*) following shortly on its heels, and with other new works such as Anton Rubinstein's *Ocean* Symphony gathering momentum, the symphonic floodgates had opened. As Richard Pohl had predicted, the history of art—in the form of Wagnerian music—had indeed moved westward. The country's musical future was at hand.

CHAPTER 9

⚭

The Rivalry of Generations

During the surge of Wagnerian proselytizing led by conductors Carl Bergmann and Theodore Thomas after the Civil War, George Frederick Bristow's personal musical future was still bright. He was quite active as a composer during the 1860s and 1870s, especially considering his prolific activities as a public school teacher and choral conductor. He even served briefly as interim president of the New York Philharmonic during the 1866–1867 season.[1] His compositional outlook also took a dramatic turn following the premiere of his Third Symphony in 1859. Most of his later large-scale works have specifically American-themed titles and, in some cases, make use of descriptive or narrative devices. They are more evocative than his earlier oeuvre and align more closely with the music of "modern Germany," to say nothing of William Henry Fry's progressive agenda of the 1850s.[2]

Bristow's decision to move in a Wagnerian direction had mixed results in an era when critics were still coming to terms with stylistic innovation. A highly programmatic overture, *Columbus* (1861), proved especially divisive. After a New York Philharmonic performance in 1866, Henry Cood Watson claimed that the overture "was a great relief from the choleric symptoms left by the 'Zug' [i.e., from Franz Liszt's *Zwei Episoden*]," provided "evidence of a master mind, with imagination to invent," and "stamped Mr. Bristow with eminence as a composer."[3] The audience, Watson noted, agreed. Following an 1870 performance given by the Brooklyn Philharmonic, however, a critic for the *Daily Eagle* took a different stance: "It is a pity [. . .] that the feeble and worn-out device of making the big drum do ordnance duty had not been omitted. Composers should have learned by this time that such realistic clap-trap, which always makes an audience laugh, does not rise above the level of burlesque. The introduction of the gun trick in descriptive music ought to be made a penal offense."[4] Unlike Watson, this critic was bothered by the work's representational elements, its most innovative features. Yet Bristow, the critic added, "deserves solitary eminence from the fact that he is the only American composer who has written an overture worthy a place in a Philharmonic programme." Despite such disagreements over technique, Bristow's star continued to rise on the heels of his Third Symphony, the programmatic overture, and an oratorio called *Daniel*, which had premiered to great acclaim in 1867.[5]

Bristow had been a member of the Brooklyn Philharmonic since its establishment in 1857, about a year after he had reconciled with its New York cousin. As a rank-and-file violinist sitting at the first desk, he became a well-known figure among subscribers. The 1870s marked a turning point in his relationship with the ensemble. The orchestra performed both *Columbus* and the Third Symphony in 1870 and 1871, respectively, and each was received warmly. This success was as much political as it was artistic, for the Philharmonic had a music committee tasked with assessing new works for addition to the repertoire. Bristow's facility with this process filtered into press accounts, which congratulated him on breaking the orchestra industry's "Teutonic rings."[6] Bristow, who had once expressed vitriolic nativist sentiment, had apparently learned how to work within the German-dominated system rather than against it.

Bristow's crowning achievement with the Brooklyn Philharmonic came in 1872, when the orchestra offered him a $100 commission for a new symphony, the *Arcadian*. Noting that vocalists could command that sum several times over for a single performance, one commentator scoffed at the paltry amount but applauded the orchestra for moving in the right direction.[7] It was in all probability the first commission that a standing municipal orchestra in the United States had offered any native-born composer. In 1872, Bristow was the most well-respected and well-known U.S. composer, and therefore the most deserving. He was also nearing fifty years of age.

Bristow forged the *Arcadian* Symphony in the standard four-movement arrangement and provided a descriptive topic for each in addition to a tempo marking. He had affixed short, poetic texts to the movements of his previous symphony, but the music was not meant to represent or depict the images from these texts as precisely as it was here. For the new symphony, Bristow provided a printed analysis at performances that the press often reprinted—a strategy borrowed from Fry (and, of course, Berlioz and Spohr). This analysis explained how the formal structure and the narrative plot were intertwined. As Bristow moved from the 1850s into the 1870s, he was also attempting to engage in a dialogue with the most up-to-date composer who had attained success among U.S. audiences: Joachim Raff. The work's structure bears a remarkable resemblance to Raff's *Im Walde* Symphony, which had premiered a mere nine months before Bristow finished the *Arcadian*. As table 9.1 shows, both works contain a nightfall scene, a dance featuring exotic musical figures, and a three-part finale. Bristow's narrative is more integrated across the four movements; Raff's is more picturesque.

Table 9.1. STRUCTURAL AND NARRATIVE COMPARISON OF JOACHIM RAFF, SYMPHONY NO. 3, *IM WALDE* AND GEORGE FREDERICK BRISTOW, SYMPHONY NO. 4, *ARCADIAN*.

Raff, Symphony No. 3, *Im Walde*	Bristow, Symphony No. 4, *Arcadian*
I. Allegro—"Daytime: Feelings and Impressions"	I. Allegro appassionato—"Emigrants' Journey across the Plains"
II. Largo—"At Dusk: Dreaming"	II. Andante religioso—"Halt on the Prairie"
III. Allegro assai—"Dance of the Dryads"	III. Allegro ma non tanto—"Indian War Dance and Attack by Indians"
IV. Allegro—"Night: Stillness of the Night in the Forest. Entry and Departure of the Wild Hunt. Daybreak"	IV. Allegro con spirito—"Arrival at the New Home, Rustic Festivities, and Dancing"

The vivid coloration in the *Arcadian* exceeded that of his previous efforts. The first movement is an expansive sonata form. It opens with a dry viola solo evoking the desolation of the imagined westward journey (example 9.1). The full orchestra later takes up the melody in a profound statement of the theme. A more lyrical secondary theme, cast in G major, follows a broad and strident transition that includes a foreshadowing of the tune in the remote key of C♯ major. Following a lengthy development and full recapitulation, the movement closes with the settlers slowing down for the evening as the solo viola line returns, this time dropping into its husky low register. The movement was so long that some listeners wanted to "cut the heart out" of it. But to Bristow's credit, he claimed that it was supposed to depict a journey through the "unbroken waste, with its weariness and monotony."[8] Evidently he had succeeded.

Example 9.1: Dry Viola Solo. Bristow, Symphony No. 4, *Arcadian*, I: Allegro appassionato, mm. 1–20.

Example 9.2: "Tallis's Evening Hymn." Bristow, Symphony No. 4, *Arcadian*, II: Andante religioso, mm. 17–25 (trombones).

Later movements heighten the work's sense of pictorialism and narrativity. In the second movement, a quotation of the well-known "Tallis's Evening Hymn" scored for trombones serves as a framing device for the broad adagio depicting the settlers at rest, as if they were singing the tune communally before bedtime (example 9.2). This meditative use of a trombone choir harkened back to Schumann's *Rhenish* Symphony of 1850, a part of Bergmann's portfolio that had been heard most recently in New York in 1871. (And Brahms would employ the sonority for a similar purpose in the opening of the finale to his First Symphony just a few years later.) The settlers are awakened by the sounds of an "Indian War Dance" (the third movement), whose thumping drumbeats in the low strings, augmented by a triangle, underscore a march-like line in the woodwinds. The scene gains emotional intensity across the movement, particularly after a brassy trio depicting the settlers' resistance (example 9.3). The symphony closes with a raucous and rustic finale in ⁶/₈ that concludes with a bombastic Presto celebrating the journey's end.

Example 9.3: Primary Theme. Bristow, Symphony No. 4, *Arcadian*, III: Allegro ma non tanto, mm. 13–24 (full orch.).

Anticipation for the symphony ran high during the Philharmonic's 1872–1873 season. The lineup included a wide array of orchestral works (in addition to the requisite solo instrumental and vocal numbers), ranging in style from Haydn's "Military" Symphony to Liszt's *Mazeppa*. Some observers trumpeted the new symphony's explicitly American theme. William Cadwalader Hudson, the new critic for the *Daily Eagle*, praised Bristow's "native independence and originality, which prove his manliness and patriotism" and applauded his "impulse toward saving something of the romance of pioneer life from the destructive march of material improvement."[9] Brooklyn's *Daily Union* concurred, remarking that "the subject is eminently American, and Mr. Bristow has treated it so ably and truthfully, that no person at all acquainted with the experiences of the early-day emigrants, in their journeying across the plains, can possibly fail to understand and enjoy its delivery."[10] At the moment, critics seemed willing to support Bristow's programmatic intentions.

The favorable press energized the public, but anticipation quickly transformed into discontent after the Philharmonic began its rehearsals. Hudson, who had been enthusiastic just two days earlier, gave a tempered assessment of the rehearsal using a tone that echoed Bristow's mid-century critics. With an air of pomposity, he defaulted to familiar claims of derivativeness:

> The symphony is reminiscential. It is not meant to be said that Mr. Bristow is a conscious plagiarist. He is a student, and the fruits of his studies appear in his writing. At times classically conservative, they also have occasional traces of the New School. Here is a faint flavor of Wagner, there is a suggestion of Schumann, and once a hint of Liszt.[11]

Whereas Bristow had faced unwarranted complaints about staleness before, Hudson's two-pronged assessment of the work as classical yet progressive betrayed the fact that Raff was the only other well-known composer who had also attempted to reconcile older and newer styles in his symphonies. Hudson's review otherwise provided a detailed account of the ways in which the work's descriptive elements (settlers traveling along the plains, setting up camp, etc.) unfolded within standard formal constraints. Listeners did not know many symphonies, even from the new school, marked by this unification of musical form and narrative content. As far as they knew, Bristow was a symphonic pioneer.

Following the symphony's official concert premiere, the conversation became much more philosophical as Hudson unleashed his full fury on the very idea of a pictorial musical narrative. First, he denied that the work's American identity, however construed, was important at all: "Art is cosmopolitan," he claimed, and "it ought to make no difference in our acceptance of a good thing whether it is the work of an American or a Hindoo." Cutting into the work's patriotic ethos, he added that a "thoughtful art-lover" would derive "little satisfaction" from the work's American subject. The assertion that music somehow transcended nationality—a position also expressed by Willis, Dwight, and Paine—set up a damning dismissal of the work's programmatic elements:

> Mr. Bristow enters upon his work at this disadvantage that, in the nature of things and by inflexible artistic limitations, it is simply impossible for him or anybody to describe a journey across the plains or anywhere else. [The truth of this proposition] is instinctively felt by every intelligent person. [. . .] Musical description begins and ends with the representation of broad and general emotions. [. . .] He only failed where every composer must fail.[12]

Likewise, a correspondent for *Dwight's* "regretted" that "Mr. Bristow has placed, or endeavored to place, his composition under the head of 'programme music,' in which each part illustrates, or is supposed to illustrate, not the progress and development of an *idea*, but certain events or material objects which it is not within the province of music to describe." Composers who take this approach either "do not comprehend [the] art" or "[set] a trap to catch the applause of unreasoning and unmusical people."[13] Bristow had made no attempt to hide these elements prior to the work's performance, making these responses all the more baffling. And in the program itself, he noted that "[the synopsis] is not pretended to give more than an outline of the composer's meaning; enough, simply, to enable the attentive listener to understand and appreciate the composition." He did not intend the work to be purely representational, as his critics had argued.

After sweeping aside the work's national pretenses and light programmaticism, however, critics agreed that the music itself was quite good. It is a "fluent and finished work," Hudson maintained, while "the controlling themes are easily apprehended and the progress of each movement is readily followed." The writer for *Dwight's* added that "the interest for the most part [was] well sustained, and the instrumentation throughout masterly." The work, readers learned, would "rank among the best that have been produced in America." Still, Hudson excoriated certain facets of the piece, including the hymn quotation in the second movement (supposedly the "first" instance of quotation in symphonic writing!), the dancelike qualities of the third (which reminded him of ballet), and the lightness of the fourth (as if no symphony had ever ended with a light finale). Such haywire criticism revealed more about the biases of the critics and the widespread aversion to "programmaticism" than about the work itself.

Bristow had faced misdirected criticism many times before and would weather it with stoicism as his star continued to rise despite the negativity. The Brooklyn audience had applauded the composer on three separate occasions during the performance, and the president of the society stopped the concert to give a speech congratulating him.[14] The event generated international interest as well. The *Musical World* of London, where Bristow had maintained a reputation as the leading American composer since the days of Jullien, reprinted the entire review from *Dwight's*, while the city's *Musical Standard* published excerpts.[15] Conductor Carl Bergmann, whose musical opinion mattered as much as any critic's, esteemed the symphony highly enough to revive it the following year at a New York Philharmonic concert; a critic for the *Spirit of the Times* would support the "ancient" orchestra for the progressiveness of the decision.[16] And Asger Hamerik (1843–1923), the new director of Baltimore's Peabody Institute and a Danish composer who had no particular investment in Bristow's career, would revive it a second time a year later.[17]

THE CLASSICIST COMMENTS

John Knowles Paine, meanwhile, had been drafting his own new large-scale work, an oratorio called *St. Peter*. As with Bristow's *Arcadian*, critics did not receive the piece with unanimous feelings, and their disagreements centered on the very issue that he had raised in his lectures: the proper future of music. One critic praised Paine for demonstrating that modern composers had not lost all sight of good counterpoint, while another belittled the piece for its Bach-like "dryness." William F. Apthorp, a Bostonian and Paine's friend, argued that his devotion to Bach heightened the religiosity of his music, surpassing even Mendelssohn. Dwight, however, condemned the oratorio for flickering between the styles of Bach, Handel, and Mendelssohn and, worse, conveying "the chill of the 'new school' and 'the future,'" euphemisms for Wagnerism.[18]

Despite their differences, critics did agree on one point: *St. Peter* was the greatest oratorio, if not the greatest work of music, written by an American composer to date. John Fiske, one of Paine's Harvard colleagues, remarked after a performance that "with the exception of Mr. Paine, we know of no American hitherto who has shown either the genius or the culture requisite for writing music in the grand [oratorio] style."[19] The young Fiske was likely unaware that New York critics had said the same thing about Bristow's *Daniel* in 1867.[20]

As the controversy over *St. Peter* unfolded two months after the Brooklyn premiere of Bristow's *Arcadian* Symphony, Paine offered his own thoughts on Wagner and the new school in a review of the composer's *Gesammelte Schriften*, which had recently been published in Leipzig.[21] Borrowing ideas from his final historical lecture, Paine critiqued Wagner's philosophical positions as morally bankrupt and his views of musical history as skewed beyond redemption. Paine also carefully delineated the specific features of Wagner's music that he found wanting. "The so-called 'infinite melody' is a falsity," he stated bluntly. "As exemplified by Wagner in his latest operas, it is nothing more or less than a kind of accompanied *recitative* or *arioso* style." The technique lacked balance and proportion, but, more importantly, it eschewed "a definite motive or theme, which must be expanded, imitated, and varied, for the purpose of intensifying the particular mood of feeling which the motive has awakened."[22] Wagner's melodic meanderings and use of leitmotifs (which Paine criticized as substitutes for "real delineation of character") paled in comparison to the motivic development found in Beethoven's instrumental music. Mere repetition without an internally driven formal structure was meaningless and redundant.[23]

Paine averred, however, that Wagner's technical command of the orchestra was "wonderful" and noted that some of the themes in his earlier operas were "noble, characteristic, and pleasing." But when heard next to the music of his contemporaries, they fell short of the mark: "If we compare his music composed in the *free thematic form* with similar works by recent masters like Mendelssohn and Schumann, we are struck by the want of refined beauty in the music of Wagner. This is not compensated for by a real grandeur of style."[24] The words that Paine himself emphasized represented the core of his dispute with Wagner's school: It was formless. The dazzling orchestral techniques favored by the school, he argued, "fail to convey to the musical understanding the clearness and beauty of design through the organic development of motives, without which the sense of proportion, as addressed to the ear, cannot be gratified, and the deep moods of feeling awakened in the soul of the hearer."[25] He concluded by speculating about who might take up the banner that Schumann and Mendelssohn had allowed to fall and that the Wagnerian camp had since trampled on. "Who knows," he asked, "but that another and younger people may yet rejuvenate the life of music? As patriotic and art-loving Americans, [. . .] let us hope that this will be the mission of our own land. May it lift the veil that now shrouds the future of this beautiful art."[26] Paine did not reveal which Americans he had in mind.

THE STALWART REGROUPS

Bristow had no reason to believe that he himself might not fill the role. The premiere of his latest symphony in Brooklyn had garnered international attention, and Bergmann had agreed to perform it again in New York in 1874—a decision that afforded Bristow yet another opportunity to shine. Like their Brooklyn counterparts, New York critics focused on the work's dialectic of form and content, an issue of increasing interest after programmatic symphonies such as Raff's *Im Walde* and *Lenore* had entered more fully into the public consciousness over the preceding year. The general consensus was that Bristow had successfully navigated treacherous compositional waters.

Agreeing with Bristow's commentary in the program, the *Times* believed that the composer had confined himself to "a description of incidents which can be illustrated, not infelicitously, by the means at the disposal of a composer." Not finding its programmaticism problematic in the least, the writer dubbed the work a "tone-picture of decided merit."[27] Departing from critics' earlier qualms about the overt borrowing in the second movement, a writer for *Appletons'*, a monthly magazine, called it "especially striking."[28] The *Herald's* notoriously finicky Myron Cooney also approved, claiming that the symphony reflected "the highest credit on the renowned composer and on the society for presenting before the metropolitan public a musical picture of Western life"—and therefore it had earned a place alongside David's *Le désert* as a descriptive piece of exceptionally high value.[29] And though he was more skeptical of the work's programmatic elements than the others, John Hassard wrote a Romantic apologia in the *Tribune*:

> It is something very different from [program music]—conceived in a higher spirit, and executed with a true musician's appreciation of the beautiful and

poetic. Mr. Bristow has not attempted to be picturesque, but has produced a work which is eminently sentimental—using that word in its best and most honorable sense.[30]

Bristow, Hassard thought, had transcended the division between old and new. His style *was* the future of music.

But Henry Cood Watson, the powerful doyen of New York critics, was the most enthusiastic of all. Generally supportive of Bristow's later career, he claimed that the *Arcadian* was "the finest of all his compositions." Bristow had "written a work which ranks with the best of modern symphonies, and will surely hold its place in the concert-room." After describing certain specific characteristics in the piece, Watson continued to gush about its potential position in the burgeoning canon of masterworks: "It evinces a degree of genius which, if not of the first creative order, is in so far excellent that it can claim to occupy a niche among the classics of symphonic writing. It places him in a position far beyond any orchestral writer in this country, and on a level with those modern writers of Germany whose works are forced upon the public here by their talented German confreres."[31] He could only have been referring to Raff.

Evidently offended by Watson's suggestion and marring what was otherwise a banner moment for Bristow, the *New-Yorker Staats-Zeitung*, the city's leading German-language newspaper, panned the work with overwhelming national chauvinism:

> There is little to say about Bristow's symphony, because the work, written by a competent, trained musician who understands his craft and handles his art as such, deserves virtually any title, just not that of "symphony." One searches in vain for new and original ideas in this so-called "Arcadian Symphony," a work that would be more properly called a very American "tone painting." Bristow's ideas are all old acquaintances. His motives demand thinking out—that is, one ponders whence the American composer has taken (or, in good German, stolen) each of them.

Accusations of imitation had been an old standby for Bristow's critics, but rarely accusations of outright plagiarism. The reviewer closed the piece with a condescending and blasé dismissal: "In the name of art lovers and friends of art, we must give polite thanks for the concessions to its native American members that the Society finds it necessary to make through the performance of such works."[32] Superseding the plainness of Watson's jab at the German community, memories of Bristow's anti-German tirades of the 1850s had bubbled their way into this review.

Hatchet work aside, perhaps the most important criticism of the symphony appeared in London's *Musical Standard*, which Dwight reprinted in his journal (a reversal of the previous year's transatlantic exchange). While skeptical of the work's programmatic elements, the magazine's New York correspondent affirmed Watson's position and closed the review by saying that Bristow's "countrymen may well point to him as a proof that they possess a man quite able to hold his own against many greatly inferior composers, who, mainly owing to their Teutonic origin, are lauded to the skies—especially in New York."[33] With comments like these reaching London readers, Bristow's international reputation should have been sealed.

The reviews following the symphony's New York premiere contained exceptionally high praise, especially considering that Bristow had made no attempt to hide the work's national pictorial narrative. New York critics wanted to like it—and did—despite what might have been a major stumbling block given the Brooklyn response. Unlike their Brooklyn counterparts, they believed Bristow had pushed beyond mere "claptrap," or dazzling effects. Their tacit neglect of the work's overtly national program affirmed that they were neither seeking nor hearing a national identity that required a distinctly American soundscape. They considered the American-themed narrative a transparent layer over the music itself, which in turn was meant to amplify the listener's feelings and imagination. They had heard Raff's music in the same way, but of course he was not an American. Bristow found as much success as could be afforded to any new symphonist in the early 1870s, in the United States or abroad. But it would not last.

OLDER CRITICS POUNCE

While Bristow was enjoying this newfound success, a result of his clever compositional maneuvering, John Sullivan Dwight and another well-regarded critic, Shakespeare scholar Richard Grant White, mounted an aggressive assault on Wagnerism at the close of the 1874 concert season. Dwight wrote in May that he appreciated the abundant opportunities to hear fresh music (thanks to Theodore Thomas), but he questioned the "propriety" of stuffing programs with newer works. "Is there no need," he asked, "of something else to keep the taste for music from running after every fashion, with no ever-present, sure corrective, no ideal, pure authoritative models of important Art to turn to?" Ratcheting up the moral force of his position, he added that "our dear old masters are ill mated in such company; they seem to shiver and grow dull in the unwonted and ungenial sphere; if they could speak, would they not each and all say, like one of our statesmen, 'take me out of that crow,' if you love me?"[34] New works tainted the old, he thought.

Beginning in June, White published a series of essays on Wagner's theories in a New York magazine called *The Galaxy* while Dwight offered ongoing commentary in intervening issues of his own journal. White's fundamental thesis was that any unification of the arts (Wagner's position) diminished the value of each one individually. "If music is to be the medium of expression," he claimed, "it should be music only. Whatever is added, either of other arts or imitation of real life, by so much does the result sink in the scale of art."[35] Concurring with this aesthetic position, Dwight added that separation of the arts was important since spiritual growth as a listener followed a path toward appreciation of instrumental music:

> Most persons, we incline to think, arrive at the love and taste for pure, or instrumental music, as the final stage. [. . .] First one cares chiefly for the singer; only later does he begin to care more for the music. [. . .] and finally it ends with finding the ne plus ultra, the very crowning glory, the very music of the music in a Beethoven Symphony. [. . .] And this is one of those revolutions which do not go backward.[36]

In Dwight's mind, Wagner was a figure to fear, a usurper of individual and collective progress. Drawing on Dwight's momentum, White directed his later essays toward the moral dimensions of Wagnerian and Lisztian theories. Using instrumental music to depict external objects or actions would be "worse than savage or childish," he spat, and as far as Liszt's orchestral works were concerned, "It would have been so much easier, as well as more humane, to let it alone."[37]

White continued to explore instrumental music in a later essay aptly titled "Absolute Music." His impetus for writing on this subject stemmed from his bewilderment at critics who would respond to a piece of music as "absolute music" on the one hand and, on the other, as "the intention of the composer, as set forth in a printed programme that was furnished to the audience." Critics had taken this very approach with Bristow's *Arcadian*. The distinction was false, he claimed, for the music existed independently of any intentions the composer had for it. (But critics were only doing their jobs by assessing the music on its own terms.) With harsh vitriol and Lisztian prolixity, White pulled out all of his rhetorical stops while attacking composers of program music:

> It seems to me that absolute music is the only music—at least the only music worthy of high consideration—and that when we are asked to accept as music a succession of sounds or a combination of tones that has little or no charm in itself, and no value until we are told, with introductory remarks, and essays, and notes, and comments, what the composer meant us to understand by it, we are abrogating from music the chief and the highest function of art, which is not relation or even illustration, but expression; expression, moreover, chiefly of beauty—beauty which takes its character from emotion, but which weeds

out and casts aside even from emotion all that cannot be made to minister to itself. It seems to me also that the composers in whose works we are called upon to admire chiefly the skilful adaptation of the sounds of certain courses of events, certain persons, and certain prescribed themes, are those who fail, under any inspiration or in any situation, to evolve from the depth of their moral consciousness anything which recompenses us for the absence of those melodies and harmonies the strong, clear, well-defined forms of whose intrinsic beauty constitute the chief charm of those great composers who delight us, we know not exactly how, by something that they uttered, they themselves knew hardly why.[38]

Although he was directing his furor at Liszt, composers such as Raff and Rubinstein—and now Bristow—were implicated. "Absolute music is simply—music," he concluded, "and music not absolute is absolutely not music." The critics and audiences who loved Bristow's music obviously disagreed.

THE CLASSICIST PARRIES

Whether he agreed or not, John Knowles Paine was paying attention. Over the next several months, he aligned himself with Dwight and White as he completed his First Symphony. The work premiered in 1876, nearly two years after Bristow's *Arcadian* had created such a splash in New York. The symphony is clearly indebted to Beethoven's Fifth, from its C-minor key to the characteristic short-short-short-long motive found in the first movement (example 9.4). Its four movements are likewise in the sequential arrangement of Beethoven's Eighth and Ninth, which reverse the conventional order of the inner two. The outer movements are in the traditional sonata form, and their scale is quite large, both in terms of the harmonic palette (third relations abound) and the sheer length of the developmental passages.

Although there was mild public furor that a local Boston ensemble did not premiere the work, Paine was fortunate that Theodore Thomas had agreed to perform it three times in rapid succession—first in Boston in late January, then in New York City, and again in Boston, all over a period of four weeks.[39] The critical response to this initial round of performances was overwhelmingly positive and nothing like the mockery, controversy, and condescension that Fry and Bristow had both endured when their first symphonies premiered in the 1850s.

Unlike Bristow's evocative *Arcadian*, Paine's symphony is self-consciously ordinary and inoffensive.[40] For the majority of the work's critics, this conservatism was its greatest strength. Most critics praised the work's supposedly

Example 9.4: Beethovenian Motivic Reminiscence. Paine, Symphony No. 1, I: Allegro con brio, mm. 105–118 (full orch.).

"masculine" qualities, an echo of typical responses to Beethoven. Their agreement was astounding:

> It is fresh, vigorous and self-consistent, and full of healthful life. (George Osgood, *Dwight's*)

> [It] is so full of strength, of vigor and refinement; it shows such a mastery of the resources of harmony and orchestral effect; it is so full of thought, brilliancy and solid worth, that it merits the highest praise as a harbinger of noble promise in its composer. (*Saturday Evening Gazette*)

> Clearness of thought, elegance of arrangement, and vigor of expression are conspicuous from the outset. (Hassard, *New York Tribune*)

> It is melodious, natural, spirited, with that strength that comes from perfect equilibrium. (Apthorp, *Atlantic Monthly*)

> In nearly the whole of every movement it was vigorously and aggressively interesting. [. . .] [The final Allegro] is always spirited, and it ends with much vigor and fire. (*Boston Daily Advertiser*)[41]

Though lacking any gendered commentary, a writer for the *Boston Post* agreed with the general sentiment shared by these authors: "It shows not only study, but, what is better, genius, or at least a fresh and glowing talent. If the smoke of the lamp is on the pages of the score, the light is there as well."[42]

Unable to resist the common urge to find sources of imitation (an itch that Bristow's critics had never failed to scratch), the *Daily Advertiser* called out passages in the finale for being "palpable reminiscences of phrases in the seventh and eighth symphonies of Beethoven." But, to Paine's credit, they were "of course unconscious."[43] Most critics enjoyed the third movement, the adagio, best of all (example 9.5). Osgood remarked that the more he became acquainted with it, "so much the more warmly does it glow with the *sacré feu* of genius," while Hassard gushed that "if Mr. Paine had written nothing else, this alone would stamp him a master of the orchestra." The responses included further commentary on Paine's "beautiful" and "pregnant" themes, but not one critic noted the obvious motivic debt to Beethoven in the first movement. Thomas's scheduling had created a ring of success that crossed state lines.

Paine's critics were preparing the way for him to become Beethoven's symphonic heir, as they had reached a remarkable consensus that the New Englander had followed squarely in the footsteps of Beethoven, Mendelssohn, and Schumann while avoiding the nefarious influence of Wagner and his ilk. Osgood noted that the work's unity soothes "the lover of legitimate musical effect in contradistinction to the feverish excitement which much of our modern music produces." Dwight, whose review was especially circumspect, remarked that "the arts of counterpoint and thematic treatment" were masterfully displayed—indicating connections to both Bach

Example 9.5: Warm Counterpoint. Paine, Symphony No. 1, III: Adagio, mm. 83–90 (strings).

and Beethoven—and that "the work is free from modern extravaganza and mere straining for effect."[44] Paine's orbit of friends and amicable acquaintances, especially in New England, was large by 1876. It is impossible to know how many critics were among them, but the *Daily Advertiser* added that the audience's "manifestations of delight" at the premiere "were so spontaneous and hearty as to prove the feeling to be no mere outgrowth of friendly prejudice." Even so, Dwight would not concede that the work was a true success: "Whether it be a work of *genius*, is a question always better left to time."

The key terms used to describe what Paine's music did *not* sound like—excitement, extravaganza, and modern effects—were euphemisms for stylistic features reminiscent of the new school and programmaticism.

Reviewing Rubinstein's *Dramatic* Symphony, which Thomas had directed in Boston just days before the premiere of Paine's First, Dwight had commented,

> The Third Symphony Concert of Theodore Thomas was chiefly remarkable for an exceedingly long (a whole hour) and an exceedingly fantastical, extravagant, spasmodic, incoherent and chaotic symphony (so at least we found it on a single hearing), called "Dramatic," by Rubinstein. There was beauty and continuity of melody in the first half of the *Adagio*, but the rest seemed like the improvisation of a mad orchestra in Bedlam; brilliant and dazzling *effects* in detail, wonderful difficulties splendidly executed, but tending nowhere, leaving nothing in mind; and yet we doubt not it is all grammatically written and in the highest degree ingenious,—but to what end? Why should it be called dramatic we could not see. Traverses the whole range of human passions and emotions? Heaven save us from some of these passions, these emotions, if there can be any like them![45]

The "vigor," beauty, grace, restraint, and learnedness of Paine's work could not have contrasted more sharply. By 1876, listeners were well aware that European composers of Paine's generation, including Rubinstein and Raff, had begun to make strong claims over the future of the symphony as a genre. Brahms had not yet completed a symphony of his own, and Bristow's name, surprisingly, did not appear anywhere, even in the New York papers.

It was a critic from New York, however, and therefore someone unlikely to be in Paine's immediate circle, who made one of the strongest claims in the Bostonian's favor. Readers learned that "there are no modern 'effects' in it, and it may not suit ears accustomed to the accumulating richness of Schumann's or Beethoven's adagios, but for what it assumes to be it is beyond criticism." Reflecting on the future, the writer added, "He has written an American symphony that will probably bear the test of the severest criticism by adherents of the old school, a symphony that will live as a beautiful work of art, simple and unaffected. If it is not strikingly original, the author is assuredly no plagiarist; if it does not astonish, it will never fail to please."[46] By calling the work "American," this critic echoed a subdued patriotic sentiment found across all the reviews, but the suggestion that it would live on was an assertion of its transcendence—Paine's precise goal.

Like any good premiere, however, Paine's symphony did not escape controversy. Predictably, questions about Wagner's influence stood at the center. The *Sunday Evening Gazette* remarked that the adagio "flows calmly and sweetly after the manner of those continuous melodies with which Wagner has made us so familiar, and it has much of the rich sensuousness that marks that composer in his placid moods."[47] Despite the apparent innocuousness of these remarks, which readers might have interpreted as praise, the accusation that Paine had made use of the suspicious technique of "end-less melody" was also potentially damning. In the minds of many, including Paine himself, it was the essence of Wagner's profane ideology. Paine's supporters felt that his compositional integrity had been impugned and responded by reasserting his position within the conservative lineage of Beethoven and Mendelssohn.

Writing for the *Nation*, John Fiske appealed directly to technique. Paine had maintained a sense of originality despite adopting Beethoven's symphonic molds, he argued, including sonata form. The composer had also skillfully circumvented all of the problems associated with Beethoven's potential "heirs" by writing a work that manifested Beethoven's spirit while speaking with an original compositional voice. The "extravagances" of "modern" music, by contrast, were the direct result of slipshod contrapuntal technique and a lack of conventional thematic treatment masked by overly dramatic modulations and "sensuous" instrumentation. Paine's symphony, he concluded, was a "protest against the inferences which might be too hastily drawn from the recent prevalence of compositions in the various styles of Raff, Rubinstein, and Liszt," as well as an implicit rejection of "the methods of composition of which Wagner is the great representative."[48]

Further defenses, one by William F. Apthorp and a second by Fiske, appeared later in the season in two successive issues of the *Atlantic Monthly*.[49] Apthorp argued that Paine's symphony, unlike bombastic and superficial works such as Rubinstein's, resisted verbal description and displayed motivic elaboration to great effect. For as a work of "absolute music, developing itself from a thematic germ," the symphony was "a fair epitome of all organic and cosmic development in the physical world." [50] Fiske took the discussion in a more pointedly nationalist direction. The premiere had been the most important event of the season, he contended, because Americans had never before listened "to a noble composition, classic in dimensions as well as in form, in the highest department of instrumental music [the symphony]."[51]

Following a lengthy technical description of the piece, Fiske concluded his second commentary by affirming the work's lineage, and therefore the vision of an American musical future that Paine had outlined in his writings. Fiske's argument followed Paine's lectures to the letter. Bach's transcendent counterpoint served as a foundation upon which composers should construct the future of instrumental music. Beethoven had provided ideal symphonic molds for his successors to fill. Mendelssohn and Schumann, though noteworthy in their own right, had failed to achieve true greatness as symphonists. Only an American was able to lift the veil shrouding the German symphony. As far as Fiske was concerned, Paine was that American.[52]

But for all of his anti-Wagnerian rhetoric, Fiske noted that despite Paine's "close adherence to classical form, [he] has drawn upon modern sensuous resources of instrumentation to no less an extent than Wagner."[53] Wagner, it seemed, could be both good and bad. The ideological battle over a progressive compositional style and its potential moral effects on listeners would intensify with an internecine conflict among Wagner's supporters in the years following the premieres of Bristow's *Arcadian* and Paine's Beethovenian First. And the place of American composers would again stand at the center.

CHAPTER 10

༒

Ellsworth Phelps, Brooklyn Patriot

Richard Wagner's two most tireless promoters during the 1870s were Carl Bergmann, long-time director of the philharmonics in Brooklyn and New York, and Theodore Thomas, director of his own entrepreneurial touring ensemble and Bergmann's eventual successor (in 1873 and 1876, respectively). In addition to German *Zukunftsmusik* ("Music of the Future"), Bergmann actively supported local composers. He had premiered two of Bristow's symphonies in New York following the Philharmonic fracas of the 1850s (see chapter 5) and continued to program works by Bristow and Frédéric Louis Ritter (the Vassar professor and music historian) in Brooklyn. His support appealed to listeners. Reporting on the first Brooklyn Philharmonic concert of the 1870–1871 season, the *Daily Eagle* applauded Bergmann for his "catholic liberality which includes Beethoven and Wagner, Mendelssohn and Liszt, Weber and Berlioz." More important, the *Eagle* believed him "free from the narrow national prejudices which prevent many of his countrymen from discovering any good musical thing outside of Germany—and especially in America."[1] Bergmann (figure 10.1) died in 1876, the year Theodore Thomas (figure 10.2) premiered Paine's First Symphony. Opportunities for the continued success of local composers died with him.

Thomas far outlived Bergmann and Bristow. But while Bergmann was still active, the two engaged in a friendly rivalry over who would premiere new works. Each conductor tried to get his hands on manuscripts as quickly as possible. And whereas Bergmann was applauded for his support of American composers, Thomas's relationship with them remained the subject of debate throughout the period. As the New York Philharmonic was preparing for the second performance of Bristow's *Arcadian* Symphony in 1874, for example,

Figure 10.1: Carl Bergmann. Courtesy of the New York Philharmonic Leon Levy Digital Archives, New York, NY.

one interested listener, calling himself "Medoc," reported to the *Daily Eagle* on a conversation with Bristow on this very topic:

"What are you doing for native worth (meaning native composers) over in the City of Churches this season?" inquired the genial, jovial and talented Bristow.

Now, to me that question was a "poser" and "George" knew it, and to add to my confusion continued to "maul in" his wedge by saying, "I understand that the Brooklyn Society, so noted in former years for its encouragement extended to American composers, this season entirely ignores the claims of all except the well known and so called old masters, while the New York Society is anxious to bring out the work (if meritorious) of any new composer, no matter what his nationality may be. Why, would you believe it, even my poor work (though my pet) the 'Arcadian' symphony, is in rehearsal. The Brooklyn Society paid me for the privilege of performing the 'Arcadian' for all of which I heartily thank

Figure 10.2: Theodore Thomas, ca. 1876. Courtesy of the American Antiquarian Society, Worcester, MA.

it—but this season things are different—queerly different somehow—why is 'this thus,' my Medoc?"[2]

Why *were* things thus? What they were not saying is that Theodore Thomas had squelched local music. Bristow and Paine were already engaged in a brewing ideological and aesthetic conflict about musical style and the future of symphonic music in the United States, but this conversation accentuated the fact that they also depended heavily on institutions and individuals who could support or hinder their careers.

Without Bergmann's help, another aspiring symphonist from Brooklyn, Ellsworth C. Phelps, was left to founder while Paine continued to thrive with the aid of Thomas and his orchestra. Despite having written hundreds of works, including two major symphonies, the enigmatic Phelps (1827–1913) remains entirely outside of our collective consciousness today, even among musicologists. As with Bristow's *Arcadian*, and unlike Paine's, Phelps's symphonies bore distinctly American-oriented titles and subject matter: *Hiawatha* (1878) and *Emancipation* (1880). Not buying the universalist rhetoric of White, Dwight, and Paine, Phelps's critics showed no ambivalence toward the "Americanisms" found in these works and hailed them as truly American. They even noted his ability to capture the essence of Native American and African American song within the larger fabric of a classical composition—well before prominent figures like Antonín Dvořák and critic Henry Krehbiel articulated the same idea.

Phelps (figure 10.3) hailed from Rockfall, Connecticut, and moved to Springfield, Massachusetts, as a young boy. His tradesman father discouraged him from becoming a professional musician, but his curiosity got the best of him. As the story goes, he taught himself how to play instruments and to compose, all by lantern light, while guarding a music shop at night.[3] He moved to Brooklyn in 1857, three years after the Fry controversy and the very year that Bergmann organized the city's Philharmonic. The group's concerts inspired Phelps to compose orchestral music. Bergmann, who had already facilitated Bristow's career in New York, occasionally programmed Phelps's early works during his tenure. Also like Bristow, Phelps had a multifaceted career extending beyond composition. He was a church organist and private tutor and eventually became a forty-year veteran music teacher in the public school system. And like Jerome Hopkins, he was actively involved in the promotion of concerts devoted to U.S. composers, a pursuit he continued into his twilight years.[4] After falling into obscurity, he died peacefully in his stepdaughter's home in 1913, over three decades after the successful premieres of his symphonies, which writers recalled in press obituaries.[5]

THE PATRIOT SNUBBED

The success of Bristow's *Arcadian* in Brooklyn inspired Phelps to try his hand at a new symphony on the related subject of Longfellow's *Song of Hiawatha*, the first since Robert Stoepel's effort of 1859. An anonymous acquaintance of Phelps gave the *Daily Eagle* the public's first glimpse of the piece. It would contain five movements, each inspired by particular sections of the poem. Exhibiting typical anxieties over style, the confidant explained its relationship to contemporary trends:

> The composer evidently believes in subordinating the resources of the orchestra to the demands of the poem, a contrary procedure with most of the New School composers. [. . .] Although Mr. Phelps has been charged with Wagnerism

Figure 10.3: Ellsworth Phelps. Image reproduced from Ross and Pelletreau, *History of Long Island*, 177.

in some of his previous efforts, we do not believe any such tendencies will be discovered in the present work. It reminds us of Beethoven and Mendelssohn, which is the highest praise that can be given to any composer.[6]

With these remarks in mind, the public was set up for a work in the vein of the *Arcadian*—an evocative symphony, but not necessarily programmatic.

No amount of caution could have prepared the public for what happened next. The Brooklyn Philharmonic announced the work as part of its 1873–1874 concert season, but the symphony never saw the light of day.[7] By late winter it had become clear that the orchestra was not going to rehearse or perform the piece. Invested members of the public expressed their dissatisfaction to the press. One commentator, "Whole Note," wondered what had happened to the new symphony and hoped that the Philharmonic might play at least one American work before season's end—perhaps Bristow's overture on Christopher Columbus or Phelps's *Winter Melody* (1867).[8] Another, signed "M. H. H.," took a firmer stance:

> If we have an original and talented composer living among us in Brooklyn, his merits ought to be recognized now, and not a hundred years hence, for glory, and precious little of that, is all the compensation composers of orchestral music have ever received. It cost Bristow two hundred dollars for private rehearsal of his "Arcadian" Symphony, and he received only half that sum for the privilege of producing it, by the Philharmonic Society. Mr. Phelps has written a good work, and it would gratify him as well as his numerous friends, to hear it performed by Thomas's orchestra, and if it is not played they would like to know why.[9]

This commentary echoed the tussle over Stoepel's *Hiawatha*: If talent is there, let it be heard and recognized. Fifteen years later, even the public had begun to make this case on behalf of American composers.

But the reason for the cancellation was clear enough to all. Theodore Thomas, Bergmann's recent successor, did not want to perform American works. Phelps was displeased. By late fall, he had already planned a concert series featuring only American works.[10] And he eventually took his grievance directly to the press. In a letter to the *Eagle*, written just two weeks before Thomas premiered Paine's First Symphony in Boston, Phelps pointed out that Carl Bergmann was the engine driving the success of American composers in Brooklyn. Recalling an incident surrounding one of his earlier works, he explained, "There were some protests from the orchestra and the audience. But Mr. Bergmann put his foot down and the work was produced with considerable success." Thomas was a different character altogether:

> There was for a time a hope that the Brooklyn Philharmonic Society would distinguish itself as the exceptional friend of American composers, but since Mr. Thomas has taken the baton nothing has been done in that direction. "The idol of the hour" is monarch of all he surveys, and carries the B. P. S. in his vest pocket. There was an effort made last season to have him produce my new symphony, "Hiawatha," but he did not find it at all in his way. It is easy to say that there are no American compositions worthy [of] his august attention. Let the public decide the matter. Mr. Thomas is the servant, not the master, of the musical interests of the country.[11]

One observer claimed that Thomas's excuse was simply that he was "too busy" to study the score and that the Philharmonic programs had "already been arranged."[12] Phelps did not see the situation from this perspective. He believed the public had a right to hear new music without the interference of untrustworthy gatekeepers.

THE CLASH OF CLASSICISTS

Paine had no trouble with gatekeepers. Thomas had always supported him. Following the premiere of his First Symphony in 1876 and possibly sensing the value of updating his public persona, he began to navigate the potentially treacherous waters of Wagnerism in the later 1870s. Critics had applauded the symphony as a masterful continuation of the classical Germanic tradition, but several had also remarked favorably on the work's Wagnerian elements, including lush orchestration and traces of endless melody. While Paine had consciously avoided Wagnerism, the idea of a stylistic mixture sat comfortably within the general conception of history he had outlined in his review of Wagner's writings.

Paine had argued that Wagner represented an antithesis to Beethoven and that his ideas needed to be reconciled according to "laws of growth." The era inaugurated by Wagner would be perfected by a healthy and natural reaction to its extremes, he claimed, while "all that is truthful in Wagner's principles of art, and all that is worthy of imitation in his operas, will not be thrown away."[13] In this model of history, which vaguely echoed Fry's translational approach, composers would be able to synthesize old and new in a stylistic dialectic that moved naturally toward authentic progress. It was the path that Bristow and Phelps (and Raff) were already following.

Paine attempted to join them in two Shakespeare-inspired works written shortly after the premiere of his symphony: a concert overture to *As You Like It* and a "symphonic fantasy" on *The Tempest*. The fantasy became the source of still another debate about modern tendencies and influence. Dwight claimed that the work, which comprises four *attaca* movements and contains leitmotifs representing specific characters, had the form "of the modern *Symphonische Dichtung* [symphonic poem]" (if it had one at all).[14] John Fiske, Paine's reliable advocate in the press, reacted strongly to Dwight's criticism and attempted to interpret the work by enfolding its progressive qualities within a more conservative lineage. The piece's freedom lived within its fluid formal arrangement, he argued, not in the haphazard use of themes evident in the music of Liszt and Wagner (the very criticism that Paine had also leveled at those composers).[15] Probably not wishing to smear his protégé, Dwight later retreated from his original critique and pointed out that his chief concern was not the work's form after all, but "the warning that we were to be looking out for Ariel, for Caliban, for Prospero, for Miranda and Ferdinand"—a typical dig at musical pictorialism.[16] All involved in the debate would soon realize, however, that Paine's championing of the German tradition would soon be challenged by a figure who had played no role in American musical discourse up to that time: Johannes Brahms.

Brahms's First Symphony premiered in Karlsruhe in November of 1876, nearly a year after the premiere of Paine's. Responses ranged widely, but as far as Americans knew, it was not a success. Dwight had reprinted a report from the *London Times* that claimed, "The Symphony in C minor [. . .] seems to us to make a great deal of too much out of too little." In the same issue in which Fiske had defended Paine's *Tempest*, however, Dwight gave notice of the American premiere of the symphony by appending a positive review from Vienna along with negative remarks from Leipzig. With the conflicting European perspectives in mind, American audiences were ready for a stimulating event, even if they did not know exactly what to expect.[17]

Filling the role of Thomas's rival after Bergmann's death, conductor Leopold Damrosch (1832–1885) scooped Thomas by rushing to premiere Brahms's symphony during the 1877–1878 concert season. The results were grim. A critic for the *New York World* gave a tempered assessment by noting that it was better than Raff—and "nearer to genius than anything we have had since Schumann"—but was marred by too many reminiscences of older composers.[18] Americans like Bristow had certainly heard their fair share of this criticism. Composer Jerome Hopkins, ever the crank, dropped a bombshell of his own that had nothing to do with lack of originality:

> But the whole work convinces us that Brahms has still less invention than Liszt. If one man crack a walnut with one hammer, it is hardly to be taken as evidence of genius for him to crack ten walnuts with ten hammers. To crack ten with *one* hammer would be something of an advance; but truly, many of our new composers resemble a man who should try to crack *one* walnut with *ten* hammers, and should yet fail to do it. Ears are not as tough as walnuts however—the more's the pity—and are easier cracked, at least *ours* are.[19]

From Hopkins's perspective, the music was simply terrible whether it was original or not.

Things would only get worse for Brahms. Following the symphony's Boston premiere, critic William F. Apthorp wrote that it "sounds for the most part morbid, strained and unnatural; much of it even ugly." A writer for the *Evening Gazette* was even more disgusted: "This noisy, ungraceful, confusing, and unattractive example of dry pedantry before the masterpieces of Schubert, Schumann, Mendelssohn, Gade—or even of the reckless and overfluent Raff! Absurd! In all that Brahms has written he has shown himself to be a composer without a heart."[20] Dwight, perhaps the most likely of all listeners to appreciate it, was left cold. Even after a second hearing, he claimed that "it was still depressing, over-labored, unspontaneous, with more of will than genius in it, more of enterprise and calculation than of the creative spark" and noted with satisfaction that Thomas had decided to drop the work from his future programs.[21] And although they had the perfect opportunity, none of these critics mentioned the name of John Knowles Paine, or George Frederick Bristow for that matter. In the shadow of a German, they had ceased to matter.

THE PATRIOT REGROUPS

But the Brahms debacle did not prevent interest in Ellsworth Phelps's *Hiawatha* Symphony from rekindling that same season, when the *Eagle* announced that Thomas's orchestra (not the Philharmonic, but his own players) would premiere it at the opening of Brooklyn's newly constructed Music Hall. The prospect of a performance once again energized the public while press accounts lauded the enterprise. Speaking about the work itself, one commentator reminded readers that, "while following the original line of the old school rules of symphonic composition, the composer has not feared to tread in the path of the more advanced school of the art." Local critics were still concerned with the work's place on a fabricated stylistic spectrum between classicism and Wagnerism. In this case, the writer held it up as an example of the "rising school of American composition" as well. The subject matter was most appropriate, readers learned, for "no musician of any imaginative power would read [Longfellow's poem] and not be inspired to give musical expression to the thoughts the story suggests."[22]

Departing from Robert Stoepel's lengthy and literal setting of 1859, Phelps chose to illustrate only five key moments of Longfellow's epic. Structured loosely on the poem's opening number, the introductory adagio depicts the Great Spirit summoning the tribes, while the allegro proper illustrates the flurry of activity as the tribal leaders convene. The adagio returns mid-movement as the Great Spirit, represented by a solo bass trombone, implores the leaders to "be at peace henceforward" (example 10.1). Here Phelps's setting was reminiscent of Stoepel's own Great Spirit, whom he had represented with a baritone vocalist accompanied by low brass. Following this interlude, the allegro resumes as the tribal leaders drop their weapons and cleanse themselves of war paint.

Phelps selected musical scenes in the poem for depiction in the inner movements. The second, a lullaby sung by Hiawatha's forlorn grandmother Nokomis, comprises two plaintive melodies accompanied by rolling arpeggio figures in the low strings. Reflecting the old woman's grief-stricken state following the death of her daughter, the movement exhibits a fluidity of tempo and expression more commonly reserved for opera (example 10.2). The third and fourth movements depict scenes from Hiawatha's wedding: the frenetic

Example 10.1: The Voice of the Great Spirit. Phelps, *Hiawatha*, I: "The Peace Pipe" (Adagio), mm. 302–318 (solo bass trombone accompanied by full orch.).

dance of Pau-Puk-Keewis and the "songs of longing" performed by Hiawatha's musical friend Chibiabos. Mirroring the poem, the dance becomes increasingly furious as it culminates in a coda marked "Prestissimo accelerando." Occasional exoticisms such as open fifths and trills add color (example 10.3). The fourth movement returns to the lyricism of the second with a series of lushly orchestrated tunes featuring harp accompaniment and adventurous harmonies (example 10.4).

Example 10.2: "Song of Nokomis." Phelps, *Hiawatha*, II: Andantino, mm. 3–10 (full orch.).

As one commentator put it, the finale "is more complex" because it depicts three separate scenes from the poem's final canto.[23] The first, a playful tune in the first violins, reportedly illustrates Hiawatha waiting in the doorway of his wigwam on a pleasant summer morning: "All the air was full of fresh-ness/All the earth was bright and joyous." The mood eventually gives way

Example 10.3: Slithering Movements. Phelps, *Hiawatha*, III: Dance of Pau Puk Keewis (Allegro vivace), mm. 105–113 (full orch.).

to a moment of somberness as a solo French horn embodies the voice of the Christian missionary (the "Black-robe Chief, the Pale Face"), who visits Hiawatha and proselytizes in the village. Upon the missionary's departure, the earlier music returns in several transmutations but eventually gives way to a sweeping melody that belies the quick tempo (example 10.5). As Hiawatha disappears into the "Great Hereafter," a solitary chord sustained by the bassoons, clarinets, horns, and cellos fades to nothingness.

The work was a major success, much like Stoepel's *Hiawatha* had been two decades earlier. Throughout the series of public rehearsals, the critic for the *Eagle* commented repeatedly on the ways in which the music manifested the "spirit of the poem," all while avoiding "realistic effects" (code for Wagnerism).[24] After the official concert, the critic was ecstatic in a lengthy commentary on the work. Every element—the conception of the poem and the treatment of its theme, the grace of the melodies, the "harmony of the groundwork," and the "pictorial force of the composer's fancy embodied in sound"—was worth a remark. Responding to a naysayer in the audience who had claimed that Wagner

Example 10.4: Wedding Song. Phelps, *Hiawatha*, IV: Song of Chibiabos (Andante con moto), mm. 7–17 (oboe solo and harp).

Example 10.5: Soaring Melody. Phelps, *Hiawatha*, V: Hiawatha's Farewell (Allegro molto), mm. 418–432 (full orch.).

would have done better, the critic went on to praise Phelps's distinctly American spirit:

> That a German composer, foreign to the soil and atmosphere of an American theme, would have introduced a crash of drums and cymbals and brasses to express his idea of the situation, which an American presented with cellos and reeds, is, of course, to assume, and therefore, according to Wagnerian logic, to prove, that the American was commonplace. But Mr. Phelps may rest satisfied, we think, whatever may be the German, Hindoo, or even Chinese judgment of his last movement, that to American ears it was music of the sweetest, most picturesque and affecting character.[25]

The musicians of Thomas's own orchestra reportedly applauded Phelps again and again during the series of public presentations—an honor they did not always confer. "At its close but one opinion, we venture to say, prevailed in the house, namely that Mr. Phelps has written a classic worthy to rank after Beethoven."

Beyond the overwhelmingly positive response to the music, one curious element of the concert lingered with listeners: Phelps himself, rather than Thomas, directed the orchestra. Thomas was not even present. His absence might not have mattered, but at least one commentator complained that Thomas would have conducted a better performance.[26] The complaint resurfaced the following season when the public clamored to hear the *Hiawatha*

Symphony again, this time in the Brooklyn Philharmonic's regular concert season, and *not* at Phelps's own expense. If they had to suffer through Brahms's First, one writer argued, surely Phelps's music would be a welcome improvement.[27]

As the season wore on without word as to why the symphony was not being programmed, accusations over whom to blame were tossed from all sides: Was it Thomas, the Philharmonic's music committee, or even Phelps himself?[28] The Philharmonic finally agreed to perform only two movements under Thomas's baton at its final concert in May, an atypically late date caused by the controversy. Critics were predictably disappointed. The *Eagle* wanted to hear more, while Frederick Schwab at the *Times* called the work "incomprehensible," undoubtedly because of the piecemeal presentation.[29]

No matter. Phelps had already garnered a rock-solid reputation and was hard at work on an even bigger (and supposedly better) project: a megalithic six-movement choral symphony with the subtitle *Emancipation*, a work designed to illustrate the country's triumph over the evils of slavery. This subject would have pleased William Henry Fry and could not have been more politically potent three years after the official conclusion of Reconstruction in the South. Nor could it have been more distinctively American since it drew on the country's own political history. Public enthusiasm and anticipation for the piece were astronomical by the work's premiere on March 2, 1880. Beginning the previous November, both the *Daily Eagle* and the *Daily Union-Argus* of Brooklyn provided a series of descriptive announcements that trumped up the work as a monument of epic proportions guaranteed to enflame patriotic passions and nationalist fervor.

The symphony's six movements depict the struggle to end slavery and comprise two distinct halves. The first three movements represent "the long night of slavery," life on the plantation, and a slave girl's dreams of freedom, respectively. Movements four and five depict the conflict of the Civil War and a funeral march for Abraham Lincoln. The finale is a grand choral setting of "Laus Deo," a triumphant verse by august abolitionist poet John Greenleaf Whittier (1807–1892). Although other symphonies, including Spohr's Fourth and Seventh, carried explicit chronological or "lifecycle" narratives across movements, using the genre to tell an openly political, historical narrative was a rare choice, even among Europeans. Raff's First Symphony (*An das Vaterland*) was the only such work that had premiered within recent memory, but it did not have the performance lifespan of his later works.[30] Even so, Phelps had made a similar political gesture long before the Raff premiere in a memorial overture to the Battle of Gettysburg. But, according to Phelps, the anti-American contingent of the Brooklyn Philharmonic—this time *before* Bergmann had taken the helm—did not allow the work to be performed.[31]

The *Emancipation* Symphony would be Phelps's chef d'oeuvre, meant to silence any lingering naysayers. Unfortunately, the full score is now lost. Only a published piano reduction of the third movement, "Slave Girl's Dream," has survived. Yet press accounts of the work uncovered how evocative it must have been. The most revelatory commentary appeared in the *Eagle* well before the work's premiere. Readers learned that "the profound pathos of all the negro melodies, which haunts one with a sense of suffering long drawn and almost hopeless, characterizes the first and second movements, the latter giving way to an exquisite tone picture of the light and shades of Southern slave life." Although the author did not clarify whether or not Phelps had quoted slave songs directly, the notice went on to argue that quotation was not necessary:

> Our readers who remember how exquisitely Mr. Phelps preserved in his "Hiawatha" symphony the characteristic features of the Indian songs and grotesque dances, how vividly descriptive and yet how utterly free from any attempt at mere reproduction of the elements of nature was the sad farewell of Hiawatha, will abundantly trust him to express in these two movements the dominating sentiment of profound melancholy which finds utterance in the crude yet melting songs of an oppressed people.[32]

The degree to which Phelps incorporated slave music (or what anyone might have believed to be slave music) into the symphony may never be known.

But the third movement offers a clue. The score in fact matches descriptions provided by the press, potentially affirming their reliability. The movement itself consists of a series of episodic tableaux framed on either end by a broad, haunting French horn melody (example 10.6). The tune's

Example 10.6: Haunting French Horn Solo. Phelps, *Emancipation*, III: Slave Girl's Dream (Allegretto con moto), mm. 1–11.

pentatonicism lends it an exotic character that Phelps might have intended to represent the melancholy of music on the plantation. Following the introduction, the melody is rhythmicized with a gospel-like swing and orchestrated (apparently for strings) in a section that recurs as a grounding refrain (example 10.7). The intervening sections contrast dramatically in character. Both in minor keys, they are nervous but have a Chopinesque quality that blends Italianate melodic shapes with subtle chromaticism and rhythmic fluidity (example 10.8). Like Fry, Phelps drew from several familiar musical languages that would have appealed widely.

Critics remarked on the work's projection of a national identity even more passionately than in their responses to Bristow's *Arcadian* or Phelps's own *Hiawatha*. The *Union-Argus* introduced the *Emancipation* by rehashing the well-worn argument that "America's contribution[s] to the domain of music have been meagre [. . .] and thus far as a people we have been compelled to go to philosophical and domestic Germany, sparkling Italy, and sunny France for all our great compositions for orchestra or voice." But, the announcement

Example 10.7: Hymn-like Refrain. Phelps, *Emancipation*, III: Slave Girl's Dream (Allegretto con moto), mm. 12–17.

Example 10.8: Emotionally Intense Contrasting Section. Phelps, *Emancipation*, III: Slave Girl's Dream (Allegretto), mm. 115–127.

went, "on the 2d of March an event of importance in the history of music will take place at the Academy of Music. It will be the production of a new and DISTINCTIVELY AMERICAN COMPOSITION." The writer claimed that Phelps's *Hiawatha* Symphony had marked the beginning of a new era of American composition (the same was said of Stoepel's *Hiawatha*), but the new work "promises to surpass it in breadth, treatment, and conception." Offering obligatory commentary on the work's style relative its German counterparts, the critic added:

THE FORM OF THE "EMANCIPATION" is such that classicists will possibly dispute the composer's claims for it to the title of symphony [as they had Bristow's]. But Mr. Phelps belongs to the new school, so far as at least asserting the right of the composer to freedom of form is concerned, and therefore he has departed in many respects from the canons of Beethoven and Schumann, upon the theory that form should be subordinate to subject.[33]

Phelps had created the ultimate synthesis: a composition that was both American and globally progressive, and therefore worthy of national attention.

The work *did* receive national attention. Given the preponderance of reviews in the city of a work's premiere, it is easy lose sight of the fact that music periodicals such as Richard Storrs Willis's *Musical World* had large subscription lists that reached across the country. Likely tens of thousands of readers across the United States had digested his debate with Fry. After the Civil War, wire services such as the Associated Press helped distribute news far and wide, and important announcements about local music often traveled overseas. The *Sheffield Daily Telegraph* (U.K.), for example, reported on the completion of Bristow's *Arcadian* in 1872, as did the *Milwaukee Sentinel*. Benefiting from rapid urban growth after the war, Henry Cood Watson's *Art Journal*, easily the largest music periodical in the country, had a readership extending from Central Europe to San Francisco.

In Phelps's case, word of the *Emancipation* Symphony reached at least as far west as Cincinnati (ironically one of Thomas's strongholds) through another news-sharing medium: an out-of-town correspondent. Writing from Brooklyn, a visiting Cincinnatian penned a letter to the *Daily Star* recounting a chance encounter with a morose Phelps, who had just decided to defer the premiere of his symphony for a few more days. The writer, signed "Cras.," went on to introduce readers to Phelps and his goal of giving musical works a "national and distinctively American turn." The rest of the letter reiterated many of the themes found in local press accounts. The *Hiawatha* Symphony had ushered in a new era of American music and would have given Phelps a high reputation in Europe; the *Emancipation* broke free from the bonds of classicism and therefore had "historical as well as art value"; and, finally, that "genius deserves recognition and encouragement, especially where found united to singular modesty."[34] This outlook could not have diverged more sharply from Dwight's, who tended to greet any new music, even Paine's, with grave skepticism. All the while, readers throughout the country were developing the notion that the United States was cultivating new composers of distinction. And they were being led to believe that Phelps was one of them.

The performance of the *Emancipation* Symphony elicited impassioned responses. The *Eagle* affirmed that it had lived up to all of the detailed advance notices, especially given the fact that the applause from the audience grew with every succeeding movement. "It is clearly the most ambitious work attempted by an American composer," the critic added, "a theme, indeed, which might have called forth the genius of Beethoven."[35] The finale had indeed transplanted Beethoven's celebration of universal brotherhood with a religious panegyric celebrating the emancipation of slaves, a distinctly national reinterpretation of the same theme.

As in the case of Paine's First, news of the work's success traveled beyond the confines of Brooklyn. A critic for the *New York Herald* (one of a few New York writers to make the journey across the river) described the symphony as a "musico-politico composition, by turns grotesque, electric, eccentric, melodic, spasmodic, and patriotic. Yet it is likewise original, and in many portions meritorious, inasmuch as in this originality the writer exhibits considerable fertility of resources and dramatic power in his treatment of a novel theme that is productive of very effective results."[36] The writer was disappointed with Phelps's treatment of slave music—it apparently "sounded more Oriental than African"—but thoroughly enjoyed the "Slave Girl's Dream" movement. The *Times-Picayune* of New Orleans, picking up a story from the *St. Louis Republican*, reported that "the first production of the symphony was an unqualified success."[37] In a modest speech given at the work's conclusion, Phelps remarked that he hoped his work "would be of permanent value, and a recognized addition to the rapidly growing musical literature of this country." The *Brooklyn Union-Argus* agreed: "Mr. Phelps has produced a work that will live."[38]

THE CLASSICIST REGROUPS

Nothing of the sort had been said about Brahms's music (at least in the United States), which might have led John Knowles Paine to believe that he, like Bristow and Phelps, might be safer adopting a compositional identity that blended Wagnerism with tradition, rather than retaining his earlier conservative style. Following the controversy in the wake of his symphonic fantasy on *The Tempest*, Paine indeed expanded his experimentation with Wagnerism in his Second Symphony, *Im Frühling* (*In the Springtime*), which premiered just weeks after Phelps's *Emancipation*.

Paine's new symphony followed the same conventional formal outline as his previous work, with the inner movements reversed. The opening introduction is immediately reminiscent of the prelude to Wagner's *Tristan und Isolde* as the strings create a slow-moving contrapuntal fog while repeating a characteristic motive with an ambiguous tonality (example 10.9a). This brief section ends with a fleeting moment of harmonic resolution that is quickly interrupted by a *quasi recitativo* passage for the lower strings—an obvious debt to Beethoven's Ninth (example 10.9b). A third idea, stated in

Example 10.9: Motives and Primary Theme. Paine, Symphony No. 2, *Im Frühling*, I:
(a) "Winter Motive" (Adagio sostenuto), mm. 1–10 (strings).
(b) Instrumental Recitative, mm. 11–15 (strings).
(c) "Awakening Motive," mm. 24–28 (clarinets and cellos).
(d) Rustic Primary Theme (Allegro ma non troppo), mm. 73–82 (full orch.).

the clarinet, moves away from the brooding minor mode in favor of a bright C major (example 10.9c). This section dissolves into passagework for the strings and returns to the previous instrumental recitative. The entire introduction concludes with a truly Wagnerian gesture: a dense stretto presentation of the opening motive that ends without resolution. After sustaining a sole, mysterious tone, the first violins usher in a change of tempo and character as they transform a four-note melodic motive into a rolling accompaniment for the allegro's exuberant primary melody (example 10.9d). The overall effect matches the rustic and joyous sounds of Beethoven's *Pastoral* or Mendelssohn's *Scottish*.

The stylistic fluidity of the slow introduction is a microcosm of the whole symphony, which vacillates between Wagnerism and the symphonic language of middle Beethoven, Mendelssohn, and Schumann. The first movement is patterned in sonata form with key areas related by thirds, while the winter motive (example 10.9a) appears throughout as a leitmotif. The motive supplants the brief "theme" presented in the secondary key area, for example, and becomes a conversation partner with the clarinet figure from the introduction (example 10.9c), which one analyst from the time called the "awakening motive."[39] Paine's presentation of the winter motive in new contexts resembles Liszt's and Raff's efforts at thematic transformation, but it never serves a germinal purpose by growing into a full-fledged melody. It merely evokes the icy bite of winter.

The remaining three movements likewise bounce narrowly between traditional and progressive languages. The second movement is a minor-key scherzo with a rhythmic drive that seems indebted to the trio of Beethoven's Fifth. The adagio, by contrast, is an emotionally charged romance of moderate proportions that bears the intensity of Mahler's slow movements, particularly in its rhythmic density, harmonic complexity, and lush orchestration (example 10.10). The finale returns to a more conservative melodic and harmonic language, as well as the traditional sonata form (this time undisturbed by interloping leitmotifs). The most noteworthy aspect of the finale, however, is the hymn-like secondary theme, a gesture clearly reminiscent of the finales to Beethoven's Ninth and Brahms's First (example 10.11). Countering Brahms directly, Paine's hymn is presented in full force by the entire orchestra each time it is heard—Wagnerian bombast at its finest.

After hearing performances of the new symphony on two successive days—one given in Cambridge, the other in Boston—critics welcomed it even more spiritedly than they had greeted his earlier work. Dwight called it "a success in every way," characterized it as "very long, elaborate, and thoughtful," and noted its "wealth of contents, breadth of plan, and mastery of form."[40] A writer for the *Saturday Evening Gazette* remarked that it was "a great advance upon anything [Paine] has previously given to the world in flexibility, easy and prolific flow of idea, profound, yet graceful scholarship

Example 10.10: Gripping Wagnerian Melody. Paine, Symphony No. 2, *Im Frühling*, III: Adagio, mm. 23–30 (full orch.).

thoroughly under control, poetic fancy, refined imagination, and that effect of spontaneity in thought which is credited to inspiration."[41] Critics also commented (sometimes unfavorably) on the work's length, to which Dwight retorted, "Mozart, when the emperor complained of too many notes in one of his works, replied: 'Sire, it has precisely the right number.'"[42] Despite this quibble, audiences reacted with unqualified enthusiasm. One reviewer

Example 10.11: Triumphant Hymn-Like Finale. Paine, Symphony No. 2, *Im Frühling*, IV: Allegro giojoso—Meno mosso e maestoso, mm 99–115 (full orch.).

predicted that "the ovation showered upon the modest composer last evening was but the first fruits of a new fame to be won for him by this masterpiece." And legend has it that "ladies waved handkerchiefs, men shouted in approbation, and the highly respected John S. Dwight, arbiter in Boston of criticism, if not manners, stood in his seat, frantically opening and shutting his umbrella as an expression of uncontrollable enthusiasm."[43]

The work's general effect pleased audiences, but reviewers also had deeper concerns about its position relative to contemporary stylistic trends. Dwight wrote an uncharacteristically long and detailed analytical description that focused on its traditional, "classical" features, especially the melodic content. "The first movement," he claimed, is laid out on a very broad scale, and swarms with musical ideas, all springing naturally from a few leading motives, which worked up together into a complex whole, is thoroughly consistent, while it is richly varied, and always fascinating, though it is exceedingly elaborate and very long. With such wealth of pregnant matter (*Inhalt*) claiming development, it could not well be shorter.[44]

His description of the slow introduction was even more poetic. The "wintry motive" is soon joined by instruments that

swell the harmony, or rather polyphony, which grows more frigid and more wild and restless; then gathers itself into a little ganglion (three bars), of tranquil subtly woven string quartet, and subsides to a low protracted tremolo of the middle strings, while the clarinet, in a warm melodic passage, sings the hope and prophecy of Spring.[45] (example 10.9c)

Dwight carefully eliminated the possibility of programmatic interpretation and frequently remarked on the music's emotional interiority ("one of the ways of Beethoven!" he claimed, probably referring to the *Pastoral* Symphony), though he playfully noted that the winter theme's reprisal in the third movement represents an authentic New England spring.

Other writers did not place the symphony so squarely within Beethoven's classical lineage. A reviewer for Boston's *Musical Record* claimed that "the treatment of the brass [in the finale] is in the Wagnerian method." The *Courier* of Boston agreed: "Here we have a broad choral melody for the brass which reminds one somewhat of a like movement in the introduction to the *Meistersingers*."[46] Using phrases more commonly applied to "New German" music, the same author responded to the work's melodic content in direct opposition to Dwight: "If we were asked to name the chief characteristics of the work, we should say, a want of repose. We are constantly tantalized by bits of melody of the most exquisite form which comes to the surface like the crests on foam tipped billows, then disappear before we are hardly aware of their presence"—an insinuation that the melodies are more like leitmotifs than structurally grounding forces, and that they dissolve almost as quickly as they appear (certainly an apt description of the slow introduction and the third movement). A critic for the *Boston Daily Advertiser* nevertheless remarked that "the symphony is not a 'programme' work in the fantastically minute sense of some modern authors, but it is a vital and convincing illustration of the true composer's power of infusing music with poetic thought and feeling."[47]

For a writer for the *Daily Transcript*, the symphony's stylistic duality was precisely its strength. It was "classic and solid in form and matter, and yet enriched with the modern style and vitalized with the modern spirit of musical art." The combination of old and new made it all the more noteworthy: "As it marks a new departure in his own career, it also marks an epoch in the development of art in America, and sets the standard of excellence on the very highest plane." Such a positive account of the work's synthesis of classical and modern styles must have pleased Paine, for it seemed to align precisely with his vision for the future of music, which, as he had remarked in several contexts, was the future of American music. Refusing to put a damper on the occasion, Dwight reversed his intellectual position of nearly thirty years by claiming that Paine's symphony was "the highest point yet reached in these early stages of American creative art in music" and "could hold a place among the works of masters." His protégé would not need to wait for time to determine the work's fate.

THE CLASSICIST CONTRA THE PATRIOT

Theodore Thomas, Paine's staunch advocate, programmed the new symphony with relative frequency after its 1880 premiere.[48] On two successive nights in late March of 1883, Thomas handed Paine the baton of the Brooklyn Philharmonic so that he could direct the symphony himself. This marquee event featuring a Harvard professor conducting and interpreting his own music caused a stir in the press. The interest generated by these performances was comparable to the flurry of discussion attending the work's double premiere in Massachusetts three years earlier.[49]

As before, critics gave the symphony high marks. The *Daily Eagle* reported that "Mr. Paine has given to the world a work which marks a long step in advance in the progress of musical art in this country" and noted its "profound scholarship," its "graceful and poetic fancy, spontaneity of thought and originality" and its "richness of instrumentation."[50] Henry Krehbiel, John Hassard's replacement at the *New York Tribune* distilled this description into one simple phrase: "serious, important, and beautiful."[51] A writer for the *Nation*, presumably Henry T. Finck, quipped elliptically that "the immense superiority of spring music over spring poetry will at once strike everyone in listening to this fine composition."[52]

Critics again attempted to situate the piece within the symphonic tradition, particularly with respect to Beethoven's heritage. "In the second part of the first movement [after the introduction]," Frederick Schwab of the *Times* noted (and as Dwight had suggested three years earlier), "there are reminiscences of a passage in the *Pastoral Symphony* so marked as to excite instant attention, and at other points there are indications of a study of Beethoven's methods."[53] Finck explained further, "Professor Paine, like Beethoven in the case of the *Pastoral Symphony*, doubtless intended them to be 'more an expression of feeling than an attempt to paint in tones.'" This comment was a direct allusion to Beethoven's own description of the Sixth as "mehr Ausdruck der Empfindung als Malerei."

Others emphasized the work's modern qualities. Krehbiel detected hints of innovation in the second and third movements, which evidently bore traces of "three masters, Beethoven, Wagner, Berlioz," but "this implies formative influence upon the composer merely, not slavish imitation in his work."[54] Paine had found inspiration; he hadn't copied. The *Daily Eagle* noticed the same middle path and described the piece in language reminiscent of Paine's own dialectical understanding of history:

> Mr. Paine has been happily successful in shaping a safe course between the new school and the old; and while the tendencies of the symphony are perhaps more in the direction of the former than the latter, there are yet unmistakable evidences that the author is strongly imbued with the influences of the older masters, particularly Beethoven.[55]

Only Finck commented on Paine's use of contrapuntal leitmotifs in the combination of spring and winter motives that created "a mixture of sad and joyous feelings," but he made no direct reference to Wagner.

Critics' preferences for the work's Beethovenian elements were not unusual, but their openness to its innovative qualities, particularly in the finale, reflected their shared belief that it marked authentic forward progress within the symphonic tradition. The *Daily Eagle* remarked enthusiastically that "the finale, as its title indicates, is a glorious outburst of joyousness, while its stately theme, a triumphant choral, is a fitting culmination to this undoubted work of genius." Evocation of Beethoven's Ninth was subtle here, but others made the connection more explicit. Krehbiel was swept away. "The sudden introduction and return of a chorale-like pæan is simply thrilling," he gushed, "especially since the scoring produces almost a vocal effect."[56] But Finck was the most moved of them all and directly invoked a parallel to Beethoven's Ninth:

> The last movement, on the other hand, marks the climax not only of the Spring Symphony, but of its author's creative power. It introduces a sort of hymn to joy in the last movement for full orchestra, the grand harmonies and stirring, vigorous rhythm of which irresistibly make the audience vividly feel the "Glory of Nature."[57] (example 10.11)

Reading this superlative description, any reader familiar with Beethoven's music might come to believe that Paine had successfully merged the subtle pictorialism of the Sixth with the integration of voices in the Ninth, two of the most hotly contested elements of symphonic writing over the past half-century. As an example of authentic forward progress, the work seemed destined to live.

Despite the predictions made by the *Daily Union-Argus*, Phelps's *Emancipation* did not live for long. His compositions received little critical acclaim after

1880, as his smaller pieces continually flummoxed critics. Krehbiel had not joined the *Tribune* staff in time to cover the *Emancipation* Symphony's premiere, but he later said of Phelps's tone poem *American Legend* that "it is American only in name, and creates the impression of a striving after sounding things with small means. The principal melody is a conventional violin melody, without a tinge of American color."[58] By 1885, Krehbiel had set his sights on the development of a folk-based school of composition. Phelps nevertheless gave him an opportunity to hear such a style when C. Mortimer Wiske (1853–1934), a supporter of local composers, revived the "Slave Girl's Dream" movement from the *Emancipation* at an all-American concert in February of 1891. Krehbiel, who wrote a lengthy review of the event, had only negative remarks about the whole enterprise. He also did not mention Phelps's name at all, despite the movement's folk character.[59]

Phelps took offense at the snub. Rekindling the conflict between composers and critics that had boiled over in the 1850s, he wrote to the editor of the *Daily Eagle* to complain specifically about Krehbiel's review. Though not typically one to protest, he claimed, the review compelled him to respond:

> The attitude of certain critics, especially of the New York press, toward American composers and their works has been so unfair and reckless as to demand a protest. If native art is in such a deplorably hopeless condition as these censors claim, it ought to be suppressed. The public have rights, and their tastes ought not to be demoralized by such bad examples.[60]

The public had a right to hear American works so that listeners could make their own decisions, he thought, despite such negativity from the press. Critics, furthermore, held American composers to an impossible standard (just as they had always done). Phelps fired back with the zeal of Heinrich and Fry:

> Now, while America has not yet been vouchsafed a genius and perhaps not a single work has been produced of permanent importance there is much ability, industry, lofty aim and some creditable composition. We have fallen upon a higher critical era. Your true Wagnerian's eyes are so dazzled with the incomparable brilliance of that genius that he can see nothing else. All musicians know its dangers, but because of this most brilliant orb in the musical firmament may not the poor little outside stars twinkle a little? There have been greater critics than these scintillant savans [sic] of the New York press, but we do not ask them to step down and out.[61]

Phelps wondered who granted critics any authority at all, especially when the public's response to a work or a performance could diverge so drastically from that of the so-called experts.

Phelps's letter exposed the balance of power within the symphonic enter-prise. Critics and institutions wielded far more authority over public taste than the public itself. Critics could always decry an uncultivated public, and they frequently did. When a composer had to fund performances from his (or her) own pocket, including the expense of advertising in newspapers for ticket subscriptions, there was virtually no way to compete with entrepre-neurial forces such as Thomas, who performed so many concerts that suc-cessful ones subsidized the failures. Ensembles such as the philharmonics of New York and Brooklyn were funded by membership dues and annual sub-scriptions, while the newly formed Boston Symphony Orchestra boasted a philanthropic donor who insulated the ensemble from losses. If a composer were stuck outside this institutional system—as Phelps frequently found himself to be—virtually nothing could be done to change one's fortune. Dwight's sanction of time was an impossible dream (unless, of course, he made an exception to the rule).

CHAPTER 11

༄

The Winds of Change

John Knowles Paine glimpsed the sanction of ages. The overwhelmingly positive responses to his two symphonies in the 1880s contrasted sharply with the reviews of George Frederick Bristow's first two in the 1850s. In Paine's case, critics approached his music largely on its own terms, a sentiment expressed most clearly by Henry Krehbiel: "To call it scholarly or learned may be necessary to convey a part of its total impression, [. . .] and then the use of [these terms] is much like praising a piece of literature for being good English. Professor Paine's score may be assumed to be good musical 'English,' and makes that impression."[1] Bristow's critics, by contrast, concerned themselves with the grammar of the music, as if it were such a novelty for an American to be speaking the Germanic symphonic language that they wondered if it could be done at all. They had drawn this conclusion despite the composer's immersion in that very language as a well-rounded violinist and conductor.

Paine's symphonic success moved quickly into the popular imagination and in turn raised his historical profile well beyond his death. Commenting on the relative "youth" of the country's "native school of music," Rupert Hughes (1872–1956) remarked that "before Mr. Paine there had never been an American music writer worthy of serious consideration in the larger forms." Not long thereafter, composer Arthur Foote (1853–1937) claimed that Paine was the first to compose any "worthwhile" American music. Daniel Gregory Mason (1873–1953) stated just as plainly that Paine was "the first serious American composer in the larger forms." Chicago critic Glenn Dillard Gunn rightly pointed out that "the first American symphonist whose fame has endured was John Knowles Paine." Historian John Tasker Howard agreed, noting, "The fact that [Paine] was the first American composer to win serious consideration abroad is enough to deserve a monument." By mid-century, the popular British musical author Percy Young had written that Paine was the "first American symphonist, impeccably academic and German." If we believe these authors, the history of serious American music had begun in 1876 with the First Symphony of John Knowles Paine (figure 11.1).[2]

This perspective emerged in 1876. Six months after the premiere of Paine's symphony, Thomas revived it at Philadelphia's Centennial Exhibition for a retrospective program highlighting the history of American composition. Appropriately, the concert also included Fry's *A Day in the Country* (1852), which Thomas himself had likely performed as a member of Jullien's orchestra (how or why he acquired the manuscript is a mystery). A correspondent for *Dwight's* who had attended the concert posited that Fry and

Figure 11.1: John Knowles Paine. Courtesy of the Music Division, Library of Congress, Washington, D.C.

Paine represented two identifiable eras in the development of American music: "the one when it whistled as it went for 'want of thought,' the other the culture of half a generation had set up the American art intellect on something like a level with that of other nations."[3] In the space between these two generations, this reviewer thought, American musical culture had grown from a happy-go-lucky amateurish affair to the more professionalized milieu characteristic of European musical centers. Only then had the history of American classical music truly begun.

But Paine had benefited from full integration into Boston's broad institutional networks, such as they were, during the 1870s and had been presented with opportunities that were not available to Fry in the 1850s. He had entered into Theodore Thomas's inner circle and had won Dwight's favor. He was also a professor at Harvard, a position that increased his public profile. For his part, Bristow enjoyed parallel benefits in New York and Brooklyn, though in a less integrated fashion. He was a violinist in two major local orchestras, conducted well-respected choral ensembles, played the organ at prominent churches, directed a fledgling music conservatory, and became a beloved teacher in New York's public school system. As fate would have it, though, the institutional network supporting Bristow was incapable of fusing him into a collective national memory, despite his acquisition of an international reputation.

Only Boston wielded that power. Henry Higginson (1834–1919), a wealthy businessman of Paine's generation, founded the Boston Symphony Orchestra in 1881, just a year after the premieres of Paine's quasi-Wagnerian *Im Frühling* Symphony and Phelps's gigantic *Emancipation*. It was the country's first ensemble with a complete roster of full-time musicians. Higginson, like Thomas, was an art worshipper and an ardent believer in music's power to uplift a community. He offered low ticket prices to entice new audiences and covered any deficits. He also retained control over the hiring of conductors but relinquished power over programming and personnel to the conductors themselves, all of whom were foreign-born during his tenure. His goal was to ensure the highest quality of performances for the largest number of people.[4] The philharmonics of New York and Brooklyn, by contrast, retained older organizational models in which decisions about programming were made by a committee of musicians and subscribers (though autocratic conductors such as Thomas could thwart the committee's efforts).

This new Boston institution opened doors for younger composers, but only if they played their cards properly. One of the first to benefit was George Whitefield Chadwick (1854–1931), who, like Paine, became immersed in the city's institutional infrastructure. He eventually assumed the directorship of the New England Conservatory and would have performers at his disposal for much of his career. Despite these advantages, he still failed to acquire the cachet of his European contemporaries in the popular imagination as critics continually questioned his ability to compose a legitimate symphony. Institutional help could take him only so far. By the late 1920s, Chadwick would forsake season tickets to the Boston Symphony for programming too many so-called modern works. He died of heart failure just weeks after attending a winter rehearsal. Not long after the rehearsal, incidentally, he had complained in his diary about the New England winter's chill.[5]

A BOSTON SYMPHONIST

Coming of age in New England at a time when attitudes such as Dwight's veneration of Beethoven were commonplace, Chadwick, like many composers before him, felt the weight of Beethoven's legacy on his shoulders. In an essay written for the New England Conservatory's 1907 senior class, he recounted a dream in which Thomas Crawford's statue of Beethoven (see chapter 8) came to life in his private study. Like the ghosts haunting Ebenezer Scrooge, it called to mind Chadwick's own first encounter with the master. Beethoven's spirit told him,

> "It was at a Thomas concert in the old Music Hall, where I used to be when I first came to Boston, you know. [. . .] You stared about in wonder, especially at me, and at Apollo in the second balcony. [. . .] Pretty soon Thomas began with my Eroica, and how you did prick up your ears! [. . .] Well, I happened to look at you just then. You have a great gulp, your nose began to leak, and your eyes too, and they kept on leaking '*sempre piú sino al Fine!*'" He grinned and chuckled to himself. "Then the lady sitting by you said, sympathetically, 'What's the matter, little boy?' And when you got your nose dry enough to let you, you said 'O, it is so beautiful!'"[6]

The remainder of the conversation went on to illustrate how Beethoven had always watched over Chadwick through his various musical endeavors (like the proud father he never had).[7] Turning the tables on his student readers, Chadwick then warned that Beethoven had been ever watchful over their activities at the conservatory as well, so much so that Beethoven complained that the soles of his "Crawford shoes" had worn thin. "I feel at home where I am respected," Beethoven told Chadwick, just as a night watchman roused him. Chadwick demanded this respect from his students.

True to form for a New Englander, Chadwick had indeed fallen in love with the German musical tradition early in his career. The concert introducing Chadwick to Beethoven had taken place in 1871, a few months after the Beethoven Centennial celebrations. He developed a taste for European classicism that Theodore Thomas and his orchestra represented. His appetite was whetted again when he heard the premiere of Paine's First Symphony in

1876, after which he sought lessons with the older (but still relatively young) composer. Taken by the work's traditionalism, he remarked later in life that "the simple and benighted music lovers of those days had not been taught by blasé critics that the sonata form was a worn-out fetich, that noble and simple melody was a relic of the dark ages, and that unresolved dissonance was the chief merit of a composition." The symphony had "been a stimulus and an inspiration to more than one ambitious musician of that time," including Chadwick himself.[8]

Like his role model, Chadwick continued his training in Germany, where he studied with Salomon Jadassohn (1831–1902) and Carl Reinecke (1824–1910) at Leipzig's Royal Conservatory. He later endured lessons with the severe contrapuntist Josef Rheinberger (1839–1901) in Munich. As part of his studies, he secured performances of two string quartets, as well as an overture inspired by Washington Irving's *Rip van Winkle* (the subject of Bristow's only opera, written in 1855). All three works exhibit a buoyancy of character that would become a hallmark of his mature style. He even claimed to have introduced a traditional American dance tune into the scherzo of the first quartet, and the works received high praise in the German press. While abroad, Chadwick had missed the premieres of Phelps's two symphonies in Brooklyn but had crept into a rehearsal of Brahms's Second, which premiered in Leipzig just two months before Phelps's *Hiawatha*.[9]

Chadwick's career as an orchestral composer had an auspicious start. American audiences heard his works even before he returned from Germany. Following a performance of the *Rip van Winkle* overture, Dwight remarked that the work "more than justified the interest with which it was anticipated" and that Chadwick had begun cautiously to forge his own compositional path, having avoided both "Wagnerism," as well as "Mendelssohnian echoes." Yet it sounded a bit like the music of Julius Rietz, he added—a typically snide remark designed to project his own breadth of knowledge along with a general coldness toward new works of any sort.[10] A year and a half later, a Boston correspondent to *Church's Musical Visitor*, a Cincinnati magazine, was much more enthusiastic: "We predict for our countryman a brilliant career, if his present successes do not overcome him. From what we know of him, we have no fears in that direction, and shall watch his progress with much interest." The next step would be to write a symphony.[11]

Dedicated affectionately to his mother, Chadwick's First Symphony rests comfortably within the conservative tradition of Mendelssohn, Schumann, and by that point Paine and Brahms. The first movement's opening theme is a soft but soaring line marked by hemiola. It evokes the strident opening of Schumann's *Rhenish* (example 11.1). Likewise, Chadwick chose E minor over the traditional G major for the movement's secondary key, a strategy Brahms had recently employed in his Second. Critic Louis Elson remarked that the scherzo was the "finest, or rather most spontaneous movement"

Example 11.1: Strident Opening Theme. Chadwick, Symphony No. 1, I: Allegro molto e sostenuto, mm. 5–20 (strings).

and noted the contrast between the "appropriate" opening melody and the "tender, almost devotional" trio—a hymn-like moment akin to one he had employed in the finale of his first string quartet (example 11.2). The third movement, a lengthy adagio, is lyrical but rhythmically dense in the manner of Mendelssohn's (and Bristow's) slow movements. It also displays significant contrapuntal complexity, a facet Elson praised. An appropriately pompous finale closes the work.

Example 11.2: Hymn-Like Trio. Chadwick, Symphony No. 1, II: Scherzo, mm. 98–113 (clarinets and bassoons).

The symphony's premiere on February 23, 1882, which was given by Dwight's Harvard Musical Association, not Higginson's Boston Symphony, jolted critics into believing that Chadwick would become a significant force in the American musical world. William F. Apthorp of the *Boston Evening Transcript* remarked that "it was apparent, for instance, that the composer had endeavored to produce a work which should be truly symphonic; one, that is, in which the theme should be regularly developed or treated, as one may say, with genuine symphonic respect."[12] He had also avoided any suspicion of "new school" excesses since he had employed color "solely for the purpose of bringing his forms into fine relief, and to be neither lavish nor niggardly in his resources." A correspondent to the *American Art Journal* of New York remarked that "Mr. Chadwick has done one thing that deservedly entitles him to fame; that is, he has written music. It is easily understood and appeals earnestly to the heart and mind."[13] Writing to *Church's Musical Visitor*, Elson took his comments in a patriotic direction, noting (with willful ignorance) that "one can count the American symphonies upon one's thumbs [. . .] but the work is an important addition to the native list."[14] Writing for the *Boston Times*, James Mortimer Keniston nodded in assent, "With men like Mr. Chadwick, we need not fear for American music."[15] The piece had generated nothing if not forward momentum for Chadwick's career as a symphonist.

LOSING SYMPHONIC DIGNITY

Chadwick was not the only recent Boston arrival whose career was on the upswing. Louis Maas (1852–1889), a pianist and professor at the Leipzig Conservatory, had been lured by Eben Tourjée (1834–1891), founder and director of the New England Conservatory (and Chadwick's predecessor in that role), to take a position there in 1881. Maas quickly acquired a reputation as an outstanding recital pianist with a prodigious memory. His programs featured works by an eclectic array of composers, including Vassar College professor Frédéric Louis Ritter. Amid internal conflict and competition with the newly established Boston Symphony Orchestra, the Boston Philharmonic engaged Maas to be its conductor, a position that secured his place in the city's spotlight.[16] With such visibility and opportunity, writing a symphony would have been a natural choice for him. In October of 1882, while President Chester Arthur was visiting Boston, he gave Maas his permission to be the dedicatee of the composer's latest work, a piece called *On the Prairies* that he explicitly dubbed an "American Symphony."[17]

As in the case of Ellsworth Phelps's *Emancipation*, the score for Maas's magnum opus did not survive. Yet the *American Art Journal* provided readers with an unusually detailed synopsis of the work that included several musical examples from all four movements. The overarching scheme bears a remarkable resemblance to Bristow's *Arcadian* Symphony in both subject matter and its finer details, such as the three-part finale (table 11.1). Maas was a close personal friend of Joachim Raff, and it is possible that he, like Bristow, found inspiration in Raff's *Im Walde*.

The published analysis revealed to readers that Maas attempted to follow Raff-like procedures of cyclic integration and thematic transformation, noting that a "strange and weird passage for three trumpets" in the slow introduction is "heard again in the third and fourth parts [movements], as in fact all four parts are closely welded together, by themes and motives which reappear here and there, every time in a different aspect and with a different meaning" (example 11.3).[18] Following the brief brass chorale, the symphony continues with a mysterious pentatonic melody in the winds. The mood gradually intensifies as the section culminates in a tutti Eb major chord signaling the beginning of the first movement proper. The primary theme, which

Table 11.1. STRUCTURAL AND NARRATIVE COMPARISON OF JOACHIM RAFF, SYMPHONY NO. 3, *IM WALDE*; GEORGE FREDERICK BRISTOW, SYMPHONY NO. 4, *ARCADIAN*; AND LOUIS MAAS, *ON THE PRAIRIES*

Raff, *Im Walde*	Bristow, *Arcadian*	Maas, *On the Prairies*
I. Allegro— "Daytime: Feelings and Impressions"	I. Allegro appassionato— "Emigrants' Journey across the Plains"	I. Allegro con moto—"Morning on the Prairies"
II. Largo—"At Dusk: Dreaming"	II. Andante religioso—"Halt on the Prairie"	II. "The Chase"
III. Allegro assai—"Dance of the Dryads"	III. Allegro ma non tanto— "Indian War Dance and Attack by Indians"	III. Adagio—"An Indian Legend"
IV. Allegro—"Night: Stillness of the night in the forest. Entry and departure of the wild hunt. Daybreak."	IV. Allegro con spirito— "Arrival at the New Home, Rustic Festivities, and Dancing"	IV. Allegro, moderato, andante, maestoso—"Evening, Night, and Sunrise"

Example 11.3: Opening Trumpet Chorale. Maas, *On the Prairies*, I: "Morning on the Prairies" (Andante moderato), mm. 1–4.

matches the contour of the earlier melody, forms the basis of an extended sonata form exposition that passes through G♭ major to a grandiose theme in B♭ major (example 11.4).

The two inner movements, whose order Maas reversed from Raff's model, depict a horse chase on the prairie with a snappy melody in the violins and an old storyteller reciting a legend around a campfire, with the trumpet chorale serving as a musical framing device (example 11.5). The symphony concludes with another extended sonata form that opens with a horn chorale and closes with a juxtaposition of the two first movement themes transformed into a "triumphal hymn" (example 11.6).

Responses to the work were mixed. In a report to the New York magazine *Music and Drama*, Louis Elson expressed disappointment that the work was "hardly" evocative enough for "programme music of this character" except in the second movement, "where the galloping rhythm was strongly suggestive of the chase." William F. Apthorp, who had applauded Chadwick's symphony, was turned off by the work's length but found the third movement to be "the most picturesque and the most genially musical." As for the

Example 11.4: Themes with Matching Contours. Maas, *On the Prairies*, I: "Morning on the Prairies":
(a) Introduction (Andante moderato).
(b) Primary Theme (Allegro con moto).

Example 11.5: Chase Theme. Maas, *On the Prairies*, II: "The Chase" (violins).

Example 11.6: Horn Chorale. Maas, *On the Prairies*, IV: "Evening, Night, Sunrise."

other movements, "we are still rather in the dark. For one thing, we rather wondered at the constantly somber orchestral coloring of this symphony. We think Mr. Maas has rather abused the lower register of his wind instruments. The work was plainly 'all Greek' to the majority of the audience." The critic for the *Daily Advertiser* agreed that the piece's chief weakness was an "occasional cloudiness" of scoring but liked it overall: "The several subjects are illustrated with a good deal of vivid realism, according to the modern conventional methods for this class of writing, and some of the descriptive effects are very beautiful and skillfully worked up—notably the tone-picture of sunrise." He, like Apthorp, believed the third movement was best. Turning the discussion in a different direction, he also noted that he failed "to perceive any 'American' flavor to the work," a stylistic omission that had not bothered critics in the past—certainly not Paine's.[19]

The conflicting opinions prompted Calixa Lavallée (1842–1891), a well-regarded French Canadian composer who had recently relocated to the Boston area, to send a lengthy commentary to William Thoms, editor of the *American Art Journal*. He noted that critics had wondered if such a vividly descriptive work could be legitimately symphonic, a question reminiscent of William Henry Fry's debate with Richard Storrs Willis in 1854. He argued that "it can be done," citing Beethoven's Sixth as the quintessential example. Maas, he claimed, had achieved the union of music and "poetic conception" that the subject matter demanded. Indeed, the first movement was "truly symphonic," the very phrase Apthorp had used to describe Chadwick's First. Lavallée closed by turning his attention to the question of American identity:

> This is called an "American" symphony, although it is said to have no "American" color in its music. But I would venture to ask if the United States has as yet any musical tradition that would give a *peculiar* color to their native music. So we might as well adopt the color inaugurated by Dr. Maas as American music, and cultivate the public taste so as to eventually kill the cheap and trashy ballad American (so-called) music.[20]

From Lavallée's perspective, Maas's dark and evocative modern style should be the way forward for native composers.

Not long after the premiere of Maas's *On the Prairies* and the rousing success of Paine's Second in Brooklyn, an interested reader wrote to the editors of Boston's *Musical Record*, asking, "Who are the principal American composers of important works?" To which the editors replied, "Paine, Buck, Chadwick, Pratt, Bristow, Gilchrist, Woolf, Whiting, Millard and others."[21] Chadwick was fortunate to be included in a group with the likes of Bristow and Paine, whose achievements and successes far outweighed his own. Phelps, the Brooklynite, was not on the list. Neither was Maas, the German.

The tireless Chadwick began composing a new symphony in 1884 and released the work piecemeal by premiering the scherzo (eventually the second movement) far in advance of the rest. Critics received it amiably. Apthorp called it a "gem" and felt that its "piquant charm is irresistible." He even detected a hint of ethnic flavor in its primary theme (example 11.7), which,

Example 11.7: "Irish" Oboe Melody. Chadwick, Symphony No. 2, II: Allegretto scherzando, mm. 5–12.

"with its quasi-Irish humorousness (it positively winks at you), is peculiarly happy."[22] Though lighthearted, such a critique was dual-edged: Apthorp welcomed the music's ethnic exoticism—and by extension its potential as "national" expression—but his snide evocation of the stereotyped Irish wink suggested that he considered the whole affair more trivial than serious.

Boston was apparently in a serious mood later that year. "Symphony! Symphony! Symphony!" Elson exclaimed. "The Bostonian gets symphony with his breakfast, he whistles the 9th symphony with his dinner, he takes the Raff symphonies as a nightcap after his suppers." Fed on this hearty diet, Elson was especially concerned with defining symphonic character and allowing this character to determine a work's placement on a concert program—a broad theoretical point rarely broached in the press. Wilhelm Gericke (1845–1925), the newly appointed conductor of the Boston Symphony, had made new plans "to put symphonies last in each concert, for he believes that the impression made by a great masterpiece should not be disturbed by following it with something more trivial." Although common today, the standard late nineteenth-century practice was to follow a heavy symphony with lighter fare, such as an overture. For Elson, though, "There are some symphonies which, because of the nature of the finale, are not well suited to close a program with, and such will be given in the centre of the program. The new Brahms symphony [No. 3] is of this class."[23] As was Chadwick's initial effort.

Gericke must have believed that Chadwick's next symphony had the potential to be a great masterpiece, for it closed the concert at its premiere in December of 1886. It is indeed a heavy work marked by rich orchestration, sweeping melodies, and expansive formal structures. The most striking characteristic, however, is the prevalence of jaunty pentatonic figures that seem to mark it as exotic when compared to contemporary symphonies, such as those by Brahms. The motivic basis for these melodies appears in the work's opening, a haunting solo horn call (example 11.8). The gesture is directly reminiscent of the third movement of Phelps's *Emancipation* (example 10.6), but Chadwick did not know the work. Instead, he was following Maas, whose symphony had opened with a similarly evocative call

Example 11.8: Horn Call. Chadwick, Symphony No. 2, I: Andante non troppo, mm. 1–5.

Example 11.9: Horn Call Reprise in Coda. Chadwick, Symphony No. 2, IV: Presto.

in the trumpets. Chadwick inserted modified versions of the call in later movements at the precise locations where Maas had utilized the same technique: at the opening of the third movement and near the end of the finale. But whereas Maas had been criticized for repeating too much of the opening at the end, Chadwick carefully disguised the motive at the beginning of an exuberant coda (example 11.9). He had learned from Maas's mistake.

Although the work engaged in a clear dialogue with *On the Prairies*, which had generated intense debate among critics, Chadwick may not have realized that critics would listen to his new symphony with questions about the very nature of the genre. They had already forgotten about Maas and did not think to compare the two works. Echoing Charles Burkhardt's critique of Fry's *Santa Claus* in the 1850s, Apthorp compared Chadwick's new symphony to an opera:

> The general lack of true seriousness in the music; the light, almost operatic, character of the thematic material; the constant changes of rhythm; the frequent solo passages—not merely incidental phrases for this or that instrument, but often full-fledged solos of considerable length—all contribute to make the work fall short of what may be called symphonic dignity.

Richard Hurd of the *Boston Post* claimed that "the symphony, to a certain extent, usurps its title" and that it more closely resembled a suite. Another added that the piece had "more a rhapsodical than symphonic character."[24] Making an about-face after calling Chadwick's earlier effort "truly symphonic," Apthorp synthesized all of these impressions:

> And yet there is that in the general character and animus of the symphony which baffles all attempts at comparing it with known models of any school. We, for one, cannot remember any music of this character being written in the symphonic form. One feels like saying, with Friar Lawrence, "Art thou a symphony?" Thy form cries out, thou art.[25]

The work had fallen flat. Whereas lightness had been a boon for the scherzo at its earlier premiere, Chadwick had overstepped his bounds by writing an entire work breathing the same spirit. It came across as a spoonful of sugar after listeners' recent diet of the beefier Raff and Brahms. Chadwick had finally experienced the challenge to his abilities that had plagued Bristow throughout his early career.

Most critics conceded, however, that the work was not without some merit. Adopting the standard critical posture of situating the work within its European lineage, one writer noted, "What is plainly avoided by the composer is the realistic method; Mr. Chadwick is no improver of Wagner. He writes after the precepts of Mendelssohn and with something of Gade's vigor and sense of color."[26] Like Paine, he had successfully navigated the boundary between the old and new schools of German composition while leaning toward the old. The *Boston Herald* claimed that the new symphony was a marked improvement over his first and, with a hint of patriotism, remarked that "no more satisfactory effort in this line of writing has yet been put before the public by a native born citizen."[27] But there was no mention of Paine—or Phelps and Bristow, for that matter. And as a non-native, Louis Maas was excluded from consideration.

Critics also remarked on what they perceived as distinctively American musical qualities, a topic that had remained an elephant in the room following the premiere of Bristow's *Arcadian* but that had finally received attention in discussions of Phelps's and Maas's definitively American-themed works. Philip Hale, whose aversion to Brahms was notorious, delighted in the "smell of American soil in this same scherzo: a suggestion of the good-natured recklessness of the citizens of these states." The opening measures, he claimed, "might serve to beat out the time of the heavy feet of Roustabouts dancing on the levy." A correspondent to *Kunkel's Musical Review* in St. Louis likewise pointed out that Chadwick had "caught the style of the folksong." Commenting on the slow third movement, yet another writer remarked that "if one finds restlessness and motion where quiet would have been preferred, the result is an evidence of the composer's affection for the brasses, without which he could scarcely be called American." Boston's critics seemed poised to accept subtle assertions of a stylistic Americanism, but they did not appreciate that it came at the expense of "symphonic dignity." If Bostonians wanted symphonic dignity, they would have to wait for a new voice to appear.[28]

AN AMERICAN WAGNERIAN ABROAD

That voice would come in the form of George Templeton Strong (1856–1948), son of the prominent New York lawyer (and diarist) of the same name who had fallen in love with Beethoven's symphonies in the 1840s (see chapter 1).

An aspiring composer, Strong traveled to Leipzig in 1879 and began studies with Chadwick's former teacher Salomon Jadassohn. Chadwick had moved on to Munich by this time. The young man was soon introduced to another visiting student, Edward MacDowell (1860–1908), by a mutual acquaintance, Joachim Raff, whose reputation in the United States remained iron-clad. Along with their families, Strong and MacDowell both moved to Wiesbaden in the mid-1880s, where Strong would begin writing his second symphony, *Sintram*, not long after the move.[29]

The piece was unquestionably going to be serious. Strong based the work's program loosely on the novella *Sintram and His Companions* by Baron Friedrich Heinrich Karl de la Motte Fouqué (1777–1843), a writer of romantic legends who became famous for creating one of the first modern realizations of the Nibelung tale that inspired Richard Wagner's *Ring* cycle. Fouqué's story describes the twofold struggle between paganism and Christianity on the one hand, and love and duty on the other—hence the symphony's subtitle: "The Struggle of Mankind against the Powers of Evil." The first three movements illustrate this tale, while the fourth, inspired by a verse from Part II of Goethe's *Faust*, is a transcendent paean in the aftermath of Sintram's epic struggle. The music is Wagnerian in character throughout and includes thematic reminiscences in the vein of Liszt, Raff, Maas, and Chadwick, particularly in a motive for French horn that Strong dubbed "Satan's Horn Call."

The work proved to be difficult for Strong to finish because of its size. He wrote to MacDowell that it was so "'fat,' it verily looks as if it were going 'to have a little one.'"[30] As he was completing the final drafts with full orchestration, Strong had acquired the published score of Chadwick's Second, which he greeted with antipathy in a letter to MacDowell. He called it too "thick" and "gelehrt" ("scholarly") and compared Chadwick's status as a composer and pedagogue to that of Cherubini. But he also heard the lightness that had disturbed Chadwick's critics:

> Chadwick seems to want to do fine things and, judging from the sinfonie, to avoid ear tickling: for this I respect him. Somebody ought—in kindness to him—tell him that there are portions of his sinfonie and others of his works that are touched with vulgarity. As this is a trait *that foreigners expect and look for in American work*, every American ought to do his utmost to avoid even the ghost of it.[31]

He continued to work on *Sintram* well into 1889 and asked MacDowell to finish it in case he met with an early death, or even to complete it from sketches should his full score be destroyed in a calamity. "You must pardon my attaching so much importance to the *Sintram Symphony*," he wrote to MacDowell, "but it is (to *me* only, perhaps) so important, that everything else I have thus far done dwindles away into utter insignificance (which 'ain't' saying so much after all). As for the other sinfonie [Strong's First], it seems child's play in comparison."[32]

Strong eventually shared parts of the score with Leipzig-based conductor Arthur Nikisch (1855–1922), who liked it. Nikisch would become the director of the Boston Symphony Orchestra in 1889. *Sintram*, with its highly dramatic subject matter, seemed destined to assuage the city's thirst for seriousness and symphonic dignity.

THE WINDS OF CHANGE

Strong's efforts notwithstanding, American symphonic writing fell fallow in the later 1880s. But the decade marked the high point of a movement taking hold in certain musical quarters to support U.S. composers by staging concerts dedicated exclusively to their works. One scholar likened this movement to a "tidal wave" of encouragement. If orchestras such as the New York Philharmonic would not program American compositions, someone else needed to step in. Theodore Presser (1848–1925), a musician who had befriended Chadwick in Boston and had studied alongside him in Leipzig, established the Music Teacher's National Association (MTNA) in 1876 with the purpose of cultivating music nationwide. By 1884, MTNA conventions had become welcome venues in which American composers could share their work. At roughly the same time, two entrepreneurial conductors of German parentage and Chadwick's generation, Frank van der Stucken (1858–1929) and Franz Xavier Arens (1856–1932), supported the MTNA's efforts by leading all-American concerts both in the United States and abroad.[33]

The music of Paine, Chadwick, Bristow, and Phelps appeared together frequently on these programs. Following one such performance at the MTNA annual convention of 1886, Presser could not have been more satisfied. "It was a most gratifying surprise to see so many young Americans come forward with compositions in the larger orchestral forms," he remarked with pride, "works, too, of such excellence that we might well be proud to place them beside any similar works by men of like age and attainments in Germany elsewhere." Then, with an air of defiance: "It is no longer open to European musicians to look down patronizingly on their American brethren."[34] For Presser at least, American music had finally come of age.

The first thorough catalog of American symphonic compositions appeared in print soon thereafter. Fry, Bristow, Gottschalk, Paine, and Chadwick all were in it. Even Ellsworth Phelps, whom the compiler dubbed a "voluminous composer," made the list. One of the compiler's stated goals was to help dispel the notion that American music "has no past." And although he cautioned his readers to bear in mind that most of the names were of recent vintage, he held out hope that "if this rate of progress be maintained during the next twenty years America will indeed be a leader in art." The compiler, surprisingly, was a British organist named Stephen Samuel Stratton (1840–1906), one of the least likely figures to care about or know many details concerning the history of American musical culture. Yet facts about American symphonic music had traveled across the Atlantic and sparked an interest among the British.[35] And even the French were interested: In 1891, Le Ménestrel of Paris reprinted portions of a fiery pro-American article from the Chicago Inter Ocean, noting that "America, tired of being dependent on foreigners in musical matters, finally claims its place in the sun of art."[36]

Anton Seidl (1850–1898), a conductor and an art worshipper who epitomized German cultural ascendency, agreed with Presser and Stratton. In a lengthy opinion essay written for the Forum in May of 1892, Seidl argued at length that the American public's longstanding approach to opera—as an amusement for the rich rather than an ennobling force for the many—had been flawed. Wagner, at least in spirit, had offered a way out by creating an art form that became a "vehicle not merely for pretty voices, but for the highest forms of music." Wagner's theories, he argued, "have now been widely accepted, his example followed by many imitators, and there is no doubt that the future development of music will be on the lines he has laid down." This future included, of course, music by Americans, who, "notwithstanding all that has been said about them, are a musical people."[37]

Seidl went on to argue that in order for American music to thrive, American composers must write English operas with the support of all willing sympathizers—the very argument Fry had made nearly fifty years before. Composers were already well on their way, he added, for "the achievements of J. K. Paine, who has done admirable work, of E. A. MacDowell, whose compositions seem to me to be superior to those of Brahms, of G. W. Chadwick, Templeton Strong, and others augur well for the future productions of American composers." Seidl's legitimacy as a cultural broker was inviolable. Even Germans could think that American composers were on the rise.

Unsurprisingly, then, it was Seidl, not Arthur Nikisch, who acquired Templeton Strong's Sintram at some point before its completion in 1889. In April of 1892, he also led its American premiere in Brooklyn at one of the Seidl Society concerts held in Brighton Beach. In true Wagnerian fashion, the concert also featured spiritually transcendent excerpts from Parsifal and Tristan in order to match the seriousness of the symphony's triumph over evil.

Seidl's Wagnerian proselytizing over the past several years had borne fruit, for Brooklyn critics greeted the work warmly despite its obvious debts to Wagner and the New German School. "The very freedom of his form," the *Daily Eagle* remarked, "the dramatic fervor of his emphases, the diversity of his orchestration are results of artistic conditions that Wagner was principally instrumental in establishing." But, most important for a disciple such as Seidl, the critic added that "there is a deep intent in the symphony, an undertone of ethical purpose running through its themes."[38] It stood far above mere entertainment. After making the trip across the river for the performance, the *Herald* critic reflected, with a hint of patriotism: "Mr. Strong is a young composer who comes of an excellent school and may reflect high credit upon his native country."[39] The work could not have contrasted more sharply with Chadwick's Second, but it was typical fare for the ladies of the Seidl Society—and it was American to boot.[40] The Bostonians craving seriousness must have been jealous.

The positive attitudes of figures such as Presser, Stratton, and Seidl was not as widely shared among interested parties as American composers might have hoped. Following Antonín Dvořák's arrival in the United States later in 1892 (described in more detail in the next chapter), the National Conservatory he was now directing announced a competition for the best entries in a number of genres, including the symphony. Three thousand dollars were at stake, five hundred of which were available to the winning symphonist, a figure five times the size of Bristow's commission for the *Arcadian*. After nagging delays, the press finally announced the winners in late March of 1893.

Unsatisfied with the choice made by a panel of experts, critics panned the winning work, the so-called *Rural* Symphony by Chicago composer Henry Schoenefeld (1857–1936). Henry Krehbiel, one of Dvořák's most vocal supporters, leveled particularly harsh criticism at Schoenefeld in the *Tribune*. Following a lengthy introduction of the winners' biographies (and a requisite tip of the hat to Dvořák for assiduously studying indigenous music with the hope of inspiring young composers), he dismissed the work with two simple words: "programme music." It was also not very good, readers learned. "Had Mr. Schoenefeld composed the work under the eyes of Dr. Dvorak he would have realized most strikingly the advantages spoken of in the early part of this review. The need of contrast in mood and key, in thought and expression, would have been pointed out to him." Dvořák, he noted smugly, would have shown Schoenefeld how to write in an American style. (Critic Rupert Hughes would later retort that "Schoenefeld's negroes do not speak Bohemian."[41])

Such general negativity toward American composers persisted. Following a performance of exclusively American music at the World's Columbian Exposition in Chicago (1893), which included Chadwick's ill-fated Second Symphony, critic W. S. B. Mathews silenced him: "Mr. Chadwick's symphony upon the present occasion did not quite bear out the composer's reputation of a man who has something to say. Or more properly, while he evidently had something to say, it by no means appeared that the something to say needed such a deal of noise for saying it." Commenting on the concert as a whole, another listener added, "From a musical point of view America has as yet no message to deliver to the world."[42] Such remarks embodied willful ignorance and pessimism. Works by Bristow, Stoepel, Paine, Chadwick, and a host of others had been performed to critical and audience acclaim throughout Europe and the United States during the previous several decades. Critics such as Mathews, who had written a sympathetic history of music in the United States and had served as one of the MTNA's charter founders, now wanted to forget them.

But the focus of musical thought in the United States had changed. No longer satisfied with the prospect of producing works on par with European composers, certain writers became increasingly concerned with the specific musical language that an American composer might adopt. Direct questions about the construction of a national musical style came to the fore by the century's end. Writing from Milwaukee, conductor Arthur Weld (1862–1914) put a damper on the entire conversation: "In all human probability those persons who are at present so noisily demanding an 'American School of Music,' will never see their apparently hopeless, and possibly undesirable, ambition gratified; no, not they, nor generations of similar 'patriots,' after them, in this century or many others to come." His reasoning was at least a century old: The United States had no national "race" and therefore no national music.[43]

Weld contended that the music of Paine, Chadwick, and others was essentially German: "Being gifted with a distinct inborn talent for music as an absolute art, but having no inborn racial characteristics strong enough to transform this absolute art-force into a special and particular one, they must *par force majeur* become members of whatever 'school' they selected as their means of education, for later it must inevitably become also their channel of expression." According to Weld, even a truly idiosyncratic musician could not develop a national style, "for its peculiarities would not arise at all from any characteristic materiality which [such a composer] might possess *as an American*." Steeped in prevailing racial theories and writing fifty years after Henry Russell Cleveland, Weld did not consider the possibility of a "nationalization" process fostered by cultivation or translation.[44]

Theodore Roosevelt (1858–1919), who was merely beginning his national political career as a member of the U.S. Civil Service Commission under President Grover Cleveland, offered his own perspective on "Americanism" in April of 1894, the very month in which Weld's article appeared (and in the same magazine as Seidl's commentary on American music). "There is one quality which we must bring to the solution of every problem," Roosevelt offered, "an intense and fervid Americanism." After explaining that Americans must first transcend local parochialism in politics, literature, and art, he argued that they should look inward for an identity rather than outward: "The man who becomes Europeanized [. . .] is not a traitor; but he is a silly and undesirable citizen. [. . .] Nothing will more quickly or more surely disqualify a man from doing good work in the world than the acquirement of that flaccid habit of mind which its possessors style cosmopolitanism." Setting his target on artists who attempted to transcend nationality, including musicians, Roosevelt next channeled Ralph Waldo Emerson:

> It is in those professions where our people have striven hardest to mold themselves in conventional European forms that they have succeeded least; [. . .] the failure being of course most conspicuous where the man takes up his abode in Europe; where he becomes a second-rate European. [. . .] He must content himself with aiming at that kind of mediocrity which consists in doing fairly well what has already been done better.[45]

Though laced with masculinist and xenophobic trappings characteristic of the Gilded Age, Roosevelt's essay brimmed with the optimism and forcefulness of William Henry Fry's missives from half a century earlier.

At least one interested reader, Herbert J. Krum of Pontiac, Illinois, had perused these two articles side by side before writing a response to the editor of *Music*, where Weld's pessimistic grumblings had originally appeared. Presenting a more moderate assessment, Krum pointed out that music can be both a "universal language" and one that "speaks through many tongues." Far from denying the prospect of a truly "native" music, he reiterated Fry's essential position that "as we surround ourselves more and more by a more esthetic environment, as we have greater opportunities for liberal culture and investigation, we shall have a constantly approaching art-life, which shall eventually produce its legitimate off-spring, an art atmosphere, and then we shall have American Art." American national life, he continued, "is as separate and distinct and unique in its character as that of any nation on the face of the earth." Concluding with the flair of both Fry and Paine, he prognosticated:

> Soon there will spring up among us that appointed being who will breathe through his transcendent genius the life, hopes, fears, peculiarities of the American people, and we shall then have American music. He may use old forms, he may avail himself of every influence, but the land of his birth, the freedom of our institutions, the marvelous resources that appear everywhere around him, will so shape his character and mold his art instinct, that they shall become part of his very nature and through it will reflect upon his music the stamp of what he is, a true American.[46]

In other words, an American composer, baptized by democracy and filled with the air of freedom, would be the great hope for American music. Fry would certainly have been pleased with Krum's idea, had he not been forgotten. But for Krehbiel, one of Fry's many successors at the *New York Tribune*, the country's best hope, Antonín Dvořák, had already arrived.

CHAPTER 12

✥

Antonín Dvořák, Bohemian Prophet

Antonín Dvořák's arrival in the United States coincided with the four-hundredth anniversary of Christopher Columbus's storied "discovery" of the New World. It was also fifty years after Anthony Philip Heinrich, a fellow Bohemian, had presided over the establishment of the New York Philharmonic. Their concerns, coincidentally, overlapped. Both wanted to improve the general state of musical cultivation in the United States. And both grappled with questions of musical style and national expression. But times were different now. The very orchestra Heinrich had helped found, and that had publicly rebuffed requests to perform his music, leaped at the opportunity to give the premiere of Dvořák's latest symphony, *From the New World*, in 1893.

Like Heinrich, Dvořák was no stranger to controversy. He ruffled feathers, particularly in Boston, after making public pronouncements about how to construct an American national style. The controversy swirled around whether or not American composers ought to seek inspiration in the music of African American "plantation songs" (or "Negro melodies," as they were sometimes called) and Native American music, to the extent that musicians trained in the Western classical tradition understood these styles at all. Dvořák's new symphony purportedly manifested this approach and was generally well received. Some critics even hailed it as the dawning of a new era in American composition. Dvořák's success as a European artist and his concomitant celebrity status granted his ideas and his music credence among a wide audience—or if one disagreed, at least the patina of legitimacy.

Symphonists had already addressed questions of national identity for over fifty years. William Henry Fry had attempted to translate Italian opera into American symphonies through the filter of democracy. Louis

Moreau Gottschalk had attempted to unite the Americas through a fusion of styles. Though he tended toward the supposed universalism of German music and even denied the possibility of a national style, John Knowles Paine believed that the United States would be the new home of great music. Ellsworth Phelps had written a monument to the country's political history. George Frederick Bristow and Louis Maas had celebrated westward expansion. Anthony Philip Heinrich and Robert Stoepel had found inspiration in Native America, however imaginary their conceptions were. And Chadwick, who erred toward Paine's perspective, had developed a stylistic lightness that seemed American enough to his critics, at least in 1886. Then Dvořák stirred the proverbial pot, leading interested musicians such as Arthur Weld and Herbert Krum to wonder again if the country would ever have a truly national music. Henry Schoenefeld's evidently terrible *Rural* Symphony had not convinced anyone that the matter was solved.

Questions concerning the sources of a folk-derived musical style (and whether these sources were authentically American or not) received the lion's share of attention during the debate. Such issues have since formed the cornerstone of our understanding of the impact of Dvořák's brief U.S. residency. But such single-minded focus has obscured the fact that questions about how to create a national school of composition had already occupied American musical discourse for decades. Swept up in the headiness of a celebrity's visit, many participants in the debate seemed to forget. Upon Dvořák's arrival, National Conservatory founder Jeannette Thurber's mission of fostering a "national musical spirit," which had originally meant training excellent performers, suddenly enveloped the creation of a national style of composition, whether or not one already existed.[1] Once again, the American compositional past seemed virtually inconsequential for its future.

THE PROPHET ARRIVES

New York City pulled out all the stops for Dvořák's arrival in late October of 1892, not long after the Brooklyn premiere of George Templeton Strong's *Sintram*, with a splendid concert designed to display local musical talent. It featured a robust rendition of a national hymn, two new works from the composer's own hand, and, inexplicably, Liszt's *Tasso*. All were executed admirably. Less well executed, however, was the introductory speech given by one of Boston Symphony founder Henry Higginson's older cousins, the abolitionist, poet, and social reformer Col. Thomas Wentworth Higginson (1823–1911). He was an improbable choice for a guest speaker. In his long speech, which drew parallels between the dawning of America and the dawning of music, Higginson asserted that the history of music had begun with Palestrina, who he then claimed was one of Christopher Columbus's contemporaries. Not aware of the historical inaccuracy, he proceeded calmly and eventually delivered his primary thesis that music was destined to find new shores following the Bohemian's arrival.[2]

But the damage had been done: The press panned Higginson's gaffe and needled him for it. Even so, the error actually sparked reflection on the nature of national compositional styles. A few days after the event, Henry Krehbiel wondered if the Bohemian visitor would indeed prove to be a good model and mentor for American composers. Could he help them develop a much-desired American school of composition? Krehbiel claimed that recent writers had denied the possibility of such a school because Americans lacked the sine qua non of a national style: "aboriginal peculiarities of rhythm or melody"—in essence, shared folk songs. Taking Higginson's blunder as a launching pad, he pointed out that many groups of composers, ranging from the Renaissance school of the Netherlands (Columbus's actual contemporaries) to the classical Viennese school of the eighteenth century, used no such "aboriginal" elements yet somehow managed to coalesce into a stylistically unified cluster.

But this definition of "school" needed revision, he claimed: "In the old sense a school is the product of a successful man who has invented or developed a style which has pleased the popular taste and proved to be a fit vehicle for his thoughts." This was Dwight's position. "If the American people of the future are bound to be a composite people," Krehbiel continued,

> so in all likelihood will their art be a composite art. If the spirit of the Folk-song is to be set down as essential to the vivification of their artistic creations in music, then the American composers of the future will have a richer storehouse to draw upon than ever had any of their predecessors, for already, though ignored, there is a body of Folk-song in this country of a most varied kind.[3]

Krehbiel believed that national schools *should* be based on folk songs and that Americans had plenty of musical material at their disposal. He had been making this argument for several years, and he stood in direct opposition to Dwight, who believed in the power of great figures to exert timeless influence. Dwight epitomized the essence of the old school.[4]

Dvořák's suitability as a mentor came into question because critics did not find his new works very praiseworthy. He was not at his compositional peak, they claimed. After naming the composer's commercial success in Great Britain as detrimental to his art, Krehbiel contended that he "has acquired a fatal ability in composition and, like Rubinstein, seems unable to stay his hand when he has only platitudes to utter."[5] Perhaps this was not the most hospitable way to treat a guest. Dvořák responded in kind. Later that fall, he stated publicly that the United States had produced very little "great" music, a gesture that quickly earned the ire of some of the country's more renowned composers, including Bostonians George Whitefield Chadwick and Amy Beach.[6] Krehbiel probably agreed with Dvořák. "Our chief want," he had once claimed, "is not theoretical learning or technical cleverness. It is originality, strength, and beauty of ideas."[7] These were the very properties that John Knowles Paine's critics, including Krehbiel himself, had perceived in his two symphonies.

The New York Philharmonic, under the Wagnerian and pro-American Anton Seidl's direction, gave the New York premiere of *Sintram* in March of 1893, only a few months after Dvořák's arrival. W. J. Henderson (1855–1937), the card-carrying Wagnerian critic of the *New York Times*, was enamored. Comparing the work favorably to music by Richard Strauss, "the horrible example of what may be done in this prostitution of a noble art to a nasty realism," he noted that "there is a mental and emotional field within which music may legitimately seek to excite the imagination by its endeavor to voice emotions of a sombre nature." Far from being realistic program music, all a listener needed to know to appreciate Strong's symphony was that "this is a tale of the conquest of evil and unbridled passions by Christianity." Following a brief description of the work itself, Henderson went on to praise Strong's individuality, treatment of themes, bold coloration, mastery of harmonic subtlety, and "perfect fluency" with chromatic modulation. Yet the gloom of the work, for Henderson, detracted from its overall effect, which was redeemed only by the scherzo.[8]

Others dismissed the symphony with a familiar charge: It was program music. Writing for the *Independent*, E. Irenaeus Stevenson asserted that "Mr. Strong has written a very long, ambitious and labored symphony with too close a kinship to 'program-music' to be acceptable, in the first place. [. . .] As music it is tiresomely lugubrious and unbeautiful and full of sheer noise: and its strength is that of the technician, with his pages laboriously worked out into a complex and turgid self-assertiveness."[9] Taking up much more space, Krehbiel recounted the story of Sintram in great detail but, as if he had set up a long joke, added, "It is a pity that entire appreciation of Mr. Strong's symphony must wait upon a knowledge of all we have said about his programme." After labeling Strong "an undisguised follower of Raff," he went on to deride the third and fourth movements as being overly dependent on the program, whereas the first and second were "sufficient unto themselves, from a musical point of view, alone." Following from this distinction, Krehbiel predictably praised the opening as the "strongest part of the work" and added that "it might fairly be questioned whether it has ever been equaled by an American symphonist in strength and fitness of idea and mastery of treatment."[10]

But for all of their pontificating about the value (or not) of writing deep, emotional music tied to a story, both Henderson and Stevenson wagged a finger at Strong over the fact that *Sintram* would not appeal to most concertgoers. With an impeccably serious symphony at hand, suddenly the average listener mattered despite being ignored for decades by critics. Fry would have fumed at the inconsistency.

THE PROPHET'S MISSION

Krehbiel did not care one way or the other. Both he and Dvořák were on what turned out to be a shared mission. The composer's lukewarm reception in October had likely faded from memory by the following May, when a new story leaped off the pages of the *New York Herald*: Dvořák finally broke his silence on the question of a national style when he famously remarked in an interview:

> [T]he future music of this country must be founded upon what are called negro melodies. This must be the real foundation of any serious and original school of composition to be developed in the United States. [. . .] These beautiful and varied themes are the product of the soil. They are American. [. . .] These are the folk songs of America and your composers must turn to them.[11]

These melodies could be used to express virtually any "mood or purpose," he added, and naturally move American listeners, making them both useful and powerful tools. One of his students had already attempted to write large-scale works in this style, and Dvořák had encouraged him to continue despite opposition from classmates. Krehbiel must have been pleased, for the Bohemian had strongly affirmed his own position on the matter.

Herald reporter James Creelman (1859–1915), Dvořák's supposed interviewer, framed the question of American national music in terms of its transatlantic importance. It was no mere localized issue, as Krehbiel seemed to believe. Using a personal connection to Anton Rubinstein as a way to acquire credibility, Creelman claimed that Dvořák's suggestions would be an auspicious method for combating Wagnerism, which many Americans had viewed with suspicion for decades. For those who remembered, Rubinstein's successful American piano tour in the early 1870s also granted his voice a high degree of authority.[12]

The transatlantic nature of the discussion was not limited to Creelman's savvy comments. The Paris edition of the *Herald* featured responses to Dvořák's ideas gathered from several European luminaries, including Rubinstein himself. A slightly confused Joseph Joachim (1831–1907), one of the world's leading violinists and a close friend of Brahms, remarked that "it may be a very good idea to try and merge the American negro melodies into an ideal form, and that these melodies would then give the tint to the national American music." A similarly perplexed Rubinstein believed it was a "fantastic idea" but felt that Americans—North Americans at least—had already surpassed a need to look for inspiration among a supposedly exotic group of people. According to an interviewer, Anton Bruckner (1824–1896), incidentally a year Bristow's senior, frowned on the idea as he took a German universalist position much closer to Paine's:

> [Bruckner] is an elderly man, has been brought up amid the traditions of the strictest school, and I was therefore little surprised when he asserted that the basis of all music must be found in the classical works of the past. German musical literature, he declared, contained no written text emanating from the negro race, and however sweet the negro melodies might be, they could never form the groundwork of the future music of America.[13]

Although these opinions had very little residual effect in Europe, they had achieved the most desirable result for the *Herald*: People were talking.

The sensationalism worked. The acquisition of European commentary in the week following the initial exposé allowed the *Herald's* New York editors to compile a blockbuster Sunday edition that included excerpts from the European remarks, as well as a letter from Dvořák affirming the comments made in his interview with Creelman.[14] The *Boston Herald* also benefited from the time lag and printed a major story on Dvořák that featured a wide variety of opinions from local musicians. The spectrum essentially mirrored that of the Europeans. John Knowles Paine predictably disagreed with the whole prospect of a national music, upholding his belief that art music was universal. Edward N. Catlin (1835?–1926), a well-known theater musician, embraced Dvořák's suggestions fully. Still others questioned the degree to which plantation songs were "American" at all. B. J. Lang (1837–1909), one of Boston's most distinguished conductors, remained skeptical but optimistic and encouraged Dvořák to illustrate his theories, "which, if followed, might beget for the dark race of our southern states and its history, what Liszt was for the Hungarian, Chopin for the Pole and Dvořák himself has been for the Bohemian."[15]

Dvořák took up Lang's challenge in his new symphony. Krehbiel thought that the composer had risen to meet it and believed the piece foretold a new age. Writing with insider information granted by Dvořák himself, Krehbiel wrote a lengthy and penetrating analysis of the work that included nearly a dozen handwritten musical illustrations—a highly unusual element in a daily newspaper. He concluded that each movement had a key stylistic facet ranging from rhythmic gestures to scales and coloration that marked it as peculiarly American. Responses to the work's premiere were also exceptionally enthusiastic and included positive remarks from luminaries such as Victor Herbert (1859–1924), the Philharmonic's principal cellist, and Anton Seidl himself. Krehbiel was elated, Creelman vindicated. Each hailed the work as a massive success for both Dvořák and the future of American music. But the greatest encomium came from the pen of *New York Times* critic W. J. Henderson: "We Americans should thank and honor the Bohemian master who has shown us how to build our national school of music." The whole event was a collective sigh of relief since American composers had purportedly been failing at the project for decades.[16]

Unlike the other reviewers, Henderson remarked openly on American composers' previous failures, a potentially touchy subject: "The composers, the critics, and the musical public all labored under the delusion that Dr. Dvořák was going to take a pinch of 'Bell da Ring,' 'Marching Through Georgia,' and 'Way Down Upon the Suanee Ribber' and try to make a symphony with unsymphonic and inflexible melodies. The American composers had tried such tunes and—if we may be pardoned the word—they would not symphonize."[17] To which composers he was referring remains a mystery, but his general thrust was that earlier attempts to manifest a national spirit had involved only the mere quotation of minstrel tunes; this of course was entirely false. A mere teenager when Bristow's *Arcadian* premiered, Henderson did not know any better.

THE PROPHET CHALLENGED

George Whitefield Chadwick entered the Dvořák debate when he publicly dismissed the Bohemian's ideas. He said he would be "sorry to see Negro melodies become the basis of an American school of musical composition."[18] Later writers have nevertheless tried to portray Chadwick as one of the originators of a distinctively American style, much as contemporaries of Gottschalk, Stoepel, Bristow, and Phelps had argued to their credit. In an essay on American symphonists written in 1900, for example, the typically negative Louis Elson remarked that "Chadwick's symphonic work has an especial interest from the fact that he has managed to impart a distinctly American character. [. . .] The scherzo of his first symphony (C major) indicates a path which Dvořák generally receives the credit for having discovered for us."[19] Elson's memory must have been failing him; he had said nothing of the sort in his review of the premiere (see chapter 11). And the fact that Dvořák's recommendations involved engaging with the music of marginalized populations, the very element Chadwick had rejected in the press, did not seem to occur to him.

In May of 1893, the National Conservatory announced a second round of competitions for American works. This time Chadwick decided to try his hand with a new symphony. It was an easy decision, for he had been working on one since (at least) the premiere of Henry Schoenefeld's earlier work. The committee even made accommodations to raise the maximum age of potential entrants so that Chadwick could participate; Krehbiel himself had made this suggestion. The prize, incidentally, had been reduced to $300, a number that might have enticed Bristow had he not been too old. It was three times what he made as a commission for the *Arcadian*. Dvořák notified Chadwick that he had won the following April, the very month that Weld's and Roosevelt's articles passed across the desks of countless readers. With the prize awarded, the stage had once again been set for a "true" American composer to emerge.[20]

But Chadwick was not destined to be that composer. Following the work's premiere in October, critics greeted his symphony with a mélange of mostly negative responses. Warren Davenport of the *Boston Herald* lamented that "one is induced to conclude that Mr. Chadwick has failed to achieve a success." Returning to Chadwick's ability to write a symphony, he concluded with a dismissal: "If the masterpieces in this form of composition by Mozart, Beethoven, Schumann, Mendelssohn, Schubert, Brahms, Paine, Raff, and Dvorak are symphonies, then this work of Mr. Chadwick's must be placed in some other class of composition."[21] Louis Elson compared the music to Brahms: "In the first movement the composer leads one into a development that is a jungle made up of fragments. The composer falls into the style of Brahms in giving many small thoughts rather than one continuous one, but Brahms's piece-work is more intelligible."[22]

Philip Hale, writing to New York's *Musical Courier*, simply called the work a "disappointment."[23] Equally anti-Brahms and anti-Dvořák, he also twisted his knife: "Mr. Chadwick has been sitting at the feet of Mr. Johannes Brahms. He has also listened—no doubt unconsciously—to the pleasing performance of Mr. Anton Dvorak on the celebrated instrument known as the Negro-Indian American pipe, which I believe is the invention of Messrs. Krehbiel & Company." And damning with faint praise, he added: "Not that he has in any degree whatever copied either of these men." Of course the reason for the work's lack of inspiration was clear to both: It was a "prize" symphony. "The road to the Temple of Fame is paved with prize compositions trodden under foot," Hale spat, "forgotten by the cutthroat band that rush toward the closed door."

Not everyone found so much to discredit. William F. Apthorp waxed at length that "it would take more than a prize to kill this symphony" and enjoyed the unexpected rhythmic and tonal transformation of the first movement's primary theme at the beginning of the recapitulation (example 12.1).[24] He also detected traces of an American sound, noting that Chadwick had harnessed the seriousness of his earlier works "but has lost not a whit of his native charm and fascination by so doing." The scherzo in particular sounded American, Hale nodded, adding, "Mr. Chadwick has avoided the mistake of trying deliberately to turn a serious work of art into a wandering booth where alleged folk songs are labeled and pointed out by the stick of the showman" (example 12.2). This comment was an oblique reference to the

Example 12.1: Transformation of Primary Theme. Chadwick, Symphony No. 3, I: Allegro sostenuto:
(a) Exposition, mm. 5–13 (violin I).
(b) Recapitulation, mm. 276–88 (flute).

Example 12.2: Jaunty Scherzo Melody. Chadwick, Symphony No. 3, III: Vivace non troppo, mm. 1–21 (violin II).

Columbian Exposition of Chicago, one of Dvořák's central sources of musical inspiration. From Apthorp's perspective, Chadwick's music was authentically American.[25]

Critics would later change their tune as Chadwick's profile continued to rise after Dvořák's departure. Following an all-Chadwick concert staged by the Boston Symphony in 1904, one writer remarked that "the first movement of this is full of learned musicianship, the development of themes being the most carefully carried out that we know of in any American instrumental work." The "rollicking" scherzo proved that Chadwick was "emphatically the American master."[26] A year later, the *Boston Globe* reported that Paul Zschörlisch, a Berlin critic, gave it exceptionally high praise: "I declare that I consider this symphony the best of all that has been written since Brahms. [. . .] From this symphony, I hold George W. Chadwick to be the most important living Anglo-American composer—Edward Elgar not excepted."[27] Speaking for the work's original audience, however, Elson had shaken his head: "All in all, one finds much to praise in the work, but at the end one must confess that the great American symphony is not yet written."[28] But there would be still more attempts before century's end.

THE PROPHET REINTERPRETED

Amy Beach (1867–1944), a young but respected musical voice in 1893, became involved in the Dvořák controversy when the *Boston Herald* published her finely wrought response to the Bohemian's theories alongside those of Paine, Chadwick, and other leading lights. While not denying Dvořák's stylistic accomplishments, she claimed that "negro melodies" were "not fully typical of our country," nor were they of a "native" American people. Instead, she pointed out:

> We of the North should be far more likely to be influenced by old English, Scotch or Irish songs inherited with our literature from our ancestors. [. . .] In order to make the best use of folk-songs of any nation as material for musical composition, the writer should be one of the people whose songs he chooses, or at least brought up among them.[29]

For a folk melody to move a listener, the individual needed a close personal relationship with the culture from which the music arose. Dvořák was not wrong about the means—folk song—but rather its meaning for potential listeners. Taking her theory and combining it with Dvořák's spirit, Beach moved into action by writing her first symphony, *Gaelic*, just days after hearing the Boston premiere of the "New World" Symphony. She would become one of the first American composers to make a symphonic debut following the fracas.

Had the discussion taken place any sooner, Beach would have been an unlikely candidate to enter it at all. Despite showing great proclivity for music as a child, she faced immense prejudices and difficulties early in her career that revolved around her identity and status as a woman. When her parents approached Wilhelm Gericke, the newly appointed director of the Boston Symphony, for advice about pursuing further compositional training, he suggested that she become an autodidact while studying the great works of the past, rather than traveling abroad to study at one of Europe's prestigious conservatories. In other words, he would deny her the path that Paine and Chadwick had been able to follow. Furthermore, she abandoned her career as a performer after marrying a Boston physician and directed her musical focus exclusively toward composition. Though it stifled her performance career, this new arrangement gave her ample opportunity to familiarize herself with the intimate details of a vast number of scores.[30] Such careful study allowed Beach to acquire a distinct and rare historical acumen that shone in her works. With the financial backing of her husband, she also did not face the same institutional challenges that vexed Fry, Bristow, and Phelps.

Upon hearing Dvořák's symphony, Beach complained privately about it in notes she kept to herself. It seemed to her to be

> light in caliber, [. . .] and to represent only the peaceful, sunny side of the negro character and life. Not for a moment does it suggest their sufferings, heartbreaks, *slavery*. It is all active, bright, cheery, and domestic, the slow movement especially suggesting the home life to me, with the baby being sung to sleep. From this point of view it is admirable, but there is much more that might have been added, of the dark, tragic, side!![31]

She had not heard Phelps's *Emancipation*, which critics believed had effectively captured the pathos of slavery. Even so, she began her work armed with fresh ideas about national music and musical realism, areas where she believed Dvořák had fallen short.

Beach entered into a clear dialogue with Dvořák's "New World" while addressing what she perceived as its flaws. Whereas the Bohemian's melodies hinted at an exotic otherness that listeners were supposed to intuit as American (or at least that was Krehbiel's argument),[32] Beach quoted folk tunes taken directly from older printed sources and used them as the basis for further elaboration. The second movement of the *Gaelic* Symphony opens with a broad French horn solo that melts into a full presentation of a jaunty tune called "Goirtin Ornadh" ("The Little Field of Barley") played by the oboe, perhaps with a nod to the "winkin'" oboe line in the analogous portion of Chadwick's Second (example 12.3). Over the course of the movement, the tune appears in various guises, including in a substantial duet between

Example 12.3: Quotation of "The Little Field of Barley." Beach, Symphony in E Minor, *Gaelic*, II: Alla Siciliana, mm. 5–12 (oboe).

the oboe and the English horn, which was Beach's response to the haunting melody of Dvořák's famous "New World" largo.

Beyond asserting musical and cultural authenticity by quoting folk tunes, Beach also attempted to project greater emotional realism, particularly in the expansive third movement. She again chose two Celtic tunes as primary themes: a lullaby and a melancholy song of longing. Both tunes appeared alongside critical commentary in issues of the *Citizen*, a Dublin magazine, dating from 1841. The original setting of the lullaby "Paisdin Fuinne" ("The Good Child") presented the ethereal tune in the high tessitura of a violin's lower strings, granting it a strained quality.[33] Beach adapted this sonority by scoring the melody for a solo cellist introduced by an intense violin recitative (example 12.4a). The somber mood created by this setting extends forward into the second song, "Cia an Bealach a Deachaidh Si" ("Which Way Did She Go?"), also known as "The Mother's Lamentation," which depicts a mother grieving the death of her child. The writer for the *Citizen* had noted that this particular tune had assumed nationalist connotations following the failed Irish Rebellion of 1798.[34] But in succession with the lullaby, it creates a larger narrative arc of sleep and death that engenders a single emotional thrust (example 12.4b).

The Boston Symphony, under the direction of Emil Paur (1855–1932), premiered Beach's symphony in October of 1896, the year following Dvořák's departure from the United States. Beach furnished William F. Apthorp, the orchestra's program annotator, with a detailed description of the work that he adapted to fit the length of the booklet. There were no remarks about tune quotation in either case. Apparently oblivious, Apthorp described the opening melody of the third movement (example 12.4a) as "a melody of strongly-marked Gaelic character," having "the characteristic Keltic closing

Example 12.4: Tune Quotations. Beach, Symphony in E Minor, *Gaelic*, III: Lento con molto espressione:
(a) "The Good Child," mm. 15–23 (solo violin and solo cello).
(b) "Which Way Did She Go?" mm. 55–58 (violin I).

cadence, from the third degree of the scale to the tonic."[35] He left no further remarks about the work's national identity.

Most reviews of this performance were highly congratulatory and noted Beach's "scholarly" approach to the genre, a result of her careful score study. While critics did not make the connection explicit, this designation would have had the rhetorical effect of placing her in a category with Paine and Chadwick, whose works critics had described with the same term. Writing for the *Boston Courier*, a delighted Howard Ticknor believed the work might find a place in the permanent canon but focused special attention on its projection of a "Gaelic" spirit. Wondering why it had been given the title, he speculated,

> Probably, as we would guess, rather because its moods are significant of those which history and poetry have roused in the composer's mind and heart, and are intended to hint to the hearer the windy waste, the gloomy world, the strange sadness, the scarcely less strange gayety and the restless combative spirit of the land and life of the ideal Gael.[36]

If his only knowledge of the work's background derived from Apthorp's notes, he might not have known Beach quoted and developed actual Celtic songs, more or less according to Dvořák's prescription. For Ticknor, the symphony projected a national ethos without necessarily embodying national musical values.

Other early reviewers, including Apthorp and Philip Hale, likewise did not comment at any length on the expression of a national identity, even given the work's clear dialogue with Dvořák. Apthorp focused his attention on the work's orchestration.[37] But the most negative critics displayed heightened anxiety over the emergence of a truly valid American symphonic voice capable of speaking to international audiences. Louis Elson, who had denied the label of "great American symphony" to Chadwick's latest effort, remarked that Beach's work was "a far cry, even from such a high position in art, to the successful creation of symphonies; neither the male nor the female native composers have as yet produced a musical composition in this large, heroic form, that is going to stand the test of time." And if once were not enough, he made the point again:

> A Paine (foremost of all American composers) may give learned development of themes, a Chadwick the spontaneity and brilliancy of a true Scherzo, a Beach the delicate beauty and tenderness of a slow movement, but the "Admirable Crichton," who is to shine in all these fields has not yet appeared in the native symphonic repertoire.[38]

The question of a style-based nationalism animating the Dvořák debate was of no concern to Elson, who believed that musical greatness was transcendent and nationless. He also showed little acknowledgment of the enthusiastic response of the audience, which overwhelmed Beach with applause after every movement. He described this response as "cordial appreciation."

After several sporadic performances over the next six months, Paur and the Boston Symphony brought out the work again in Brooklyn alongside a new overture by Ellsworth Phelps. Though skeptical of Phelps's overture, the *Daily Eagle* critic was taken by Beach's symphony and, echoing Apthorp, compared the orchestral writing to that of Joachim Raff and Camille Saint-Saëns, two figures with established American reputations. Despite finding certain "flaws," the critic remarked that "we may pride ourselves on being the only nation that has a woman composer of symphonies at this writing."[39] Her identity as a woman notwithstanding (a subject that the critic could not help but mention), she had made headway toward an international reputation—a boon for the country at large.

Curiously, Henry Krehbiel was unmoved. Returning to the well-worn Beethoven problem, he began with the observation that "all the composers who have lived since Beethoven have lived in vain so far as their influence in his manner of musical thought is concerned." In accordance with the general dislike of Phelps that Krehbiel had expressed elsewhere, he added that she had bested the Brooklynite in that regard. Damning the symphony with faint praise, however, he also noted that only minor improvements were needed to transform it from a curiosity (a symphony by a woman) into a work demanding a performance "for its own sake." More surprising, though, Krehbiel did not appreciate Beach's incorporation of Irish folk tunes. The gesture had justified the work's title, he claimed, but did not "stamp [it] with a spirit which would be recognized as characteristically Gaelic." He concluded, "In this respect, as well as in the development of the national material the symphony falls short of Dr. Stanford's symphony called 'Irish.'"[40] To Krehbiel's ears, the work certainly was not American. Though with a different value system entirely, he, like Elson, was still waiting for a great American symphony.

Despite the vehemence of naysayers such as Elson and Krehbiel, Beach and Chadwick are the only two composers appearing in this book who have become subjects of scholarly biographies published in the last twenty years. Such attention is partly a consequence of the fact that their works have made small headway into the canonical repertoire of contemporary symphony orchestras. Like Chadwick, Beach garnered the support of much of Boston's critical establishment, the Boston Symphony Orchestra, and the publishing firm of Arthur P. Schmidt, which had also published major works by Paine and Chadwick and with which she eventually entered into an exclusive relationship. Such support translated into far more performances of their works than most of their compatriots, which in turn left a larger print record of their accomplishments. Beach also left an extensive collection of manuscripts, notes, and correspondence after living well into the twentieth century. Born two years after Robert E. Lee's surrender at the Appomattox courthouse, she died of heart disease just five months before Nazi Germany's surrender to the Allies in World War II.

THE STALWART'S LAST STAND

Henry Krehbiel did not openly acknowledge the existence of older composers at any point early in Dvořák's residency. The omission may be excusable because of his age. Having been born in 1854, he could not have had any clear memory of the Philharmonic contretemps or Stoepel's 1859 *Hiawatha*; he did not move to New York until many years later. But there can be no doubt that Krehbiel knew of the existence of Bristow's mid-century symphonies, as well as the more recent *Arcadian*. All are listed in the appendix to his retrospective catalog of the New York Philharmonic's performance history, which he had compiled for the orchestra's fiftieth anniversary.[41] The omission was a conscious neglect.

Not all of the debate's participants were so forgetful. Responding to Dvořák's initial comments from May of 1893, Boston composer and organist

George Whiting (1840–1923) remarked that he had "advocated the same thing: that is, that, failing to find anything in the shape of American folk songs the native composer would do well to avail himself of these negro melodies for hint of local color."[42] Whiting's advocacy was one thing; implementation was quite another. Writing to the *New York Herald* later that spring, a writer named "A. Thompson" was even more rattled by the discussion's ignorance of the past:

> This idea may be original with Dr. Dvořák, but George F. Bristow advanced that theory ten years ago and was laughed at for it. Bristow's idea was that the American school of music would partake more of the character of negro melody in the South than the so-called negro melodies sung at minstrel shows. [. . .] To prove Bristow's claim in being the first to put forth this idea, about five years ago he wrote a piano piece called a "Walk Around" (a decidedly original composition). Also in a new symphony Bristow has put a "Breakdown." So you see it is only just that as Bristow, an American and one of our best musicians, should be recognized as the first to put forth this idea.[43]

Thompson, like the reader who exposed Dwight's coldness during the Stoepel *Hiawatha* affair, wanted to be sure that the public was aware that critics were controlling these discussions, and that these figures were not necessarily trustworthy keepers of history.

The gap across the river to Brooklyn may also help explain Krehbiel's neglect. The musical cultures of Brooklyn and New York, while overlapping heavily, were distinct. It was, in fact, a Brooklyn critic who made the strongest case for remembering "forgotten" composers after hearing the local premiere of Dvořák's symphony:

> Those who heard it delightedly exclaimed that, though not written by an American, it was the first one composed in the United States and heard in this city. The last assertion is hasty and mistaken. The name of E. C. Phelps will at once occur to every local music student and listener. Earlier, George F. Bristow was associated with like composition.[44]

Brooklynites knew these familiar names. The critic also noted that there was nothing particularly American about Dvořák's music; play Bristow's last symphony side by side with it, and no one could have any doubts about which was the more authentic.

Bristow, now nearly seventy years old, had undoubtedly witnessed the Dvořák controversy unfolding in the press. He could have heard the "New World" and Beach's *Gaelic* in concert. By all accounts, he was still quite vivacious despite having resigned from performing as a Philharmonic violinist in 1882. During the controversy itself, he had been hard at work on one final symphony, an expansive work with a choral finale rivaling Phelps's *Emancipation* in grandiosity, if not in formal dimensions. He completed this four-movement work, subtitled *Niagara*, in September of 1893, three months before the premiere of Dvořák's "New World."

For reasons that may never be ascertained, *Niagara* did not premiere for another four and a half years, in April of 1898. There is little extant information about the performance itself. Important local figures had planned to mount an extravagant Niagara Falls celebration in mid-spring with Bristow's new symphony as the centerpiece. But Anton Seidl, who had been engaged to conduct, died unexpectedly two weeks before the event. Swept up by the drumming of impending war with Spain, few major dailies covered the performance, which Bristow himself directed in Seidl's place. The work was the final statement made by one of the country's most distinguished composers, and it was heard in one of New York's newest and best venues, Carnegie Hall.[45]

When Thompson wrote his message to the press during the Dvořák debate, Bristow had only just finished the work, suggesting that the two had shared ideas privately. By this time, Bristow had become a member of the Manuscript Society of New York, an organization whose purpose was to allow composers to share their works with others in a safe, congenial environment (a purpose reminiscent of Jerome Hopkins's effort of the mid-1850s). Although the Manuscript Society performed new pieces by over one hundred different composers during its brief existence, including Phelps, Paine, Beach, and Chadwick, the press panned it repeatedly while its members fell into complacency about its future, much like its mid-century forebear.[46]

Bristow constructed the symphony to mirror the awesome size of Niagara Falls. Though it is in four movements, the first three serve as an instrumental prelude to a grandiose multipart choral finale. The closest model would have been Mendelssohn's *Lobgesang*, but the work was unfamiliar to New Yorkers.[47] The first movement of *Niagara* begins with a solo trumpet call that immediately gives way to an earnest unison theme in C minor sounded by the low strings. The solo trumpet was reminiscent of Ellsworth Phelps's *Emancipation* and Louis Maas's *On the Prairies*, whereas the low string melody had become a signature for Bristow. Molded into sonata form, the movement assumes a *per aspera ad astra* trajectory as it closes with a coda in C major marked "furioso." Undulating eighth-note figures in the strings underpin a triumphant woodwind and brass chorale. The second movement, a succulent adagio, is the most conventional and exhibits the textural and rhythmic density of Bristow's earlier works.

As Thompson noted, Bristow called the third movement "A Breakdown," a rowdy fiddle dance with bawdy connotations that cut across racial, gender, and class boundaries alike.[48] Patterned loosely on the two-strain structure of fiddle tunes, the movement alternates between statements of the primary strain and episodic passages. The colorful introduction features shrill woodwind punches and heavy syncopated figures in the strings that build momentum as they tumble into the fiendish primary strain (example 12.5a). The whirlwind character of this section persists for several bars before blending seamlessly into a contrasting strain, in which the first violins play a lyrical tune in A♭ major—a folksy cowboy rendition of a hymn-like melody—to the accompaniment of slow-moving strings and clucking, syncopated woodwinds (example 12.5b). Following a full restatement of the primary strain, the next episode contains a placid tune in $\frac{6}{8}$ accompanied by a rolling clarinet line (example 12.5c). Instead of returning to the primary theme in full, however, Bristow treated it with a four-part fugato in the strings. The movement closes with a strident coda featuring a rich orchestration of the primary strain sounding on a foundation of driving eighth notes. The final gesture anticipates Aaron Copland's "Hoe Down" by nearly fifty years (example 12.5d).

Despite the intensity of the preceding movements, they pale in comparison to the cantata-like finale. Structurally similar to Mendelssohn's *Lobgesang*,

Example 12.5: Bristow, Symphony No. 5, *Niagara*, III: "Breakdown" (Allegro):
(a) Primary Strain, mm. 9–16 (full orch.).
(b) Folksy Hymn Tune, mm. 34–49 (full orch.).
(c) Rollicking Clarinet Melody, mm. 142–151 (clarinet 1 and strings).
(d) Concluding Gesture (full orch.).

Example 12.5: (Continued)

(b)

it comprises six numbered sections that include arias, duets, and choruses. The first number begins with a majestic double-dotted instrumental section serving an overture-like function. The full choir, joined by trumpet and trombone, suddenly begins singing a century-old hymn by Nathan Strong (1748–1816) praising God for the glory of nature. Following convention, Bristow set the words to the august tune "Old Hundredth" (example 12.6a).

Example 12.5: (Continued)

Bristow's choice to set the final strophe of of the hymn, which describes choral singing ("Let ev'ry power of heart and tongue/Unite to swell the grateful song"), mimics the self-referentiality of the text Beethoven appended to
Schiller's "An die Freude" in the finale of the Ninth ("Let us strike up more

Example 12.6: Choral Quotations. Bristow, Symphony No. 5, *Niagara*, IV:
(a) "Old Hundredth," No. 1: Maestoso, mm. 43–47 (full chorus and orch.).
(b) *Messiah*, No. 2: Allegro, mm. 124–132 (full chorus and orch.).

pleasing/and more joyful [sounds]"). The second number, a lyrical tenor aria, gives way to another unexpected quotation. As the vocalist finishes his line, the choir joins the texture, singing "King of Kings, Lord of Lords" to the instrumental accompaniment in Handel's famous setting in *Messiah* (example 12.6b). Later numbers include an ode to the Great Lakes and a final paean to Niagara Falls.[49]

The movement concludes violently with an instrumental coda depicting the roaring of the waterfalls. The maelstrom is interrupted briefly by a pianissimo restatement of the trumpet motive that opened the entire work. As the music regains intensity for a final grandiose codetta, this motive, which outlines dominant and tonic, slips into the lower sections of the ensemble as the full orchestra insistently blasts a C-major triad. William Henry Fry's ill-fated *Niagara*, which was never performed during his lifetime, contains a similar moment near the end of its first movement. It is even in the same key. But while Bristow probably did not know the piece, his finale closed a loop that connected the turn of a new century to the launch of the American symphonic enterprise.

Epilogue

In the introduction, I compared nineteenth-century American symphonic enterprise to an endless winter in which early-blooming perennial flowers, anticipating warmth, broke through the soil only to find that the air was still too cold. The first several chapters illustrated the vitality and variety of symphonic composition throughout the antebellum era in spite of institutional obstacles. Later chapters demonstrated how changing values led to willful ignorance of the country's compositional past as a new generation of composers vied for space on increasingly crowded programs. In many cases, however, they too experienced denunciation or outright neglect as critical and institutional goals continued to change. None of this music survived as part of the standard performance repertoire after the turn of the century because its most powerful potential cultivators—critics and conductors—had maintained inhospitable attitudes toward it before it had a chance to thrive.

The elements of this frigid winter persisted into the twentieth century and would continue to have negative effects on aspiring composers. As musical values continued to change rapidly, especially those concerning national identity and stylistic innovation, critics relegated the music of nineteenth-century American composers to the dustbin of history while applying mutable standards of criticism to each new crop. During the search for a so-called Great American Symphony, which flourished during the period between the two world wars, U.S. composers such as Roy Harris eventually found a small niche among the musical mainstream—an achievement their nineteenth-century forebears had long sought. Even so, their identities as white men earned them the relatively privileged status held by not-quite-canonical German composers such as Carl Goldmark and Joachim Raff during the latter part of the nineteenth century. Composers who were not white or male, such as Florence Price, became the excluded equivalent of U.S.-born composers of the nineteenth century, such as Ellsworth Phelps. As Price's story illustrates, race and gender had overtly and nefariously replaced a composer's country of origin as targets of prejudice during this period.

To close the institutional loop opened in the introduction, I conclude with reflections on the remarkable fact that U.S. orchestras continued (and continue) to favor nineteenth-century European (and mostly German) symphonic music even after they welcomed a new class of native-born composers into the fold. Given patterns established in the nineteenth century, this fact should not be surprising at all. Mirroring the New York Philharmonic's decisions of the late 1840s and 1850s, the choice not to support new, local music has become institutionally entwined in the very fabric of our national orchestral music culture.

NOT AMERICAN ENOUGH

As we saw in the opening of chapter 11, many writers dubbed John Knowles Paine the first great American symphonist. Achieving this label required at least some concession that he had successfully entered the German tradition, as well as the tacit admission that previous composers had failed. If we return for a moment to Theodore Thomas's retrospective concert of American music given in 1876, we can witness one of the first explicit dismissals of earlier work. Commenting on William Henry Fry's *A Day in the Country*, the reviewer observed, "Mr. Fry had many fine qualities and much ability; but as a composer he was not great. At a time when the aesthetic condition of the whole country was a feeble copy of that in other countries, he produced *Leonora*, the first opera ever written by an American."[1] As a feeble imitator apparently incapable of originality, Fry had failed. Paine, the supposed innovator, had moved the country in the right direction. As earlier chapters demonstrate, neither characterization was accurate.

Paine's supposed entry into the German tradition might have earned him prestige among thinkers who believed in its universality, but composers of his generation would later stand on the receiving end of the same sweeping criticism leveled at Fry's generation in the 1870s. In one of Leonard Bernstein's Young People's Concerts from 1958, for example, the conductor described music from the later nineteenth century in the same vein in which Fry's critic had described his—essentially as a "feeble copy":

> Actually, our really serious music didn't begin until about seventy-five years ago [ca. 1880]. At that time the few American composers we had just imitated the European composers, like Brahms, Liszt, and Wagner. We might call this the kindergarten period of American music. For instance, there was a very

fine composer named George W. Chadwick, who wrote expert music, and even deeply felt music; but you almost can't tell it apart from Brahms or Wagner.[2]

How the tables had turned! Chadwick's initial audiences believed his music was distinctively American, and they criticized it for not being serious enough. The antebellum era did not figure into Bernstein's formulation at all. And one is left to wonder that if Chadwick's music really sounded like Brahms or Wagner, why Bernstein did not program more of it.

In a lecture given to a more mature audience earlier in the 1950s, Aaron Copland presented the plight of nineteenth-century American composers with greater empathy. He explained that, at around the turn of the twentieth century, the music of local composers was not readily available, either in performance or in published scores. The composers themselves had studied in Europe and, "like us, they came home full of admiration for the treasures of European musical art, with the self-appointed mission of expounding these glories to their countrymen." So far his statements were accurate. "But," he continued,

> When I think of these older men, and especially of the most important among them—John Knowles Paine, George Chadwick, Arthur Foote, Horatio Parker—who made up the Boston school of composers at the turn of the century, I am aware of the fundamental difference between their attitude and our own. Their attitude was founded upon an admiration for the European art work and an identification with it that made the seeking out of any other art formula a kind of sacrilege. The challenge of the Continental art work was not: can we do better or can we also do something truly our own, but merely, can we do as well.[3]

Copland likely would not have made this assessment had he known the idiosyncratic works of Heinrich, Fry, Stoepel, Phelps, and the later Bristow, but of course he did not know them. They were already "dead." With some aplomb, he added, "Meeting Brahms or Wagner on his own terms one is certain to come off second best." Working on their new symphonies of the early 1870s, how could Bristow and Paine have known that Brahms was in the middle of writing a "better" one? And what of the many U.S. critics who railed against Brahms's First in direct opposition to the positive European accounts published in advance of its premiere? For Copland, Brahms's entry into the symphonic canon was a foregone conclusion.

The importance of these comments lies in the fact that Bernstein and Copland were not chauvinist German musicologists steeped in idealist or formalist aesthetics. Rather, they enjoyed a great deal of symbolic authority as well-respected public figures. Bernstein directly influenced the performing canon, and both were composers themselves. The marginalization or typecasting of earlier generations bolstered their own claims of originality and distinctiveness, particularly *as* Americans. In the lecture quoted above, Bernstein later remarked that a "truly American" music did not arise until composers attempted to create an "American-*sounding*" music. In his perception of history, which matched the stance taken by historian Gilbert Chase at the same time, Antonín Dvořák's arrival in 1892 had spurred this effort.[4]

Bernstein and Copland found success by writing in what many listeners have considered an accessible and American-sounding style, but they are the ones who presumed that creating such a style was a self-evident goal. Paine, as we saw, believed the country's destiny was to reinvigorate the classical German tradition. Anton Seidl and Calixa Lavallée believed that American music should be Wagnerian. William Henry Fry believed it should be Italian. One was no more right than the others.

NOT NEW ENOUGH

Copland's and Bernstein's comments illustrate how the conferral of value upon composers and works, both old and new, had increased in complexity during the twentieth century as ideologies diversified. Outside of the positions held by the two composers, German-speaking performers continued to dominate instrumental ensembles, while conductors and the academy tended to favor the universalist disposition of Paine and Dwight. These groups were not wholly indifferent to the place of American composers; they simply made no concerted effort to change the status quo.

Complicating matters further, critical discourse concerning the search for an American sound included not only the remnants of Dvořák's influence and questions about "folk" elements, as Bernstein suggested, but also the rise of modernism.[5] This new mentality led writers to propose any number of figures as the first national composer while casting aside those whose music did not embody some new and modern national (or international) ideal.[6] After claiming that the Civil War had left the country bereft of "potencies in any field," prominent American critic Paul Rosenfeld asserted in 1929 that "musicians, men like Paine . . . were forceless; weak personalities."[7] But Paine's original critics, as we saw, praised the masculinity and vigor of his music using the same turns of phrase they had used to describe Beethoven's music, thus making implicit connections.

Rosenfeld's vision of national identity was distinctively forward-looking. He went on to identify Edward MacDowell as the progenitor of an American musical spirit and described its development in chronologically overlapping stages that included, in order of American-ness: the "eclectic" immigrants Charles Loeffler, Leo Ornstein, and Dane Rudhyar; the "eclectic" natives Roger Sessions, Adolph Weiss, Virgil Thomson, and Carl Ruggles; the "autonomous" Horatio Parker, Deems Taylor, Roy Harris, and Aaron Copland; the "primitive" but ruggedly idiosyncratic Carlos Chávez; and, finally, Edgard Varèse, whose works contained the "greatest fullness of power and of prophecy yet to come of music in America."[8] The last two names might surprise us today, particularly since we do not think of them as American composers cut from the same cloth as Harris or Copland. But the author of the rules greatly affects the outcome. And the rules had certainly changed: George Chadwick and Amy Beach were still active when Rosenfeld was writing. Paine's and Chadwick's students, such as Henry Hadley, likewise must have been too conservative—too foggily Germanic—to warrant mention. They were not new enough.

Rhetoric that held the nineteenth century in a state of perpetual infancy or utter dependence on Europe also benefited Charles Ives, both during his lifetime and in his posthumous reception. For those seeking a folk-derived national music, including Henry Cowell and Rosenfeld himself, Ives's quotation or integration of hymnody and other vernacular styles fit the bill.[9] In earlier eras, listeners greeted these specific techniques differently. Bristow was called a plagiarist in the 1870s for quoting "Tallis's Evening Hymn" in the *Arcadian* Symphony, while audiences sat transfixed as they listened to the "Adeste fideles" finale of Fry's *Santa Claus* in 1853. For other writers, Ives has represented a belated manifestation of New England transcendentalism. This perspective is most ironic, however, because the actual transcendentalists who cared about classical music—John Sullivan Dwight and Margaret Fuller—worshiped Beethoven and appropriated his music as American. The question of how to construct a distinctively American music did not have any urgency for them.[10]

Several writers, furthermore, have rightly called into question the originality of Ives's techniques when compared to the European classical tradition or to earlier American symphonic music.[11] The charge of ignorance can nevertheless be used as a failsafe in order to justify his seminal position. If Ives did not know (or know of) works by Heinrich, Fry, Bristow, Phelps, and others, then his music seems all the more idiosyncratic and self-reliant. But if Ives truly did not know this music (and can we ever be sure with Ives?), it was because it had already fallen out of collective memory. We should bear in mind that Bristow's *Niagara*, with its fiddle-driven breakdown and extravagant collage-like choral finale, premiered in 1898, the same year that Ives began writing his own first symphony. Due to the unfortunate circumstances of its premiere, the *Niagara* Symphony faded from view as quickly as it appeared. Ives was not as far removed from the previous two generations of American composers as we might presume.

NOT GOOD ENOUGH

The metaphorical winter I have proposed was not only rhetorical; it also had tangible effects on composers' lives. While planning for the

1876 Centennial Exhibition, conductor Theodore Thomas gave $5,000 to Richard Wagner for a grand ceremonial work to open the festivities. This figure was fifty times Bristow's commission for the *Arcadian*. Had Thomas given Bristow (or any American) this money, it naturally would have made a huge material difference to his well-being; Wagner pocketed the cash and gave Thomas a terrible potboiler in return. For his part, Bristow did end up writing a piece for the ceremony—for its high point on Independence Day, no less—but Thomas did not conduct the performance. Yet Thomas programmed Wagner's piece nearly twenty times over the next year alone. Again, a different choice might have made a significant difference for Bristow and those who wished to follow in his footsteps.

The separation of supposed wheat from chaff, based largely on arbitrary ideas about musical quality, continued to plague American composers. During the first half of the twentieth century, the purported quest for an American musical identity, whether folksy or modernist, buttressed an accompanying desire for the "Great American Symphony," a work that could supposedly stand as an icon for the nation's musical achievements. Critic Louis Elson had helped inaugurate the sentiment when he claimed after hearing Chadwick's Third Symphony that the Great American Symphony "has yet to be written." This new symphonic quest, instigated by critics, would swallow up even the most vigilant composers.

One such figure, Florence Price (1887–1953), wrote at least two symphonies manifesting the values sought by several factions in the quest, but she encountered the same cold air that had frozen Bristow and Phelps.[12] Incidentally, she had been one of Chadwick's students at the New England Conservatory and therefore had direct ties to their earlier milieu. Under the direction of Frederick Stock (1872–1942), Theodore Thomas's successor and himself a German immigrant, the Chicago Symphony premiered Price's First Symphony in June of 1933, a moment when the quest for the Great American Symphony was in full swing. Notice of the work was given throughout the region, particularly in the African American press.

Since it was a major performance, all the leading newspapers in the Chicago area reviewed it. Writing for the *Chicago Defender*, a newspaper in the African American community, Robert Abbot remarked on the awe-filled experience of an all-white orchestra performing music by an African American woman. He noted that upon the work's conclusion, "the large auditorium, filled to the brim with music lovers of all races, rang out in applause for the composer and the orchestral rendition." The evening "could hold no greater thrills."[13] This reaction had mirrored the responses to Bristow's and Phelps's symphonies of the 1870s. Emotion overflowed from the audience, which seemed convinced of the work's greatness and power.

Price's music immediately became a malleable tool for calculated ideological use, not a potential symbol of national achievement. Writing for the *Chicago Tribune*, critic Edward Moore praised her effective employment of "racial folk song idioms" and her ability to be concise without "overloading and elaboration."[14] Moore's focus on the work's inner construction reflected the common critical interest in situating new works within the symphonic tradition, but he did not frame its stylistic idiosyncrasies within broader discourses about nationality. Ignoring the "juba" dance rhythms in the third movement, the "Dean of the Harlem Renaissance," Alain Locke, erased its ethnic character entirely by claiming that Price had vindicated "a Negro's right, at choice, to go up Parnassus by the broad road of classicism rather than the narrower, more hazardous, but often more rewarding path of racialism."[15] As far as he was concerned, Price had written a work that transcended both racial and national identities. Reviewing the symphony for the *Chicago Daily News*, Eugene Stinson found a way to dismiss Price by damning her with faint praise: "It is a faultless work cast in something less than modernist mode and even reminiscent at times of other composers who have dealt with America in tone. But for all its dependence upon the idioms of others, it is a work that speaks its own message with restraint and yet with passion."[16] The echoes of nineteenth-century critics, who judged works by an unstated and eminently mutable standard, could not have been clearer. No matter how good the work was, it was not good enough for some reason or other.

Price's symphony at times shares sonic similarities with those of her teacher Chadwick, and even with Dvořák. Yet neither the generally supportive reception of the piece on "purely musical" terms nor the radically positive response from the audience was enough to secure a place for it in the orchestral canon. Nor was she able to earn respect for it among certain prominent musicians, the vast majority of whom were white and male. Although Frederick Stock had championed her music as part of a general program supporting American composers, Price wrote several letters to Serge Koussevitzky (1874–1951), director of Henry Higginson's Boston Symphony, inquiring if he might perform her works. If he had said yes, it would have given her a much broader audience. He never did, and he most certainly knew she was a woman of color: She had told him so.[17] As Ellsworth Phelps might have told her, if he had the chance, Stock was her Carl Bergmann, Koussevitzky her Theodore Thomas.

Just at the moment when an African American woman was able to penetrate into the country's notoriously closed orchestral infrastructure, the stylistic path she had chosen, Dvořák's path, was passé among the country's musical intelligentsia. When they were seeking a modern American sound, a concept that rarely had a precise meaning, anything else was derivative or not American enough. The Great American Symphony had still not been written, even though it had.[18]

AN ALTERNATE PORTRAIT OF JOHN SULLIVAN DWIGHT

The twentieth-century episodes highlighted here illustrate the ways in which nineteenth-century composers and works, as well as the act of composition itself, have accrued negative value throughout the history of the American symphonic enterprise. Generally speaking, these processes have causes and residual effects that fall outside conventional understandings of canon formation. In the case of Bernstein and Copland, their own assertions of American national identity and their concomitant devaluation of earlier music relied on the extrapolation of critic John Sullivan Dwight's universalist disposition across the entire nineteenth century. Because of what Dwight represented to many thinkers in the twentieth century—along with the fact that certain public figures kept replicating his point of view—we have fundamentally misunderstood the eclecticism and diversity of nineteenth-century American orchestral music and musical thought. Correcting this misunderstanding requires a brief reassessment of Dwight himself.

The impulse shared by Bernstein and Copland to paint the nineteenth century with such broad strokes is understandable since Dwight's pointed views seemed so thoroughly anti-American that they were easy to present as evidence of Teutonic intellectual dominance. The persistence of Dwight's universalist outlook among high-profile conductors like Arturo Toscanini and prominent New York critics like Olin Downes and Lawrence Gilman did not help make him and his ilk more sympathetic to innovators such as Bernstein or Copland.[19] But throughout his career, Dwight's beliefs were frequently in fierce competition with both Wagnerism and American exceptionalism—two ideas that were more pressing for composers fashioning individual stylistic voices than for critics, who stood to gain little from supporting either.

A wide array of figures challenged Dwight directly. As we saw in chapter 6, one of Dwight's most sympathetic readers, ostensibly an average music lover, held significant reservations about his judgments of new music. In the midst of the 1869 National Peace Jubilee, discussed in chapter 8, critic Henry Cood Watson wrote this poem:

> 'Twas D——, the great critic, who growled on alone;
> He found none to join him, not even one.
> But still, like a patriarch mourning his flock,
> He boldly stood forward, encountering the shock
> Of ridicule—knowing that he 'twas who brought
> Great Beethoven up with a spoon, and who taught
> That Handel was great upon Fugues—that, in short,
> He knew more than all the world else could or ought.
> He vetoed the Festival—called it a hum—
> From the "Hallelujah" down to the drum:

He roared out that anvils and cannon and all
The ten thousand voices, would end in a bawl.
So Dogberry like, it thus came to pass,
The great critic D—— wrote himself down an a—.[20]

And Jerome Hopkins, introduced in chapter 6 as the founder of the first organization dedicated to American composers, penned these reflections in 1876:

> His creed has been to rub up, burnish and brighten, venerate and adore, feed and honor skeletons and to allow his living, breathing, eager, palpitating, enthusiastic and earnest fellow art-lovers and art-sufferers and artistic work- ers to remain unnoticed, uncared for and unknown. They may starve, and who would care? [. . .] Surely not Dwight. [. . .] Do not contemporaries pick their teeth with their forks after the great Beethoven has picked his teeth with his fork?[21]

Dwight nevertheless appears frequently in scholarship as the century's most powerful tastemaker. Views similar to Dwight's became prevalent among a certain class of listeners in the twentieth century. But we should not let this fact lead us to conclude that he was the sage of his era, as if he prophesied the eventual outcomes of music history. Contemporaries from all corners of the musical world disagreed with his perspective, and, as always, history had every opportunity to turn in a different direction.

AN ALTERNATE PORTRAIT OF THEODORE THOMAS

In the case of the American symphonic enterprise, the real history makers were performers. Though important, critics like Dwight wielded less power than we tend to think. The fact that they left a sizable historical record in print can skew our perceptions. During the nineteenth century, virtually everyone highlighted in this book, critics included, understood the fact that music was lifeless without performance. Nothing seemed to anger compos- ers more than refusals to have their works performed. Bristow, for exam- ple, weathered negative reviews throughout his long career without a single complaint to the press, but he led a tirade in 1854 when he perceived that his music was unfairly excluded from performance (see chapter 5). In the nineteenth-century balance of power, performers held ultimate control over a symphonic composer's entry into public consciousness.

The vast majority of the music discussed throughout this book, with the notable exception of music by Anthony Philip Heinrich, was in fact performed shortly after it was written. Theodore Thomas programmed new works by

Brahms just as he programmed those by Paine, while Carl Bergmann performed Bristow alongside Liszt. But conductors and organizations typically placated local composers with only a single performance, not several. Before recordings, repeated live hearings were vital for sustained engagement with a piece of music. Critics lamented this fact time and again, particularly when commenting on large orchestral works. Eager listeners who fawned over Ellsworth Phelps's *Emancipation* had no reason to believe that it would not "live," because there was no self-evident reason that it would not be performed again. The same held true for those who loved Florence Price's music. The clamor for more performances went unheeded, however, and composers naturally felt wronged. One performance was not enough.

But the fact remained that entrepreneurial conductors such as Thomas held ultimate sway over programming decisions. Like Serge Koussevitzky or Leopold Stokowski in the early twentieth century, Thomas's opinion of new works—seemingly encapsulated in his programs—has come down to us as the only one that mattered, as if he were the ultimate arbiter of quality.[22] As in Dwight's case, however, Thomas also had vocal detractors, notably William Thoms of the *American Art Journal*. As Henry Cood Watson's critical protégé, Thoms selectively reported bad news about Thomas from around the country and provided a counterpoint (though sometimes unfairly) to the general praise the conductor received elsewhere.

To cite one example among many: Frederick Mollenhauer, a violinist from Germany who had settled in the United States after arriving with Louis Antoine Jullien's orchestra in 1853, stated frankly in an 1879 interview with the *New York Herald* (which Thoms reprinted) that "Theodore Thomas possessed the wand of success, energy. He is not much of a musician, and no composer; and he cannot play—he has a stiff 'back arm' as we say, instead of bowing only from the wrist. Besides, he lacks education."[23] Thomas was so upset that he reportedly fired Mollenhauer's son Emil from the Brooklyn Philharmonic. A writer for *Kunkel's Musical Review* in St. Louis, a thousand miles away, commented on the situation: "We suspect the sting of Mr. Mollenhauer's estimate of the musical ability of Mr. Thomas lies in its truth. Accident has assigned Thomas to a prominent place in his profession." William Thoms gleefully reprinted the piece in order to heighten its circulation.[24]

As with Dwight, Thomas's skeptics and the many reports concerning his mismanagement of finances and personnel printed throughout his career should entice us to question other facets of his judgment, as well as his personal motivations. (Of course, his critics also had motivations worth questioning.) Recent scholarship suggests that Thomas was an important supporter of U.S. composers, especially given the high number of premieres he led.[25] In terms of pure statistics, his efforts certainly fit the generally open-minded program presented in this scholarly portrait. As we have seen, though, key composers repeatedly accused him of prejudice.

Were they justified? While preparing for a May Festival in 1882, Thomas himself spoke on the matter in an interview printed in Boston's *Musical Review*. When asked why so many "ladies and gentlemen" might be hurt that no American composers were on the program, Thomas replied,

> I have to say in my defense that it was with no desire to crush American talent, which I have heretofore been instrumental in bringing out. [. . .] But, with all due respect to the American composers, *a festival like this is not the place to bring out the compositions of Young America to compete by comparison with such masters as Beethoven, Bach, and Handel.* [. . .] This is not a country fair, where every local housewife is expected to make and exhibit a homemade little pat of butter, but it is like an art collection, where *the masterpieces of the world's labor are shown.*[26]

If not a festival, then where should local composers have been promoted? He had refused Ellsworth Phelps a position on a Brooklyn Philharmonic program. We will never know what might have happened if any of the works that Thomas (or Koussevitzky) ignored had been performed more frequently. They were never given a chance to "live." Once their initial public exposure had faded, they became targets of facile stereotyping, when they were remembered at all.

AN ALTERNATE PORTRAIT OF ORCHESTRAS

The situation of nineteenth-century American symphonic composers that I encountered while researching this book led me to consider that performers, including conductors, might have had motivations that worked at cross purposes with those of composers. We tend to assume that musicians are all "in it" together. While looking for these motivations as well, sociologist Samuel Gilmore attributed the persistence of canonical repertoires to the alignment of "administrative rationality" (i.e., reducing organizational costs while increasing efficiency) with performers' general "interest in virtuosity and interpretation" (or sounding their best while displaying a wide range of technical and interpretive abilities).[27] He concluded that repeating familiar works benefited both performers and organizations because it increased rehearsal efficiency while allowing performers, who already "knew the notes," to focus on elements such as perfect intonation, articulation, phrasing, and so on—the things they were trained to do. In today's musical world, these conclusions make sense at face value: efficiency rules all.

They also have roots in the very circumstances illustrated in this book. The claims of composers such as Fry, Bristow, and Phelps that New York's orchestras were inhospitable to American composers were self-serving. As composers themselves, they wanted more exposure. In 1879, however, twenty-five years after Bristow's tussle with the Philharmonic, Harvey Dodworth (1822–1891), a famous band director whose family had been key organizers of the Philharmonic, reiterated Bristow's complaints in an interview. He claimed that "one especial object which we had in view was the founding, if possible, of an American school of composition, and it was required that at least one American work should be performed during each season."[28] He went on to describe how the founders "worked manfully" during the first few seasons, adding, "At the start the Philharmonic was the most cosmopolitan thing you ever saw. There were in it Italians, French, English, Germans, and Americans. Not one-fourth of them were Germans. Now it is exclusively a German organization." He was implying that the growth of German musicians in the orchestra effectively eliminated this "especial object." From today's vantage, it seems unquestionable that canon formation included a heavy dose of German national chauvinism, which, as we saw in the case of Bristow's *Arcadian*, could become uncomfortably intertwined with perceptions of inherent musical quality.

Dodworth's comments appeared just a few weeks after critic William Thoms had already complained about New York's major orchestras not supporting local talent. Their neglect was noteworthy, he claimed, since these orchestras depended on anywhere from fifty to ninety percent English-speaking ticket buyers (the "American element") for support. In the same article, he went on to reprint Bristow's screed against the Philharmonic while reminding readers that Bristow was "a musician who stands in the front rank of native composers to-day."[29] Thoms seemed to believe that the box office should rule programming decisions. Otherwise he had no reason to point out who patronized these orchestras.

But Thoms was not considering that receipts were only one part of a complex sociological equation that also included performers and their self-interests as practicing musicians, not just as professional workers in need of an income. Jerome Hopkins argued in 1888 that the musical aims of rank-and-file orchestral musicians (aside from the conductor) most certainly did affect programming decisions, and thus the prospects of aspiring composers. His target was musical unions, which he believed reduced excellent players "to a level but a little higher than that of a street-paver or hod-carrier," while a composer (or "original investigator") is "compelled to submit to terrible extortion, or else be denied the privilege of hearing his own works." His explanation hinged on the fact that the unions required payment of the same amount ($7.00) for the concertmaster, as well as the triangle player. On top of that, a composer had to pay each musician an extra $2.00 per rehearsal (i.e., *for learning to play his Music*").

What irritated Hopkins the most, however, was that this financial structure gave performers no incentive to agree to perform new works. "Wretched players" who get the fee will not want to learn the music, whereas "superior players" will not want to improve since "he can take no more than $7.00 a concert." This system, he claimed, "has virtually shut out every new orchestral achievement unless the composers humiliate themselves to curry favor with the Conductors of organized orchestras and 'beg' a hearing. A new Beethoven would have to beg all the same."[30]

Outside of this incentive structure for performers, conductors such as Thomas premiered new works despite whatever resistance (if any) they faced from their players. "Premieres are attractive to performers," Gilmore writes, because they "indicate the performer is in touch with the contemporary music world." In Thomas's case, rivalries with Carl Bergmann and Leopold Damrosch over premieres of the latest works by Raff, Rubinstein, Goldmark, Brahms, and others generated public curiosity and reflected what critics of the time called "liberality." In turn, premieres potentially generated greater revenue and worked to enhance a conductor's reputation. They still fulfill the same function: What savvy performer's biography today does not include a statement about how much he or she supports contemporary music? Gilmore adds that orchestral premieres also tend to be low-risk enterprises since critics will likely focus attention on the new work rather than the performance; or if the performance is poor, they will shift blame away from the conductor and onto lack of rehearsal time or poor orchestral writing. Achieving second performances is always more difficult, even today, leading to a situation in which very few performers have constructed international careers primarily as advocates of new music. When they have, it has almost always been as a soloist or chamber musician, not as an orchestral conductor.

This situation is not news to anyone affiliated with a university school of music. It was John Knowles Paine who became the first professor of music at a university, and that university was Harvard. Of all the figures highlighted in this book, the Berlin-trained composer was the most likely to develop a university music curriculum that placed German music and musical pedagogy at its center. Unsurprisingly, he did in fact choose to do so. His students then went on to populate university music faculties elsewhere. Beginning around the turn of the twentieth century, many of these same universities created schools of music that functioned in large part as training grounds for musicians dedicated to performing or teaching canonical European masterworks, particularly for the orchestra. Theory, composition, and history, subjects that Paine initially emphasized, became ancillary for students of musical performance, while the young but German-dominated field of musicology attempted to distance itself from undergraduate instruction altogether.[31] University music curricula rapidly approximated those of American conservatories, the first of which had appeared in the 1860s and continued to thrive into the twentieth century. Contemporary university degree tracks in performance, including those at the doctoral level, attest that this educational model is alive and well.

If, as Gilmore suggests, a particular repertoire is tied to one's self-identification as a performer because it formed a core part of one's education, then we cannot ignore the tremendously influential roles that applied instruction and performance pedagogy at universities have played and continue to play within U.S. orchestral music culture. Ethnomusicologist Alejandro Madrid has argued pointedly that "[n]early all music departments in the U.S. serve in fact as music 'conservatories,' programs for the study and reproduction of the values of the European learned music tradition, invested in 'conserving' that tradition regardless of the lack of Europe in their names."[32] Orchestras are symbiotic extensions of this function. And as of this writing, incidentally, all of Harvard's music degrees still have a foundation in the liberal arts.

THE FUTURE OF THE ENTERPRISE

The elements that ultimately led to the canonization of a narrow body of symphonic pieces occupied precarious and contested positions throughout most of the nineteenth century. John Sullivan Dwight's unflappable reverence for Beethoven was a minority position. Theodore Thomas controlled up to three major orchestras at any given time, including a touring ensemble that essentially defined the current U.S. repertoire. Most orchestral players happened to be native German speakers who probably learned how to play their instruments while studying German music and who preferred to rehearse in German. Appeals to inherent or universal musical values do not account for any of these factors, though perceptions of those values certainly figured prominently in each.

Alter any one of them and things might have gone differently. How much would be different now if the New York Philharmonic had lived up to its original charge to support American composers and made this its core mission? What if Bristow had been elected conductor in 1850, or upon Carl Bergmann's death in 1876? A significant number of critics supported the creation of an American school of composition. Audiences often greeted new American works with unbridled enthusiasm. What if there had been fewer obstacles to the symphonic enterprise? Would institutions and audiences today demand new music? Would quality musicianship itself be defined by someone's ability to adapt rather than to achieve supposed perfection, or to make something new rather than to recreate something old? These results are precisely the opposite of what happened in the world of orchestral music, where new works are predominantly short fanfare-type compositions performed at the beginning of a program, so as not to dislodge the featured soloist and symphonic warhorse from their conventional positions.

Since we are stuck with what happened in the past, what about the future? The beauty of the music described in this book, I think, lies in the fact that one can hear just about anything in it one wants. Everyone else certainly has. It is American and not American, serious and not serious, German and not German, symphonic and not symphonic. Another attendee at the preconcert lecture I described in the introduction remarked that the fairylike scherzo of Bristow's Third Symphony sounded like "diet Mendelssohn." I am sure that many of today's listeners would agree. Others might be surprised that American composers were writing music that was so "good" in 1859, a year off the radar for anyone who believes in Paine's or Ives's primacy. Like Fry's critics from 1853, we might hear *Santa Claus* as an entertaining addition to a Christmas pops concert. It certainly would be. Others might be moved by the simple religiosity of the Lord's Prayer recitative and the "Adeste fideles" finale. And what American music lover wouldn't move to the jazziness of Gottschalk's Cuban dance music? A listener's frame of reference and value system matter a great deal. One lesson of this book is that the experience of music reflects the listener as much as the composer, and I think listeners today might enjoy much of this music.

As we become increasingly skeptical of universalist claims, the enterprise of reifying canons in performance, and the entire concept of art music, perhaps this repertoire is doomed for eternity and will never live. After all, it was inextricably intertwined with the cultural ascent of these very things. Some of its creators believed in them! But let us not forget that other musicians actively resisted the cultural forces that led to the marginalization of this repertoire. Though they had flaws and intellectual inconsistencies of their own, Fry, Bristow, and Phelps understood that German musical chauvinism, girded by the pretense of universalism, was not merely an abstract philosophical position. It was a cultural practice with potentially damaging effects, which they experienced firsthand. Fry believed that his own social function was in fact to *counteract* these effects by introducing audiences to pieces that were accessible and instructive. If he could disclose deeper truths in the process, it was all the better.

After writing this book, I find that I rarely read about today's orchestras or have a conversation about orchestral music without thinking at least once: "That comment sounded so much like Dwight." It was probably what jumped into my mind when the gentleman at my lecture asked if Beethoven's music would bring world peace. I even occasionally catch myself echoing the "Boston oracle" (as Dwight was sometimes called) and wincing on the inside. If we cling to old values, these composers, and any composer of new orchestral music, will continue to freeze. Maybe some of them should. It is not my place here to judge. But even in their silence, they tell us something about who we are as orchestral music lovers and about the condition in which we find ourselves, if only we listen.

NOTES

INTRODUCTION

1. On symphonic canons, see Weber, "The Rise of the Classical Repertoire"; Street, "The Modern Orchestra and the Performing Canon," in Horton, ed., *The Cambridge Companion to the Symphony*, 396–414; Dowd et al., "Organizing the Musical Canon"; and Kremp, "Innovation and Selection." See also Citron, *Gender and the Musical Canon*, 15–43; Goehr, *The Imaginary Museum*; and Weber, "The History of Musical Canon."
2. On cultural and symbolic capital, see Bourdieu, "The Forms of Capital" and "The Production of Belief."
3. See Taruskin, "Agents and Causes and Ends," 279.
4. See Pederson, "On the Task of the Music Historian," 12–24; Morrow, *German Music Criticism*, 45–65; and Applegate and Potter, "Germans as the 'People of Music,'" in Applegate and Potter, eds., *Music and German National Identity*, 1–34.
5. See Applegate, "How German," 275–277; and Potter, *Most German of the Arts*, 258–261.
6. See Taruskin, "Some Thoughts," 325–326; Taruskin, "Is there a Baby in the Bathwater?"; and Bonds, *Absolute Music*, 269–289.
7. Hepokoski, "Beethoven Reception," in Samson, ed., *Cambridge Companion to Nineteenth-Century Music*, 424–459; Holoman, ed., *The Nineteenth-Century Symphony*; Horton, ed., *The Cambridge Companion to the Symphony*; and Brown, ed., *The Symphonic Repertoire*.
8. On twentieth-century American symphonies, see Schnepel, "The Critical Pursuit"; Taruskin, *Oxford History*, 4:637–649; and Tawa, *Great American Symphony*.
9. See, e.g., Howard, *Our American Music*, 310–403.
10. Chase, *America's Music*, 325; for a thorough comparison of these two positions, see Crawford, *The American Musical Landscape*, 3–37.
11. On parallel issues in Russia, see Taruskin, *Defining Russia Musically*, especially parts I and II.
12. See the contributions of Katherine K. Preston and Michael Broyles to Nicholls, ed., *The Cambridge History of American Music*; see also Crawford, *America's Musical Life*, 272–350.
13. Cf. the "All the Music in Full Context Paradigm" in Locke, *Musical Exoticism*, 59–64.
14. On the value of this historiographical approach, see Burkholder, "Music of the Americas," 418–419.
15. Historians have increasingly adopted similar positions; see, e.g., Fleche, *Revolution of 1861*; and Rodgers, *Atlantic Crossings*.

16. See Benner, "Nationalism: Intellectual Origins," 41–48.

17. See Gelbart, *The Invention of "Folk Music" and "Art Music,"* 204.

18. For three classic studies, see Anderson, *Imagined Communities*; Gellner, *Nations and Nationalism*; and Hobsbawm, *Nations and Nationalism*.

19. On the fluidity of the nation concept, see Bhabha, *Nation and Narration*, 1–7; on nationalism and music, see Samson, "Nations and Nationalism," in Samson, ed., *Cambridge Companion to Nineteenth-Century Music*, 568–600; and Bohlman, *The Music of European Nationalism*, 81–160.

20. On early expressions of American national musical identity, see Crist, " 'Ye Sons of Harmony.' "

21. See Yokota, *Unbecoming British*, 226–242.

22. See in particular Howe, *What Hath God Wrought*.

23. See A. Levy, *Musical Nationalism*; and Tischler, *American Music*.

24. Sponheuer, "Reconstructing Ideal Types in of the 'German' in Music," in Applegate and Potter, eds., *Music and German National Identity*, 39.

25. Thomson, "On Being American," *NYDT*, Jan. 25, 1948, reprinted in *A Virgil Thomson Reader*, 305.

26. Garrett, *Struggling to Define a Nation*, 1–16.

27. Broyles, *Beethoven in America*.

28. Cavicchi, *Listening and Longing*.

29. For a related approach in Russian opera studies, see Frolova-Walker, "A Ukrainian Tune in Medieval France"; on the symphony as public genre, see Sisman, "Symphonies and the Public Display of Topics"; and Bonds, "The Symphony as Pindaric Ode."

30. Frisch, *Brahms*, 145–147.

31. For the European story, see Bonds, *After Beethoven*; and Fifield, *The German Symphony*.

32. On opera, see Ahlquist, *Democracy at the Opera*; on popular song, see the second half of Finson, *The Voices that are Gone*.

33. See Irving, "The Viennese Symphony 1750 to 1827," in Horton, ed., *Cambridge Companion to the Symphony*, 25–27.

34. See Deaville, "Critic and Conductor in 1860s Chicago," in Spitzer, ed., *American Orchestras*.

35. Osterhammel, *The Transformation of the World*, 911–914.

CHAPTER 1

1. For data on U.S. premieres of major symphonies, see Johnson, *First Performances*; for data on longevity, see Mueller, *The American Symphony Orchestra*, 182–252.

2. See Lowe, *Pleasure and Meaning*, 3–7.

3. See Weber, *Great Transformation of Musical Taste*; and Wyn Jones, *The Symphony in Beethoven's Vienna*.

4. [E. T. A. Hoffman], "Recension," *AmZ* (July 4, 1810 and July 11, 1810): 630–642 and 652–659; translated in Hoffmann, *E. T. A. Hoffmann's Musical Writings*, 235–251.

5. See Kramer, "The Idea of *Kunstreligion*"; Burnham, *Beethoven Hero*; and Goehr, *Imaginary Museum*, 208–218.

6. M. Fuller to William H. Channing, Apr. 5, 1841, in *Letters of Margaret Fuller*, 2:206.

7. Saloman, "Margaret Fuller on Beethoven in America," 102.

8. Gienow-Hecht, *Sound Diplomacy*, 8.

9. See Buell, "Postcolonial Anxiety in Classic U.S. Literature."

10. See Burstein, *The Original Knickerbocker*, 293–294; R. W. Emerson, "The American Scholar," in *Complete Works of Ralph Waldo Emerson*, 1:114; Watts, *Writing and Postcolonialism in the Early Republic*, 5–6; and Haynes, *Unfinished Revolution*, 51–76.

11. Dana, *Discourse*, 14; C. Emerson, *Discourse*, 8.

12. Dana, *Discourse*, 18; C. Emerson, *Discourse*, 7–8 (emphasis in original).

13. Handel and Haydn Society, *Constitution*, 3–4.

14. "Music," *Port-Folio* (May 1819): 432.

15. "Review of First Number Boston Handel and Haydn Society Collection Sacred Music," *Euterpiad* (June 24, 1820): 51; see also Crawford, "'Ancient Music' and the Europeanizing of American Psalmody," in Crawford, Lott, and Oja, eds., *A Celebration of American Music*, 225–255.

16. On the perception of European products as instruments of cultivation, see Yokota, *Unbecoming British*, 74–106.

17. For the full program, see Madeira, *Annals of Music in Philadelphia*, 71–77.

18. All of the extant materials of the Musical Fund Society are in MFS and MFSSR; at one time the Historical Society of Pennsylvania held some of these records, but they have since been relocated.

19. On his career, see Sciannameo, *Phil Trajetta*.

20. See Swenson-Eldridge, "Charles Hommann," lviii–lxiv and lxv–lxviii; Johnson, *First Performances*, 28; Claypool, "Archival Collections"; and Knouse, "The *collegia musica*."

21. Report from the Annual Meeting, May 5, 1835, *Minutes of the proceedings of the Musical Fund Society of Philadelphia, at their stated annual and other meetings, May 1, 1827–May 1, 1866*, MFS.

22. Swenson-Eldridge, "Charles Hommann," xxxv.

23. Winthrop, "Music in New England," in *Addresses and Speeches*, 2:334.

24. Appiah, "Cosmopolitan Patriots," 618.

25. [J. S. Dwight], "Musical Review," *Harbinger* (Aug. 16, 1845): 154–155.

26. On the oratorio's early nineteenth-century status in the German-speaking world, see Applegate, *Bach in Berlin*, 188–200.

27. See Wyn Jones, *The Symphony in Beethoven's Vienna*.

28. On performing ensembles and their repertoire in Britain and the United States before 1820, see Butler, *Votaries of Apollo*.

29. "Music," *New-England Magazine* (Dec. 1831): 460.

30. For the group's original constitution and acts of incorporation, see Boston Academy of Music, *First Annual Report*, 9–12.

31. [T. Hach], "On Concerts," *Musical Magazine* (May 25, 1839): 164.

32. [T. Hach], "The Late Musical Season," *Musical Magazine* (Jul. 20, 1839): 236.

33. Boston Academy of Music, *Ninth Annual Report*, 4; Boston Academy of Music, *Tenth Annual Report*, 4; Broyles, *"Music of the Highest Class,"* 203.

34. Krehbiel, *The Philharmonic Society*, 76; see also Faust, *The German Element in the United States*.

35. The orchestra's complete performance history is also available at the New York Philharmonic website; see also Block, "Thinking about Serious Music in New York," in Spitzer, ed., *American Orchestras*.

36. See Madeira, *Annals of Music in Philadelphia*, 144–147.

37. Report from the Annual Meeting, May 6, 1845, *Minutes of the proceedings of the Musical Fund Society of Philadelphia, at their stated annual and other meetings May 1, 1827–May 1, 1866*, MFS.

38. Dwight, "Haydn," *United States Magazine, and Democratic Review* (Jan. 1844): 20–21.
39. "Music," *Albion* (Feb. 3, 1849): 56.
40. Quoted in Lawrence, *Strong on Music*, 1:359 (emphasis in original).
41. Schumann, *On Music and Musicians*, 62.
42. See Hepokoski, "Beethoven Reception," in Samson, ed., *The Cambridge Companion to the Symphony*, 425–458; and Laudon, *The Dramatic Symphony*.
43. See Koch, *Kurzgefaßtes Handwörterbuch*, 166–167, and A. B. Marx, *Über Malerei in der Tonkunst*.
44. Bonds, *Absolute Music*, 69–78.
45. On these and similar figures of the 1830s and 1840s, see Fifield, *The German Symphony*, 7–124.
46. Several others fell into this camp: Eduard Sobolewski, Emile Douay, Georges Kastner, Louis Lacombe, Théodore Wackerlin, Ernest Reyer, and the mercurial Robert-Nicolas-Charles Bochsa (see chapter 5), all of whom wrote descriptive works but did not always use the label "symphony" to describe them; see Laudon, *The Dramatic Symphony*, 52–54 (Bochsa), 57–60 (Douay), 93–94 (Sobolewski), and 120–131.
47. R. Schumann, "Sinfonie von H. Berlioz," in *Gesammelte Schriften*, 1:83. My translation.
48. [R. Schumann], "Kalliwoda," *NZfM* (May 5, 1834): 38.
49. Alex. Br., "Parallelen: Politik und Musik," *NZfM* (Sep. 9, 1836): 84.
50. See Bonds, *Music as Thought*, 88–93; Gienow-Hecht, *Sound Diplomacy*, 34; and D. Levy, "Wolfgang Robert Griepenkerl and Beethoven's Ninth Symphony."
51. "Das Feld der Symphonie gehört seit langer Zeit unbestritten den Deutschen, dieser das Gebiet der Instrumentalmusik überhaupt beherrschenden Nation, ein Gebiet, worin die Symphonie gleichsam die vornehmste Provinz bezeichnet. Frankreich und Italien verstehen, bei aller Mühe, die sie sich geben, diese Traumwelt der Töne nicht, welche sich der Deutsche geschaffen hat, wo es keiner Worte bedarf, welche die Phantasie des Hörers durch einen bestimmten Gedanken leiten, sondern wo die freien Formen der Tongestalten sich selbst zu Gesetzgebern machen." A[ugust] K[ahlert], "Rescension. Felix Mendelssohn-Bartholdy. Symphonie No. 3, Op. 56," *AmZ* (May 10, 1843): 341. My translation.
52. On this shift in general, see Pederson, "A. B. Marx."
53. On Schiller's influence on Dwight, see Saloman, *Beethoven's Symphonies and J. S. Dwight*, 19–43.
54. Dwight, *Lecture on Association*, 5.
55. "Musical Review. Music in Boston during the Last Winter.—No. IV," *Harbinger* (Aug. 30, 1845): 189.
56. "Musical Review. Music in Boston. Beethoven's Pastoral Symphony," *Harbinger* (Nov. 1, 1845): 330.
57. Cooke, ed., *Early Letters*, 134.
58. [M. Fuller], "Entertainments of the Past Winter," *Dial* (July 1842): 61; later in the review she commented more favorably on the Fifth: "Here with force, and ardent, yet deliberate approach, manifold spirits demand the crisis of their existence."
59. See Howard, "The Hewitt Family," 26–31.
60. See Waldstreicher, *In the Midst of Perpetual Fetes*.
61. Brackenridge, *The Battle of Bunkers-Hill*.

62. See Purcell, *Sealed with Blood*.

63. See Newman, *Good Music for a Free People*, 25.

64. Ibid., 26.

65. Johnson, "The Germania Musical Society," 92.

66. Skinner, *Discourse on Music*, 5.

67. Gelbart, *The Invention of "Folk Music" and "Art Music,"* 98–102.

68. "On Musical Expression," *Blackwell's Edinburgh Magazine* (Aug. 1819): 558; it was reprinted with the same title in *Belles-Lettres Repository* (Jan. 1, 1820): 187–190 and *Euterpiad* (May 20, 1820): 30–31.

69. "On National Music," *Euterpiad* (Aug. 5, 1820): 75.

70. [R. La Roche], "Italian Music," *AQR* (June 1827): 400; La Roche's authorship of these articles is established in Aderman, "Contributors to the *American Quarterly Review*" and Woodall, "More on the Contributors to the *American Quarterly Review*."

71. [R. La Roche], "Musical Style," *AQR* (Mar. 1834): 101–104; [R. La Roche], "Music and Musicians of Europe," *AQR* (Mar. 1830): 216.

72. [R. La Roche], "The French Opera," *AQR* (Mar. 1832): 64.

73. "Music," *New-England Magazine* (Dec. 1831): 463.

74. [R. La Roche], "National Music," *AQR* (June 1835): 277.

75. Ibid., 278.

76. [R. La Roche], "The French Opera," 65–66.

77. See Applegate, *Bach in Berlin*, 74–77 and 116; Sponheuer, "Reconstructing Ideal Types of the 'German' in Music," in Applegate and Potter, eds., *Music and German National Identity*, 46–48.

78. [H. R. Cleveland], "National Music," *North American Review* (Jan. 1840): 4–5. Cleveland's authorship is established in Cushing, *Index to the North American Review*, 124.

79. [H. R. Cleveland], "National Music," 11–15.

80. On the parallel attitude in German culture, see Gramit, *Cultivating Music*.

CHAPTER 2

1. Preface to Heinrich, *The Dawning of Music in Kentucky* (emphasis in original).

2. A. P. Heinrich to John Rowe Parker, Sep. 1, 1820, JRPC.

3. [J. R. Parker], "Criticism. *The Dawning of Music in Kentucky*," *Euterpiad* (Apr. 13, 1822): 46.

4. On Belcher, see Edwards, *Music and Musicians of Maine*, 20.

5. On Heinrich's opportunism, see Broyles, *Mavericks*, 39–68.

6. *Boston Daily Advertiser*, May 29, 1823, quoted in Upton, *Anthony Philip Heinrich*, 70.

7. Heinrich to Albert Gallatin, n.d., APHS, 189–190, quoted in Maust, "Symphonies," 31.

8. APHS, 966, quoted in Upton, *Anthony Philip Heinrich*, 110.

9. See Upton, *Anthony Philip Heinrich*, 118–128.

10. Heinrich to Richard Hughes, Apr. 10, 1833, APHS, 241, quoted in Upton, *Anthony Philip Heinrich*, 129–130.

11. "Vermischtes," *NZfM* (Jan. 15, 1836): 22.

12. "Anton Philipp Heinrichs," *AmZ* (Feb. 17, 1836): 102. This report closely matches an entry on Heinrich in Gustav Schilling's musical encyclopedia (published in Stuttgart around the same time), but it is difficult to tell which came first; Schilling, ed., *Encyclopädie*, 3:543–544. My translation.

13. Upton, *Anthony Philip Heinrich*, 136–137.

14. Quoted in translation in Upton, *Anthony Philip Heinrich*, 143.

15. For further analytical remarks, see Maust, "Symphonies," 96, 112–113, 135–137, 162–165.

16. Heinrich, *The Columbiad, Grand American National Chivalrous Symphony*, APHC.

17. See, e.g., "Grand Musical Festival. Father Heinrich," *Brother Jonathan* (Apr. 16, 1842): 436–37.

18. See Lawrence, *Strong on Music*, 1:120–124.

19. For reviews, see APHS, 1053, quoted in Upton, *Heinrich*, 166; APHS, 879, quoted in Maust, "Symphonies," 74; see also Lawrence, *Strong on Music*, 1:168–170.

20. APHS, 37.

21. McIntosh, *Origin of the North American Indians*, 104–109.

22. See also Maust, "Symphonies," 117–118, 139–140.

23. McIntosh, *Origin of the North American Indians*, 170–175.

24. Andrew Stiller, preface to Heinrich, *The Mastodon* (Philadelphia: Kallisti Press, 2000).

25. See "Indian Eloquence," *Niles' Literary Register* (Oct. 14, 1815): 113; Outalissa, "Fragments from the Woods," *New Monthly Magazine and Literary Journal* (Jan. 1, 1821): 60–71; and McIntosh, *Origin of the North American Indians*, 225, 246–247. On the early impact of these speeches on literary culture, see Franklin, *James Fenimore Cooper*, 475–476.

26. Wied-Neuwied, *Travels in the Interior*, 211–212.

27. See Hewitt, *Shadows on the Wall*, 82–85.

28. Stiller, preface to *The Mastodon*.

29. See Child, *Hobomok and Other Writings on Indians*.

30. Bulwer-Lytton, *Zanoni*, 1:15; see also "Memoir of a Remarkable Man," *NYDT*, Nov. 19, 1845.

31. "Father Heinrich's Concert," *NYEP*, May 6, 1846; see also "Father Heinrich's Concert," *NYDT*, May 5, 1845.

32. APHS, 320, quoted in Upton, *Anthony Philip Heinrich*, 188–191.

33. Ibid.

34. "City Items," *NYDT*, May 7, 1846.

35. On these changes in European criticism, see Burnham, "Criticism, Faith, and the *Idee*"; and Watkins, "From the Mine to the Shrine."

36. APHS, 1063, quoted in Upton, *Anthon Philip Heinrich*, 198; for another review, see "Music in Boston," *American Journal of Music* (June 30, 1846): 189.

37. [J. S. Dwight], "Musical Review. 'Father Heinrich' in Boston," *Harbinger* (July 4, 1846): 58–59.

38. APHS, 517, quoted in Waters, "John Sullivan Dwight," 78–79.

39. Ibid.

CHAPTER 3

1. CJHJ, Jan. 14, 1856.

2. Fry, *Republican "Campaign" Text-Book*; Fry to Lincoln, Aug. 4, 1860, Abraham Lincoln Papers, Library of Congress.

3. Fry, *Republican "Campaign" Text-Book*, 108.

4. "Mr. Meignen's Concert," *PPL*, Apr. 21, 1845.

5. On Meignen, see Swenson-Eldridge, "The Musical Fund Society," 151–160; and "Death of a Distinguished Musician," *DJM* (June 28, 1873): 43.

6. [Untitled], *PPL*, Apr. 17, 1845.

7. Cicero, *Epistulae*, VII.9.1–4, quoted in Montgomery, *Science in Translation*, 34; see also 31–36.

8. "Obituary," *NYT*, Sep. 4, 1855.

9. On Walsh's literary career, see Griswold, *The Prose Writers of America*, 196–198.

10. On the growth of opera in the United States, see Ahlquist, *Democracy at the Opera*; Dizikes, *Opera in America*; and Preston, *Opera on the Road*; on Fry's earliest compositions, see Upton, *William Henry Fry*, 18–22.

11. On what music Fry might have heard in Philadelphia, see Izzo, "William Henry Fry's *Leonora*," 8–10; and Upton, *Fry*, 14–16. For a more detailed account, see Curtis, *A History of Opera in Philadelphia*; and Curtis, "A Century of Grand Opera in Philadelphia."

12. See "William Henry Fry, The Composer. Biography and Phrenological Character," *American Phrenological Journal* (Mar. 1856): 51–53; *Aurelia* survives intact, but only a small excerpt from *The Bridal of Dunure* is extant.

13. Preston, *Opera on the Road*, 19.

14. For a detailed comparison of Joseph Fry's translation to the Italian original, see Izzo, "William Henry Fry's *Leonora*," 10–11.

15. Sill Diary, Jan. 11, 1841; a letter to the *National Gazette* (Jan. 21, 1841), signed "A Music Admirer," confirmed Sill's impressions.

16. Sill continued to patronize the Fry production; see Sill Diary, Feb. 4, 1841.

17. See Curtis, "A History of Grand Opera in Philadelphia," 140–141.

18. See Lawrence, *Strong on Music*, 1:132–133.

19. "The 'Norma' of Romani," *Knickerbocker* (Apr. 1841): 356.

20. "The Dramatic World," *New World* (Apr. 30, 1842): 289.

21. Hogarth, *Musical History*, 312–313.

22. Rush, *The Philosophy of the Human Voice*, 497.

23. Fry, *Leonora*, iii–v; reprinted in Upton, *Fry*, 327–331; and Chase, ed., *The American Composer Speaks*, 47–52.

24. "The Concert Room," *Broadway Journal* (June 21, 1845): 397–398. Other comments in the series appeared in the June 14 and July 12 issues of *Broadway Journal*.

25. Fry, *Leonora*, iv.

26. Rush, *The Philosophy of the Human Voice*, 497.

27. Fry referenced Rush's treatise in a lecture given in New York on Dec. 28, 1852; see "Music," *NYDT*, Dec. 30, 1852.

28. Fry, *Leonora*, v.

29. *PPL*, Aug. 22, 1851.

30. "European Affairs," *NYDT*, Jan. 12, 1850.

31. *PPL*, Apr. 27, 1852.

32. "Letter from Paris," *PPL*, June 2, 1851.

33. See, e.g., "Europe by an American, No. LII," *NYDT*, Jan. 21, 1851; and "Europe by an American, No. LIII," *NYDT*, Jan. 31, 1851.

34. "Europe by an American, No. VI," *NYDT*, Apr. 12, 1850; and *PPL*, July 11, 1851.

35. *Message Bird* changed its title several times while Fry was in Europe: *Journal of the Fine Arts* (1851), *Musical World and Journal of Fine Arts* (early 1852), and *Musical World and New York Musical Times* (July 1852).

36. "Musical Art in France, England, and America," *Message Bird* (Oct. 15, 1850): 492–493.

37. Ibid.

38. See Widmer, *Young America*.

39. [J. L. O'Sullivan], "Introduction," *United States Magazine, and Democratic Review* (Oct. 1, 1837): 14.

40. *MWMT* (June 15, 1852): 338; similar ads appeared widely.

41. The contents of the lectures remain mysterious because significant remnants of only two of them are extant: a conductor's score from the first lecture and a transcript of the seventh lecture printed in "The English Language for Lyrical Uses," *MWMT* (Jan. 29, 1853): 69–70. The press accounts are generally good; see also Lawrence, "William Henry Fry's Messianic Yearnings."

42. Lawrence, "William Henry Fry's Messianic Yearnings," 390–391.

43. [R. S. Willis], "Mr. Fry's Lectures," *MWMT* (Feb. 19, 1853): 115.

44. Ibid., 116.

45. [J. S. Dwight], "Mr. Fry's 'American Ideas' about Music," *DJM* (Mar. 12, 1853): 182.

46. Ibid., 181.

47. "Communication from Mr. Fry," *MWMT* (Mar. 26, 1853): 196.

48. Apthorp, *Musicians and Music-Lovers*, 280.

CHAPTER 4

1. Hoplit [Richard Pohl], "Ein Blick nach dem 'fernen Westen'. Offenes Sendschreiben an Mr. J. S. Dwight," *NZfM* (June 17, 1853): 269–273; [J. S. Dwight], "A Greeting from Germany," *DJM* (July 30, 1853): 132–134.

2. [J. S. Dwight], "A Greeting from Germany," 134.

3. Ibid.

4. Ibid.

5. Ibid., 133.

6. "Music Teacher Dies in School," *New York Sun*, Dec. 14, 1898.

7. "George Bristow's Pranks," *BDE*, Sep. 23, 1888.

8. Philharmonic Society of New-York, *Constitution and By-Laws*, 14.

9. "The Philharmonic Society," *Saroni's Musical Times* (Nov. 17, 1849): 88.

10. "New York Philharmonic Society," *Message Bird* (Nov. 15, 1849): 130 (emphasis in original); see also Lawrence, *Strong on Music*, 1:572; and Preston, "American Orchestral Music," xlix–l.

11. *Saroni's Musical Times* (Nov. 24, 1849): 99.

12. See Preston, "American Orchestral Music," liii.

13. "Art National and Art Universal," *Journal of the Fine Arts* (May 1, 1851): 51.

14. [H. C. Watson], "Concert of the Philharmonic Society," *Albion* (Jan. 16, 1847): 36; and *New York Mirror*, Jan. 13, 1847, quoted in Lawrence, *Strong on Music*, 1:424.

15. *New York Courier & Enquirer*, Jan. 16, 1847, quoted in Lawrence, *Strong on Music*, 1:424.

16. Quoted in Lawrence, *Strong on Music*, 1:422.

17. "Domestic Compositions," *Saroni's Musical Times* (June 1, 1850): 422.

18. Ibid.

19. His translation appeared in 1852 under the title *Theory and Practice of Musical Composition* and ran through at least seven editions over the next decade.

20. "New York Philharmonic Society. Mr. Bristow's Symphony," *Message Bird* (June 15, 1850): 362.

21. [F. N. Crouch], "Symphony in E♭ Major. Composed by Geo. F. Bristow," *Message Bird* (July 1, 1850): 377; on Crouch's authorship, see Lawrence, *Strong on Music*, 2:4.

22. [H. C. Watson], "Music," *Albion* (Dec. 10, 1853): 596.

23. [F. N. Crouch], "Symphony in E♭ Major," *Message Bird* (July 1, 1850): 377 (emphasis in original).
24. [H. C. Watson], "Music," *Albion* (Dec. 10, 1853): 596.
25. Preston, "American Orchestral Music," lii.

CHAPTER 5

1. See Lawrence, *Strong on Music*, 2:86.
2. "Knaebel's National Concert," *BDE*, Apr. 15, 1851.
3. See Graziano, "Invisible Instruments," in *Spitzer*, ed., *American Orchestras*, 109–129; and Koegel and Westover, "Beethoven and Beer," in ibid., 130–155.
4. Lawrence, *Strong on Music*, 2:229.
5. Lawrence, *Strong on Music*, 2:284–285.
6. Preston, "American Orchestral Music," lxii–lxix.
7. "Music. Jullien," *NYDT*, Oct. 14, 1853.
8. "A Letter from Mr. Fry," *MWMT* (Jan. 21, 1854): 29.
9. [J. S. Dwight], "Mr. Fry and His Critics," *DJM* (Feb. 4, 1854): 141–142.
10. "Rejoinder from Mr. Fry," *MWMT* (Feb. 18, 1854): 75.
11. "The Philharmonic Society," *MWMT* (Mar. 4, 1854): 100.
12. Ibid.
13. Ibid.
14. "Letter from Mr. W. H. Fry," *DJM* (Mar. 18, 1854): 186–187.
15. "The Philharmonic Society," *MWMT* (Mar. 18, 1854): 121–122.
16. "The Philharmonic Again," *MWMT* (Mar. 25, 1854): 133.
17. "Second Letter from Mr. Bristow," *MWMT* (Apr. 1, 1854): 153 (emphasis in original).
18. Ibid.
19. "New York Philharmonic Society," *DJM* (Mar. 11, 1854): 181–182; reprinted in *MWMT* (Apr. 15, 1854): 172.
20. "Letter from Mr. Bristow," *MWMT* (Apr. 22, 1854): 183.
21. Ibid., 184 (emphasis in original).
22. Bristow was mostly right; see Haws, "Ureli Corelli Hill and the New York Philharmonic," in Spitzer, ed., *American Orchestras*, 362–364.
23. On Know-Nothingism, see Wilentz, *The Rise of American Democracy*, 668–706.
24. Carroll, *The Great American Battle*, 355–356.
25. [H. E. Krehbiel], "Musical Matters," *NYDT*, Dec. 18, 1898.
26. "Second Letter from Mr. Bristow," *MWMT* (Apr. 1, 1854): 153.
27. "New York Philharmonic Society," *DJM* (Mar. 11, 1854): 181–182.
28. On the status of the scores, see Upton, *William Henry Fry*, 317–319; Harvey, "Rethinking William Henry Fry"; and Carse, *The Life of Jullien*, 87–88.
29. See Lowens, *Music and Musicians in Early America*, 212–222; Butterworth, *The American Symphony*, 15; and Potter, *Food for Apollo*, 154.
30. "Letter from Paris," *Message Bird* (Jan. 15, 1851): 595.
31. See Miller, *Empire of the Eye*, 217.
32. A review indicated that the specific passage depicted in the symphony was canto III, stanza 3; see "Fry's New Symphony," *MRCA* (June 8, 1854): 201.
33. "A Letter from Mr. Fry," *MWMT* (Jan. 14, 1854): 31; for the program, see *Prospectus and Programmes of the New-York Musical Congress, 20*.
34. On Berlioz, see Johnson, *First Performances*, 59–70; and Saloman, "Presenting Berlioz's Music in New York," in Graziano, ed., *European Music and Musicians*.

35. An original printed copy of the synopsis is among the Fry manuscripts at the Library Company of Philadelphia; it is reprinted in full in Upton, *William Henry Fry*, 335–338.

36. [C. Burkhardt], "Music. Jullien's Concerts: Mr. Fry's New Symphony," *Albion* (Dec. 31, 1853): 632; on Burkhardt's authorship, see Lawrence, *Strong on Music*, 2:239.

37. Hafiz [G.W. Curtis], "Music in New York," *DJM* (May 1, 1852): 28.

38. "A Literary Curiosity," *Albion* (Jan. 14, 1854): 21.

39. See "Musical News From Everywhere. New York," *MWMT* (Jan. 7, 1854): 6.

40. Fry's penchant for coloration is also evident in his fondness for the newly invented saxophone, which he featured in *Santa Claus, Hagar,* and *The Dying Soldier.*

41. "The Eleventh and Final Lecture of W. H. Fry," *NYDT*, Feb. 11, 1853; and "Amusements. Jullien's Concerts," *NYT*, Dec. 29, 1853.

42. "Fry's New Symphony," *MRCA* (June 8, 1854): 201.

43. [C. Burkhardt], "Music. Jullien's Concerts: Mr. Fry's New Symphony," *Albion* (Dec. 31, 1853): 632.

44. [C. Burkhardt], "Music. Jullien's Concerts: Mr. Fry's New Symphony," 632; and R. S. Willis, "Musical News from Everywhere. New York," *MWMT* (Jan. 7, 1854): 6.

45. "A Letter from Mr. Fry," *MWMT* (Jan. 21, 1854): 29.

46. "Reply to Mr. Fry of the Tribune," *MWMT* (Jan. 28, 1854): 38.

47. On the aesthetic debate between Fry and Willis, see Shadle, "How Santa Claus Became a Slave Driver," 512–520.

48. "Music. Concert of the Philharmonic Society," *NYDT*, Jan. 16, 1854.

49. Ibid.

50. Kemp, "*Romeo and Juliet* and *Roméo et Juliette*," 48–50.

51. Saffle, "An Introduction to Liszt's Symphonic Poems," 25.

52. On writing or implying a symphonic choral finale, see Bonds, "Beethoven's Shadow," in Horton, ed., *The Cambridge Companion to the Symphony*, 339–341.

53. "Musical News from Everywhere. New York," *MWMT* (Jan. 7, 1854): 5.

54. Ibid., 6.

55. "Musical. The Philharmonic Society," *NYDT*, Mar. 3, 1856.

56. "The Philharmonic Society," *MWMT* (Mar. 8, 1856): 110; on Jullien, American popular musical culture, and the polka, see Foreman, "The Remarkable Monsieur Jullien."

57. "The World of New York," *Putnam's Monthly Magazine* (Mar. 1856): 333.

58. "Musical Correspondence. New York, Mar. 3," *DJM* (Mar. 8, 1856): 180.

59. [T. Hagen], "Third Philharmonic Concert," *MRG* (Mar. 8, 1856): 68.

60. Josef Küffner (1776–1856) wrote at least seven symphonies during his lifetime; see Rosenkranz, *Novello's Catalogue of Orchestral Music*, 56.

61. Webster, *Haydn's "Farewell" Symphony*, 180–181.

62. "Mr. Jullien's Concert at the Philharmonic Hall," *Manchester Times*, Feb. 14, 1855.

63. See Preston, "American Orchestral Music," lxxxii–lxxxiii.

64. "Au dernier concert philharmonique, on a exécuté une symphonie de Bristow, compositeur américain." See "Nouvelles Diverses," *Le Ménestrel* (Apr. 4, 1856): 4.

65. See Lawrence, *Strong on Music*, 1:551.

66. APHS, 776, quoted in Maust, "Symphonies," 43.

67. "Grand Farewell Concert of Anthony Philip Heinrich," *MWMT* (Dec. 18, 1852): 251.

CHAPTER 6

1. See Lawrence, *Strong on Music*, 2:577.
2. "The Cause of American Music," *MWMT* (June 16, 1855): 79.
3. "Concert of American Music," *NYT*, Feb. 16, 1856.
4. "Musical Intelligence," *MWMT* (Apr. 12, 1856): 173.
5. CJHJ, Sep. 16, 1856.
6. "Musical Correspondence. New York, Dec. 16," *DJM* (Dec. 20, 1856): 93.
7. CJHJ, Jan. 26, 1856.
8. CJHJ, Oct. 25, 1856.
9. CJHJ, Nov. 11, 1856.
10. "American-Music Association," *MWMT* (May 8, 1858): 291.
11. "Amusements," *NYT*, Feb. 16, 1858; for more details, see Jackson, "An American Muse."
12. "The Man About Town. Summer Music," *Harper's Weekly* (Aug. 22, 1857): 531; see also Shadle, "How Santa Claus became a Slave Driver," 526–530.
13. Cf. Lowens, *Music and Musicians in Early America*, 222; Butterworth, *The American Symphony*, 15; and Zuck, *A History of Musical Americanism*, 25.
14. "National Music," *North American Review* (Jan. 1840): 15.
15. On Lind's American tour, see Ware and Lockard Jr., *P. T. Barnum Presents Jenny Lind*.
16. On organ grinding, see "The Modern Troubadours. Our Democratic Opera and Its Votaries," *NYDT*, Mar. 27, 1855. On bel canto arias as popular songs and on Foster's indebtedness to them, see Hamm, *Yesterdays*, 62–88, 219–222. On the transformation of operatic numbers into minstrel pieces, see Norris, "Opera and the Mainstreaming of Blackface Minstrelsy"; and Mahar, *Behind the Burnt Cork Mark*, 101–156 (Fry, 126–144).
17. "Italian Opera," *MWMT* (Jan. 15, 1853): 33 (emphasis in original).
18. "Lectures on Music. By W. H. Fry," *NYDT*, Jan. 21, 1853.
19. See, e.g., "Music. Concert of the Philharmonic Society," *NYDT*, Mar. 7, 1854; and "The Harmonic Society," *NYDT*, May 14, 1856.
20. Fry wrote Johnson's eulogy for the *Public Ledger*; see Jones, *Francis Johnson*, 244–245.
21. [R. S. Willis], "Jullien's Strong Points," *MWMT* (Sep. 17, 1853): 17. Dwight's correspondents responded similarly; see "Jullien's Concerts," *DJM* (Sep. 3, 1853): 175; and "Jullien's Concerts," *DJM* (Sep. 24, 1853): 198–199.
22. Graziano, "Jullien and His *Music for the Million*," in Crawford, Lott, and Oja, eds., *A Celebration of American Music*, 214–215.
23. Cavicchi, *Listening and Longing*, 4–7.
24. [R. S. Willis], "Jullien's Strong Points," 17.
25. See Cavicchi, *Listening and Longing*, 79; see also Howe, *Making the American Self*.
26. Cavicchi, *Listening and Longing*, 102.
27. See Bonds, *Music as Thought*, 73–78.
28. [Samuel Atkins Eliot], "Music and Politics," *DJM* (Jan. 28, 1860): 345. On the orchestra as a metaphor for civil polity, see Spitzer and Zaslaw, eds., *The Birth of the Orchestra*, 512–514.
29. "Jullien's Concerts," *DJM* (Oct. 29, 1853): 30.
30. "A Letter from Mr. Fry," *MWMT* (Jan. 21, 1854): 34.
31. "Mr. Meignen's Concert," *PPL*, Apr. 21, 1845.
32. "Editorial Notes. Music," *Putnam's Monthly Magazine* (May 1854): 564; see also *Strong on Music*, 2:235.

33. "A Letter from Mr. Fry," *MWMT* (Jan. 21, 1854): 29.

34. *Empress Queen of the Magyars*, Part I, APHC, Vol. 19.

35. See Audubon, *Ornithological Biography*, 319–327; and Wilson, *American Ornithology*, 2:293–306.

36. Quoted and translated in Upton, *Anthony Philip Heinrich*, 232–233.

37. See Bonds, *Absolute Music*, 210–218.

38. For Stoepel's early biography, see Pisani, "Longfellow," 51–52.

39. "Mr. Stoepel's 'Hiawatha' Music, *DJM* (Jan. 15, 1859): 332; and "Mr. Stoepel's Romantic Symphony 'Hiawatha,'" *DJM* (Jan. 15, 1859): 334.

40. For other accounts of the Boston newspaper reviews, see "Mr. Stoepel's 'Hiawatha,'" *MWMT* (Jan. 29, 1859): 66–67; and "Stoepel's 'Hiawatha,'" *MWMT* (Jan. 29, 1859): 67.

41. "Mr. Robert Stoepel's 'Hiawatha,'" *DJM* (Jan. 15, 1859): 334–335.

42. "Musical," *New York Evening Express*, Feb. 22, 1859.

43. [T. Hagen], "Academy of Music. 'Hiawatha.' Romantic Symphony by Robt. Stoepel," *MRG* (Mar. 5, 1859): 67.

44. [R. S. Willis], "Hiawatha," *MWMT* (Feb. 26, 1859): 131.

45. "Music," *Frank Leslie's Illustrated Newspaper*, Jan. 22, 1859.

46. See "Musical Intelligence," *NYDT*, Jan. 27, 1859; "Mr. Stoepel's Hiawatha," *NYDT*, Feb. 23, 1859; and "Israel in Egypt Again," *DJM* (Mar. 5, 1859): 391.

47. "The 'Hiawatha' Music Again," *DJM* (29 Jan. 1859): 350–351; all quotations in this section are taken from this article.

48. See Lawrence, *Strong on Music*, 3:290.

49. See also Fried, "A Study of the Orchestral Music of George Frederick Bristow," 55.

50. On the origins and popularity of this style, see Brittan, "On Microscopic Hearing."

51. "New York. Mar. 27," *DJM* (Apr. 2, 1859): 6.

52. [C. B. Seymour], "Amusements," *NYT*, Mar. 28, 1859.

53. [T. Hagen], "Music in New York. Fourth Philharmonic Concert," *MRG* (Apr. 2, 1859): 98–99.

54. [R. S. Willis], "The Philharmonic Society," *MWMT* (Apr. 2, 1859): 210.

INTERLUDE

1. See Huneker, *The Philharmonic Society*, 8.

2. On these issues, see Lawson, *Patriot Fires*; and Smith, *Listening to Nineteenth-Century America*.

3. On the war's impact on intellectual life, see Menand, *The Metaphysical Club*; on literature, see R. Fuller, *From Battlefields Rising*.

4. On sacralization, see Levine, *Highbrow/Lowbrow*; and Horowitz, "Music and the Gilded Age," 241–245; on fans and art worship, see Cavicchi, *Listening and Longing*, 107–148.

5. Gienow-Hecht has called this bond an "elective affinity"; see *Sound Diplomacy*.

CHAPTER 7

1. On Dwight's programming practices as manager of the Harvard Musical Association, *see* Davidson, "John Sullivan Dwight," in Spitzer, ed., *American Orchestras*, 251–257.

2. H. Didimus [Edward Henry Durell], "L. M. Gottschalk," *Graham's American Monthly* (Jan. 1853): 61–69.

3. On the San Francisco incident, see Jackson, "More Notes of a Pianist," 364–375; on his death, see Starr, *Bamboula!*, 435–437.
4. See "Gottschalk," *Watson's Art Journal* (Oct. 8, 1870): 255.
5. "Music," *Albion* (Feb. 19, 1853): 92.
6. Complicating matters further, nineteenth-century commentators often noted Gottschalk's paternal Jewish heritage, but this seemed to play little or no role in interpretations of his music during his lifetime; see Korn, "A Note on the Jewish Ancestry of Louis Moreau Gottschalk"; and Starr, *Bamboula!*, 18–25.
7. His other patriotic work, *Columbia, caprice américaine*, Op. 34 (1859), is a shortened version of the second part of the (now lost) *Grand National Symphony*, which was supposed to depict American life after the Revolution; Starr, *Bamboula!*, 139 and 283.
8. Preceding a performance in New Orleans on Feb. 1, 1854, a description of the work appeared in the *Courrier de la Louisiane*, Jan. 31, 1854, reprinted in Starr, *Bamboula!*, 157.
9. *Daily Orleanian*, Feb. 5, 1854, quoted in Pruett, "Louis Moreau Gottschalk," 98. For other reviews, see *Courrier de la Louisiane*, Feb. 2, 1854, quoted in Starr, *Bamboula!*, 157; and "Gottschalk's Concert," *L'Abeille de la Nouvelle Orleans/ New Orleans Bee*, Feb. 2, 1854.
10. For a summary of reactions to *L'Union*, see Starr, *Bamboula!*, 320.
11. Dwight did not mention the work in his review of Gottschalk's return to Boston in 1862 after a nine-year absence from the city; "Gottschalk's Concerts," *DJM* (Oct. 18, 1862): 230–231.
12. He also composed a symphony for ten pianos, *El sitio de Zaragoza* (*The Siege of Saragosa*, 1852), but the music is now lost.
13. Cf. Starr, *Bamboula!*, vii, 35–36, 364.
14. Gottschalk, *Notes of a Pianist*, 236.
15. "News from Gottschalk," *WAJ* (Dec. 19, 1868): 108–109.
16. "News from Gottschalk," 109; see also Hensel, *Life and Letters*, 165–167.
17. Gottschalk, *Notes of a Pianist*, 343–344, 396.
18. Ibid., 397.
19. Quoted in Starr, *Bamboula!*, 406.
20. Gottschalk, *Notes of a Pianist*, 261.
21. Trollope, *The West Indies and the Spanish Main*, 114–115; on the commercial relationship between Cuba and the United States, see Gott, *Cuba*, 67–68.
22. Gottschalk, *Notes of a Pianist*, 30–31.
23. "Jenny Lind," *NYEP*, Nov. 27, 1850.
24. For more on Maretzek in Cuba, see Maretzek, *Crotchets and Quavers*, 149–172.
25. Raimond, "Music," *Albion* (July 18, 1857): 344.
26. "Correspondence," *WAJ* (Oct. 17, 1868): 337.
27. Gottschalk, *Notes of a Pianist*, 106.
28. See Starr, *Bamboula!*, 269.
29. Gottschalk, *Notes of a Pianist*, 106 (emphasis in original).
30. Ibid., 108 (emphasis in original). In this modern edition, the editor changed the phrase "whole physical economy" found in the essay's original publication in 1865 to "whole being." I have retained the original because Gottschalk's focus in this passage is clearly the body, not the whole human being; see Gottschalk, "Notes of a Pianist," *Atlantic Monthly* (Feb. 1865): 179.
31. Gottschalk, *Notes of a Pianist*, 106.

32. Ibid., 106–107.
33. Ibid., 110–111.
34. For more on Gottschalk's stay in Matouba, see Starr, *Bamboula!*, 272–288.
35. Starr, *Bamboula!*, 290–295.
36. On the possible origin of this title, see Starr, *Bamboula!*, 285.
37. Gottschalk, *Notes of a Pianist*, 103.
38. Cf. Korf, *Orchestral Music*, 73.
39. Gottschalk, *Notes of a Pianist*, 183; see also Korf, *Orchestral Music*, 67–78.
40. "Correspondence," *AAJ* (Sep. 27, 1866): 364.
41. Carpenter, *Music in Cuba*, 150.
42. Chasteen, *National Rhythms, African Roots*, 76–77.
43. This technique was not new for Gottschalk, who had quoted or suggested Foster in several works; see Pruett, "Louis Moreau Gottschalk," 70–109.
44. "Ejecutóse la grandiosa sinfonía *Noche de los Trópicos*, obra de concepcion gigantesca, de génio brillante, de plan vastísimo, en la cual Gottschalk á pesar de demostar un elevadísimo grado de belleza estética y selecta, se amolda en sus ritmos é índole á todos los giros caracterísicos del pais, hasta el punto de satisfacer el gusto musical más exigente." Fors, *Gottschalk*, 111. My translation with the assistance of Matthew Shadle.
45. Starr, *Bamboula!*, 285.
46. See Salgado, *The Teatro Solís*, 46.
47. On French comic opera, see Marshall, *The French Atlantic*, 260–297.
48. See Gibbons, "'Yankee Doodle' and Nationalism."
49. See Leuchars, *To the Bitter End*.
50. "Gottschalk's Festival of 350 Musicians!!!" *WAJ* (Jan. 23, 1869): 170.
51. "Music in South America. Gottschalk in Brazil," *NYT*, Oct. 24, 1869.

CHAPTER 8

1. Gilmore, *History*, 409.
2. "The Peace Jubilee Summed Up," *DJM* (July 3, 1869): 62–63.
3. [H. C. Watson], "Review of the Boston Musical Festival, and the Men Who Worked for It," *WAJ* (July 17, 1869): 139.
4. Ibid., 140.
5. "Music in American Universities," *Nation* (June 8, 1905): 452.
6. On Paine's last years, see Schmidt, *Life and Works*, 192–255.
7. Schmidt, *Life and Works*, 17–23.
8. "The Musical Festival," *NYDT*, June 29, 1858.
9. See Schmidt, *Life and Works*, 24–29; and Bomberger, "Charting the Future of 'Zukunftsmusik,'" 351.
10. *Boston Musical Times* (Aug. 10, 1861): 166, quoted in Broyles, "Haupt's Boys," 40.
11. "Mr. John K. Paine," *DJM* (Nov. 9, 1861): 254.
12. "Music at Harvard," *DJM* (July 7, 1866): 270.
13. See "John K. Paine," *DJM* (Nov. 24, 1866): 352. For a translation of a performance review written by Godard in the *Berlinische Nachrichten*, see "Music Abroad. Berlin," *DJM* (Mar. 16, 1867): 413.
14. George L. Osgood, letter to the editor, *Boston Daily Evening Transcript*, Mar. 16, 1867, quoted in Schmidt, *Life and Works*, 73.
15. Smith, *Extracts*, 100.
16. For the entire poem, see Story, *Poems*, 296–305.

17. See "The Great Musical Jubilee and Beethoven Centennial," *WAJ* (June 18, 1870): 63–66; "The Great Musical Jubilee," *WAJ* (July 2, 1870): 86–87; and "Geo. F. Bristow's Public School Centennial," *WAJ* (July 2, 1870): 87–88.
18. "The Centennial Celebration," *DJM* (Dec. 17, 1870): 366.
19. "Beethoven," *DJM* (Jan. 14, 1871): 380.
20. See Nagler, "From Culture to *Kultur*."
21. [Untitled], *WAJ* (Dec. 5, 1868): 84.
22. Paine, *The Musical Profession: A Plea for thorough musical culture* (Sept. 1869), National Musical Convention Speech, reprinted in *Boston Musical Times* (Oct. 1869): 58–59, quoted in Schmidt, *Life and Works*, 83–84.
23. Ibid.; see also "The National Musical Congress," *WAJ* (Oct. 2, 1869): 262.
24. "The History of Music," *DJM* (Mar. 25, 1871): 420.
25. Ibid., 421.
26. Schlüter, *Allgemeine Geschichte der Musik*, 51: "Als Componist musste er, gewiss der universellste Musiker vor Mozart, wie dieser überall mit kunstlerische Freiheit in die herrschende Geschmacksrichtung einzugehen und den Erfolg an seine Schritte zu fesseln." My translation.
27. Ibid., 101.
28. Ritter, *History of Music*, 1:87–88; Ritter gave the lectures that formed this book's narrative foundation in New York in 1869. See "Lectures on the History of Music," *WAJ* (Oct. 23, 1869): 288.
29. "The History of Music," *DJM* (Mar. 25, 1871): 420; on transcendence, see chapter 6 of Goehr, *The Imaginary Museum*.
30. "The History of Music," *DJM* (Apr. 8, 1871): 8.
31. "The History of Music," *DJM* (Apr. 22, 1871): 11.
32. Ibid.
33. "The History of Music," *DJM* (Apr. 22, 1871): 11.
34. Ritter, *History of Music*, 2:207–208.
35. "The History of Music," *DJM* (Apr. 22, 1871): 11–12.
36. On asymmetrical information exchanges in earlier transatlantic musical discourses, see Shadle, "How Santa Claus Became a Slave Driver."
37. On the European context, see Frisch, *Brahms*, 1–27.
38. E. R. [Edmund Remack], "New York," *Boston Musical Times* (Dec. 29, 1860): 366.
39. [H. C. Watson], "New York Philharmonic Society First Concert—25th Season," *AAJ* (Nov. 22, 1866): 67–68.
40. [J. S. Dwight], "Concerts. Harvard Musical Association," *DJM* (Mar. 11, 1871): 414.
41. [J. S. Dwight], "Fifth Symphony Concert," *DJM* (Jan. 14, 1871): 382.
42. See Johnson, *First Performances*, 289–290, 299–300.
43. "Philharmonic," *BDE*, Nov. 21, 1870.
44. See Williamson, "The Symphony as Programme Music," in Horton, ed., *The Cambridge Companion to the Symphony*, 351–353.
45. [H. C. Watson], "New York Philharmonic Society," *WAJ* (Jan. 15, 1870): 84; see also "Music," *NYDT*, Feb. 10, 1870; and "Music and the Drama," *NYDT*, Feb. 28, 1870.
46. [J. Hassard], "Music. Thomas's Symphony Concert," *NYDT*, Mar. 31, 1873; "Musical and Dramatic Notes," *Philadelphia Inquirer*, Jan. 6, 1873; and "Musical Correspondence [Philadelphia]," *DJM* (Feb. 8, 1873): 380.

CHAPTER 9

1. See Shanet, *Philharmonic*, 133; and Schabas, *Theodore Thomas*, 33.

2. On his later career, see Rogers, "Nineteenth Century Music in New York City," 82–121; on his teaching career, see Dox, "George Frederick Bristow."

3. [H. C. Watson], "N.Y. Philharmonic Society First Concert—25th Season," *AAJ* (Nov. 22, 1866): 68.

4. "Fourth Philharmonic Concert," *BDE*, Feb. 28, 1870.

5. See [H. C. Watson], "George F. Bristow's Oratorio, 'Daniel,'" *WAJ* (Jan. 4, 1868): 158; Watson continued to fête the work in two later issues.

6. "Merging Nationalities," *BDE*, June 29, 1871; "Philharmonic. Should the Orchestra Rehearse for Rehearsals?" *BDE*, May 29, 1872.

7. "Concerning Music," *BDE*, Oct. 4, 1872.

8. See "Amusements. The Philharmonic Rehearsal," *Brooklyn Daily Union*, Jan. 16, 1873.

9. [W. C. Hudson], "Philharmonic," *BDE*, Jan. 14, 1873; on Hudson's tenure at the *Eagle* (1872–1876), see "Personal Gossip about Writers," *Author* (July 15, 1890): 107.

10. "Amusements. The Philharmonic Rehearsal," *Brooklyn Daily Union*, Jan. 16, 1873.

11. [W. C. Hudson], "Philharmonic," *BDE*, Jan. 16, 1873.

12. "Philharmonic. Seventy-Sixth Concert," *BDE*, Feb. 10, 1873.

13. "Musical Correspondence," *DJM* (Mar. 8, 1873): 399.

14. "Amusements. Third Philharmonic Concert," *Brooklyn Daily Union*, Feb. 10, 1873.

15. "Bristow's 'Arcadian' Symphony," *Musical World* (Mar. 29, 1873): 197.

16. "Musical Matters," *Spirit of the Times* (Feb. 7, 1874): 616.

17. "Eleventh Peabody Concert—American Night," *Baltimore Sun*, Mar. 15, 1875.

18. *New York World*, Mar. 31, 1873, reprinted in "Mr. Paine's Oratorio," *DJM* (May 17, 1873): 20–21 (quote at 21); and Mathews, "American Oratorios," *Nation* (Feb. 13, 1873): 116–117.

19. "Music," *Atlantic Monthly* (Aug. 1873): 248.

20. See Smither, *The History of the Oratorio*, 4:479–481.

21. Paine, "The New German School of Music," *North American Review* (April 1873): 217–245; see also "The North American Review for April," *Nation* (Apr. 24, 1873): 289.

22. Paine, "The New German School of Music," 245.

23. Ibid., 231.

24. Ibid., 237.

25. Ibid., 240.

26. Ibid.

27. "Record of Amusements," *NYT*, Feb. 15, 1874.

28. "Music," *Appletons' Journal* (Mar. 7, 1874): 317.

29. [M. Cooney], "Amusements," *NYH*, Feb. 7, 1874.

30. "Music and the Drama," *NYDT*, Feb. 16, 1874; see also "Classical Music," *New York Daily Graphic*, Feb. 17, 1874.

31. "The Fourth Philharmonic Concert," *WAJ* (Feb. 21, 1874): 202–203.

32. "Von der Bristow'schen Sinfonie läßt sich wenig sagen, denn das Werk eines tüchtig geschulten Musikes, der sein Handwerk versteht und die Kunst auch als solches behandelt, verdient jedenfalls jeden anderen Titel, nur den einer Sinfonie nicht. Neue originelle Ideen wird man in dieser arcadischen Sinfonie, richtiger gesagt, in diesem recht amerikanischen Tongemälde, vergeblich suchen. Es sind lauter alte Bekannte, die Bristow'schen Ideen; seine Motive fordern das

Nachdenken heraus, d.h. man grübelt bei jedem derselben nach, woher sie der amerikanische Componist genommen, auf gut Deutsch, gestohlen hat. Wir müssen im Namen der Kunstkenner und Kunstfreunde für solche Concessionen, welche die Gesellschaft ihren eingeborenen amerikanischen Elementen durch die Aufführung solcher Werke zu machen für nöthig hält, doch höflichst danken. Bergmann und seine Philharmoniker gaben sich zwar die größte Mühe, das Ding über Wasser zu halten, aber es wollte ihnen doch nicht recht gelingen." *New-Yorker Staats-Zeitung*, Feb. 22, 1874; the review is quoted in Reichert, "Carl Bergmann in New York," 910–911. My translation.

33. "Mr. Howard's 'Lohengrin'—'The Musical Season in America' (Meaning New York)," *DJM* (June 27, 1874): 251.

34. [J. S. Dwight], "'Monotony' of Good Things—New Music," *DJM* (May 2, 1874): 222.

35. White, "Richard Wagner, and His Theory of Music" *Galaxy* (June 1874): 786.

36. [J. S. Dwight], "Richard Wagner and his Theories," *DJM* (July 11, 1874): 263.

37. White, "Franz Liszt, and His Relations to the 'Music of the Future,'" *Galaxy* (Sep. 1874): 390.

38. White, "Absolute Music," *Galaxy* (May 1875): 398.

39. "Music in Boston," *Boston Post*, Feb. 5, 1876; see also Schmidt, *Life and Works*, 113–116; and Davidson, "John Sullivan Dwight," in Spitzer, ed., *American Orchestras*, 260–261.

40. See also Schmidt, *Life and Works*, 340–342.

41. Osgood, "Mr. Paine's Symphony.—A Technical Analysis," *DJM* (Feb. 5, 1876): 173; *Boston Saturday Evening Gazette*, Jan. 29, 1876; "Music," *NYDT*, Feb. 7, 1876; and *New York World*, Feb. 6, 1876; all reprinted in "Prof. Paine's Symphony.—Shades of Opinion," *DJM* (Feb. 19, 1876): 181–182; W. F. Apthorp, "Music," *Atlantic Monthly* (May 1876): 633; and "Music and the Drama," *Boston Daily Advertiser*, Jan. 27, 1876.

42. "Entertainments," *Boston Post*, Jan. 27, 1876.

43. "Music and the Drama," *Boston Daily Advertiser*, Jan. 27, 1876.

44. [J. S. Dwight], "Concert Review," *DJM* (Feb. 5, 1876): 175.

45. [J. S. Dwight], "Concerts," *DJM* (Jan. 22, 1876): 167.

46. *New York World*, Feb. 6, 1876, reprinted in "Prof. Paine's Symphony.—Shades of Opinion," 182.

47. *Sunday Evening Gazette*, Jan. 29, 1876, reprinted in "Prof. Paine's Symphony.—Shades of Opinion," 181.

48. [J. Fiske], "Fine Arts. Paine's Symphony in C Minor," *Nation* (Mar. 30, 1876), 216–217; Fiske's authorship is affirmed in Haskell, ed., *The Nation*, 56.

49. Their authorship is affirmed in the *Atlantic Index*, 160.

50. [W. F. Apthorp], "Music," *Atlantic Monthly* (May 1876): 633.

51. [J. Fiske], "Music," *Atlantic Monthly* (June 1876): 763.

52. Ibid., 764.

53. [J. Fiske], "Fine Arts," *Nation* (Mar. 30, 1876): 217.

CHAPTER 10

1. "Philharmonic," *BDE*, Nov. 21, 1870.

2. "Philharmonic," *BDE*, Feb. 18, 1874.

3. See Ross and Pelletreau, *History of Long Island*, 3:177–181.

4. See Bomberger, *Tidal Wave*; and Phelps, "New Music Society of America," *BDE*, Mar. 27, 1906.

5. See "Prof. E. C. Phelps, Dies" *NYT*, Dec. 1, 1913; "Prof Ellsworth C. Phelps," *New York Sun*, Dec. 1, 1913.

6. "Musical," *BDE*, Oct. 18, 1873.

7. See, e.g., "The Brooklyn Philharmonic Society," *NYEP*, Nov. 7, 1873.

8. "The Fourth Philharmonic Concert a Brilliant Promise," *BDE*, Feb. 27, 1874.

9. "Phelps's 'Hiawatha' Symphony," *BDE*, Mar. 7, 1874.

10. "A New Musical Enterprise in Brooklyn," *NYEP*, Oct. 29, 1874.

11. "An American Composer's Trials. America an Inviting Field for Foreign Musical Adventurers," *New York Sun*, Jan. 16, 1876.

12. "The 'Hiawatha' Symphony," *BDE*, Mar. 7, 1878.

13. Paine, "The New German School of Music," *North American Review* (April 1873): 244–245.

14. [J. S. Dwight], "Orchestral Concerts," *DJM* (Nov. 24, 1877): 135.

15. "Professor Paine's Symphonic Fantasy," *DJM* (Dec. 22, 1877): 148.

16. [J. S. Dwight], "Orchestral Concerts," *DJM* (Dec. 22, 1877): 150.

17. "The New Symphony by Brahms," *DJM* (Apr. 28, 1877): 9; and "The C-Minor Symphony by Brahms," *DJM* (Dec. 22, 1877): 149–150.

18. Quoted in "Music in New York," *DJM* (Jan. 5, 1878): 160.

19. [C. J. Hopkins], "Musical Items," *Philharmonic Journal and Orpheonist* (Jan. 1878): 6–7.

20. Quoted in "After-Thomas Opinions of the Brahms Symphony," *DJM* (Feb. 2, 1878): 170–171.

21. "Fifth Harvard Symphony Concert," *DJM* (Jan. 19, 1878): 166–167; "Concerts," *DJM* (Feb. 2, 1878): 174; "Concerts," *DJM* (Feb. 16, 1878): 182.

22. "An American Symphony," *BDE*, Feb. 11, 1878.

23. "The 'Hiawatha' Symphony," *BDE*, Mar. 5, 1878.

24. "An American Symphony," *BDE*, Feb. 11, 1878; "A Symphony Rehearsal," *BDE*, Mar. 13, 1878.

25. "The Brooklyn Music Hall," *BDE*, Mar. 15, 1878.

26. "Come to an End," *BDE*, Apr. 28, 1878.

27. "Musical," *BDE*, Sep. 17, 1878.

28. See "The 'Hiawatha' Symphony," *BDE*, Jan. 2, 1879; "The 'Hiawatha' Symphony," *BDE*, Jan. 26, 1879; "The 'Hiawatha' Symphony," *BDE*, Jan. 27, 1879; "Mr. Phelps and the Philharmonic Society," *BDE*, Jan. 28, 1879; and "The 'Hiawatha' Symphony," *BDE*, Jan. 30, 1879.

29. "The Last Philharmonic Concert," *BDE*, May 11, 1879; and "Musical and Dramatic," *NYT*, May 11, 1879.

30. On Raff, see Brodbeck, "The Symphony after Beethoven after Dahlhaus," in Horton, ed., *The Cambridge Companion to the Symphony*, 74–76; Brown, ed., *The Symphonic Repertoire*, IIIa:831–841; and Johnson, *First Performances*, 289.

31. See "Mr. Phelps and His Overture," *BDE*, May 16, 1864; and "Native versus Classic Composers," *BDE*, Sep. 23, 1865.

32. "A Brooklyn Composer," *BDE*, Nov. 16, 1879.

33. "The Emancipation," *Brooklyn Daily Union-Argus*, Feb. 2, 1880.

34. "Brooklyn Letter," *Cincinnati Daily Star*, Feb. 26, 1880.

35. "Dramatic and Musical," *BDE*, Mar. 3, 1880.

36. "Brooklyn Academy of Music—Symphony Concert," *NYH*, Mar. 3, 1880.

37. "A Great Musical Event," *New Orleans Times-Picayune*, Mar. 6, 1880.

38. [Untitled], *Brooklyn Daily Union-Argus*, Mar. 3, 1880.

39. Goodrich, *Complete Musical Analysis*, 286.

40. [J. S. Dwight], "Mr. J. K. Paine's New Symphony," *DJM* (Mar. 27, 1880): 53.

41. *Saturday Evening Gazette* (n.d.), quoted in Schmidt, *Life and Works*, 137.

42. [J. S. Dwight], "Mr. J. K. Paine's New Symphony," *DJM* (Mar. 27, 1880): 53.

43. See Aldrich, "Paine, John Knowles," in Malone, ed., *Dictionary of American Biography*, 14:152.

44. [J. S. Dwight], "Mr. J. K. Paine's New Symphony," 53–54.

45. Ibid.

46. "Music in Boston," *Musical Record* (Mar. 20, 1880): 389. The reviews from the *Gazette, Courier*, and *Daily Transcript* may be found in the A. A. Brown Music Collection, Boston Public Library, and are quoted in Schmidt, *Life and Works*, 137–139.

47. "Music and the Drama," *Boston Daily Advertiser*, Mar. 11, 1880.

48. See Thomas, *Memoirs*, 569. For a performance list, see Nelson-Strauss, "Theodore Thomas and the Cultivation of American Music," in Spitzer, ed., *American Orchestras*, 427–428.

49. See "Mr. Paine's 'Spring' Symphony," *BDE*, Mar. 28, 1883.

50. "Seventh Philharmonic Concert," *BDE*, Apr. 1, 1883.

51. [H. E. Krehbiel], "The Brooklyn Philharmonic Concert," *NYDT*, Apr. 1, 1883.

52. [H. T. Finck], "Notes," *Nation* (Apr. 5, 1883): 298; on Finck as critic for *The Nation* beginning in 1877, see Lind, "Music in *The Nation*," 11–12.

53. [F. A. Schwab], "Amusements," *NYT*, Mar. 31, 1883.

54. [H. E. Krehbiel], "The Brooklyn Philharmonic Concert," *NYDT*, Apr. 1, 1883.

55. "Seventh Philharmonic Concert," *BDE*, Apr. 1, 1883.

56. [H. E. Krehbiel], "The Brooklyn Philharmonic Concert," *NYDT*, Apr. 1, 1883.

57. [H. T. Finck], "Notes," *Nation* (Apr. 5, 1883): 298.

58. [H. E. Krehbiel], "Music," *NYDT*, Apr. 1, 1885.

59. [H. E. Krehbiel], "A Concert of American Music," *NYDT*, Feb. 24, 1891.

60. "American Music," *BDE*, Mar. 4, 1891.

61. Ibid.

CHAPTER 11

1. [H. E. Krehbiel], "The Brooklyn Philharmonic Concert," *NYDT*, Apr. 1, 1883.

2. Foote, "Thirty-Five Years of Music in Boston"; Mason, *The Dilemma of American Music and Other Essays*, 3; Gunn, *Music*, 296; Howard, *Our American Music*, 316; and Young, *A Critical Dictionary*, 245.

3. "Music in Philadelphia," *DJM* (Aug. 5, 1876): 280.

4. See Horowitz, *Moral Fire*, 19–73.

5. See Faucett, *George Whitefield Chadwick* (II), 331–338.

6. Chadwick, "A 'Touch' of Beethoven"; thanks to Bill Faucett for forwarding this article to me.

7. See Faucett, *George Whitefield Chadwick* (II), 28–29, 90–91.

8. Chadwick, "American Composers," in Hubbard, ed., *American History and Encyclopedia of Music: A History of American Music*, 2; see also Faucett, *George Whitefield Chadwick* (II), 85.

9. Faucett, *George Whitefield Chadwick* (II), 46–72.

10. [J. S. Dwight], "Music in Boston," *DJM* (Dec. 20, 1879): 205.

11. "Here and There," *Church's Musical Visitor* (May 1881): 218.

12. *Boston Evening Transcript*, Feb. 24, 1882, quoted in Faucett, *George Whitefield Chadwick* (I), 33.

13. "Boston Musical Events," *AAJ* (Mar. 4, 1882): 369.

14. Proteus [L. C. Elson], "Music in Boston," *Church's Musical Visitor* (Apr. 1882): 187.

15. Quoted in "Boston Musical Events," *AAJ* (Mar. 4, 1882): 369.

16. "Musical Matters in Boston—Debut of Dr. Louis Maas as Conductor," *AAJ* (Nov. 19, 1881): 65.

17. "'On the Prairies,'" *AAJ* (Oct. 14, 1882): 509.

18. "'On the Prairies.' An 'American' Symphony by Louis Maas," *AAJ* (Dec. 16, 1882): 146.

19. L. C. E., "Boston," *Music and Drama* (Dec. 23, 1882): 26; [W. F. Apthorp], "Theatres and Concerts," *Boston Evening Transcript*, Dec. 15, 1882; and "The Old Bay State Concert," *Boston Daily Advertiser*, Dec. 15, 1882.

20. Lavallée, "Dr. Louis Maas' Symphony, 'On the Prairies,'" *AAJ* (Jan. 20, 1882): 242–243.

21. "American Composers," *Musical Record* (May 19, 1883): 47.

22. [W. F. Apthorp], "Theatres and Concerts. Boston Symphony Orchestra," *Boston Evening Transcript*, Mar. 10, 1884; see also Proteus [L. C. Elson], "Music in Boston," *Musical Visitor* (Apr. 1884): 97.

23. Proteus [L. C. Elson], "Boston," *Musical Visitor* (Nov. 1884): 292.

24. *Boston Post*, Dec. 13, 1886; and *Boston Herald*, Dec. 12, 1886, quoted in Faucett, *George Whitefield Chadwick* (I), 53, 56.

25. [W. F. Apthorp], "Theatres and Concerts," *Boston Evening Transcript*, Dec. 13, 1886.

26. Unidentified clipping, quoted in Faucett, *George Whitefield Chadwick* (I), 56.

27. *Boston Herald*, Dec. 12, 1886, quoted in Faucett, *George Whitefield Chadwick* (I), 55.

28. Hale and "brasses" quoted in Faucett, *George Whitefield Chadwick* (I), 56–58; and Comes, "Correspondence. Boston," *Kunkel's Musical Review* (Jan. 1887): 34.

29. Loring, *American Romantic-Realist*, 28–33.

30. Ibid., 37.

31. Ibid., 37–39.

32. Ibid., 53–54.

33. On this movement, see Bomberger, *Tidal Wave*.

34. [T. Presser], "M.T.N.A.," *Etude* (July 1886): 158.

35. Stratton, "American Composers and Their Works," *Quarterly Musical Review* (Aug. 1888): 148–159.

36. "Nouvelles Diverses," *Le Ménestrel* (June 28, 1891): 206 (my translation); for the article it cites, see "Americanism in Art," *Chicago Inter Ocean*, May 17, 1891.

37. Seidl, "The Development of Music in America," *Forum* (May 1892): 386–393.

38. "Seidl Society Concert," *BDE*, Apr. 13, 1892.

39. "Last Seidl Society Concert," *NYH*, Apr. 13, 1892.

40. On the Seidl Society, see Horowitz, *Wagner Nights*.

41. [H. E. Krehbiel], "Music. Some American Compositions," *NYDT*, Apr. 1, 1893; and Hughes, *Contemporary American Composers*, 131.

42. [W. S. B. Matthews], "Music at the Fair," *Music* 4 (1893): 226; and unidentified clipping, quoted in Faucett, *George Whitefield Chadwick* (I), 59; on American music at the Exposition, see Bomberger, *Tidal Wave*, 127–144.

43. Weld, "A Contribution to the Discussion of 'Americanism' in Music," *Music* (Apr. 1894): 633–640.

44. Ibid., 637.

45. Roosevelt, "What 'Americanism' Means," *Forum* (Apr. 1894): 196–206.

46. Krum, "Americanism Musically," *Music* (Sept. 1894): 544–547.

CHAPTER 12

1. See Rubin, "Jeannette Myers Thurber," 294–298.
2. See "Dr. Dvorak's Reception," *NYDT*, Oct. 22, 1892; and "Antonin Dvorak Leads at the Music Hall," *NYH*, Oct. 22, 1892.
3. [H. E. Krehbiel], "Some Observations after the Fact," *NYDT*, Oct. 24, 1892.
4. See "Character and Music," *Musical Courier* (Sep. 18, 1889): 250; and Krehbiel, "Music in America," 959–960.
5. [H. E. Krehbiel], "Some Observations after the Fact," *NYDT*, Oct. 24, 1892.
6. "American Music. Dvorak Thinks Little Has Been Done Here," *Boston Daily Traveler*, Dec. 10, 1892.
7. [H. E. Krehbiel], "Some Observations after the Fact," *NYDT*, Oct. 24, 1892.
8. "A Week's Musical Topics," *NYT*, Mar. 5, 1893.
9. Stevenson, "Music," *Independent* (Mar. 9, 1893): 9.
10. [H. E. Krehbiel], "Music. The Philharmonic Concert," *NYDT*, Mar. 5, 1893.
11. [J. Creelman?], "Real Value of Negro Melodies," *NYH*, May 21, 1893; on Creelman's possible involvement, see Beckerman, "The Real Value of Yellow Journalism."
12. See, e.g., A. K. Gardner, "The Music King, Rubinstein," *WAJ* (Nov. 2, 1872): 9–10.
13. On Joachim: "American Music," *NYH*, European Edition–Paris, May 26, 1893; on Rubinstein: "Herr Rubinstein Is Sceptical," *NYH*, European Edition–Paris, May 27, 1893; on Bruckner: "America's Musical Future," *NYH*, European Edition–Paris, May 28, 1893.
14. "Dvorak's Theory of Negro Music," *NYH*, May 28, 1893.
15. "American Music. Dr. Antonin Dvorak Expresses Some Radical Opinions," *Boston Herald*, May 28, 1893.
16. [H. E. Krehbiel], "Dr. Dvořák's Symphony," *NYDT*, Dec. 17, 1893; [A. Steinberg], "Dr. Dvořák's Great Symphony," *NYH*, Dec. 16, 1893; [J. Creelman], "Dvořák's Symphony a Historic Event," *NYH*, Dec. 17, 1893; [W. J. Henderson], "Dr. Dvořák's Latest Work," *NYT*, Dec. 17, 1893.
17. Ibid.
18. "American Music," *Boston Herald*, May 28, 1893.
19. Elson, "Some Orchestral Masterpieces," in Elson and Hale, eds., *Famous Composers*, 2:194.
20. See [H. E. Krehbiel], "Some American Compositions," *NYDT*, Apr. 1, 1893; "Real Value of Negro Melodies," *NYH*, May 21, 1893; and Faucett, *George Whitefield Chadwick* (II), 117.
21. Quoted in Faucett, *George Whitefield Chadwick* (I), 81–83.
22. [L. C. Elson], "The Symphony," *Boston Daily Advertiser*, Oct. 22, 1894.
23. Hale, "Music in Boston," *Musical Courier* (Oct. 24, 1894): 18.
24. [W. F. Apthorp], "Theatres and Concerts," *Boston Evening Transcript*, Oct. 22, 1894.
25. See Peress, *Dvořák to Duke Ellington*, 29–32.
26. Unidentified clipping, quoted in Faucett, *George Whitefield Chadwick* (I), 84–85.
27. *Boston Globe*, Dec. 29, 1905, quoted in Faucett, *George Whitefield Chadwick* (I), 85–86.
28. [L. C. Elson], "The Symphony," *Boston Daily Advertiser*, Oct. 22, 1894.
29. "American Music," *Boston Herald*, May 28, 1893.
30. On Beach's training and marriage, see Block, *Amy Beach*, 21–53.

31. Amy Beach, Music Reviews, Vol. 2, Oct. 1894. Amy Beach Papers, Milne Special Collections and Archives, University of New Hampshire, quoted in Gerk, "A Critical Reception History," 19.

32. See "Dr. Dvořák's American Symphony," *NYDT*, Dec. 15, 1893.

33. "The Native Music of Ireland," *Citizen* (Mar. 1841): 203–204.

34. "The Native Music of Ireland," *Citizen* (Jan. 1841): 64.

35. For the analysis, see Jenkins, *The Remarkable Mrs. Beach*; on its connection to the program, see Block, "Dvořák, Beach, and American Music," in Crawford, Lott, and Oja, eds., *A Celebration of American Music*, 263–264; the program notes were reprinted in "Things Here and There: A New Symphony by Mrs. H. H. A. Beach," *Music* (Dec. 1896): 200–202.

36. *Boston Courier*, Nov. 1, 1896, quoted in Jenkins, *The Remarkable Mrs. Beach*, 38; Ticknor's authorship confirmed in "Things Here and There," 203.

37. Hale, "With Musicians: Women in the List of Symphony Makers," *Boston Journal*, Nov. 4, 1896; and "Music in Boston," *Musical Courier* (Nov. 11, 1896): 15; Apthorp, "Music and Drama," *Boston Evening Transcript*, Nov. 2, 1896; see also Gerk, "A Critical Reception History," 28–33.

38. [L. C. Elson], "Musical Matters," *Boston Daily Advertiser*, Nov. 2, 1896.

39. "Symphony Orchestra Matinee," *BDE*, Mar. 28, 1897.

40. [H. E. Krehbiel], "Musical Comment," *NYDT*, Mar. 29, 1897.

41. Krehbiel, *The Philharmonic Society of New York*, passim.

42. "American Music," *Boston Herald*, May 28, 1893.

43. "Criticisms on Dvořák's Theory," *NYH*, June 4, 1893.

44. "Music in Brooklyn," *BDE*, Jan. 14, 1894.

45. On Seidl's death, see Horowitz, *Wagner Nights*, 11–18; on the premiere, see Von Glahn, *Sounds of Place*, 50–63.

46. See Bomberger, *Tidal Wave*, 145–164.

47. Fried, "A Study of the Orchestral Music of George Frederick Bristow," 86–87.

48. See Cockrell, *Demons of Disorder*, 87–88.

49. See Von Glahn, *Sounds of Place*, 60–61.

EPILOGUE

1. C. H., "Music in Philadelphia," *DJM* (Aug. 5, 1876): 280.

2. Leonard Bernstein, *Young People's Concerts*, 139.

3. Copland, *Music and Imagination*, 100.

4. See chapter 12 and Chase, *America's Music*, 386–390.

5. On Dvořák's influence, see Block, "Dvořák, Beach, and American Music," in Crawford, Lott, and Oja, eds., *A Celebration of American Music*, 256–280; Broyles, "Art Music from 1860 to 1920," in Nicholls, ed., *The Cambridge History of American Music*, 249–253; B. Levy, *Frontier Figures*, 2–6; Peress, *Dvořák to Duke Ellington*; Sullivan, *New World Symphonies*; and Tibbetts, ed., *Dvořák in America*.

6. On internationalism and nationalism among modernists, see Oja, *Making Music Modern*.

7. Rosenfeld, *An Hour with American Music*, 39.

8. Ibid., 160.

9. See Paul, *Charles Ives in the Mirror*, 53–58.

10. Paul, *Charles Ives in the Mirror*, 97–100; and Burkholder, *Charles Ives*, 27–29.

11. See Bruce, "Ives and Nineteenth-Century American Music," 38–41; Burkholder, "Ives and the Nineteenth-Century European Tradition"; and Horowitz, *Moral Fire*, 197–199.

12. On the style of these works, see Brown, "Lifting the Veil"; and Brown, "Selected Orchestral Music."
13. *Chicago Defender*, June 24, 1933, quoted in Brown, "Lifting the Veil," xli.
14. *Chicago Tribune*, June 16, 1933, quoted in Brown, "Selected Orchestral Music," 125.
15. Locke, *The Negro and His Music*, 115.
16. *Chicago Daily News*, June 16, 1933, quoted in Brown, "Lifting the Veil," xlii.
17. Brown, "Lifting the Veil," xxxv–xxxvi; on Stock's advocacy, see Epstein, "Frederick Stock and American Music."
18. On the dimensions of gender and race in this enterprise, see B. Levy, "The White Hope of American Music."
19. See Horowitz, *Understanding Toscanini*, 95–132.
20. "Editorial Correspondence," *WAJ* (July 3, 1869): 114.
21. "Jerome Hopkins on the Boston Oracle," *AAJ* (Apr. 1, 1876): 128.
22. On Koussevitzky's luster as a leader of premieres, see Copland, "Serge Koussevitzky," 256; on Stokowski, see Oja, *Making Music Modern*, 34–35; on Thomas's programs, see Vol. 2 of Thomas, *Theodore Thomas*.
23. "Interview with Frederick Mollenhauer," *AAJ* (Feb. 8, 1879): 229.
24. "Thomas and His Critics," *AAJ* (May 3, 1879): 3.
25. See Nelson-Strauss, "Theodore Thomas and the Cultivation of American Music," in Spitzer, ed., *American Orchestras*, 427–428.
26. "Great Festivals Here and Elsewhere," *Musical Record* (Apr. 22, 1882): 474 (emphasis in original).
27. Gilmore, "Tradition and Novelty."
28. "Founding of the Philharmonic—Interview with Harvey Dodworth," *AAJ* (July 5, 1879): 150.
29. "A Plea for American Art. Are We a Hessian Colony?" *AAJ* (Mar. 22, 1879): 323.
30. Hopkins, *Music and Snobs*, 27 (emphasis in original).
31. See Lohman, "Orchestral Extraliteracy," 5–27.
32. Madrid, "American Music in Times of Postnationality," 701; on the culture of conservatories and university music departments, see also Kingsbury, *Music, Talent, and Performance*; Nettl, *Heartland Excursions*; and Landes, "On Being a Music Major."

WORKS CITED

ARCHIVAL AND SPECIAL COLLECTIONS

Abraham Lincoln Papers, Library of Congress

Anthony Philip Heinrich Collection, Music Division, Library of Congress (APHC)

Anthony Philip Heinrich Scrapbook, Music Division, Library of Congress (APHS)

Charles Jerome Hopkins Journals, Houghton Library, Harvard College Library, Harvard University (CJHJ)

George Frederick Bristow Collection, Music Division, New York Public Library for the Performing Arts

John Curtis, *A History of Opera in Philadelphia* (1922), seven-volume typescript, Historical Society of Pennsylvania

John Rowe Parker Correspondence, Rare Book & Manuscript Library, University of Pennsylvania (JRPC)

Joseph Sill Diaries (1831–1854), Historical Society of Pennsylvania

Louis Moreau Gottschalk Collection, Music Division, New York Public Library for the Performing Arts

Musical Fund Society of Philadelphia Records (ca. 1820–1994), Rare Book & Manuscript Library, University of Pennsylvania (MFS)

Musical Fund Society of Philadelphia Supplementary Records, Rare Book & Manuscript Library, University of Pennsylvania (MFSSR)

Theodore Thomas Collection, Rosenthal Archives, Chicago Symphony Orchestra

William Henry Fry Collection, Library Company of Philadelphia

NINETEENTH-CENTURY PERIODICALS

L'Abeille de la Nouvelle Orleans/The New Orleans Bee

The Albion, A Journal of News, Politics, and Literature

Allgemeine musikalische Zeitung (AmZ)

American Art Journal (AAJ)

American Journal of Music

American Phrenological Journal

American Quarterly Review (AQR)

Appletons' Journal of Literature, Science, and Art

The Atlantic Monthly

The Author: A Monthly Magazine for Literary Workers

Baltimore Sun

Belles-Lettres Repository, and Monthly Magazine

Blackwell's Edinburgh Magazine

Boston Daily Advertiser
Boston Daily Evening Transcript
Boston Daily Traveler
Boston Evening Transcript
Boston Herald
Boston Musical Times
Boston Post
Broadway Journal
Brooklyn Daily Eagle (BDE)
Brooklyn Daily Union (also *Union-Argus*)
Brother Jonathan
Chicago Inter Ocean
Church's Musical Visitor
Cincinnati Daily Star
The Citizen: A Dublin Magazine
The Dial: A Magazine for Literature, Philosophy, and Religion
Dwight's Journal of Music (DJM)
The Etude
The Euterpiad; or Musical Intelligencer, and Ladies Gazette
The Forum
Frank Leslie's Illustrated Newspaper
The Galaxy
Graham's American Monthly Magazine of Literature, Art, and Fashion
The Harbinger, Devoted to Social and Political Progress
*The Independent, Devoted to the Consideration of Politics, Social and Economic
    Tendencies, History, Literature, and the Arts*
Journal of Fine Arts
The Knickerbocker, or New York Monthly Magazine
Kunkel's Music Review
Manchester Times (UK)
Le Ménestrel
The Message Bird
Music: A Monthly Magazine Devoted the Art, Science, Technic and Literature of Music
Music and Drama
The Musical Courier
The Musical Magazine, or Repository of Musical Science, Literature, and Intelligence
The Musical Record
The Musical Visitor, a Magazine of Musical Literature and Music
The Musical World (London)
Musical World and New York Musical Times (MWMT)
The Nation
National Gazette and Literary Register (Philadelphia)
Neue Zeitschrift für Musik (NZfM)
The New-England Magazine
The New Monthly Magazine and Literary Journal
New Orleans Times-Picayune
The New World
New York Daily Graphic
New York Daily Times (NYT)
New York Daily Tribune (NYDT)

New York Evening Express
New York Evening Post (NYEP)
New York Herald (NYH)
New York Musical Review and Choral Advocate (MRCA)
New York Musical Review and Gazette (MRG)
New York Sun
Niles' Literary Register
North American Review
Philadelphia Public Ledger (PPL)
The Port-Folio
Putnam's Monthly Magazine of American Literature, Science and Art
The Quarterly Musical Review (Manchester, UK)
Saroni's Musical Times
Spirit of the Times
The United States Magazine, and Democratic Review
Watson's Art Journal (WAJ)

BOOKS AND ARTICLES

Aderman, Ralph G. "Contributors to the *American Quarterly Review*, 1827–1833." *Studies in Bibliography* 14 (1961): 163–176.

Ahlquist, Karen. *Democracy at the Opera: Music, Theater, and Culture in New York City, 1815–60*. Urbana: University of Illinois Press, 1997.

Anderson, Benedict. *Imagined Communities: Reflections on the Origin and Spread of Nationalism*. Rev. ed. London and New York: Verso, 2006 [1983].

Appiah, Kwame Anthony. "Cosmopolitan Patriots." *Critical Inquiry* 23 (1997): 617–639.

Applegate, Celia. *Bach in Berlin: Nation and Culture in Mendelssohn's Revival of the* St. Matthew Passion. Ithaca, NY: Cornell University Press, 2005.

———. "How German Is It? Nationalism and the Idea of Serious Music in the Early Nineteenth Century." *19th-Century Music* 21 (1998): 274–296.

Applegate, Celia, and Pamela Potter, eds. *Music and German National Identity*. Chicago: University of Chicago Press, 2002.

Apthorp, William F. *Musicians and Music-Lovers, and Other Essays*. New York: Charles Scribner's Sons, 1894.

The Atlantic Index: A List of Articles, With Names of Authors Appended, Published in "The Atlantic Monthly," from Its Establishment in 1857 to the Close of Its Sixty-Second Volume in 1888. Boston and New York: Houghton, Mifflin, and Co., 1889.

Audubon, John James. *Ornithological Biography, or an Account of the Habits of the Birds of the United States of America*. Philadelphia: E. L. Carey and A. Hart, 1832.

Beckerman, Michael B. "The Real Value of Yellow Journalism: James Creelman and Antonín Dvořák." *Musical Quarterly* 77 (1993): 749–768.

Benner, Erica. "Nationalism: Intellectual Origins." In *The Oxford Handbook of the History of Nationalism*, edited by John Breuilly, 36–55. New York: Oxford University Press, 2013.

Bernstein, Leonard. *Young People's Concerts*. Revised and expanded edition. New York: Simon and Schuster, 1970.

Bhabha, Homi K. *Nation and Narration*. London: Routledge, 1990.

Block, Adrienne Fried. *Amy Beach, Passionate Victorian*. New York: Oxford University Press, 1998.

Bohlman, Philip V. *The Music of European Nationalism: Cultural Identity and Modern History*. Santa Barbara, CA: ABC-CLIO, 2004.

Bomberger, E. Douglas. "Charting the Future of 'Zukunftsmusik': Liszt and the Weimar Orchesterschule." *Musical Quarterly* 80 (1996): 348–361.

———. *"A Tidal Wave of Encouragement": American Composers' Concerts in the Gilded Age*. Westport, CT: Praeger, 2002.

Bonds, Mark Evan. *Absolute Music: The History of an Idea*. New York: Oxford University Press, 2014.

———. *After Beethoven: The Imperative of Originality in the Symphony*. Cambridge, MA: Harvard University Press, 1996.

———. *Music as Thought: Listening to the Symphony in the Age of Beethoven*. Princeton, NJ: Princeton University Press, 2006.

———. "The Symphony as Pindaric Ode." In *Haydn and His World*, edited by Elaine R. Sisman, 131–153. Princeton, NJ: Princeton University Press, 1997.

Boston Academy of Music. *First Annual Report of the Boston Academy of Music*. Boston: Perkins, Marvin, & Co., 1835.

———. *Ninth Annual Report of the Boston Academy of Music*. Boston: T. R. Marvin, 1841.

———. *Tenth Annual Report of the Boston Academy of Music*. Boston: T. R. Marvin, 1842.

Bourdieu, Pierre. "The Forms of Capital." In *Handbook of Theory and Research for the Sociology of Education*, edited by John G. Richardson, 241–258. Westport, CT: Greenwood Press, 1986.

———. "The Production of Belief: Contribution to an Economy of Symbolic Goods." *Media, Culture, & Society* 2 (1980): 261–293.

Brackenridge, Hugh Henry. *The Battle of Bunkers-Hill. A Dramatic Piece, of Five Acts, in Heroic Measure*. Philadelphia: Robert Bell, 1776.

Brittan, Francesca. "On Microscopic Hearing: Fairy Magic, Natural Science, and the *Scherzo fantastique*." *Journal of the American Musicological Society* 64 (2011): 527–600.

Brown, A. Peter. *The Symphonic Repertoire*, 4 vols. Bloomington: Indiana University Press, 2002–2012.

Brown, Linda Rae. "Lifting the Veil: The Symphonies of Florence B. Price." In *Symphonies Nos. 1 and 3*, by Florence Price, edited by Linda Rae Brown and Wayne Shirley, xv–lii. Middleton, WI: A-R Editions, 2008.

———. "Selected Orchestral Music of Florence B. Price (1888–1953) in the Context of Her Life and Work." Ph.D. diss., Yale University, 1987.

Broyles, Michael. *Beethoven in America*. Bloomington: Indiana University Press, 2011.

———. "Haupt's Boys: Lobbying for Bach in Nineteenth-Century Boston." In *Bach in America*, edited by Stephen A. Crist, 37–55. Urbana: University of Illinois Press, 2003.

———. *Mavericks and Other Traditions in American Music*. New Haven, CT: Yale University Press, 2004.

———. *"Music of the Highest Class": Elitism and Populism in Antebellum Boston*. New Haven, CT: Yale University Press, 1992.

Bruce, Neely. "Ives and Nineteenth-Century American Music." In *An Ives Celebration: Papers and Panels of the Charles Ives Centennial Festival-Conference*, edited by H. Wiley Hitchcock and Vivian Perlis, 29–43. Urbana: University of Illinois Press, 1974.

Buell, Laurence. "Postcolonial Anxiety in Classic U.S. Literature." In *Postcolonial Theory and the United States: Race, Ethnicity, and Literature*, edited by Amritjit Singh and Peter Schmidt, 196–219. Jackson: University Press of Mississippi, 2000.

Bulwer-Lytton, Edward. *Zanoni*, 2 vols. New York: Harper & Bros., 1842.

Burkholder, J. Peter. *Charles Ives, The Ideas Behind the Music*. New Haven, CT: Yale University Press, 1985.

——. "Ives and the Nineteenth-Century European Tradition." In *Charles Ives and the Classical Tradition*, edited by Geoffrey Block and J. Peter Burkholder, 11–33. New Haven, CT: Yale University Press, 1996.

——. "Music of the Americas and Historical Narratives." *American Music* 27 (2009): 399–423.

Burnham, Scott. *Beethoven Hero*. Princeton, NJ: Princeton University Press, 1995.

——. "Criticism, Faith, and the *Idee*." *19th-Century Music* 13 (1990): 183–192.

Burstein, Andrew. *The Original Knickerbocker: The Life of Washington Irving*. New York: Basic Books, 2007.

Butler, Nicholas Michael. *Votaries of Apollo: The St. Cecilia Society and the Patronage of Concert Music in Charleston, South Carolina, 1766–1820*. Columbia: University of South Carolina Press, 2007.

Butterworth, Neil. *The American Symphony*. Aldershot, UK, and Brookfield, VT: Ashgate, 1998.

Carpentier, Alejo. *Music in Cuba*, edited by Timothy Brennan, translated by Alan West-Durán. Minneapolis: University of Minnesota Press, 2001.

Carroll, Anna Ella. *The Great American Battle; or the Contest Between Christianity and Political Romanism*. New York: Miller, Orton, and Mulligan, 1856.

Carse, Adam. *The Life of Jullien*. Cambridge, UK: W. Heffer and Sons, 1951.

Cavicchi, Daniel. *Listening and Longing: Music Lovers in the Age of Barnum*. Middletown, CT: Wesleyan University Press, 2011.

Chadwick, George Whitefield. "A 'Touch' of Beethoven." *Neume* 3 (1907): 35–37.

Chase, Gilbert. *America's Music: From the Pilgrims to the Present*. New York: McGraw-Hill, 1955.

Chase, Gilbert, ed. *The American Composer Speaks: A Historical Anthology, 1770–1965*. Baton Rouge: Louisiana State University Press, 1966.

Chasteen, John Charles. *National Rhythms, African Roots: The Deep History of Latin American Popular Dance*. Albuquerque, NM: University of New Mexico Press, 2004.

Child, Lydia Maria. *Hobomok and Other Writings on Indians*, edited by Carolyn L. Karcher. New Brunswick, NJ: Rutgers University Press, 1986.

Citron, Marcia. *Gender and the Musical Canon*. Cambridge: Cambridge University Press, 1993.

Claypool, Richard D. "Archival Collections of the Moravian Music Foundation and Some Notes on the Philharmonic Society of Bethlehem." *Fontes Artes Musicae* 23 (1976): 177–190.

Cockrell, Dale. *Demons of Disorder: Early Blackface Minstrels and Their World*. Cambridge: Cambridge University Press, 1997.

Cooke, George Willis, ed. *Early Letters of George Wm. Curtis to John S. Dwight: Brook Farm and Concord*. New York: Harper & Bros., 1898.

Copland, Aaron. *Music and Imagination*. Cambridge, MA: Harvard University Press, 1952.

——. "Serge Koussevitzky and the American Composer." *Musical Quarterly* 30 (1944): 255–269.

Crawford, Richard. *America's Musical Life: A History*. New York: W. W. Norton, 2001.

——. *The American Musical Landscape: The Business of Musicianship from Billings to Gershwin*. Berkeley and Los Angeles: University of California Press, 1993.

Crawford, Richard, R. Allen Lott, and Carol Oja, eds. *A Celebration of American Music: Words and Music in Honor of H. Wiley Hitchcock*. Ann Arbor: University of Michigan Press, 1990.

Crist, Elizabeth B. "'Ye Sons of Harmony': Politics, Masculinity, and the Music of William Billings in Revolutionary Boston." *William and Mary Quarterly* 60 (2003): 333–354.

Curtis, John. "A Century of Grand Opera in Philadelphia." *Pennsylvania Magazine of History and Biography* 44 (1920): 122–157.

Cushing, William. *Index to the North American Review, Vols. I–CXXV, 1815–1877*. Cambridge, MA: John Wilson and Son, 1878.

Dana, Daniel. *A Discourse on Music Addressed to the Essex Musical Association, at Their Annual Meeting, at Boxford, Sept. 12, 1803*. Newburyport, MA: Edmund M. Blunt, 1803.

Dizikes, John. *Opera in America: A Cultural History*. New Haven, CT: Yale University Press, 1993.

Dowd, Timothy J., Kathleen Little, Kim Lupo, and Ann Borden. "Organizing the Musical Canon: The Repertoires of Major U.S. Symphony Orchestras, 1842–1969." *Poetics* 30 (2002): 35–61.

Dox, Thurston. "George Frederick Bristow and the New York Public Schools." *American Music* 9 (1991): 339–352.

Dwight, John Sullivan. *A Lecture on Association: In Its Connection with Education, Delivered Before the New England Fourier Society, in Boston, February 29th, 1844*. Boston: Benjamin H. Greene, 1844.

Edwards, George Thornton. *Music and Musicians of Maine: Being a History of the Progress of Music in the Territory Which Has Become Known as the State of Maine, from 1604 to 1928*. Portland, ME: Southwarth Press, 1928.

Elson, Louis C., and Philip Hale, eds. *Famous Composers and Their Works*. New Series, 3 vols. Boston: J. B. Millet Co., 1900.

Emerson, Caleb. *A Discourse on Music, Pronounced at Amherst, N.H. before the Handellian Musical Society, September 13, 1808*. Amherst, NH: Joseph Cushing, 1808.

Emerson, Ralph Waldo. *The Complete Works of Ralph Waldo Emerson*, 12 vols. Boston and New York: Houghton, Mifflin, and Co., 1903–1921.

Epstein, Dena J. "Frederick Stock and American Music." *American Music* 10 (1992): 20–52.

Faucett, Bill F. *George Whitefield Chadwick: His Symphonic Works*. Lanham, MD: Scarecrow Press, 1996.

———. *George Whitefield Chadwick: The Life and Music of the Pride of New England*. Boston: Northeastern University Press, 2012.

Faust, Albert Bernhardt. *The German Element in the United States with Special Reference to its Political, Moral, Social, and Educational Influence*, 2 vols. Boston and New York: Houghton Mifflin, 1909.

Fifield, Christopher. *The German Symphony between Beethoven and Brahms: The Fall and Rise of a Genre*. Farnham, Surrey, UK and Burlington, VT: Ashgate, 2015.

Finson, Jon. *The Voices that are Gone: Themes in Nineteenth-Century Popular Song*. New York: Oxford University Press, 1994.

Fleche, Andre M. *The Revolution of 1861: The American Civil War in the Age of Nationalist Conflict*. Chapel Hill: University of North Carolina Press, 2012.

Foote, Arthur. "Thirty-Five Years of Music in Boston." *Harvard Musical Review* 1 (1912): 9–10, 19.

Foreman, George C. "The Remarkable Monsieur Jullien and His Grand American Tour." In *Wind Band Activity in and Around New York*, ca. *1830–1950*, edited by Frank J. Cipolla and Donald Hunsberger, 1–30. Van Nuys, CA: Alfred, 2007.

Fors, Luis Ricardo. *Gottschalk*. Havana: La Propaganda Literaria, 1880.

Franklin, Wayne. *James Fenimore Cooper: The Early Years*. New Haven, CT: Yale University Press, 2007.

Fried, Gregory Martin. "A Study of the Orchestral Music of George Frederick Bristow." D.M.A. diss., University of Texas at Austin, 1989.

Frisch, Walter. *Brahms: The Four Symphonies*. New York: Schirmer, 1996.

Frolova-Walker, Marina. "A Ukrainian Tune in Medieval France: Perceptions of Nationalism and Local Color in Russian Opera." *19th-Century Music* 35 (2011): 115–131.

Fry, William Henry. *Leonora: A Lyrical Drama in Three Acts*. Philadelphia: E. Ferrett & Co., 1846.

———. *Republican Campaign "Text-Book" for the Year 1860*. New York: A. B. Burdick, 1860.

Fuller, Margaret. *The Letters of Margaret Fuller*, 6 vols., edited by Robert N. Hudspeth. Ithaca, NY: Cornell University Press, 1983–1994.

Fuller, Randall. *From Battlefields Rising: How the Civil War Transformed American Literature*. New York: Oxford University Press, 2011.

Garrett, Charles Hiroshi. *Struggling to Define a Nation: American Music and the Twentieth Century*. Berkeley and Los Angeles: University of California Press, 2008.

Gelbart, Matthew. *The Invention of "Folk Music" and "Art Music": Emerging Categories from Ossian to Wagner*. Cambridge: Cambridge University Press, 2007.

Gellner, Ernest. *Nations and Nationalism*. Ithaca, NY: Cornell University Press, 1983.

Gerk, Sarah. "A Critical Reception History of Amy Beach's 'Gaelic' Symphony." M.A. thesis, California State University, Long Beach, 2006.

Gibbons, William. "'Yankee Doodle' and Nationalism." *American Music* 26 (2008): 246–274.

Gienow-Hecht, Jessica C. E. *Sound Diplomacy: Music and Emotions in Transatlantic Relations, 1850–1920*. Chicago: University of Chicago Press, 2009.

Gilmore, Patrick S. *History of the National Peace Jubilee and Great Musical Festival, Held in the City of Boston, June, 1869, to Commemorate the Restoration of Peace throughout the Land*. New York: Patrick S. Gilmore, 1871.

Gilmore, Samuel. "Tradition and Novelty in Concert Programming: Bringing the Artist Back Into Cultural Analysis." *Sociological Forum* 8 (1993): 221–242.

Goehr, Lydia. *The Imaginary Museum of Musical Works: An Essay in the Philosophy of Music*. New York: Oxford University Press, 1992.

Goodrich, Alfred John. *Complete Musical Analysis: A System Designed to Cultivate the Art of Analyzing and Criticising and to Assist in the Performance and Understanding of the Great Composers of Different Epochs*. Cincinnati, OH: John Church Co., 1889.

Gott, Richard. *Cuba: A New History*. New Haven, CT: Yale University Press, 2004.

Gottschalk, Louis Moreau. *Notes of a Pianist: The Chronicles of a New Orleans Music Legend*, edited by Jeanne Behrend. Princeton, NJ: Princeton University Press, 2006 [1881].

Gramit, David. *Cultivating Music: The Aspirations, Interests, and Limits of German Musical Culture, 1770–1848*. Berkeley and Los Angeles: University of California Press, 2002.

Graziano, John, ed. *European Music and Musicians in New York City, 1840–1900*. Rochester, NY: University of Rochester Press, 2006.

Griswold, Rufus Wilmot. *The Prose Writers of America: With a Survey of the Intellectual History, Condition, and Prospects of American Literature*. Philadelphia: Carey and Hart, 1847.

Gunn, Glenn Dillard. *Music: Its History and Enjoyment*. New York and London: Harper & Bros., 1939.

Hamm, Charles. *Yesterdays: Popular Song in America*. New York: W. W. Norton, 1979.

Handel and Haydn Society. *Constitution of the Handel and Haydn Society. Instituted April, 1815*. Boston: Stebbins, 1815.

Harvey, Joseph. "Rethinking William Henry Fry: Uncovering Two Lost Symphonies." M.A. thesis, West Chester University, 2001.

Haskell, Daniel C., ed. *The Nation, Volumes 1–105, New York, 1865–1917, Index of Titles and Contributors, Vol I: Index of Titles*. New York: New York Public Library, 1951.

Haynes, Sam W. *Unfinished Revolution: The Early American Republic in a British World*. Charlottesville, VA: University of Virginia Press, 2010.

Heinrich, Anthony Philip. *The Dawning of Music in Kentucky, or the Pleasures of Harmony in the Solitudes of Nature*. New York: Da Capo Press, 1972 [1820].

Hensel, Octavia. *Life and Letters of Louis Moreau Gottschalk*. Boston: Oliver Ditson Co., 1870.

Hewitt, John H. *Shadows on the Wall; or Glimpses of the Past*. New York: AMS Press, 1971 [1877].

Hobsbawm, E. J. *Nations and Nationalism since 1780: Myth, Programme, Reality*. Cambridge: Cambridge University Press, 1990.

Hoffmann, E. T. A. *E. T. A. Hoffmann's Musical Writings: Kreisleriana, The Poet and the Composer, Music Criticism*, edited by David Charlton. Cambridge: Cambridge University Press, 1989.

Hogarth, George. *Musical History, Biography and Criticism: Being a General Survey of Music, From the Earliest Period to the Present Time*. London: John W. Parker, 1835.

Holoman, D. Kern, ed. *The Nineteenth-Century Symphony*. New York: Schirmer, 1996.

Hopkins, C. Jerome. *Music and Snobs; or, a Few Funny Facts Regarding the Disabilities of Music in America*. New York: R. A. Saalfield, 1888.

Horowitz, Joseph. *Moral Fire: Musical Portraits from America's Fin de Siècle*. Berkeley and Los Angeles: University of California Press, 2012.

———. "Music in the Gilded Age: Social Control and Sacralization Revisited." *Journal of the Gilded Age and Progressive Era* 3 (2004): 227–245.

———. *Understanding Toscanini: How He Became an American Culture-God and Helped Create a New Audience for Old Music*. New York: Alfred A. Knopf, 1987.

———. *Wagner Nights: An American History*. Berkeley and Los Angeles: University of California Press, 1994.

Horton, Julian. *The Cambridge Companion to the Symphony*. Cambridge: Cambridge University Press, 2013.

Howard, John Tasker. "The Hewitt Family in American Music." *Musical Quarterly* 17 (1931): 25–39.

———. *Our American Music: Three Hundred Years of It*. New York: T. Y. Crowell, 1931.

Howe, Daniel Walker. *Making the American Self: Jonathan Edwards to Abraham Lincoln*. Cambridge, MA: Harvard University Press, 1997.

———. *What Hath God Wrought: The Transformation of America, 1815–1848*. New York: Oxford University Press, 2007.

Hubbard, W. L. *American History and Encyclopedia of Music: A History of American Music*. Toledo, OH: Irving Squire, 1908.

Hughes, Rupert. *Contemporary American Composers*. Boston: L. C. Page and Co., 1900.

Huneker, James Gibbons. *The Philharmonic Society of New York and Its Seventy-Fifth Anniversary: A Retrospect*. New York: Printed by the Society, 1917.

Izzo, Francesco. "William Henry Fry's *Leonora*: The Italian Connection." *Nineteenth-Century Music Review* 6 (2009): 7–25.

Jackson, Richard. "An American Muse Learns to Walk: The First American-Music Group." In *American Musical Life in Context and Practice to 1865*, edited by James R. Heintze, 265–336.

———. "More Notes of a Pianist: A Gottschalk Collection Surveyed and a Scandal Revisited." *Notes* (2nd ser.) 46 (1989): 352–375.

Jenkins, Walter S. *The Remarkable Mrs. Beach, American Composer: A Biographical Account Based on Her Diaries, Letters, Newspaper Clippings, and Personal Reminiscences*, edited by John H. Baron. Warren, MI: Harmonie Park Press, 1994.

Johnson, H. Earle. *First Performances in America to 1900: Works with Orchestra*. Detroit, MI: Information Coordinators, 1979.

———. "The Germania Musical Society," *Musical Quarterly* 39 (1953): 75–93.

Jones, Charles K. *Francis Johnson (1792–1844): Chronicle of a Black Musician in Early Nineteenth-Century Philadelphia*. Bethlehem, PA: Lehigh University Press, 2006.

Kemp, Ian. "*Romeo and Juliet* and *Roméo et Juliette*." In *Berlioz Studies*, edited by Peter Bloom, 37–79. Cambridge: Cambridge University Press, 1992.

Kingsbury, Henry. *Music, Talent, and Performance: A Conservatory Cultural System*. Philadelphia: Temple University Press, 1988.

Knouse, Nola Reed. "The *collegia musica*: Music of the Community." In *The Music of the Moravian Church in America*, edited by Nola Reed Knouse, 189–211, Rochester, NY: University of Rochester Press, 2008.

Koch, Heinrich Christoph. *Kurzgefaßtes Handwörterbuch der Musik für praktische Tonkünstler und für Dilettanten*. Hildesheim, DE: Georg Olms Verlag, 1981 [1807].

Korf, William. *The Orchestral Music of Louis Moreau Gottschalk*. Henryville, PA: Institute of Mediaeval Music, 1983.

Korn, Bertram. "A Note on the Jewish Ancestry of Louis Moreau Gottschalk, American Pianist and Composer." *American Jewish Archives* 15 (1963): 117–119.

Kramer, Elizabeth. "The Idea of *Kunstreligion* in German Musical Aesthetics of the Nineteenth Century." Ph.D. diss., University of North Carolina–Chapel Hill, 2005.

Krehbiel, Henry Edward. "Music in America." In *Famous Composers and Their Works*, Vol. 4, edited by John Knowles Paine, Theodore Thomas, and Karl Klauser, 933–960. Boston: J. B. Millet Co., 1891.

———. *The Philharmonic Society of New York: A Memorial*. New York: Novello, Ewer, and Co., 1892.

Kremp, Pierre-Antoine. "Innovation and Selection: Symphony Orchestras and the Construction of the Musical Canon in the United States (1879–1959)." *Social Forces* 88 (2010): 1051–1082.

Landes, Heather Angela. "On Being a Music Major: A Comparative Study of Student Culture in a Conservatory and a University School of Music." Ph.D. diss., Loyola University, Chicago, 2008.

Laudon, Robert Tallant. *The Dramatic Symphony: Issues and Explorations from Berlioz to Liszt*. Hillsdale, NY: Pendragon Press, 2012.

Lawrence, Vera Brodky. *Strong on Music: The New York Music Scene in the Days of George Templeton Strong*, 3 vols. Chicago: University of Chicago Press, 1995–1999 [1988].

———. "William Henry Fry's Messianic Yearnings: The Eleven Lectures, 1852–53." *American Music* 7 (1989): 382–411.

Lawson, Melinda. *Patriot Fires: Forging a New American Nationalism in the Civil War North*. Lawrence: University of Kansas Press, 2002.

Leuchars, Chris. *To the Bitter End: Paraguay and the War of the Triple Alliance*. Westport, CT: Greenwood Press, 2002.

Levine, Lawrence. *Highbrow/Lowbrow: The Emergence of Cultural Hierarchy in America*. Cambridge, MA: Harvard University Press, 1988.

Levy, Alan H. *Musical Nationalism: American Composers' Search for Identity*. Westport, CT: Greenwood Press, 1983.

Levy, Beth E. " 'The White Hope of American Music'; or, How Roy Harris Became Western." *American Music* 19 (2001): 131–167.

———. *Frontier Figures: American Music and the Mythology of the American West*. Berkeley and Los Angeles: University of California Press, 2012.

Levy, David. "Wolfgang Robert Griepenkerl and Beethoven's Ninth Symphony." In *Essays on Music for Charles Warren Fox*, edited by Jerald C. Graue, 103–113. Rochester, NY: Eastman School of Music Press, 1979.

Lind, John Dayton. "Music in *The Nation*, 1870–1935." Ph.D. diss., University of Montana, 1970.

Locke, Alain. *The Negro and His Music Negro Art: Past and Present*. New York: Arno Press, 1969 [1936].

Locke, Ralph P. *Musical Exoticism: Images and Reflections*. Cambridge: Cambridge University Press, 2009.

Lohman, Laura. "Orchestral Extraliteracy and the Foundations of American Musicology." Ph.D. diss., University of Pennsylvania, 2001.

Loring, William C., Jr. *An American Romantic-Realist Abroad: Templeton Strong and His Music*. Lanham, MD: Scarecrow Press, 1996.

Lowe, Melanie. *Pleasure and Meaning in the Classical Symphony*. Bloomington, IN: Indiana University Press, 2007.

Lowens, Irving. *Music and Musicians in Early America*. New York: W. W. Norton, 1964.

Madeira, Louis C. *Annals of Music in Philadelphia and History of the Musical Fund Society: From Its Organization in 1820 to the Year 1858*, edited by Philip H. Goepp. Philadelphia: J. P. Lippincott, 1896.

Madrid, Alejandro J. "American Music in Times of Postnationality." *Journal of the American Musicological Society* 64 (2011): 699–703.

Mahar, William J. *Behind the Burnt Cork Mark: Early Blackface Minstrelsy and Antebellum American Popular Culture*. Urbana: University of Illinois Press, 1999.

Malone, Dumas, ed. *Dictionary of American Biography*, 20 vols. New York: Charles Scribner's Sons, 1934.

Maretzek, Max. *Crotchets and Quavers: or, Revelations of an Opera Manager in America*. New York: S. French, 1855.

Marshall, Bill. *The French Atlantic: Travels in Culture and History*. Liverpool, UK: Liverpool University Press, 2009.

Marx, Adolf Bernhard. *Über Malerei in der Tonkunst: ein Maigruss an die Kunstphilosophien*. Berlin: G. Fink, 1828.

Mason, Daniel Gregory. *The Dilemma of American Music and Other Essays.* New York: MacMillan, 1928.

Maust, Wilbur Richard. "The Symphonies of Anthony Philip Heinrich Based on American Themes." Ph.D. diss., Indiana University, 1973.

McIntosh, John. *The Origin of the North American Indians.* New York: Nafis and Cornish, 1843.

Menand, Louis. *The Metaphysical Club: A Story of Ideas in America.* New York: Farrar, Straus, and Giroux, 2001.

Miller, Angela. *Empire of the Eye: Landscape Representation and American Cultural Politics, 1825–1875.* Ithaca, NY: Cornell University Press, 1993.

Montgomery, Scott L. *Science in Translation: Movement of Knowledge through Cultures and Time.* Chicago: University of Chicago Press, 2000.

Morrow, Mary Sue. *German Music Criticism in the Late Eighteenth Century: Aesthetic Issues in Instrumental Music.* Cambridge: Cambridge University Press, 1997.

Mueller, John H. *The American Symphony Orchestra: A Social History of Musical Taste.* Bloomington, IN: Indiana University Press, 1951.

Nagler, Jörg. "From Culture to *Kultur*: Changing American Perceptions of Imperial Germany, 1870–1914." In *Transatlantic Images and Perceptions: Germany and America Since 1776,* edited by David E. Barclay and Elisabeth Glaser-Schmidt, 131–154. Washington, DC, and Cambridge: German Historical Institute and Cambridge University Press, 1997.

Nettl, Bruno. *Heartland Excursions: Ethnomusicological Reflections on Schools of Music.* Urbana: University of Illinois Press, 1995.

Newman, Nancy. *Good Music for a Free People: The Germania Musical Society in Nineteenth-Century America.* Rochester, NY: University of Rochester Press, 2010.

Nicholls, David, ed. *The Cambridge History of American Music.* Cambridge: Cambridge University Press, 1998.

Norris, Renee Lapp. "Opera and the Mainstreaming of Blackface Minstrelsy." *Journal of the Society for American Music* 1 (2007): 341–365.

Oja, Carol. *Making Music Modern: New York in the 1920s.* New York: Oxford University Press, 2000.

Osterhammel, Jürgen. *The Transformation of the World: A Global History of the Nineteenth Century,* translated by Patrick Camiller. Princeton, NJ: Princeton University Press, 2014.

Paul, David C. *Charles Ives in the Mirror: American Histories of an Iconic Composer.* Urbana, IL: University of Illinois Press, 2013.

Pederson, Sanna. "A. B. Marx, Berlin Concert Life, and National Identity." *19th-Century Music* 18 (1994): 87–107.

———. "On the Task of the Music Historian: The Myth of the Symphony after Beethoven." *Repercussions* 2 (1993): 5–30.

Peress, Maurice. *Dvořák to Duke Ellington: A Conductor Explores America's Music and Its African American Roots.* New York: Oxford University Press, 2004.

Philharmonic Society of New-York. *Constitution and By-Laws of the Philharmonic Society of New-York, Adopted April, 1843.* New York: S. W. Benedict and Co., 1843.

Pisani, Michael V. "Longfellow, Robert Stoepel, and an Early Musical Setting of *Hiawatha* (1859)." *American Music* 16 (1998): 45–86.

Potter, Dorothy T. *"Food for Apollo": Cultivated Music in Antebellum Philadelphia.* Bethlehem, PA: Lehigh University Press, 2011.

Preston, Katherine K. "American Orchestral Music at the Middle of the Nineteenth Century: Louis Antoine Jullien and George Bristow's *Jullien* Symphony." In *Symphony No. 2 in D Minor, Op. 24 ("Jullien")*, by George Frederick Bristow, xv–cvi, edited by Katherine K. Preston. Middleton, WI: A-R Editions, 2011.

———. *Opera on the Road: Traveling Opera Troupes in the United States, 1825–60.* Urbana: University of Illinois Press, 2001.

Prospectus and Programmes of the New-York Musical Congress. New York: John Darcie, 1854.

Pruett, Laura Moore. "Louis Moreau Gottschalk, John Sullivan Dwight, and the Development of Musical Culture in the United States, 1853–1865." Ph.D. diss., Florida State University, 2007.

Purcell, Sarah. *Sealed with Blood: War, Sacrifice, and Memory in Revolutionary America.* Philadelphia: University of Pennsylvania Press, 2002.

Reichert, Matthew. "Carl Bergmann in New York: Conducting Activity, 1852–1876." D.M.A. diss., City University of New York, 2011.

Ritter, Frédéric Louis. *History of Music, in the Form of Lectures*, 2 vols. Boston: Oliver Ditson, 1874.

Rodgers, Daniel T. *Atlantic Crossings: Social Politics in a Progressive Age.* Cambridge, MA: Belknap Press of Harvard University Press, 1998.

Rogers, Delmer Dalzell. "Nineteenth Century Music in New York City as Reflected in the Career of George Frederick Bristow." Ph.D. diss., University of Michigan, 1967.

Rosenfeld, Paul. *An Hour with American Music.* Philadelphia and London: J. B. Lippincott Co., 1929.

Rosenkranz, A. *Novello's Catalogue of Orchestral Music: A Manual of the Orchestral Literature of All Countries.* London: Novello and Co., 1902.

Ross, Peter, and William S. Pelletreau. *A History of Long Island: From Its First Settlement to the Present Time*, 3 vols. New York and Chicago: Lewis Publishing Co., 1905.

Rubin, Emanuel. "Jeannette Myers Thurber and the National Conservatory of Music." *American Music* 8 (1990): 294–325.

Rush, James. *The Philosophy of the Human Voice: Embracing Its Physiological History; Together with a System of Principles, by which Criticism in the Art of Elocution may be Rendered Intelligible, and Instruction, Definite and Comprehensive, to which is Added a Brief Analysis of Song and Recitative*, 3rd ed. Philadelphia: J. Crissy, 1845.

Saffle, Michael. "An Introduction to Liszt's Symphonic Poems." In *The Symphonic Poems of Franz Liszt*, rev. ed., edited by Keith T. Johns, 1–82. Stuyvesant, NY: Pendragon Press, 1997.

Salgado, Susana. *The Teatro Solís: 150 Years of Opera, Concert, and Ballet in Montevideo.* Middletown, CT: Wesleyan University Press, 2003.

Saloman, Ora Frishberg. *Beethoven's Symphonies and J. S. Dwight: The Birth of American Music Criticism.* Boston: Northeastern University Press, 1995.

———. "Margaret Fuller on Beethoven in America, 1839–1846." *Journal of Musicology* 10 (1992): 89–105.

Samson, Jim, ed. *The Cambridge Companion to Nineteenth-Century Music.* Cambridge: Cambridge University Press, 2002.

Saroni, Hermann. *Theory and Practice of Musical Composition.* New York: F. J. Huntington and Mason & Law, 1852.

Schabas, Ezra. *Theodore Thomas: America's Conductor and Builder of Orchestras, 1835–1905.* Urbana: University of Illinois Press, 1989.

Schilling, Gustav. *Encyclopa̋die der gesammten musikalischen Wissenschaften, oder, Universal-Lexicon der Tonkunst*, 6 vols. Stuttgart: F. H. Kőhler, 1835–1838.

Schlüter, Joseph. *Allgemeine Geschichte der Musik in übersichtlicher Darstellung.* Leipzig, DE: Wilhelm Engelmann, 1863.

Schmidt, John C. *The Life and Works of John Knowles Paine.* Ann Arbor, MI: UMI Research Press, 1980.

Schnepel, Julie. "The Critical Pursuit of the Great American Symphony." Ph.D. diss., Indiana University, 1995.

Schumann, Robert. *Gesammelte Schriften über Musik und Musiker*, 2 vols., edited by Martin Kreisig. Leipzig: Breitkopf & Härtel, 1914.

———. *On Music and Musicians*, edited by Konrad Wolff, translated by Paul Rosenfeld. Berkeley and Los Angeles: University of California Press, 1983.

Sciannameo, Franco. *Phil Trajetta (1777–1854), Patriot, Musician, Immigrant: Commentary on His Life and Work in Context with a Facsimile Edition of His Theoretical Treatise and New Editions of Selected Compositions.* Hillsdale, NY: Pendragon Press, 2010.

Shadle, Douglas. "How Santa Claus Became a Slave Driver: The Work of Print Culture in a Nineteenth-Century Musical Controversy." *Journal of the Society for American Music* 8 (2014): 501–537.

Shanet, Howard. *Philharmonic: A History of New York's Orchestra.* New York: Doubleday, 1975.

Sisman, Elaine. "Symphonies and the Public Displays of Topics." In *The Oxford Handbook of Topic Theory*, edited by Danuta Mirka, 90–117. New York: Oxford University Press, 2014.

Skinner, Ichabod. *A Discourse on Music; Delivered February, 1796, at a Singing Lecture, in North Bolton.* Hartford, CT: Printed by Hudson and Goodwin, 1796.

Smith, Mark M. *Listening to Nineteenth-Century America.* Chapel Hill: University of North Carolina Press, 2001.

Smith, Thomas. *Extracts from the Journals Kept by the Rev. Thomas Smith, Late Pastor of the First Church of Christ in Falmouth, in the County of York (Now Cumberland) From the Year 1720, to the Year 1788, with an Appendix, Containing a Variety of Other Matters, Selected by Samuel Freeman, Esq.* Portland, ME: Printed by Thomas Todd and Co., 1821.

Smither, Howard. *The History of the Oratorio*, 4 vols. Chapel Hill: University of North Carolina Press, 2000.

Spitzer, John, ed. *American Orchestras in the Nineteenth Century.* Chicago: University of Chicago Press, 2012.

Spitzer, John, and Neal Zaslaw, eds. *The Birth of the Orchestra: History of an Institution, 1650–1815.* New York: Oxford University Press, 2004.

Starr, S. Frederick. *Bamboula!: The Life and Times of Louis Moreau Gottschalk.* New York: Oxford University Press, 1995.

Story, William W. *Poems.* Boston: Little, Brown and Co., 1856.

Sullivan, Jack. *New World Symphonies: How American Culture Changed European Music.* New Haven, CT: Yale University Press, 1999.

Swenson-Eldridge, Joanne. "Charles Hommann—America's First Symphonist." In *Surviving Orchestral Works*, by Charles Hommann, edited by Joanne Swenson-Eldridge, xiii–lxxxiii. Middleton, WI: A-R Editions, 2007.

———. "The Musical Fund Society of Philadelphia and the Emergence of String Chamber Music Genres Composed in the United States, 1820–1860." Ph.D. diss., University of Colorado, 1995.

Taruskin, Richard. "Agents and Causes and Ends, Oh My." *Journal of Musicology* 31 (2014): 272–293.

———. *Defining Russia Musically: Historical and Hermeneutical Essays*. Princeton, NJ: Princeton University Press, 1997.

———. "Is there a Baby in the Bathwater?" *Archiv für Musikwissenschaft* 63 (2006): 163–186, 309–327.

———. *The Oxford History of Western Music*, 6 vols. New York: Oxford University Press, 2005.

———. "Some Thoughts on the History and Historiography of Russian Music." *Journal of Musicology* 3 (1984): 321–339.

Tawa, Nicholas. *The Great American Symphony: Music, the Depression, and War*. Bloomington: Indiana University Press, 2009.

Thomas, Rose Fay. *Memoirs of Theodore Thomas*. New York: Moffat, Yard, and Co., 1911.

Thomson, Virgil. *A Virgil Thomson Reader*. Boston: Houghton Mifflin, 1981.

Tibbetts, John C., ed. *Dvořák in America: 1892–95*. Portland, OR: Amadeus Press, 1995.

Tischler, Barbara. *American Music: The Search for an American Musical Identity*. New York: Oxford University Press, 1986.

Trollope, Anthony. *The West Indies and the Spanish Main*. Leipzig: Bernhard Tauchnitz, 1860.

Upton, William Treat. *Anthony Philip Heinrich: A Nineteenth-Century Composer in America*. New York: Columbia University Press, 1939.

———. *William Henry Fry: American Journalist and Composer-Critic*. New York: Thomas Y. Crowell Co., 1954.

Von Glahn, Denise. *The Sounds of Place: Music and the American Cultural Landscape*. Boston: Northeastern University Press, 2003.

Waldstreicher, David. *In the Midst of Perpetual Fetes: The Making of an American Nationalism, 1776–1820*. Chapel Hill: University of North Carolina Press, 1997.

Ware, W. Porter, and Thaddeus C. Lockard Jr. *P. T. Barnum Presents Jenny Lind: The American Tour of the Swedish Nightingale*. Baton Rouge: Louisiana State University Press, 1980.

Waters, Edward N. "John Sullivan Dwight, First American Critic." *Musical Quarterly* 21 (1935): 69–88.

Watkins, Holly. "From the Mine to the Shrine: The Critical Origins of Musical Depth." *19th-Century Music* 27 (2004): 179–207.

Watts, Edward. *Writing and Postcolonialism in the Early Republic*. Charlottesville: University of Virginia Press, 1998.

Weber, William. *The Great Transformation of Musical Taste: Concert Programming from Haydn to Brahms*. New York: Cambridge University Press, 2009.

———. "The History of Musical Canon." In *Rethinking Music*, edited by Nicholas Cook and Mark Everist, 336–355. Oxford, UK, and New York: Oxford University Press, 1999.

———. "The Rise of the Classical Repertoire in Nineteenth-Century Orchestral Concerts." In *The Orchestra: Origins and Transformations*, edited by Joan Peyser, 361–386. New York: Charles Scribner's Sons, 1986.

Webster, James. *Haydn's "Farewell" Symphony and the Idea of Classical Style: Through-Composition and Cyclic Integration in His Instrumental Music*. Cambridge: Cambridge University Press, 1991.

Widmer, Edward L. *Young America: The Flowering of Democracy in New York City*. New York: Oxford University Press, 1999.

Wied-Neuwied, Maximilian, Prince von. *Travels in the Interior of North America*. London: Ackermann and Co., 1843.

Wilentz, Sean. *The Rise of American Democracy: Jefferson to Lincoln*. New York: W. W. Norton, 2005.

Wilson, Alexander. *American Ornithology; or the Natural History of the Birds of the United States*, 4 vols. Edinburgh, UK: Constable and Co., 1831.

Winthrop, Robert C. *Addresses and Speeches on Various Occasions*, 4 vols. Boston: Little, Brown and Co., 1852–1886.

Woodall, Guy R. "More on the Contributors to the *American Quarterly Review* (1827–1837)." *Studies in Bibliography* 23 (1970): 199–207.

Wyn Jones, David. *The Symphony in Beethoven's Vienna*. Cambridge: Cambridge University Press, 2006.

Yokota, Kariann Akemi. *Unbecoming British: How Revolutionary America Became a Postcolonial Nation*. New York: Oxford University Press, 2011.

Young, Percy M. *A Critical Dictionary of Composers and Their Music*. London: D. Dobson, 1954.

Zuck, Barbara A. *A History of Musical Americanism*. Ann Arbor, MI: UMI Research Press, 1980.

INDEX